Justice for Kids

FAMILIES, LAW, AND SOCIETY SERIES
General Editor: Nancy E. Dowd

Justice for Kids:
Keeping Kids Out *of the Juvenile Justice System*
Edited by Nancy E. Dowd

Justice for Kids

Keeping Kids Out *of the Juvenile Justice System*

Edited by Nancy E. Dowd

NEW YORK UNIVERSITY PRESS
New York and London

NEW YORK UNIVERSITY PRESS
New York and London
www.nyupress.org

References to Internet websites (URLs) were accurate at the time of writing.
Neither the author nor New York University Press is responsible for URLs
that may have expired or changed since the manuscript was prepared.

Library of Congress Cataloging-in-Publication Data

Justice for kids : keeping kids out of the juvenile justice system /
edited by Nancy E. Dowd.
p. cm. — (Families, law, and society series)
Includes bibliographical references and index.
ISBN 978–0–8147–2137–7 (cl : alk. paper) — ISBN 978–0–8147–2138–4 (ebook)
1. Juvenile justice, Administration of—United States. 2. Pre-trial intervention—
United States. 3. Restorative justice—United States. 4. Juvenile delinquency—
United States—Prevention. I. Dowd, Nancy E., 1949–
KF9779.J87   2011
364.360973—dc22   2011015752

New York University Press books are printed on acid-free paper,
and their binding materials are chosen for strength and durability.
We strive to use environmentally responsible suppliers and materials
to the greatest extent possible in publishing our books.

Manufactured in the United States of America

10 9 8 7 6 5 4 3 2 1

To all the kids who need our help,
and who shared their stories so we would understand.

Contents

Preface

NANCY E. DOWD

This project has been a labor of love and passion by people who care deeply about the juvenile justice system, and even more deeply about children. It is part of the Juvenile Justice Project of the Center on Children and Families at the University of Florida Levin College of Law. The project began with critical work by Shani King (the codirector of the center), Lauren Fasig, Meshon Rawls, Monique Haughton-Worrell, and Iris Burke, as well as the Center for the Study of Race and Race Relations (CSRRR) at the College of Law, directed by Katheryn Russell-Brown, together with Melissa Bamba, the CSRRR assistant director. The book has also benefited from connections with the Harvard Child Advocacy Project and the Georgetown Juvenile Justice Clinic, with critical contributions by Jessica Budnitz of the Child Advocacy Project and Kristin Henning, professor and codirector of the Juvenile Justice Clinic.

Two energetic research assistants contributed to the volume: Jessica Harrison (JD 2010) and Sarah Hensen (JD 2010). Debbie Willis, the coordinator of everyone and everything at the Center on Children and Families, also contributed enormously to the success of this project. The College of Law has been supportive of this project and this book in many tangible and intangible ways. Dean Robert Jerry and Senior Associate Dean William Page have been remarkable supports.

When you work in this area, sometimes there are particular sources of insight and inspiration, and for this book two in particular stand out: Shay Bilchik and Geoffrey Canada. Shay Bilchik has given us a road map for change. Geoffrey Canada has shown us what that looks like, in microcosm, in the Harlem Children's Zone. Both perspectives are essential, as are each of the specific pieces in the chapters here.

It has been an amazing process putting this book together. The authors have been dedicated and hard working, making this an easy task for me as the editor.

Our greatest hope is to make a difference.

Introduction: Justice for Kids

NANCY E. DOWD

Justice for kids, in the broad sense of meeting their needs, providing them with opportunities to grow, and supporting their families and communities, is rarely achieved by pushing them into the juvenile justice system. It is the contention of this book's contributors that America's juvenile justice system doesn't work: it hurts kids instead of helps them. Accordingly, the best thing we can currently do is keep kids out of the system. Better still, we should reconceptualize the juvenile justice system around children's needs. A system truly fashioned around the needs of kids has the potential to offer creative and lasting solutions to problems facing our youth.

This book focuses on preventing and reducing juvenile crime and fostering healthy child development grounded in evidence-based, effective interventions and systemic restructuring. The goal is not a Band-Aid fix or a rescue from a faulty system, but rather a complete system change. The scholars and experts featured in this book focus on what is wrong upstream, rather than how to rescue kids from a malfunctioning system that fails to bring justice to children and therefore does little to aid in their development toward healthy adults.

America's juvenile justice system is especially harmful to children of color, just as the adult criminal justice system is disproportionately weighted toward racial minorities. Indeed, as Michelle Alexander demonstrates in *The New Jim Crow: Mass Incarceration in the Age of Colorblindness* (2010), the adult criminal justice system labels, segregates, and marginalizes black and brown people, especially men. Alexander ties racial patterns in the adult system to differential policing and prosecution of drug offenses by race. The juvenile system reflects a similar pattern in the high rate of arrests and system involvement for nonviolent offenses, particularly drug offenses (Children's Defense Fund 2008).

Moreover, the racial composition of the juvenile justice system substantiates Alexander's ideas about the purpose of the adult system, and there is much evidence that the juvenile justice system feeds into the adult system.

The children who end up in the juvenile justice system disproportionately are the children who are not served, or are ill served, by other social systems, such as the child welfare, education, and mental health systems. This marginalization of children into the desired and the undesired, "our" children and "other" children, children of functional families and children of dysfunctional families, children who succeed in other social systems versus the failures, is a hallmark of the juvenile justice system. It particularly characterizes the children who end up in the deep end of the system, where offenders with long sentences and few services are more likely to continue to the adult system than to be rehabilitated for a chance at a normal adulthood.

The Context

Children and youth interact with the juvenile justice system at a significant rate. While some children move quickly out of the system and go on to live productive lives as adults, others become enmeshed in the system, moving to deeper problems linked to reoffending or more serious offending, and even to the adult criminal justice system. An encounter as a child with the juvenile justice system, therefore, can pose the potential risk of a lifelong relationship with the criminal justice system.

A high percentage of teenagers engage in acts during their teen years that could be the basis of an arrest. For example, according to national statistics gathered by the federal Office of Juvenile Justice and Delinquency Prevention, one in eight high school students has been in a fight in school, and one in three has had property stolen or damaged in school. Over half of high school seniors report that they have used illegal drugs (OJJDP 2009). In addition, teenagers are subject not only to the laws for which adults could be charged but also to status crimes (running away, ungovernability, alcohol consumption, engaging in sexual intercourse, truancy) involving conduct that is legal for adults but forbidden to minors. According to a nationally representative survey of public and private high school students, an even higher percentage of teenagers than those who have used illegal drugs have consumed alcohol: three out of four seniors have tried alcohol at least once (OJJDP 2009). One in seven kids between the ages of ten and eighteen will run away (Seith 2002). By age nineteen, seven in ten never-married teenagers have engaged in sexual intercourse (Guttmacher Institute 2010).

Whether the conduct is a conventional crime or a status crime, its frequency, according to representative national data from a broad cross-section of teenagers, reflects a simple fact: for many kids, they are simply being teenagers (ABA 2010). This conclusion rests on developmental, biological, and psychological data (Slobogin and Fondacaro 2009). Teenagers are particularly likely, as compared to adults, to fail to consider the consequences of their actions, or possible punishment. In other words, they are more reckless. Moreover, they are more strongly influenced by their peers, as evidenced by the fact that a majority of their criminal behavior occurs in groups (id.) Peer pressure may influence them, more than adults, to engage in criminal behavior. One researcher suggests that this is the case because emulating certain behaviors or certain peers makes them seem to *be* adults. Adults, for example, drink alcohol and do not have to recognize the authority of parents (Moffitt 1993).

Every day, 1,385 kids are arrested; every year, 2.11 million kids are arrested (CDF 2008; OJJDP 2009). In nearly half of those arrests, the most serious charges are larceny-theft, simple assault, drug abuse, disorderly conduct, or an alcohol violation (Snyder and Sickmund 2006, 125). Juveniles account for 16 percent of all violent-crime arrests and 26 percent of all property-crime arrests (CDF 2008). Of those who are arrested, 22 percent of arrests are handled by law enforcement and the juveniles are subsequently released (dismissed or diverted); 66 percent are referred to juvenile court; and 10 percent are directly moved to adult criminal court (Snyder and Sickmund 2006). There are two clear patterns overall. Roughly three-quarters of the kids in the juvenile justice system will only be arrested once or twice, and then they never come into the system again. For the remaining kids, a third arrest signals potentially serious, long-term involvement with the criminal justice system (ABA 2010).

The high rate of juvenile arrests is matched by a high rate of incarceration, either in pretrial detention or after sentencing. The United States has the highest rate of incarceration of any country in the world (CDF 2010). Approximately ninety-three thousand juveniles are in residential placement annually, at an estimated cost of $240.99 per day per youth, or an annual cost of $5.7 billion. The bulk of kids who are incarcerated have committed nonviolent offenses (Justice Policy Institute 2009).

The kids who are arrested and who move into the juvenile justice system disproportionately are children of color, and boys. This is visible every day in juvenile courts. Black youth are 16 percent of the population aged ten to seventeen but constitute 52 percent of juvenile violent crime index arrest rates, and 33 percent of juvenile property crime index arrest rates (OJJDP 2009). Children of color are disproportionate to their percentage of the population in every stage of the juvenile justice system: arrests, formal charging instead of diversion, transfer to the adult system for charging and prosecution, conviction, and residential placement (CDF 2007; OJJDP 2009).

Boys dominate the system, enough so that it might legitimately be called the "boys' juvenile justice system," as boys were and continue to be the focus of the system (Dowd 2010). Yet girls are now 30 percent of arrests (id.). Like boys, they are disproportionately girls of color. Boys and girls also are similar to the extent that most commit trivial offenses, and juvenile self-reports of conduct indicate a similar rate of offending except for the most serious, violent crimes, which boys commit more often. Girls' offending is strongly linked to sexual abuse and control of sexuality, with higher rates of status offenses like running away. Boys are more likely to be arrested, but girls are treated more harshly once they are arrested (Chesny-Lind and Shelden 1992; MacDonald and Chesny-Lind 2001). For example, girls are more likely to be formally processed into the system for offenses like running away. They are also more likely than boys to receive detention for status offenses (MacDonald and Chesny-Lind 2001).

Gender-nonconforming youth are an additional disproportionate group in the system, mostly invisible (Valentine, this volume). An estimated 13 percent of youths in detention are lesbian, gay, bisexual, or transgendered (Majd, Marksamer, and Reyes 2009).

These patterns within the formal juvenile justice system are connected to a broader context that strongly predicts who will enter the system. That broader context begins at birth, in what has been called by the Children's Defense Fund the "cradle to prison pipeline":

> So many poor babies in rich America enter the world with multiple strikes already against them: without prenatal care and at low birthweight; born to a teen, poor and poorly educated single mother and absent father. At crucial points in their development . . . more risks cumulate and converge. Lack of access to health and mental health care; child abuse and neglect; lack of quality early childhood education . . . ; failing schools; zero tolerance school discipline policies and the arrest and criminalization of children at younger and younger ages . . . ; neighborhoods saturated with drugs and violence; . . . rampant racial and economic disparities in child and youth serving systems; tougher sentencing guidelines; too few positive alternatives to the streets after school and in summer months. (CDF 2007, 3-4)

The link to poverty is strong, and it is well to remember the stark figures of poverty among America's children: the number of children in poverty is one in five; the number in extreme poverty is one in twelve (CDF 2010).

In an ideal world, the risk factors children face would be ameliorated by superior social supports and social services, but in reality, too often resources designed to help and support children (child welfare, foster care, education, mental health care) either fail to do so, or even worse, function as pathways to the juvenile justice system. About three million cases of abuse and neglect are reported annually; without intervention, these children are 38 percent more likely to commit violent crimes (Bender 2010, 466). A high rate of maltreated kids end up in the juvenile justice system, but few services and little coordination exist between those systems, nor is there any strategy to disrupt the connection. With respect to mental health, 10-20 percent of children meet diagnostic criteria for a mental health disorder (American Psychological Association 2008), yet services for mental health are not universally available and are even less available to children than to adults. Despite the link between physical and emotional abuse and mental health, particularly PTSD and depression, there is little treatment available for children, and 70-92 percent of delinquent youth report suffering prior experiences with trauma (Bender 2010).

The foster care system, which includes approximately half a million children, has dismal outcomes by virtually all measures. Children in foster care begin with trauma associated with removal from their families as a result of abuse or neglect. Not only does the system fail to address those issues but also these children, as compared to their peers outside the foster care system, suffer from poor educational achievement, high unemployment, mental and physical health problems, high rates of pregnancy, and high risk for poverty and homelessness (Collins 2004; Casey Family Programs 2003; Casey Family Programs 2005). Because of the high propensity for these outcomes and the correlation between these factors and criminal offending, involvement in the foster care system is a predictor for children moving from this form of state custody to juvenile justice system supervision or custodial confinement (Collins 2004).

But perhaps the most glaring sign that something is wrong with the juvenile justice system is the failure of America's public educational system. Because all children theoretically should be served by the public school system, and school is mandatory, it is a universal system for children. Yet it is a system that increasingly follows a policy of removal and exclusion rather than support and education. The rate of suspension and expulsion has increased dramatically (Bay Area Reform Collaborative 2001; Glennon, this volume). This data includes preschool, which has an even higher rate of expulsions than K-12 (NAACP 2005). Suspension and expulsion are strongly linked to dropout rates, and both often lead to involvement in the juvenile justice system; indeed, some disciplinary actions lead directly to the child being charged with a criminal offense in the juvenile system. This is the "school to prison pipeline," a label that succinctly captures the counterproductive results of current policies of educational failure and disciplinary consequences. Every day 18,493 children are suspended from public school (CDF 2010). About one in fifteen teenagers is a dropout, with 2,227 teens leaving school for good each day (id.). Not surprisingly, a third of those in juvenile corrections are identified as having special learning needs (NAACP 2005).

In schools, as in the other social service systems, negative outcomes are disproportionate among children of color. While they are in school, children of color are more likely to be enrolled in classes for students with mental disabilities, emotional disabilities, and learning disabilities; are more likely to be disciplined; and are more likely to drop out of school (CDF 2010). Black children are three times more likely than white or Asian children and twice as likely as Hispanic children to be suspended, and they are three times as likely to be expelled, in comparison to their percentage of the school population (CDF 2010; NAACP 2005).

A Vision for Change

An ecological, developmental approach can help fix our ailing juvenile justice system. The ecological approach considers both the individual child and children as a group in context, within a developmental framework. It uses an evidence-based approach to intervene early and often to ensure positive outcomes based on known risk and protective factors.

This ecological approach, grounded in the work of Uri Bronfenbrenner (1979, 1989, 1990; Bronfenbrenner and Ceci 1993) and James Garbarino (1995, 1985) and further developed by family law scholar Barbara Woodhouse (Woodhouse 2004, 2005) and many juvenile justice scholars (e.g. Slobogin and Fondacaro 2009), focuses on the interlocking systems or contexts that affect children's development. Most significant are *microsystems*, those systems that have direct impact on children, including family, peers, and community. Where those systems overlap (*mesosystems)*, they can either conflict with or mutually support each other. Children are also affected by the indirect impact of *exosystems*, such as their parents' workplaces, the juvenile justice system, and, more broadly, the legal system. Finally, these contexts are enmeshed in the *macrosystem* of cultural ideals, biases, and beliefs. When the contexts affecting children mutually support each other to achieve the positive well-being of children, then they should be made functional for all children; when they lack that goal or do not apply it to all children, they can be highly dysfunctional.

In a functional ecology—a healthy ecology for children—the value that ideally drives the system should be care and concern for all children, or what Barbara Woodhouse has identified as generist values (Woodhouse 2004). Alternatively, society's interests in reducing crime and reducing costs might be the focus of the system (Slobogin and Fondacaro 2009).

Integral to this ecological model is a developmental perspective that is sensitive to the individual and general developmental stages of children (Scott and Steinberg 2008; Dodge 2001; Borgenschneider 1996; Dahlberg and Potter 2005). Children are not static. Even if the context has some stability, the individuals within it are in constant flux, particularly in the evolution from child to young adult. Developmental data is critical to understanding the conduct of children and youth, particularly adolescents, when they commit acts that can be charged as status or criminal offenses. Perhaps more importantly, the early stages of child development prior to adolescence are essential to giving children skills to safely navigate to adulthood. Indeed, some of the most profound interventions, with the most promise of preventing delinquency, are those that occur early and often on the path to adolescence.

The factors that generate risk or protection for juvenile offending are now well known (Farrington and Welsh 2007). Just as this model is used to fight disease and foster health, so too it can be applied to attack delinquency and support children's positive development into adulthood. Risk factors include, for example, low educational attainment, poor social skills, parental conflict, and economic deprivation; protective factors include, among others, involved parents, positive peers, supportive mentoring, high-quality education, and positive neighborhoods (id.). Evaluating existing systems based on known risk and protective factors exposes the failures of existing systems as well as their tendencies to propel children toward the juvenile justice system, with negative outcomes such as arrest records that will confound children's ability to obtain employment both as minors and when they become adults (Maschi et al. 2008).

This empirically based approach to policy is epitomized by the 2001 surgeon general's report, *Youth Violence: A Report of the Surgeon General*, which outlines the research on risk and protective factors and then goes on to identify effective programs for intervention and prevention. As the report notes, in an ecological framework, interventions can be primary, secondary, or tertiary, and in a well-functioning system, these interrelate in a proactive, preventive way.

Primary interventions are preventive and universal, aimed at preventing the negative effects accompanying risk factors and strengthening protective factors. Secondary interventions focus more narrowly on at-risk children, seeking to reduce negative outcomes. Tertiary interventions focus on children who have come in contact with the system, and the goal is to prevent a reoccurrence or worsening of the situation (USHHS 2001). This approach of identifying evidence-based successful approaches to prevention is epitomized by the Blueprints Project, a violence-prevention project of the Center for the Study and Prevention of Violence at the University of Colorado, which has gathered data on model and promising programs (CSPV website).

The empirical data shows that intervention and prevention is most effective when it occurs early. The policy changes and interventions called for in this volume are particularly concentrated in the areas of primary and secondary interventions.

For many children, involvement in the juvenile justice system is linked to other problems. Those problems stem from the structure of work and family responsibilities and supports; the educational system and the "school to prison" pipeline; and family difficulties and the "foster care to prison" pipeline. Various systems and statutory structures affect the ecology of children's development, and this book considers both broad and very specific analyses of existing systems and strategies for change. The goal is to critique and disrupt existing destructive pathways in order to create the supports and strategies required for children to succeed, as well as to identify some model programs and best practices.

In this book we seek to identify ways to intervene early, either among juveniles who have not yet come into the juvenile justice system or among those who are in the "shallow" end of the system, such as those involved with a first arrest or charged with a minor offense. We identify past strategies that have been effective and critique those that have failed, in order to explore interventions that keep children from further involvement with the system while effectively addressing the problems they face. While our discussion is geared toward all children, we focus in particular on issues of race, gender, and sexual orientation that skew the likelihood of involvement in the system.

All of the chapters in this book share the belief that strengthening justice for kids must be the core principle in juvenile justice. If the system remains as it is currently structured, keeping kids out of the juvenile justice system is essential because the existing system is so problematic. But a redefined, reimagined system—one that recognizes that delinquency prevention must begin early—would play a positive role in supporting families and children in healthy development and safe passage to adulthood.

Outline of the Book

This book focuses on a reconstructed juvenile justice system that prioritizes prevention and diversion. Crossing boundaries of theory and practice, it includes the perspectives of academics from a variety of disciplines, those who have worked within the system as administrators, and those who run programs that successfully challenge dominant punitive approaches with evidence-based, successful, proactive programs and rehabilitative goals. It unfolds in four parts: "System Change"; "Race, Gender, and Sexual Orientation"; "Legal Socialization and Policing"; and "Model Programs."

Part 1, "System Change," begins with a systemic perspective that frames the entire volume. Shay Bilchik's opening chapter outlines a new footprint for a juvenile justice system that stretches far beyond the boundaries of the current system of arrest, detention, juvenile court, probation, and corrections. Using an ecological model and research supporting a risk– and protective-factor approach, Bilchik identifies the critical feature of a system reimagined according to evidence-based practices to achieve core goals for kids—love, opportunity, and hope. He outlines how to restructure the work that takes place in the juvenile justice system, as well as how to develop family and community resources to prevent delinquency, reduce recidivism, and achieve better outcomes.

Part 1 moves on to critically analyze various systems, including daycare, foster care, mental health care and special education, and education. A common theme in these chapters is how to make these systems work as preventive systems, rather than as conduits into the juvenile justice system.

David Katner focuses on the importance of quality daycare (including after-school programs through high school) for children. While U.S. policy debates about daycare tend to revolve around work/family issues, with a focus especially on supporting working parents, less attention has been paid to the link between daycare and delinquency. Katner describes several longitudinal studies that have followed participants in specialized daycare and early educational programs in various communities in the United States. These studies reach very similar findings: participants in high-quality preschool care tend to perform much better academically, and they engage in far fewer delinquent behaviors than members of the control groups. From a macroeconomic perspective, reduced expenditures for criminal justice systems, reduced spending for incarceration, and increased revenue from successful participants who generate tax dollars amount to major dollar returns for every dollar expended on daycare and early educational programs.

In addition to benefiting from the family support provided by improved daycare programs, children can also benefit from greater care and resources devoted to home environments, as Leslie Harris demonstrates in her examination of the child welfare system. Harris explores the link between the dependency system (which deals with reports of abuse or neglect) and the delinquency system, and argues for keeping children in their families as a means of preventing the movement of kids into delinquency. Numerous studies show that children who are removed from home and placed in foster care on the basis of dependency, abuse, or neglect are at significantly increased risk for a variety of negative outcomes, including being adjudicated delinquent (and later being arrested as adults). The homes of some children are so unsafe that removal is the only prudent option. However, in marginal cases, whether a child is removed depends on how decision makers, especially caseworkers, exercise discretion. Recent studies show that in these marginal cases the adverse effects of removal on children is particularly pronounced.

Next, Joseph Gagnon and Brian Barber address youth with complex educational and mental health needs. Youth with disabilities, especially youth with the special education classification of emotional disturbance (ED), are present in every school, and are a group known to be at high risk for involvement with the juvenile justice system. These youth are thirteen times more likely to be arrested than nondisabled youth. Additionally, youth with ED commonly have co-occurring mental disorders and problems with drug abuse, lack of social skills, and a history of abuse and neglect.

As Gagnon and Barber point out, difficulties for these children often surface in school, particularly in connection with zero-tolerance policies. These policies have had a disproportionately negative effect on youth with ED because they behave in ways that violate those policies. Moreover, mental health services for youth in public schools are often ad hoc, fragmented, and poorly funded. The result is that the juvenile justice system is utilized as a de facto approach to treatment of youth behavioral and mental disorders. Gagnon and Barber advocate a tiered, comprehensive approach to prevention, based on universal programs aimed at all youth, selective interventions aimed at identified at-risk youth, and intensive interventions aimed at youth with the most severe issues or those who have already come in contact with the juvenile justice system.

The final chapter in part 1, by Theresa Glennon, focuses broadly on education as a place where early intervention could make a critical difference in keeping kids out of the existing juvenile justice system, especially African American boys. Glennon explores the federal government's role in public education and its effect on African American boys at two levels. First, she examines federal policies applicable to all students—zero tolerance and No Child Left Behind—that have advanced a view of education that is fundamentally at odds with the teachings of child development theory. These policies have led to excessively high rates of school exclusions, exclusions that have an especially harsh impact on African American boys. Second, Glennon examines the misguided direction in which the federal government has led us on the issue of race. It has narrowly defined racial equality as the absence of any explicit racial legislation and has turned a blind eye to the devastating evidence of racial disparities in the lives of its citizens. In so doing, the federal government has undermined and stigmatized efforts to address the institutionalized and interactive racism that permeates the lives of racial and ethnic minorities, especially African American boys.

Glennon exhorts the federal government to take the lead in redefining educational policy to be child-centered and in accordance with child development theory. It must foster positive behavioral interventions that build communities of trust rather than climates of suspicion, and it must be dedicated to overcoming the twin barriers of institutional and interactive racism. She explores how policy might be geared toward creating an "architecture of inclusion" as the hallmark of education.

Part 2 of the book, "Race, Gender, and Sexual Orientation," extends Glennon's focus and brings to the forefront not only race but also gender and sexual orientation as critical issues in juvenile justice. This section highlights the importance of keeping these fault lines in mind with respect to every aspect of system change and program design.

Kenneth Nunn argues that the root of the pervasive pattern of disproportionate minority contact (DMC) in the existing juvenile justice system (and in other related systems) can be traced to the oppressed status of African American communities within the broader social/political/economic construct of the United States. The result is that African American children (and other communities of color with similar issues) are more likely to come into the juvenile justice system, are treated more harshly, and are more likely to end up in the deep end of the system. As the juvenile justice system is itself a societal construct, it is structured—and functions—as a mechanism of oppression.

More broadly, he argues that African American communities are oppressed by the majority culture to the extent that their group identity is suppressed, intracommunity collective action is discouraged, access to resources is cut off, and the intergenerational transmission of survival skills is impeded. Nunn suggests that adopting Black nationalist modalities would lead to the development of positive youth self-images, high community and family expectations, supportive adult involvement, and collective economic opportunities that would reduce minority contacts with the juvenile justice system.

At this point, like the juvenile justice system itself, this book will have focused more on boys than on girls, who are significantly harmed by the system's inattention. Lawanda Ravoira and Vanessa Patino emphasize the different pathways of girls into the juvenile justice system and their different needs for prevention and intervention. Girls are arrested at younger ages than boys and many enter the system with histories of abuse, trauma, and victimization. Girls are typically less violent than boys but often have higher rates of disciplinary infractions for less serious violations. Boys who have been subjected to high levels of violence in the home, either as victims of abuse or as witnesses, appear to exhibit more aggressive behavior with peers as well as violence against intimate partners. In contrast, exposure to violence for girls seems to lead to self-abusive behavior, maltreatment of their children, depression, mental illness, drug use, and suicide.

Gender-specific, gender-sensitive interventions are therefore needed system wide. Providing such interventions in the known, distinctive pathways for girls, according to Ravoira and Patino, must be the primary focus of prevention efforts. Those interventions must be early and intensive to disrupt girls' existing pathways into the juvenile justice system.

A focus on gender can sometimes leave invisible the issue of sexual orientation. Sarah Valentine's chapter ensures that we remain cognizant of this particular group within the juvenile justice system. Queer youth are defined as those who are, or are perceived by others to be, lesbian, gay, bisexual, transsexual, questioning, or gender nonconforming. Because of the heteronormativity and homophobia that pervade our culture, this population is overrepresented in the juvenile justice system, often suffers terrible abuse when in state custody, and frequently becomes homeless during or after placement. The presence of gender-nonconforming youth in the system, Valentine argues, reflects societal discrimination that treats these children as alien. Targeting that discrimination is essential to changing the mistreatment queer youth face inside and outside the juvenile justice system. Valentine advocates a public health approach toward prevention that would support family-based interventions to reunite queer youth with their families, while also providing community supports for acceptance of these children by their peers and the broader community.

Parts 3 and 4 of the book shift from a focus on broad system change and essential values to an examination of the ecology of this issue on the ground. Part 3 focuses on the most visible "face" of the juvenile justice system, the police, and the process of legal socialization. Contact with police is a universal, but differentiated, experience for youth. For many, police are rarely encountered first-hand but serve as a reminder of social and community norms. For others, police are a daily presence that generate risk irrespective of any criminal conduct. For those youth who have committed some act that subjects them to arrest, or who are thought to have done so, interactions with police are a critical interface that deeply affects their outcomes in the juvenile justice system. This reminds us that a youth's connection with the system can be glancing or significant; the system may drive the child deeper or resolve his or her issues with the kind of family-based, community-centered programs that have been identified as most successful.

It is especially challenging to improve relationships between police and youth when the latter are repeat, serious offenders. As argued by Thomas Loughran, Alex R. Piquero, Jeffrey Fagan, and Edward P. Mulvey, the goals of prevention or intervention may need to be carefully calibrated, depending not only on developmental and individual factors but also on the pattern of offending. The authors share research that shows a complex set of reactions to offending that cannot be reduced to one simple pattern, but rather depends on the history of offending and the type of offense. This makes the problem of deterrence more complex. At the same time, it underscores the value of empirically based policy even for the most serious youth offenders, and the ways in which knowledge of behavioral decision making can inform policing and deterrence strategies.

Importantly, Loughran, Piquero, Fagan, and Mulvey remind us that policies that make sense for one subgroup of offenders will not necessarily reach all youth. In addition, the focus on risk and response to risk should not be seen in isolation; the rewards of crime (financial and social) may trump rational evaluation of risks. Finally, developmental factors influence this process tremendously, a point that spans all structural and policy issues in juvenile justice.

Steve Reba, Randee Waldman, and Barbara Bennett Woodhouse focus on a different part of the policing process: the interviewing of juveniles by the police, and the role of parents in that process. While parents can guide children through a crisis situation such as a police interview or court proceeding, too often they are used by the police to obtain information or confessions, which may ultimately hurt rather than help the child. Driving a wedge between parent and child at a time when the child needs the parent's advice and counsel and the parent needs to get the honest truth from the child has highly negative public policy implications. Communications between parent and child implicate constitutional values that are based not only on history and tradition but also on developmental evidence of the importance of the parent-child bond.

Grounding their stance in both constitutional and public policy arguments, Reba, Waldman, and Woodhouse contend that parent-child communication during police interrogation should be privileged and confidential. Moreover, they recommend a series of steps to preserve the parent-child relationship when a child is in custody so that the positive role of family is not undermined.

Family– and community-based interventions, calibrated to serve individual needs, have consistently proved to be the most effective tools of prevention, as well as intervention with youth who become involved in the juvenile justice system. Part 4, "Model Programs," examines several specific initiatives that exemplify the localized, evidence-based approach discussed in part 3.

Thalia González and Ben Cairns expose the potential for avoiding violence and resolving conflicts through the use of a restorative justice model in schools. Restorative justice focuses on converting the response to misbehavior from punishment or zero tolerance to interventions that accentuate accountability, fairness, and situational responses to unique events and individuals. This includes requiring children to acknowledge wrongdoing, take responsibility, and rehabilitate relationships. School-based restorative-justice practice holds out rich possibilities for educators concerned with challenging the underlying structural causes of school violence, high dropout rates, and low graduation rates, all of which are linked to juvenile justice involvement. González and Cairns's chapter uses the restorative justice program at North High School in Denver, Colorado, as a case study of restorative justice with broader implications for more holistic educational reform.

In the next chapter, Khary Lazarre-White discusses his Brotherhood/Sister Sol (BHSS) program, founded in 1995 in Harlem. Through an intensive after-school and summer program, BHSS provides a series of interwoven and connected supports: educational, developmental, exposure, and protection related. BHSS serves a population that ranges in age from six to twenty-one, including some of New York City's most precariously situated young men. Yet none of

BHSS's alumni or members is incarcerated; less than 1 percent is on probation; and less than 1 percent of its alumni or members has a felony conviction.

To achieve these results, the program offers participants a comprehensive immersion into activities and lessons designed to raise awareness of their immediate circumstances as well as to expose them to far-flung worlds. BHSS members are schooled in leadership development and educational achievement, bias reduction, sexual responsibility, sexism and misogyny, political education and social justice, Pan-African and Latino history, and global awareness. Families, schools, and neighborhoods may be unable to introduce youth to these new experiences and concepts, but BHSS ensures that these youth are informed so that they can imagine opportunities for themselves.

The book concludes with a chapter by David Domenici and James Forman Jr. that reminds us that the connection between prevention and deterrence, and the juvenile justice system, is truly synergistic. Turning youth to a positive direction includes not only those on the perimeter of the system but also those who are mired in the system; they must be put on a path of success, not placed in a pipeline to further juvenile or adult criminal involvement. Domenici and Forman write about a unique school, in a unique setting: a school within a juvenile residential facility, the Maya Angelou Academy at New Beginnings, in Washington, D.C. Educational programs inside juvenile facilities are typically of low quality, with few resources, poorly drafted curricula, and demoralized staff. Most people simply assume that this is inevitable. Challenging that view, the leader of Washington's juvenile justice agency, Vincent Shiraldi, solicited Domenici and Forman to envision a different model. They created a program to educate incarcerated youth, facilitate their positive reintegration into the community, and support their personal success.

This chapter describes the philosophy and program components at the Maya Angelou Academy, including the core academic curriculum, career training, positive behavioral intervention model, and individualized transition planning. The authors publish here for the first time details on credit accumulation, reading and math gains, and documented changes in the way students perceive school as a place they can succeed.

Domenici and Forman also discuss the challenges inherent in creating high-quality educational options in a juvenile correctional setting. It is a program with lessons to offer other jurisdictions seeking to improve schools in their juvenile systems. More broadly, it reminds us that quality education that is responsive to individual needs is a powerful tool to help children and youth grow to be positive adults.

Together, the essays in this book offer a road map for change that can not only revolutionize the juvenile justice system in America but also, ultimately, keep children and youth out of it. Positive outcomes for children and youth benefit families and communities, and ultimately, all of us. Each of these chapters addresses the goals laid out by Bilchik's vision for a new juvenile justice system: providing love, opportunity, and hope. Our hope is that this volume represents the first step on a journey toward meeting those goals for *all* children.

REFERENCES

Alexander, Michelle. 2010. *The New Jim Crow: Mass Incarceration in the Age of Colorblindness*. New York: New Press.

American Bar Association. 2010. Juvenile Justice: Legal, Policy, and Political Issues. *Focus on Law Studies* 25: 2.

American Psychological Association, APA Task Force on Evidence-Based Practice with Children and Adolescents. 2008. *Disseminating Evidence-Based Practice for Children and Adolescents: A Systems Approach to Enhancing Care*. Washington, DC: APA.

Bay Area School Reform Collaborative. 2001. *Research Brief: The Color of Discipline: Understanding Racial Disparity in School Discipline Practices*. www.annenberginstitute. org/tools/tools/detail/php?toolid=14.

Bender, Kimberly. 2010. Why Do Some Maltreated Youth Become Juvenile Offenders? A Call for Further Investigation and Adaptation of Youth Services. *Children and Youth Services Review* 32: 466-73.

Borgenschneider, Karen. 1996. An Ecological Risk/Protective Theory for Building Prevention Programs, Policies, and Community Capacity to Support Youth. *Family Relations* 45: 2, 127-38.

Bronfenbrenner, Urie. 1990. Discovering What Families Do. In *Rebuilding the Nest: A New Commitment to the American Family*. 27-39 (D. Blankenhorn, S. Bayme, J. B. Elsthain, eds.) Milwaukee: Family Service America.

Bronfenbrenner, Urie. 1989. Ecological Systems Theory. *Annals of Child Development* 6: 187-251.

Bronfenbrenner, Urie. 1979. *The Ecology of Human Development: Experiments by Nature and Design*. Cambridge, MA: Harvard University Press.

Bronfenbrenner, Urie, and S. J. Ceci. 1993. Heredity, Environment, and the Question "How?": A New Theoretical Perspective for the 1990s. In *Nature, Nurture, and Psychology* (R. Plomin and G. E. McClearn, eds.) Washington, DC: APA Books.

Casey Family Programs. 2005. Improving Family Foster Care: Findings from the Northwest Foster Care Alumni Study, available at http://www.casey.org/NR/rdonlyres/4E7C77-7624-4260-A253-892C5A6CB9E1/300/nw alumni study full apr2005.pdf.

Casey Family Programs. 2003. Assessing the Effects of Foster Care: Early Results from the Casey National Alumni Study, available at http://www.casey.org/Resources/Publications/pdf/CaseyNationalAlumniStudy_FullReport.pdf.

Center for the Study and Prevention of Violence. Blueprints for Violence Prevention. http://www.colorado.edu/cspv/blueprints/.

Chesny-Lind, Meda, and Randall G. Shelden. 1992. *Girls, Delinquency, and Juvenile Justice*. Pacific Grove, CA: Brooks/Cole Publishing.

Children's Defense Fund. 2010. *The State of America's Children*. www.ChildrensDefense.org.

Children's Defense Fund. 2008. *The State of America's Children*. www.ChildrensDefense.org.

Children's Defense Fund. 2007. *America's Cradle to Prison Pipeline*. www.ChildrensDefense.org.

Collins, Mary. 2004. Enhancing Services to Youths Leaving Foster Care: Analysis of Recent Legislation and Its Potential Impact. *Children and Youth Services* 26: 1051, 1052.

Dahlberg, Linda L., and Lloyd B. Potter. 2005. Youth Violence: Developmental Pathways and Prevention Challenges. *American Journal of Preventive Medicine* 29: 582, 185-90.

Dodge, Kenneth A. 2001. The Science of Youth Violence Prevention: Progressing from Developmental Epidemiology to Efficacy to Effectiveness to Public Policy. *American Journal of Preventive Medicine* 20: 63-70.

Dowd, Nancy E. 2010. *The Man Question: Male Subordination and Privilege*. New York: New York University Press.

Farrington, David P., and Brandon C. Welsh. 2007. *Saving Children from a Life of Crime: Early Risk Factors and Effective Interventions*. New York: Oxford University Press.

Federal Interagency Forum on Child and Family Statistics. 2009. *America's Children: Key National Indicators of Well-Being*. Washington, DC: US Government Printing Office.

Garbarino, James. 1995. *Raising Children in a Socially Toxic Environment*. San Francisco: Jossey-Bass.

Garbarino, James. 1985. *Adolescent Development: An Ecological Perspective*. Columbus, OH: Merrill.

Guttmacher Institute. 2010. *Sexual Activity*. www.guttmacher.org.

Justice Policy Institute. 2009. *The Costs of Confinement: Why Good Juvenile Justice Policies Make Good Fiscal Sense*. www.justicepolicy.org.

MacDonald, John M., and Meda Chesney-Lind. 2001. Gender Bias and Juvenile Justice Revisited: A Multiyear Analysis. *Crime and Delinquency* 47: 2, 173-95.

Majd, Katayoon, Jody Marksamer, and Carolyn Reyes. 2009. *Hidden Injustice: Lesbian, Gay, Bisexual, and Transgendered Youth in Juvenile Courts*. www.nclrights.org.

Maschi, Tina, Schnavia Smith Hatcher, Craig S. Schwalbe, and Nancy Scotto Rosato. 2008. Mapping the Social Service Pathways of Youth to and through the Juvenile Justice System: A Comprehensive Review. *Children and Youth Services Review* 30: 1376-85.

Moffitt, Terrie E. 1993. Adolescence-Limited and Life-Course-Persistent Antisocial Behavior: A Developmental Taxonomy. *Psychological Review* 100: 674-701.

NAACP Legal Defense and Educational Fund, Inc. 2005. *Dismantling the School-to-Prison Pipeline*. www.naacpldf.org/issues/aspx?issue=3.

Office of Juvenile Justice and Delinquency Prevention. 2009. *Juvenile Arrests 2008*. Washington, DC: U.S. Department of Justice, Office of Justice Programs.

Seith, Robert. 2002. *Runaways*. www.connectwithkids.com/tipsheet/2002/79_ju103/runaway.html.

Scott, Elizabeth S., and Laurence Steinberg. 2008. *Rethinking Juvenile Justice*. Cambridge, MA: Harvard University Press.

Slobogin, Christopher, and Mark R. Fondacaro. 2009. Juvenile Justice: The Fourth Option. *Iowa Law Review* 95: 1-62.

Snyder, Howard N., and Melissa Sickmund. 2006. *Juvenile Offenders and Victims: 2006 National Report*. Washington, DC: U.S. Department of Justice, Office of Justice Programs Office of Juvenile Justice and Delinquency Prevention

U.S. Department of Health and Human Services. 2001. *Youth Violence: A Report of the Surgeon General*. Washington, DC: Office of the Surgeon General.

Woodhouse, Barbara Bennett. 2005. Ecogenerism: An Environmentalist Approach to Protecting Endangered Children. *Virginia Journal of Social Policy and the Law* 12: 409-47.

Woodhouse, Barbara Bennett. 2004. Reframing the Debate about the Socialization of Children: An Environmentalist Paradigm. *University of Chicago Legal Forum* 2004: 85-165.

I

System Change

1

Redefining the Footprint of Juvenile Justice in America

SHAY BILCHIK

Over the past twenty years, we have experienced significant changes in the philosophical underpinnings of the juvenile justice system. Laurie Garduque, of the John D. and Catherine T. MacArthur Foundation, argues that this shift represents the beginning of a fourth wave of juvenile justice policy and practice. Prior stages reflect the establishment and growth of a separate court with exclusive jurisdiction over juveniles; waning confidence in that system in the 1950s and 1960s; and the trend to a more punitive approach toward juveniles in the 1980s and early 1990s. This fourth wave is based on the strong and growing body of research concerning the pathways that youth follow into delinquent behavior, including risk and protective factors.

This swing of the pendulum is not new, but in the past we made our case for a more appropriate, proportionate, and consistent response to juvenile offending without the strong research that now exists in support of this position. This opening chapter will address our ability to use this research to create and sustain more effective responses to juvenile crime, and the policy, practice, and leadership implications related to these efforts. It will examine these issues from both a developmental and multisystem perspective, focusing on the use of data, the restructuring of the work that takes place in the juvenile justice system, and the need to collaborate in the development of family and community resources to prevent delinquency, reduce recidivism, and achieve better outcomes for our system-involved youth. The chapter will present a new footprint for juvenile justice systems in the United States.

This chapter will challenge us not only to stretch the boundaries of the juvenile justice system as we currently define it but also to stretch our thinking about where the boundaries lie among child-serving systems. There is a new kind of field building underway—it is no longer just the juvenile justice field, the behavioral health field, the child welfare field, or the youth development field. These fields are doing their work—viewing their work—in a different way: *across* systems. As some have framed this approach, those who work this way are "boundary spanners" (Steadman 1992).

What we are all striving to provide as we work across those systems is very simple, but very profound and difficult to achieve. Put simply, it is to provide love, opportunity, and hope for our children and youth. This is what we want in our own lives, and it is what we should provide for all of our children: to love and be loved back in a healthy way; to have opportunities, in particular opportunities for skill building and meaningful work; and to have hope for the future—hope that life will get better, that today is not the best life is going to be. It is these three things that are at the heart of what we do each and every day in working with some of the most challenged and challenging young people in our communities.

But we have to go further—we need to make sure that no child falls through the cracks; and too often we do not do that. I would like to amplify this point with a story a colleague once shared with me, one from a different field, but one that makes the point in a very powerful manner.

A visiting lecturer was speaking to a group of businessmen and –women on the subject of risk management. To drive home one of his points, he asked for a volunteer from the audience, and he asked the volunteer the following question: "Imagine that I have a huge steel I-beam here—fifteen feet long, six inches high, and six inches wide. If I put it on the floor in front of this audience, would you be willing to walk across it for fifty dollars?"

"Of course I would," said the volunteer.

"All right," said the lecturer, "now let's imagine that the I-beam has been suspended high above the ground between the two sides of a gorge, with a 300-foot drop down to a bed of rocks. Would you be willing to walk across that same I-beam for fifty dollars?"

"Of course not," said the volunteer.

Raising his voice dramatically, the lecturer continued. "Now imagine," he said, "that I am on one side of the gorge and I am holding one of your children over the edge. And you are on the opposite side of the gorge. If you don't come across the I-beam and get your child, I will drop him. *Now* will you cross the beam?" The volunteer hesitated for a long moment before making his reply, which was actually a question.

"Which one of my kids have you got?" he asked.

If this story seems humorous, the reason may be that a good number of those reading this book are parents who have had "one of those days" with their kids—or at one point in their lives, were one of those kids! I tell this story, however, to make a very important point. One is unlikely to ever meet an individual who says that he or she does not care about kids. All of us truly want what is best for children on some level. But the way people express this caring, and act on it, varies a great deal.

The man in my story was being asked a very clear question: exactly what steps are you willing to take to help a child? What kind of priority do children have for you when the going gets tough, when there are choices to be made? And his answer revealed what may be an even harder question: which children are you willing to help?

The truth of the matter is that the vast majority of parents would do whatever it would take to get across that I-beam—in fact, virtually every adult would do what it would take to save that child. But as a society, perhaps through our benign neglect, we do not act, and kids are slipping through the cracks and to one extent or another, falling into the gorge! And too many of them are children from families without power, living in poverty and in impoverished and disadvantaged communities; and far too many of them are children of color.

I share these thoughts in this opening chapter because the lessons learned in my career are that if we get these basics right, we will have a better chance of succeeding in our work to reduce juvenile delinquency. I saw in my work in the Miami-Dade State Attorney's Office, at the Office of Juvenile Justice and Delinquency Prevention at the U. S. Department of Justice (OJJDP), and at the Child Welfare League of America, the pathway kids too often follow—from histories of child abuse and neglect, untreated mental health problems, ungovernability, running away and truancy to minor offending (theft, substance abuse) and then to more serious offending. While I was at OJJDP, we were funding the Causes and Correlates of Delinquency Study (Thornberry et al. 2004), which highlighted for us the average seven-year trajectory that a young person follows from the first signs of acting-out behavior to his or her first arrest for a more serious delinquent offense—seven years of opportunity to intervene, to interrupt that trajectory, seven years of potentially approaching this work with a "no wrong door" perspective, one that allows us to better meet children's needs.

So how do we take those first steps that many would call prevention or early intervention? First, we must utilize the science of risk and protective factors and apply it to communities, families, and our young people. Second, we need to redefine what we consider our juvenile justice system—in other words, we need to become "boundary spanners" (Steadman 1992).

According to the work of the Causes and Correlates Study Group, and the research of Dr. David Hawkins and Dr. Richard Catalano (see Hawkins et al. 2000), risk factors are defined as predictors of problem behaviors, such as substance abuse, teen pregnancy, dropping out of school, and youth violence. Protective factors are defined as factors that counterbalance the effects of risk, such as opportunities for prosocial activities and the influence of a positive adult to whom the child or youth has bonded. Risk and protective factors are related to the domains in which a child or youth lives his or her life—family, peer group, school, community—and to his or her own individual characteristics. This ecological model allows us to see how we need to approach our work across domains and systems in a data-driven, research-informed manner. It also highlights for us some of the factors that contribute to or accelerate the pathway many young people follow into delinquency. In addition, recent research on adolescent brain development sponsored by the MacArthur Foundation helps us understand the importance of adopting a developmental frame in our work within this ecological model (Grisso and Schwartz 2003; MacArthur Foundation 2010b).

This newfound empirical data cries out for us to acknowledge the multiple factors that lead to delinquency, and to abandon our old ideas about the four corners of the juvenile justice system. We need to redefine the footprint of juvenile justice. Using data-driven/evidence-based approaches, our policy makers and system leaders need to take responsibility for a juvenile justice system that includes seven components or realms of activity, some of which are currently outside of our definition of juvenile justice.

1. Prevention/Early Childhood
2. Prevention/Early Intervention
3. Integrated Court Systems
4. Juvenile Detention Reform
5. Effective System Interventions
6. Juvenile Corrections
7. Aftercare/Parole

It is not enough for these elements to simply exist. Rather, they must be embedded within a system that adheres to principles of an effective juvenile justice system, such as those identified by the MacArthur Foundation's Models for Change juvenile justice reform initiative. These principles include (1) a commitment to fair, unbiased, and nondiscriminatory treatment, (2) a recognition of the differences between adults and juveniles that results in developmentally appropriate treatment, (3) use of the individual differences that each juvenile presents, such as culture, needs, and strengths, to affect decision making, (4) a belief in the potential of youth to change, grow, and become law-abiding, productive members of society, (5) a focus on the safety of the community and of the juvenile through managing risk and addressing needs of offenders, and (6) a culture of responsibility, including youth taking responsibility for their actions, communities taking responsibility for their youth, and systems taking responsibility for their performance (MacArthur Foundation 2010a). It is critical that these principles be kept in mind as I explore each of the seven areas of the new footprint below, and then examine the larger policy framework needed to make this new vision a reality so that better outcomes for our youth can be achieved.

Prevention/Early Childhood

The work of supporting children in a reframed juvenile justice system starts in early childhood, far outside the traditional notion of the parameters of the juvenile justice system. While a juvenile justice director or chief probation officer may not have direct responsibility in this area of practice and policy, he or she must use his or her leadership role to advocate for investment in this area.

One might ask why the development of practice and policy in this area is important for juvenile justice. One example of such work in the prevention/early childhood area is the Nurse-Family Partnership program, a community health program that focuses on first-time, disadvantaged teen mothers, particularly those who are drug involved. It aims to improve outcomes for the expectant mothers and their children by counseling the teens on good health practices, how to care for their child in a responsible and competent way, and how to make plans for their future. These components allow for the healthy development of the child as well as the improved economic well-being of the family (Nurse-Family Partnership 2010b). The results have been extraordinarily positive, reducing child abuse and neglect by 48 percent and reducing the arrests of the babies within the program, when measured fifteen years later, by 59 percent (Nurse-Family Partnership 2010c). The program also reduced the children's behavioral and intellectual problems by 67 percent when measured at age six (Nurse-Family Partnership 2010c). From an economic standpoint, the net benefit was $34,148 to society per family served, which equals a $5.70 return per dollar invested (Nurse-Family Partnership 2010a).

This level of effectiveness also holds true for early childhood programs that focus on preschool education and family strengthening as both child development and crime fighting tools. The High/Scope Perry Preschool program provided high-quality preschool services for low-income African American children aged three to four years who were at high risk of school failure. Part of the program included home visits by teachers to discuss the child's development and support the parents in the education of their children. The results for the children participating in the program include the following long-term outcomes:

- 65 percent completed high school compared to 45 percent in the control group;
- 76 percent were employed at age forty, compared to 62 percent in the control group;
- 36 percent were arrested five or more times over their lifetime, compared to 55 percent in the control group;
- an economic return to society of $258,888 (in 2003 dollars) per participant, which equals a $17.07 return on each dollar invested (Schweinhart 2005).

By addressing the risk factors propelling youth into the juvenile justice system early on, early childhood programs like the Nurse-Family Partnership and High/Scope Perry Preschool can stem the trajectory of increasingly serious delinquent behavior before it even begins. This is why it is key for such interventions to be part of the new footprint of juvenile justice.

Prevention/Early Intervention

What we also know now that we did not know twenty to thirty years ago is that bringing young people into the traditional juvenile justice system, in many instances unnecessarily, does more harm than good (Petrosino et al. 2010). A primary example of this is the implementation of zero tolerance policies in schools and their tendency to drive youth into the justice system. To counter this trend, a number of prevention/early intervention programs have been developed. These programs should also be part of the new footprint for juvenile justice.

An example of this type of programming is the School Referral Reduction Program in Georgia. The program, spearheaded by the local court, law-enforcement, and school officials, is designed to reduce the number of referrals to juvenile court for minor offenses (e.g., school fights, disrupting public school, and disorderly conduct) so that school resource officers can focus on the more serious problems in the schools. The program institutes a series of graduated responses. A warning is given for a first offense; a second offense results in a referral to a workshop; and a third offense leads to a complaint being filed. One of the goals of the program is to return the school disciplinarian function to school officials. The results have been very promising. There has been

- a reduction in school referrals to the court from a high of over twelve hundred per year (before program implementation), to approximately four hundred per year currently, and
- a reduction in felonies from a high of two hundred per year to less than one hundred per year currently (Teske 2009).

From both a school safety and ecological perspective, these results are significant. Keeping these young people in school as opposed to pushing them out onto the street has a tremendous impact on the risk and protective factor balance: prosocial connections as a protective factor as compared to school failure and association with negative peers who may also be pushed out of the school and onto the street corner as risk factors. From an economic perspective the benefits are also great. For example, increasing male graduation rates by 5 percent nationally can lead to a benefit of $8 billion each year due to crime savings and additional wages (Alliance for Excellent Education 2006).

Another example of this changing paradigm is the way we view arrest and court referral as opposed to diversion for entry-level offenders. In the 1980s and 1990s we thought it was good enough just to "divert." We understand better now that it may be even better not to arrest low-level offenders at all.

The Civil Citation program in Miami, Florida, diverts eligible juvenile misdemeanor offenders from the arrest process. Youth are referred to services on the basis of an assessment of their needs. The labeling and individual and family stress associated with arrest is replaced with a strength-based treatment and service orientation. The results have shown that there has been

- a 20 percent reduction in juvenile arrests in the county between 2007 and 2008;
- a 3 percent recidivism rate for youth who have completed the program (Walters 2009);

- a five thousand dollar cost savings per child involved in the program as compared to youth who were arrested (Miami-Dade County).

Programs like these allow for the opportunity to address the underlying cause of a child's delinquency without unnecessarily exposing him or her to the negative effects of justice system involvement, thereby preventing negative outcomes for the individual youth as well as society as a whole.

Integrated Court Systems

For youth who do become involved in the juvenile justice system, we know that we need to avoid duplication of services; therefore, the third element of this new footprint for juvenile justice is an integrated, or at least well-coordinated, court system. All child-serving agencies (including juvenile justice, child welfare, behavioral health, and others) should work together in an integrated court approach to interrupt the pathways youth follow into the delinquency system. There should be coordinated assessments, coordinated case management, high-quality legal representation, and, whenever possible, service integration.

One example of restructuring that supports this type of approach is the "one judge, one family" case assignment approach that crosses at a minimum both juvenile justice and child welfare cases. It allows one judge to hear all cases relating to one family so that issues can be holistically addressed. Evaluation results show that this approach reduces the number of redundant or conflicting judicial orders and increases compliance with court orders (Washington State Center for Court Research 2004). Dedicated dockets is another promising approach that allows for both delinquency and dependency cases to be heard on the same docket, at the same time, by the same judge for a particular youth known to both systems (Siegel and Lord 2004).

Coordination in this manner allows for the systems in which a child is involved to share information about the multitude of factors influencing his or her behavior and thereby address the problem as holistically as possible. Without this, services and interventions are often fragmented or duplicated, resulting in inefficiencies and ineffectiveness.

Juvenile Detention Reform

The fourth element of this new footprint deals with detention practice. We know that unnecessary detention leads to negative outcomes for youth who could remain and be served in the community pretrial. These include the lost opportunity to stay connected to school, family, and prosocial influences, the worsening of mental health conditions, and the higher probability of being committed to an institutional setting at disposition (Holman and Zeidenberg 2006). In this regard, we need to bar the door to detention, except for those young people for whom there is no appropriate alternative.

The Juvenile Detention Alternatives Initiative (JDAI) takes this approach in working with communities. Through the use of validated detention criteria and risk assessment instruments, the implementation of detention alternatives, and the use of improved case flow and data management, it has reduced the number of youth detained and in some instances has reduced the disproportionate representation of youth of color in detention facilities.

The results of the program have been nationally recognized, and it is now being replicated across the country with the support of the Annie E. Casey Foundation. Outcomes include

- a 35 percent reduction of the detention population in JDAI sites;
- a 23 percent reduction in commitments to state custody in JDAI sites; and
- a 22 percent reduction in the number of youth of color in detention in JDAI sites (Mendel 2009).

By reforming detention practices, the juvenile justice system can avoid adding to the multiple risk factors already affecting individual youth. In our interventions with young people, our first goal should be to "do no harm." In this area of focus, this means keeping young people out of detention facilities to the greatest extent possible.

Effective System Interventions

We also have greater knowledge today of effective system interventions, another part of this new footprint for juvenile justice. This requires both an understanding of the common traits of an effective system, as mentioned previously, as well as the identification of the specific programs that comprise that system. Effective system interventions help youth develop a positive self-image, reduce the influence of negative role models, support youth in engaging in prosocial behavior, and help youth connect to love, opportunity, and hope. They operate within the ecological model referenced earlier, and while many of them are "gold standard" programs that have been rigorously evaluated, many of them would be categorized as "promising," in that they are showing positive results, but through less rigorous evaluation designs.

Among the rigorously tested programs, Functional Family Therapy (FFT) stands out as a program that reduces a child's risk of reoffending, as well as reduces the risk of a sibling entering the justice system. Youth involved with FFT attend twelve one-hour-long sessions with their families over a three-month period. Through the therapy sessions, the counselors help the youth address maladaptive beliefs and perceptions that prevent the youth from changing his or her actions, develop behavior change plans with the youth and family, and address strategies that can be applied in a variety of difficult situations in order to prevent relapse. Studies of the program have shown that 19.8 percent of those receiving FFT committed an offense in the year following completion, compared with 36 percent in the control group (Mihalic et al. 2001).

Another effective intervention is Multisystemic Therapy (MST), a program that brings a youth and his or her family together multiple times per week for four months to reduce the risk factors contributing to the youth's deviant behavior and increase his or her protective factors. MST stresses the importance of empowering the family to help in the design and implementation of the treatment plan (Multisystem Therapy Services 2010b). Analysis of multiple studies has shown that this model reduces long-term rearrest rates by between 25 percent and 70 percent and reduces the number of days in out-of-home placements by between 47 percent and 64 percent (Multisystemic Therapy Services a).

Multidimensional Treatment Foster Care (MTFC) is yet another intervention shown to have positive outcomes for juvenile offenders. MTFC is designed for children with behavioral problems requiring out-of-home placement. Foster parents of these youth receive training on behavior management skills such as fair limits and predictable consequences for misbehavior. Youth receive individual therapy, skills training, and academic support, and the youth's biological family is provided training and counseling to facilitate a smooth transition back home and prevent future conflict from occurring (Multidimensional Treatment Foster Care Consultants, Inc.). Youth in MTFC spend 60 percent fewer days incarcerated after one year, have fewer arrests, are less likely to run away, and do better in school than those not experiencing the program (Center for the Study and Prevention of Violence 2010).

The final effective intervention is Cognitive Behavioral Therapy, an approach that is taking hold across the country in corrections, probation, and parole. CBT is based on the premise that it is our thoughts that primarily contribute to criminal behavior, not our environment, and that these thoughts can be controlled and changed. Offenders participating in CBT are taught how to monitor their thoughts and change thinking patterns that lead to their criminal behavior. This intervention has been shown to reduce recidivism by between 25 percent and 50 percent (Lipsey et al. 2007).

Worth highlighting is the fact that each of these effective interventions operates within the ecological domains in which a child lives his or her life. From ensuring success at school and building individual capacity to improving the family environment, these programs—and others like them—offer community-based options for treatment that should be available as a major part of a new footprint of juvenile justice.

Juvenile Corrections

When it is not possible or safe to treat a youth in the community, correctional facilities are required. However, we know now (and knew twenty years ago) that placing youth in large congregate facilities can cause them harm, whether because of peer contagion, the danger of physical and sexual assault, or other developmental factors. Instead, smaller community-based facilities achieve better outcomes for our delinquent youth (Zavlek 2005; Howell 1995).

Missouri is the model state for this approach. The "Missouri Model" has been shown to reduce recidivism by placing juvenile offenders in small residential facilities close to their home so their family can be involved in their rehabilitation. They separate serious offenders from less serious ones and provide day-treatment centers to help those released from the facility better integrate back into the community (Franck 2003). Additionally, youth committed to the Missouri Division of Youth Services (DYS) receive individual and group counseling, get academic support, and participate in volunteer activities (Annie E. Casey Foundation 2008).

This focus on rehabilitation, rather than punishment, as the primary "driver" of the way a juvenile corrections system should operate, is effective. Data show that Missouri's recidivism rate, as measured by reincarceration within three years upon exiting DYS custody, is 9 percent. States that measure recidivism in a similar way have much higher rates; for example, Maryland's recidivism rate is 30 percent and Louisiana's is 45 percent (Annie E. Casey Foundation 2008). Missouri has approached corrections reform from an ecological framework—recognizing the importance of maintaining connections to the areas in which a child lives his or her life: family, school, community, peer, and individual. By doing so, the state has been able to improve outcomes for youth in its care.

Aftercare/Parole

The last core element of this new footprint for juvenile justice is based on the notion that aftercare and community reentry is as important as the institutional care that precedes it. This is an area in which our knowledge has developed significantly over the last few decades.

Youth leaving residential facilities are typically ill prepared to return to their home and community, in part due to the system's failure to focus properly on criminogenic needs before release and to reinforce transferable, cognitive-behavioral skills that should be learned in the institution. A poor transition can result in a return to antisocial behavior, among other negative outcomes. To better facilitate transition, best practices now focus on Overarching Case Management (OCM), continuity of care, staffing and training, quality assurance, and monitoring performance. As described by Altschuler et al. (2009, 30), OCM "refers to the process used to identify the appropriate offenders who will receive supervision and services, to determine and integrate the supervision and services that will be provided, and to promote consistency and continuity through collaboration." This is done through the development of a case plan, designed with an ecological framework in mind; provision of services and supervision that seek to address the risk and protective factors presented by a child; a menu of graduated incentives and consequences to respond to behavior; and connection to community-based resources and supports (Altschuler et al. 2009).

OCM is a method that can be used to provide the continuity of care between residential facilities and aftercare services needed for a successful transition back to the community. As Altschuler (2008) describes, success is defined differently in residential facilities than it is in the community, and therefore "behavioral conditioning" in the facility may not translate to success in the community. For this reason, continuity of care must be established to avoid the often abrupt transition between facility and community that can negatively impact recidivism. By (1) gradually reducing levels of control, (2) ensuring community availability of services provided in the facility, (3) ensuring continuity of program content, (4) involving the family during residential placement and aftercare, and (5) maintaining attachments with prosocial individuals, systems can ease the transition between residential placement and community and can achieve continuity of care (Altschuler 2008).

OCM is associated largely with the Intensive Aftercare Program (IAP), a program for high-risk parolees that has been shown to have positive results (Wiebush et al. 2005). That program reinforced some of the core elements of effective reentry and community aftercare practices. Participants in three IAP programs were found to exhibit less substance abuse, shorter lengths of stay, and a greater likelihood for involvement in vocational training. The data was inconclusive in terms of the impact on reducing recidivism. Continued work on OCM will need to be evaluated to determine whether it will consistently lead to similar positive outcomes, as well as a reduction in recidivism, when the program is applied to a wide range of offenders.

We must also be aware that regardless of how much we improve OCM, there is the possibility of the overuse of parole. For parole to be effective, it must be used for the appropriate length of time, at the appropriate intensity, and with appropriate conditions and handling of technical violations. What is considered appropriate depends on the individual characteristics of a youth, including risk level. For example, one study recently showed that for non-high-risk offenders, parole may have no positive effect on recidivism outcomes. The Washington State Institute for Public Policy conducted a study on the effects of parole on youth released from the Juvenile Rehabilitation Administration and found no statistically significant differences in recidivism between youth placed on parole and those not placed on parole. The study was possible because the Washington legislature eliminated parole in 1998 for all juveniles who were not high-risk or sex offenders, and then reintroduced it in 1999. The researchers controlled for differences in the level of risk between the parole and nonparole groups, thereby allowing for an even comparison. They found that 32.7 percent of the juveniles released on parole were convicted of a felony within twelve months of release, compared to 30.2 percent of the juveniles who were not put on parole. Also, within thirty-six months after release, 55 percent of the juveniles released on parole were convicted of a felony, compared to 50 percent of the juveniles who were not put on parole (Washington State Institute for Public Policy 2006). While neither of these statistics is statistically significant, they do give us an indication that parole for non-high-risk and non-sex-offender youth may not have an impact on recidivism.

These findings suggest that for parole to be used most effectively and efficiently, it should be used with discretion only for those at high risk for reoffending, when special considerations are present, and for lower-level offenders only as long as is necessary to effectively transition the youth back into the community. In support of this approach, OCM prescribes that criteria for aftercare programs should be defined and juveniles should be assessed for their eligibility for the program. Instituting this type of approach would also help prevent youth on parole from being unnecessarily put at risk of being subjected to technical violations of their parole and returned to institutional placement. This is particularly important because in most instances these technical violations do not present a danger to public safety. With the research we now have about the development of the adolescent brain (Grisso and Schwartz 2003), it should not surprise us that many of our youth may not be able to abide by every technical aspect of their parole conditions. We should, therefore, view parole as a mechanism for successfully transitioning youth back to the community by stabilizing them after their return, connecting them to appropriate services and to prosocial influences in their lives, such as school and a positive peer group. This calls for the more judicious use of parole and of the violation authority—both of which would reflect a better understanding of normal youth development.

Policy Implications

So what do we do with this knowledge? What are the implications for our policies and practices? There is clearly a wealth of knowledge and experience available now that we did not have in the past. However, the good efforts being made are often done piecemeal—not through a thoughtful, coordinated effort to improve outcomes for young people. As a result, young people are falling through the cracks. I suggest that if we are going to be successful in improving outcomes for the young people coming in contact, or at risk of coming in contact, with the juvenile justice system, we must develop a national children and youth policy—a set of policies that cuts across federal agencies such as the Department of Health and Human Services, the Department of Justice, the Department of Education, the Department of Labor, and the Department of Housing and Urban Development, to name the agencies most central to this work. Some of these policies will need to be embedded in federal legislation. While this flies in the face of federalism, we need an overarching children and youth law, complemented by a strengthened and broadened Juvenile Justice and Delinquency Prevention Act (JJDPA), that creates a common set of measures and standards each federal agency is trying to support in partnership with states and local communities—standards and measures that would hold us accountable to our children and youth, regardless of the power or standing that they or their families hold within their communities or our society more broadly. With everyone working toward the same outcomes for young people, and being held accountable to those outcomes, our children and youth will not be handed off from one system to another to deal with their multitude of problems occurring simultaneously or over time and end up falling between the cracks of our disjointed systems. Every system would be responsible for ensuring positive outcomes for the whole child, not just those outcomes narrowly defined by the system in which a child is currently involved. This will give systems the incentive to work together across system lines, and thereby make the new footprint for juvenile justice a reality.

In order to do this work well, we must focus on children, youth, and families within the context of communities. We need to understand that the families and communities from which the children in our care come are not the enemy. And when we "wrap" services, support, and supervision around each child and family in an individualized way, these efforts should be based in the community and backed by strong community connections. It is in this way that we make positive long-term connections for kids and create a sense of stability in their lives.

Moreover, whether it is children and youth in our child welfare or juvenile justice systems, their families have both strengths and weaknesses—and in our work with them we need to identify and build on those strengths, and address those weaknesses. Furthermore, we need to disabuse ourselves of the notion that we can or should in most instances permanently separate these youth from their families. Whether it be a youth aging out of foster care or a youth transitioning from a juvenile institution and back into the home community, our young people need us to work with them as they reengage with their families, helping them navigate those families in a healthy way.

This push and pull around the role of families has been a focal point of this nation's juvenile justice system and the juvenile court since its inception 110 years ago. This is seen in the doctrine of *parens patriae*; in the idea of shipping youth to the West to live with farm families when their own families could not control them, as we did in the mid-twentieth century; and in the idea expressed through the Adoption and Safe Families Act that we could rush our young people into permanency (adoption, guardianship, independent living) through termination of parental rights and by establishing arbitrary time periods around familial reunification, without providing the resources to do so in a way that truly serves the child's and family's best interests. We have struggled in so many ways with the problem of how to view and place the family in our work with their children, and what we know now is that we do our best work if families are at the core of everything that we do.

With a national children and youth policy and stronger JJDPA in place, we can make this new footprint a reality, even in this difficult financial time. In fact, there can be no better time to adopt a platform for our juvenile justice systems in this country that is both effective in reducing delinquency and also cost effective. A sermon delivered several years ago by Reverend Dr. Douglas Oldenburg from Charlotte, North Carolina, shared with me by my colleague Frank Crawford, underscores this point. Dr. Oldenberg's fervent message was that we should not forget the millions of children in this country living in poverty—that every one of us must demonstrate a commitment to children. Rev. Oldenburg outlined the sad statistics that those of us working on children's issues are all too familiar with and encouraged us to remember the needs of all of our children, with special concern for those in greatest need. The fact that too many children are without permanent, loving homes, and that millions more live in poverty is, as Rev. Oldenburg pointed out, terrible and appalling. However, as he said, it is not their poverty that is most shocking and unacceptable—it is society's poverty of will.

Which brings me full circle—back to what all of this work is designed to do: support our children and youth in a way that brings love, opportunity, and hope into their lives. We must move down this path, stay focused on these basic needs, and be relentless in this work! As Albert Einstein so eloquently wrote in a letter quoted in the *New York Times* (Sullivan 1972),

> A human being is a part of a whole, called by us "universe," a part limited in time and space. He experiences himself, his thoughts and feelings, as something separate from the rest—a kind of optical delusion of his consciousness. This delusion is a kind of prison for us, restricting us to our personal desires and to affection for a few persons nearest to us. Our task must be to free ourselves from this prison by widening our circle of compassion to embrace all living creatures and the whole of nature in its beauty.

As you read the chapters of this book, I encourage you to think about how all of the ideas put forward, as they are moved from concept to practice, widen our circle of compassion and allow us to more effectively embrace all of our children and youth.

REFERENCES

Alliance for Excellent Education. 2006. Saving Futures, Saving Dollars: The Impact of Education on Crime Reduction and Earnings. Issue Brief. www.all4ed.org/files/Saving-Futures.pdf.

Altschuler, David. 2008. Rehabilitating and Reintegrating Youth Offenders: Are Residential and Community Aftercare Colliding Worlds and What Can Be Done about It? *Justice Policy Journal* 5 (1) (Spring 2008): 1-26.

Altschuler, David, Gary Stangler, Kent Berkley, and Leonard Burton. 2009. Supporting Youth in Transition to Adulthood: Lessons Learned from Child Welfare and Juvenile Justice. Center for Juvenile Justice Reform, Georgetown University. http://cjjr.georgetown.edu/ pdfs/TransitionPaperFinal.pdf.

Annie E. Casey Foundation. 2008. Missouri Juvenile Justice System Honored by Harvard University & Casey Foundation. Juvenile Detention Alternative Initiative Newsletter, December. http://www.aecf.org/MajorInitiatives/ JuvenileDetentionAlternativesInitiative/Resources/Dec08newsletter/JJNews5.aspx.

Center for the Study and Prevention of Violence. Multidimensional Treatment Foster Care (MTFC). http://www.colorado.edu/cspv/blueprints/modelprograms/MTFC.html.

Franck, Matthew. 2003. Juvenile Justice in Missouri Serves as Model for Nation. *St. Louis Post-Dispatch*, October 5.

Grisso, Thomas, and Robert Schwartz, eds. 2003. *Youth on Trial: A Developmental Perspective on Juvenile Justice.* Chicago: University of Chicago Press.

Hawkins, J. David, Todd I. Herrenkohl, David P. Farrington, Devon Brewer, Richard F. Catalano, Tracy W. Harachi, and Lynn Cothern. 2000. Predictors of Youth Violence. *Juvenile Justice Bulletin,* April. Office of Juvenile Justice and Delinquency Prevention.

Holman, Barry, and Jason Zeidenberg. 2006. The Dangers of Detention: The Impact of Incarcerating Youth in Detention and Other Secure Facilities. Justice Policy Institute. www.justicepolicy.org/images/upload/06-11_REP_DangersOfDetention_JJ.pdf.

Howell, James, ed. 1995. *Guide for Implementing the Comprehensive Strategy for Serious, Violent, and Chronic Juvenile Offenders.* Washington, DC: U.S. Department of Justice, Office of Juvenile Justice and Delinquency Prevention.

Lipsey, Mark W., Nana A. Landenberger, and Sandra J. Wilson. 2007. Effects of Cognitive-Behavioral Programs for Criminal Offenders. *Campbell Systematic Reviews* 6 (2007): 1-27.

MacArthur Foundation. 2010a. Models for Change Principles. http://www.modelsforchange.net/about/Background and principles/Principles.html.

MacArthur Foundation. 2010b. Research Network on Adolescent Development and Juvenile Justice. Available at www.adjj.org.

Mendel, Richard. 2009. Two Decades of JDAI: A Progress Report. Baltimore, MD: The Annie E. Casey Foundation. http://www.aecf.org/~/media/Pubs/Initiatives/ Juvenile%20Detention%20Alternatives%20Initiative/TwoDecadesofJDAIFromDemonstrationProjecttoNat/JDAI_National_final_10_07_09.pdf.

Miami-Dade County. Civil Citation. http://www.miamidade.gov/jsd/civil_citation.asp.

Mihalic, Sharon, Katherine Irwin, Delbert Elliott, Abigail Fagan, and Diane Hansen. 2001. Blueprints for Violence Prevention. *Juvenile Justice Bulletin* July 2001. Office of Juvenile Justice and Delinquency Prevention. http://www.ncjrs.gov/html/ojjdp/ jjbul2001_7_3/contents.html.

Multidimensional Treatment Foster Care Consultants, Inc. MTFC Program Overview. http://www.mtfc.com/overview.html.

Multisystemic Therapy Services. a. Complete Overview: Research on Effectiveness. http://www.mstservices.com/executive_summary.php.

Multisystemic Therapy Services. b. Executive Summary. http://www.mstservices.com/executive_summary.php.

Nurse-Family Partnership. 2010a. Benefits and Costs. http://www.nursefamilypartnership.org/ assets/PDF/Fact-sheets/NFP_Benefits-Cost.

Nurse-Family Partnership. 2010b. Overview. http://www.nursefamilypartnership.org/assets/PDF/Fact-sheets/NFP_Overview.

Nurse-Family Partnership. 2010c. Research Trials and Outcomes. http://www.nursefamilypartnership.org/assets/PDF/Fact-sheets/NFP_Research_Outcomes.

Petrosino, Anthony, Carolyn Turpin-Petrosino, and Sarah Guckenburg. 2010. Formal System Processing of Juveniles: Effects on Delinquency. *Campbell Systematic Reviews* 1: 1-88.

Schweinhart, Lawrence. 2005. The High/Scope Perry Preschool Study through Age 40: Summary, Conclusions, and Frequently Asked Questions. High/Scope Educational Research Foundation. https://secure.highscope.org/file/Research/PerryProject/3_specialsummary%20col%2006%2007.pdf.

Siegel, Gene, and Rachael Lord. 2004. *When Systems Collide: Improving Court Practices and Programs in Dual Jurisdiction Cases.* Pittsburgh, PA: National Center for Juvenile Justice.

Steadman, Henry. 1992. Boundary Spanners: A Key Component for the Effective Interactions of the Justice and Mental Health Systems. *Law and Human Behavior* 16 (1): 75-87.

Sullivan, Walter. 1972. The Einstein Papers: A Man of Many Parts Was Long Involved in the Cause of Peace. *New York Times,* March 29, 1972.

Teske, Steven. 2009. School Referral Reduction Program: Reducing Racial Disparities and the Criminalization of Low-Risk Youth. PowerPoint presentation presented at the DMC/Juvenile Justice Action Network Third Annual Meeting, May 15, in Washington, DC.

Thornberry, Terence, David Huizinga, and Rolf Loeber. 2004. The Causes and Correlates Studies: Findings and Policy Implications. *Juvenile Justice* 9 (1). www.ncjrs.gov/pdffiles1/ojjdp/203555.pdf.

Walters, Wansley. 2009. The Miami-Dade County, Florida Juvenile Justice Model. PowerPoint presentation presented at Innovative Community-Based Strategies That Work, October 29, in Albany, NY.

Washington State Center for Court Research. 2004. An Evaluation of Unified Family Court Pilot Sites in Washington State Executive Summary. Administrative Office of the Courts. www.courts.wa.gov/newsinfo/content/pdf/UFCExecSummary.pdf.

Washington State Institute for Public Policy. 2006. The Effects of Parole on Recidivism: Juvenile Offenders Released from Washington State Institutions: Final Report. http://www.wsipp.wa.gov/rptfiles/06-07-1203.pdf.

Wiebush, Richard, Dennis Wagner, Betsie McNulty, Yanging Wang, and Thao Le. 2005. Implementation and Outcome Evaluation of the Intensive Aftercare Program: Final Report. National Council on Crime and Delinquency. www.ncjrs.gov/pdffiles1/ojjdp/206177.pdf.

Zavlek, Shelley. 2005. Planning Community-Based Facilities for Violent Juvenile Offenders as Part of a System of Graduated Sanctions. *Juvenile Justice Bulletin*, August. Washington, DC: Office of Juvenile Justice and Delinquency Prevention. www.ncjrs.gov/pdffiles1/ojjdp/209326.pdf.

2

Delinquency and Daycare

DAVID R. KATNER

As the nation faces policy challenges over juvenile delinquency and subsequent crime, one all-but-forgotten option remains as promising as ever despite its virtual absence in recent national discussions and debates: a comprehensive daycare and after-school-care policy (Platt 2009; Tanenhaus 2004). For decades, social scientists in this country have examined various designs of early educational and daycare programs, some promising tremendous alterations in the lives of participants and others offering far more modest achievements. Today, however, long-term studies provide a much clearer picture of the way early child care programs and after-school programs offer significant benefits for communities. Longitudinal evidence suggests that early childhood intervention programs, which buffer the effects of delinquency risk factors, help prevent chronic delinquency and later adult offending. After-school care programs also provide healthy alternatives to otherwise unsupervised adolescent behavior and hopefully spare children and their communities the expense, fear, and suffering that often accompany delinquent misconduct and subsequent adult criminal misconduct. Overall, early intervention programs help reduce risk factors that contribute to delinquent behavior and later adult offending, while after-school programs create activities for juveniles during the time period when many delinquent acts occur.

Policy debates dating back to the 1970s have recognized the many benefits derived from subsidized universal child care programs. However, for decades the political climate has been less than receptive to policies that include any major federal provisions for universal access to child care (Dixon 2005). By the late 1980s, commentators were remarking that the child care problem had "grown so pervasive that it [was] now called America's child care crisis" (Zigler 1989; Kaminer 2007). Yet Congress still made significant cuts in federal funding for child care for low-income women, and comprehensive national legislation was a political impossibility (Clarke-Stewart 1993). Then in 1990, the United States Congress considered over one hundred different child care bills (id.). Although Congress eventually enacted the Child Care and Development Block Grant, it quickly became apparent that the grant was ineffective (Kaminer 2007). Since then, there have been no major policy revisions concerning daycare and after-school care despite the many recent findings by social scientists regarding the benefits of child care programs.

Although not a panacea for these issues, quality daycare and after-school programs offer cost-effective methods of reducing the number of adolescents in juvenile court proceedings and of lightening the burden on state and local governments for funding residential placements for adjudicated delinquents. Emerging long-term studies provide data that was either incomplete or non-existent during earlier national child care policy debates, revealing substantial cost-effective savings for communities that employ early child care programs (Nagle 2009; Knudsen et al. 2006; Pitegoff 1993).

I. The Private and Problematic Nature of Daycare in the United States
A. The Private Nature of American Child Care as Compared to European Public Child Care

As many have recognized, the evolution of child care in the United States is closely connected with vast increases in women's participation in the workforce over the last sixty years. Since the end of World War II, the percentage of working women who have young children has increased more than fivefold (Lombardi 2003). As of 2007, over 70 percent of women in the civilian labor force had children under eighteen (U.S. Bureau of Labor Statistics 2008).

However, as Joan Lombardi, the first director of the federal Child Care Bureau, asserts, this social movement has not been accompanied by necessary reforms to the child care system (Lombardi 2003). Although women have emerged from the private, domestic sphere, U.S. child care policy has not. By the 1970s, attempts at a belated federal response to child care policy met strong opposition from the growing social conservative movement, which remains strong today (Morgan 2006). Even as conservatives bemoaned the degradation of the American family, they opposed federal child care policy as undue state interference with private family matters.

In comparison, European public attitudes toward child care policy are fundamentally different. Some researchers have suggested that "social roots for these systems can be found in the nineteenth century, when child care evolved in response to conditions associated with industrialization, including urbanization, the breakup of traditional family structures, and the entrance of mothers into the industrial workforce" (Tietze and Cryer 1999, 176).

Demographic trends in Europe have also significantly contributed to greater acceptance of child care services provided and funded by the government. Reductions in the male workforce and declining birthrates have encouraged governments to provide child care services to ensure that able-bodied adults enter the workforce and to provide children with experiences that may be lacking in their family and local social networks (id.). In general, ethnically and religiously homogenous countries that have lost population through out-migration or war have been particularly likely to provide public support for child rearing (Morgan 2006). In the United States, on the other hand, white apprehensions about the growth of African American and Hispanic populations have discouraged policies that would encourage increased childbirth rates, even as fertility rates are steadily declining (England and Folbre 1999).

In response to these legal, social, and demographic movements, by the early 1990s, most European countries had achieved or were rapidly moving toward comprehensive early care and education for young children below compulsory school age (id.). All of the member countries of the European Union (EU) now guarantee at least two or three years of preschool (UNI-CEF 2008). And EU leaders agree that by 2010, free or government-subsidized full daycare for children should be available for at least one-third of all children under the age of three and for 90 percent of children aged three to six (id.).

B. The Problematic Consequences of Private Child Care

Child care in the United States has never been viewed as a fundamental service deserving of government provision. Rather, it has been traditionally viewed as a private familial responsibility. This is not an insignificant burden for America's families to bear. It is estimated that "[a]pproximately sixty-seven percent of American families need some kind of childcare assistance" (Medina 1994, 195). Without a comprehensive public policy to serve these families, for the most part, child care has been relegated to private providers in a competitive market system motivated by profit rather than true public need (Baker 1990; Lombardi 2003). The consequence has been the creation of a patchwork system of daycare and after-school care services plagued by high costs, inaccessibility, and unacceptably low quality.

1. High Costs of Private Child Care

The United States has more than four hundred thousand licensed and regulated child care centers and homes in operation, yet there remains a shortage of available child care, especially for low-income families (Lombardi 2003). With only 39 percent of the total national expenditure for child care coming from the government and 1 percent coming from the private sector, families must privately bear 60 percent of all costs (id.). Child care costs have risen exponentially in recent years, placing a significant strain on low-income families. In 2005, the U.S. Census Bureau found that families that are below the poverty level and that pay for child care spend 26.6 percent of their monthly income doing so, compared to only 7.7 percent for families over 200 percent of the poverty level (U.S. Census Bureau 2005). Furthermore, child care is typically more expensive in urban areas where low-income families are more likely to live (Lombardi 2003).

2. Lack of Access to Private Child Care

Since child care is predominantly available through the competitive market, rural communities without great profit potential are often left underserved (Kaminer 2007). Even in rural communities that do offer child care facilities, parents may have to travel long distances in order to reach them. High fuel prices combined with a scarcity of public transportation options constitute considerable obstacles for low-income families in particular.

To overcome lack of access to child care, many parents must rely on the goodwill of neighbors or other family members (Hooton 2002). However, "One study found that more than 60 percent of welfare families had no friend or relative, inside or outside their immediate household, who could provide child care" (Lombardi 2003, 8). Furthermore, even when families do have access to informal child care, they often pay these relatives and friends for their services (id., 6).

3. Low Quality of Private Child Care

When child care services are available, their quality is often unacceptably low. Even middle- and upper-income child care programs must frequently rely upon the services of minimum-wage-earning care providers. Child care providers typically earn annual salaries between fifteen and twenty-five thousand dollars and receive few employment benefits (Morrissey and Banghart 2007; Crary 2006). As a result of these low wages, child care jobs are not economically competitive, and thus undereducated or very young workers frequently fill these positions (Smith 2006). Since the most qualified workers can easily find more lucrative jobs, high turnover rates characterize the industry, causing service shortages, inconsistent care, and inadequate training (Lombardi 2003). In sum, "While some families can afford to pay child care's true cost, a defining characteristic of the industry is that most families cannot, without support, finance the cost of high quality care, nor can they afford to pay child care workers decent wages" (Smith 2006, 590).

Some studies suggest that the quality of child care is not associated with the provider's age or experience but rather is positively correlated with the training and education the provider has received (Morrissey and Banghart 2007). Yet, state regulation of training has been notoriously poor, with many states failing to mandate training for basic providers or even program directors (Lombardi 2003). Some estimates assert that between 82 and 90 percent of all family child care homes in the United States are effectively unregulated by state agencies, either because no regulations are in effect or because the facilities have illegally avoided oversight (id.). The lack of regulation for so many child care providers detracts from the ability to provide children with appropriately nurturing environments during their formative childhood years.

II. The Advantages of Affordable, High-Quality Child Care

A. Community Benefits: Daycare and Delinquency

The various benefits of quality child care services have been well documented (e.g., Nagle 2009; O'Connor and Parfitt 2009). Multiple studies show that high-quality child care can improve children's academic achievement, physical health, and psychological well-being. Yet little attention has been given to the broader connection between these positive effects and reduction of juvenile delinquency rates (e.g., Tremblay and Craig 1995). Studies have revealed that poverty strongly correlates with delinquency, and high-quality child care has the potential to target these interconnected problems that today's low-income families face (e.g., Biglan et al. 2004). Daycare programs for young children reduce high-risk factors, while after-school programs enhance protective factors (Flowers 2002).

1. Early Intervention and Daycare Programs

In the early 1990s, the United States Office of Juvenile Justice and Delinquency Prevention (OJJDP) developed a comprehensive strategy to respond to serious, violent, and chronic juvenile offenders, including early preventive intervention strategies (Hawkins et al. 1995). The OJJDP concluded, "Prevention approaches applied from conception through age six that seek to reduce risk and enhance protection can be effective in preventing crime, violence, and substance abuse in adolescence and young adulthood" (id., 48). The OJJDP cited "risk-focused" strategies that originated in the public health field as a possible model (Hawkins et al. 1995). In the realm of juvenile delinquency, the OJJDP found through several longitudinal studies that structured educational daycare could be an effective way to reduce risk factors (id.).

More specifically, children's academic attainment correlates with reduced delinquency. In particular, the OJJDP explained that "as a component of overall mental development, language functions as an indicator of later intelligence and is a critical factor in the relationship between intelligence and delinquency" (Parks 2004, 4). Good daycare programs contributed to language skills and thus decreased delinquency by improving children's readiness to enter school. For example, the Cost, Quality, and Child Outcomes in Child Care Centers Study concluded that children who had attended high-quality daycare programs displayed better cognitive skills, including language skills, through age eight, allowing them to take greater advantage of the opportunities available at school (Peisner-Feinberg et al. 1999). Importantly, the study revealed that while these positive effects could be seen across all families, they were stronger for children at risk of not doing well in school—namely, those with less-educated mothers. In other words, at-risk children "were more sensitive to the negative effects of poor quality child care and received more benefits from high quality child care" (id., 2).

Early educational intervention can have long-term positive effects for children from low-income families. The University of North Carolina at Chapel Hill's Abecedarian Project studied fifty-seven infants from low-income families randomly assigned to receive high-quality daycare services, along with fifty-four infants in the control group who received no services (Ramey 2000). The participants enrolled as early as four weeks after birth and remained in the program until kindergarten (Frank Porter Graham 1974). When the individuals reached the age of twenty-one, they were surveyed and found to have significantly higher scores on IQ and reading tests when compared with individuals in the control group (Ramey 2000). Thus, early-intervention daycare programs can improve academic outcomes and decrease delinquency and criminal misconduct well into a child's life.

Furthermore, quality child care can reduce the incidence of mistreatment of children, further reducing delinquency rates. Researchers have repeatedly concluded that maltreatment during childhood is predictive of later offending during adolescence (e.g., Stewart et al. 2008). Research has shown that neglect may be even more harmful to emotional development than abuse, and such emotional damage contributes to delinquency (Watson 1995). Well-trained child care providers can help detect cases of child abuse and neglect more readily, allowing for earlier and more effective intervention.

The High Scope/Perry Preschool Program, probably the most famous child care study, demonstrates the strong correlation between early child care services and reduced delinquency among children from low-income families (Schweinhart 2005; Belfield et al. 2005). The program focused on children with below-average IQs from low-income African American families from Ypsilanti, Michigan. From 1962 through 1967, 123 children in the school district assessed as being at high risk for school failure were divided into two groups: fifty-eight at ages three and four received high-quality preschool education and daycare, and sixty-five in a second group received no services (id.). The educational program lasted two and a half hours, five days a week, for seven and a half months each year for preschool education, and it included teacher visitation with each mother and child at home for ninety minutes once per week during the school year over a period of two years (id.). Data was collected from both groups from ages three through eleven, and again at ages fourteen, fifteen, nineteen, twenty-seven, and forty (id.). The Perry Preschool Program remains exceptional among longitudinal studies of early intervention daycare and preschool projects because it follows participants and the control group long after members complete high school, up to the age of forty (Campbell et al. 2001).

Most importantly, the study showed strong evidence that the Perry Preschool Program significantly reduced criminal and delinquent behaviors in participants across their lifetimes (Schweinhart 2005). The Perry Preschool Program group had significantly fewer lifetime arrests than the control group (id.). Program participants who did become involved in criminal activity as adults were sentenced to significantly fewer months in prison or jail as of age forty (id.). As one reviewer explained, "the program participants committed fewer delinquent or criminal acts, the acts they committed were less severe, and they were less likely to be chronic offenders than were control group members" (Yoshikawa 1995, 59). These findings were consistent up to the final evaluation when original participants reached age forty (Schweinhart 2005).

Similar decreases in juvenile delinquency were also documented among participants in the Syracuse University Family Development Research Program. The Syracuse Program "provided educational, nutrition, health and safety, and human service resources to 108 low-income, primarily African

American families beginning prenatally and continuing [through] elementary school age" (Yoshikawa 1995, 59). The program provided quality weekday child care and weekly home visits for participant families (id.). As in the High/Scope Perry Preschool Project, the Syracuse Program "decreased the total number, severity, and chronicity of later involvement with the juvenile justice system among participants" (id.). Only 6 percent of children in the Syracuse Program had juvenile records by the age of fifteen in comparison to 22 percent of those in the control group (Hawkins et al. 1995). In addition, even those participants with juvenile records had committed less serious and fewer offenses than the juveniles in the control group (id.).

These studies exemplify the strong longitudinal evidence showing that daycare programs permanently improve social behaviors, a benefit to both the participants and society (Crane and Barg 2003). Daycare programs by themselves may not result in crime reduction, but well-crafted preschool and daycare programs that offer an intensive educational component, are staffed by well-trained professionals, and are funded to allow full participation by at-risk children appear to offer communities an affordable mechanism to significantly reduce overall delinquency and crime (Belfield et al. 2005).

2. After-School Programs

Many states have struggled to reduce juvenile delinquency. Some communities have adopted curfew laws, believing that such tools would allow police to intervene, thus preventing or curtailing delinquent acts during evening hours. However, the curfew strategy has met much opposition. First, civil libertarians question the disparate impact of curfews on the rights of inner-city children and adolescents (Trollinger 1996). Beyond these constitutional concerns, curfews are very expensive to enforce—a problem often underestimated or simply ignored by proponents. For example, following the enactment of a curfew in New Orleans, the city experienced substantially increased costs for additional policing of curfew violations and detention of offending juveniles (Privor 1999). Furthermore, studies of delinquent misconduct suggest that money spent on curfew enforcement is not money well spent. Studies have shown that juvenile crime peaks between the after-school hours of 2:00 p.m. and 6:00 p.m., rather than later in the evening when curfews would be in effect (Gottfredson et al. 2001). As one critic argues, "Curfew laws are essentially cosmetic solutions to systemic problems. They require fewer resources than are necessary to reach the underlying social problems that contribute to juvenile crime. They are . . . desperate measures that allow cities to appear tough on crime" (Trollinger 1996, 964).

A common interpretation of the elevated crime rate during the afternoon hours is that adolescents are unsupervised during this time—between the end of the school day and the time when their parents come home from work (Gottfredson et al. 2001). With so many parents working outside the home, "An estimated five to seven million, and up to as many as 15 million 'latch-key children' return to an empty home after school" (Chung 2000, 1). These unsupervised children are at a greater risk for problem behaviors. Groundbreaking research conducted in the late 1980s "showed that eighth-grade children who care for themselves for eleven or more hours per week without an adult present are twice as likely to use drugs as those who are always supervised" (Gottfredson et al. 2001, 63). This remained true even when other variables, including socioeconomic status and number of parents in the household, were held constant (id.).

After-school programs target juvenile crime more effectively than curfews and also address underlying social problems that curfews ignore. As one researcher noted, "First and foremost, after-school programs keep children of all ages safe and out of trouble" (Chung 2000, 2). Providing adolescents with after-school alternative activities can decrease the chances that they will engage in delinquent activities and, if well-designed, provide enriching experiences. Programs that promote exercise and physical activity could also help reduce the high rate of obesity among America's children and improve their overall health (Land 2009). In addition, research has shown that "[o]verall, children from low income families spend less time in lessons, sports teams, and other extracurricular activities than do those from more affluent families" (Casey et al. 2005, 80). Thus, well-designed programs would directly reduce delinquency while compensating for this enrichment deficit and better integrating juveniles into the local community.

After-school programs can help reduce delinquency by providing supervision and meaningful relationships with adults. One of the most successful after-school programs, Big Brothers/Big Sisters, shows how community-based mentorship programs can successfully reduce problem behaviors among adolescent participants (Benard and Marshall 2001). Although all after-school programs may not be able to offer such intensive mentoring, more informal relationships with adults can still be productive. For example, caregivers can provide help with homework, strengthening attendees' academic skills, which correlate with positive behavioral outcomes (Casey et al. 2005). And children who develop relationships with adults through after-school programs are also less likely to abuse alcohol, another risk factor associated with delinquency (Gottfredson et al. 2001). Overall, after-school programs can provide children with a "safe haven" and introduce them to positive role models that can help mitigate risk factors in their lives (id.).

The Obama administration budget currently appropriates $1.1 billion for after-school programs under the No Child Left Behind Act. However, on the campaign trail, then-Senator Obama promised to double this funding (Editorial 2009). A recent study by the nonprofit advocacy group Afterschool Alliance reports that parents of 18.5 million students would enroll their children in after-school programs if one were available (Afterschool Alliance 2009). This may represent the strongest showing of public support ever for the creation and expansion of funded after-school-care programs.

B. Economic Benefits

According to the Brookings Institution, a $59 billion investment in high-quality universal preschool could add $2 trillion to annual U.S. gross domestic product by 2080 (Dickens et al. 2006). As the High Scope/Perry Preschool Program demonstrates, much of this return can be attributed to the maturation of children into more productive adults. At age forty, significantly more of the program-participant children were employed than were control group members (Schweinhart 2005). Participants also enjoyed higher median annual earnings than the nonenrolled children and were more likely to own homes by age forty (id.). One researcher calculated that "the economic return to society of the Perry Preschool Program was $258,888 per participant on an investment of $15,166 per participant—$17.07 per dollar invested" (id., 3). This study confirmed that the beneficial impact of early childhood quality daycare services had lifetime effects, with substantial financial returns for the public on its initial investment (id.).

Parents also benefit from access to quality daycare (Zigler 1989). First, parental employment is more difficult if children are too young to care for themselves and parents lack resources for child care (Wood 1995). Thus, access to child care could directly improve parents' employment opportunities. Child care would especially benefit low-income households with parents employed in entry-level wage jobs. Such jobs frequently impose inflexible work schedules not well coordinated with school day schedules (Selmi and Cahn 2006). Thus parents' employment may be compromised without reliable child care. Child care can therefore provide economic benefits for parents, who are more likely to work and continue working, and for their employers, whose recruitment and training costs would decrease with improved employee retention and stability.

Quality child care is particularly essential for low-income parents in light of the federal transition from subsidized welfare to workfare (Zatz 2006a, 2006b). Workfare programs encourage employment and provide supplemental benefits for families, but they alter family structures and parents' time at home (Casey et al. 2005). One study found that as of 2000, "nearly one million toddlers have been placed in daycare in the wake of welfare reform as single mothers move off welfare and into the workforce" (Wax 2001, 503). If workfare programs are to succeed, they must be accompanied by a robust child care policy.

The impact of any change in child care policy will be felt disproportionately by working mothers. As discussed above, women have dramatically increased their participation in the workforce since the end of World War II and particularly since the 1970s. However, men have not proportionally increased their participation in domestic and child care responsibilities. "That many other traditional obstacles to gender inequality have been overturned means that parental responsibilities loom large as a current cause of lower earnings and restrictions on career advancement for women" (England and Folbre 1999, 197). The U.S. General Accounting Office has estimated that if the costs of child care were reduced for families, the employment rate among low-income mothers would increase by as much as 35 percent (Meyers and Heintze 1999).

III. A Progressive Vision of Child Care

A. Designing High-Quality Child Care

Longitudinal studies that have reported reductions in overall delinquency and subsequent criminal misconduct provide verified measures that could be adopted as components of any high-quality daycare proposal. In addition, some independent research has helped to identify both the problematic aspects of many current daycare programs as well as the elements of the more successful high-quality daycare offerings. One study of child care services identified the following characteristics of high-quality early education programs (Fleron et al. 2006):

- *Child care providers* must be well educated and adequately compensated. This reduces the turnover of the care providers, creates an environment in which children become familiar with their care providers, and enables providers to offer consistent social and emotional support.

- *Curricula* must be age appropriate and delivered in appropriately sized groups and physical settings, with an emphasis on active engagement of children. This will reduce dependence on passive self-entertainment such as television and promote socialization skills.
- *Parents must be regularly informed* about their children's progress and development. Daycare programs should not be viewed as a substitution for parenting. Parental input regarding cultural values, religious values, and other aspects of the family lifestyle allow child care providers to better meet the needs of children.

Any daycare reform should address these fundamental components of quality child care.

After-school programs also require a great deal of planning and coordination. Emulating popular mentorship programs like Big Brother/Big Sister can be extremely difficult, so such programs should be initiated only after adequate investigation. It has been estimated that two-thirds of mentorship pairs involving high-poverty children do not survive the introductory phase. "The adults and youths are typically from extremely different worlds. . . . Unfortunately, youth fare poorly when exposed to relationships that do not last long" (Hirsch 2005, 57).

Some researchers have identified the amount of contact time between mentors and mentees in these programs as being particularly important (id.). But the reality is that most mentorship programs were started in the late 1990s, and very few have undergone extensive, empirical followup studies (id.). Funding should be restricted to those programs with clearly stated objectives and detailed designs. Funding should also be dedicated to empirical studies of after-school programs so that successful programs can be emulated and funded in the future.

B. A Comprehensive Public Policy

The 1980s marked perhaps the most active efforts to establish a national daycare policy. Many early longitudinal studies on the benefits of child care received national attention, yet legislative efforts to garner congressional support fell short. Those early studies have been supplemented by more extended documentation of the significant positive impacts of child care for program participants.

To ensure that quality child care and its attendant benefits reach all children, the government must develop a comprehensive child care policy. Leaving child care in the hands of the private market has left the United States lagging behind our European counterparts and simply will not produce the quality services needed to engender all the potential positive benefits child care has to offer. Although private companies can benefit from providing child care services for their employees, and many well-financed employers do offer programs such as flexible scheduling, on-location daycare, and parental leave (Baughman et al. 2003), many businesses simply lack the capital to provide comprehensive services for their employees. This is particularly true of small businesses and those that depend on the low-wage earners most in need of such services. The following reform suggestions are designed to aid federal and state governments in developing a comprehensive child care policy.

1. Infrastructure: Potential Federal and State Leaders

In order to implement a comprehensive child care policy, the U.S. government must first establish suitable oversight and infrastructure. It may be that a collaborative working arrangement between federal agencies would best support the creation of a national daycare and after-school-care policy. Some European countries have taken this route, electing not to create a single governmental agency to oversee all aspects of child care policy. In Denmark, for example, fifteen different ministries work under a Governmental Child Committee to provide services to children and families (Bennett et al. 2001). In the United States, similar cooperative efforts have recently emerged between the Departments of Education and Health and Human Services (Posting of Lisa Guernsey 2009).

Rather than a multiagency model, Peter W. Greenwood proposes a single-agency model. He recently reviewed the various existing federal agencies—including the Departments of Justice, Education, and Health and Human Services—that could oversee implementation of a national policy for early delinquency-prevention programs. He concluded that the Department of Health and Human Services should be responsible for early prevention programs while the Department of Justice should focus on the needs of high-risk and adjudicated juveniles (Greenwood 2006). Alternatively, David P. Farrington and Brandon C. Welsh, two of the most recognized national experts on crime and delinquency policy, have also proposed the creation a new national council on early crime prevention (Farrington and Welsh 2007). The proposed council would be similar in scope to Sweden's National Council for Crime Prevention (established in 1974) and Canada's National Crime Prevention Centre (established in 1994), which both develop evidence-based crime-prevention proposals for their respective national governments (id.).

Regardless of which existing or new agency takes the lead, the federal government should focus primarily on the creation of a national policy for daycare and after-school programs. Policy considerations could include national guidelines for child care facilities seeking federal funding. Specific policies should include requiring child care centers to maintain criminal record checks of all child care providers, comply with local and regional health codes, disclose employee wage data, and undergo periodic inspection to ensure compliance with national standards of care.

Traditionally, child care has fallen within the states' domains of education and family matters. For example, although the federal Head Start Reauthorization Act of 2007 required the creation of a coordinated system of early childhood education and care, a recent report on state compliance shows that only nineteen states have councils (called Early Childhood Advisory Councils, or ECACs), while thirteen states are in the process of developing such councils, and one state—South Dakota—has decided not to apply for any of the available federal funding (Satkowski 2009). To foster cooperation, state-run programs should also be evaluated as potential recipients of federal support once they demonstrate viability.

Successful state initiatives include Colorado's Nurse Home Visitor Program, an evidence-based delinquency-prevention strategy designed to reduce and eliminate child maltreatment by first-time mothers with incomes below the federal poverty level (Calonge 2005). New Jersey has also gained national attention for its provision of high-quality prekindergarten programs to all three– and four-year-old children in thirty-one of the state's highest-poverty districts. The state is currently expanding the program to the other 560 educational districts (Mead 2009). These programs are particularly useful models as they use quantifiable results, making it possible to assess the efficacy of programs. A national strategy for daycare and after-school care should consider funding similar projects in other jurisdictions or providing funding to continue such state programs.

2. Funding: Directly Funded Programs and Vouchers

Perhaps the most dramatic possible reform would be to mandate compulsory preschool and lengthen the school day or school year for older children. These measures would significantly decrease the amount of time all children are in need of child care or other supervision. Models from other countries exist for these large-scale reforms. In Sweden, for example, municipalities must provide preschool classes for all six-year-olds (Gunnarsson et al. 1999). Participation is voluntary, but 91 percent of all Swedish six-year-olds attend these preschool classes (id.). Germany is considering extending the length of the average school day for public schools (Falling Behind 2007). Exploring such alternatives to current practices might lead to greater reductions in juvenile delinquency, result in higher academic achievement by U.S. students, and minimize the massive numbers of latch-key children.

European practices provide viable models, as those governments have had national child care policies in place for decades (e.g., Morgan 2006). European nations have adopted various combinations of tax credits, paid family leave provisions, public daycare centers, and subsidies to and regulation of private daycare providers.

The much-acclaimed services provided by the French government offer one such model (e.g., Jenson and Sineau 2003; Martin and Le Bihan 2009; Morgan 2002). Following World War II, France quickly increased the number of daycare services. By the 1970s, these schools were universally available, and France was recognized as one of the leading providers of early childhood education in the world (Jenson and Sineau 2003; Martin and Le Bihan 2009; Morgan 2002). Three types of services are currently available for young children: community day nurseries, organized family care, and parent cooperatives (Jenson and Sineau 2003). In addition, French services provide part-time or drop-in care for children who need only occasional care (id.).

Aside from direct funding of comprehensive programs, vouchers may offer an alternative method of government-supported child care. In the United States vouchers have attracted the attention of advocates for child care providers since the 1970s (Parker 1989). Such a funding scheme appeals to conservatives, who generally oppose federal provision of child care but who might be receptive to child care centers run by religious groups. Vouchers have been a cornerstone in previous attempts at creating federally funded early child care such as the failed 1987 Act for Better Child Care (ABC) bill, which proposed mandated federal child care standards and offered a combination of grants, contracts, loans, and vouchers (Cohen 2001; Haskins and Brown 1989). Vouchers could also be employed in a composite system. For example, Professor Debbie Kaminer's proposal for a national child care policy suggests the adoption of a voucher system supplemented by contracted care in communities where there is a shortage of child care providers (2007).

No one will deny that public child care, whether implemented with direct funding or vouchers, will be very expensive. Again, we should learn from our European counterparts, who have faced serious financial challenges in running their child care programs in recent years. For example, due to shortages of publicly funded child care services in both France and

Belgium, policymakers today encourage parents to select a stay-at-home caretaker, hire a nanny, or solicit the services of other relatives (Jenson and Sineau 2003; Morgan 2002). If the experience of these European countries is predictive, genuine child care reform might require a substantial tax increase, at least until the various benefits of the reform—such as reduced numbers of incarcerated individuals and a more productive adult population—are realized.

Of course, reformers must be prepared for strong opposition to tax increases to pay for child care services. Some economists warn that affluent families in particular would oppose increases since they can already purchase high-quality private services on their own and therefore would object to subsidizing government-provided services for lower-income families (England and Folbre 1999). To earn widespread support, the government must convince parents that its services are actually superior to any that could be purchased on the private market. Since the government would be able to respond to the real needs of children and families, rather than only those needs that are profitable to meet, superior government services are far from impossible. In fact, in several European countries, including France and Sweden, "it is the wealthier families who tend to use the publicly funded daycare services more often" (Dixon 2005, 583; Jenson and Sineau 2003). This finding suggests that wealthy families, too, could benefit from publicly funded services and thus could be convinced to support tax increases to support them. In the end, the greatest resistance to tax increases can be expected to come from Americans opposed to subsidizing other people's children when their own children have already been raised on private dollars (England and Folbre 1999). Reformers must convince these and other opponents that children's well-being and development ultimately is a public obligation (id.).

3. Tax Code Reforms

Other than directly funded child care programs, the most common form of government subsidy for child care is likely to be found in the tax code. In the United States, there are currently two types of tax breaks for child care costs: the universally available child and dependent care credit, and pretax dependent care accounts available only through employers (Ebeling 2009). Tax subsidies and credits could comprise valuable components of a national policy to promote effective child care. However, these tax solutions are subject to many limitations. Generally, such proposals benefit the middle and upper classes most, as many families in need of daycare and after-school care will have incomes so low that they will have very little tax liability to begin with. For these low-income families, tax credits will do very little to increase access to child care services.

The various tax breaks and subsidies are also subject to a number of more specific limitations. First, standard tax return credits only apply to children under the age of thirteen and require that neither parent can be available to watch the child full-time (id.). In addition, *Smith v. Commissioner* established that child care expenses were personal expenses and, therefore, were not deductible as ordinary business expenses. This decision remains valid today, and it "precludes the deduction of child care expenses that would not otherwise fall under [Internal Revenue Code] Sections 21 or 129" (Shurtz 1997, 519). But these two sections of the tax code do not provide a refund for low-income taxpayers with low taxability (id.). Moreover, low-income parents cannot afford to pay market price for the child care services the credits were originally designed to promote (id.).

Some European countries currently offer subsidies that are restricted to low-income families (Tietze and Cryer 1999). And in general, European countries seem to have found success in using their tax codes to help families afford quality private child care. The French government, for example, provides subsidies for parents who use family child care and special tax breaks for parents who hire nannies (Shurtz 1997). Although these tax breaks do not address the shortcomings of private child care described above, they at least allow families to afford some child care, helping jump start the economic benefits also described above.

4. New Leave Policies

Perhaps the only major policy change in the United States concerning child care since the mid-1970s has been the creation of federally required family and medical leave, along with the adoption of similar provisions by state governments (Morgan 2006). American employers of more than fifty workers are required by the Family and Medical Leave Act (FMLA) of 1993 to provide twelve weeks of unpaid family leave. But these leaves of absence from work remain unpaid, so the parent taking the leave is dependent upon the employer's goodwill for any compensation (id.). Today, the United States remains "one of the few advanced, industrialized countries in which parents have no entitlement to a paid parental leave" (id., 151). In comparison, in European countries, mothers are typically paid 75 percent or more of their earnings while on maternity leave, and many countries also provide paid paternity and other family leave (Tietze and Cryer 1999).

The United States could improve its leave policies by mandating paid leave, especially for new parents. Of course, expanded leave provisions would increase care for infants only, but improved care during this crucial time of child and family development could yield exponentially greater benefits in the long term. It would also preserve parents' funds for child care services when the leave term concludes, while simultaneously ensuring that parents do not lose their jobs when new children are born. Thus, although expanded family leave would not address all of the deeper issues discussed here, it should be part of any comprehensive child care policy.

IV. Conclusion

A profound conceptual shift is needed in American child care policy debates. Child care must be recognized as an investment, not seen as consumption (England and Folbre 1999). While funding a comprehensive child care program presents major challenges, "Framing high quality child care and early childhood education in terms of economic development is a crucial component to economic growth and competitiveness at the national, state and local level" (Fleron et al. 2006, 2). Emerging longitudinal studies and well-established examples from our European counterparts call for serious consideration and investment by U.S. policymakers. As these models show, a national child care policy offers the Obama administration a unique opportunity to stabilize childhood experiences for millions of American children, increase productivity of American families, and, finally, reduce juvenile delinquency and subsequent criminal misconduct that has long plagued our communities.

This chapter is an edited version of an article that previously appeared at 4 *Harvard Law and Policy Review* 49-72 (Winter 2010).

REFERENCES

Afterschool Alliance. 2009. America after 3 pm: Key Findings. http://www.afterschoolalliance.org/documents/AA3PM_key_Findings_2009.pdf.
Baker, Jean. 1990. Child Care: Will Uncle Sam Provide a Comprehensive Solution for American Families? *Journal of Contemporary Health Law and Policy* 6: 239-75.
Baughman, Reagan, et al. 2003. Productivity and Wage Effects of "Family Friendly" Fringe Benefits. *International Journal of Manpower* 24: 247-59.
Begné, Patricia. 2005. Parental Authority and Child Custody in Mexico. *Family Law Quarterly* 39 (2): 527-42.

Belfield, Clive R., Milagros Nores, Steve Barnett, and Lawrence Schweinhart. 2005. The High/Scope Perry Pre-school Program: Cost-Benefit Analysis Using Data from the Age-40 Followup. *Journal of Human Resources* 41: 162-90.

Benard, Bonnie, and Kathy Marshall. 2001. Big Brothers/Big Sisters Mentoring: The Power of Developmental Relationships. The Resilience Research for Prevention Programs Series 2. http://www.cce.umn.edu/pdfs/nrrc/mentoring.pdf.

Bennett, John, et al. 2001. OECD Review Team, Early Childhood Education and Care Policy in Denmark. http://www.oecd.org/dataoecd/31/56/33685537.pdf.

Biglan, Anthony, Sharon L. Foster, Harold D. Holder, and Patricia A. Brennan. 2004. *Helping Adolescents at Risk.* New York: Guilford Press.

Bresnahan-Coleman, Theresa. 2009. The Tension between Short-Term Benefits for Care-givers and Long-Term Effects of Gender Discrimination in the United States, Canada, and France. *New England Journal of International and Comparative Law* 15: 151-83.

Calonge, Ned. 2005. Community Interventions to Prevent Violence: Translation into Public Health Practice. *American Journal of Preventive Medicine* 28: 4-5.

Campbell, Frances A., Elizabeth P. Pungello, Shari Miller-Johnson, Margaret Burchinal, and Craig T. Ramey. 2001. The Development of Cognitive and Academic Abilities: Growth Curves from an Early Childhood Educational Experiment. *Developmental Psychology* 37: 231-42.

Casey, David M., et al. 2005. Activity Participation and the Well-Being of Children and Adolescents in the Context of Welfare Reform. In *Organized Activities as Contexts of Development: Extracurricular Activities, After-School and Community Programs.* Edited by Joseph L. Mahoney, et al. Mahwah, NJ: Lawrence Erlbaum.

Chung, An-me, U.S. Department of Education. 2000. *After-School Programs: Keeping Children Safe and Smart.* http://www.ed.gov/pubs/afterschool/afterschool.pdf.

Clarke-Stewart, Alison. 1993. *Daycare.* Revised ed. Cambridge, MA: Harvard University Press.

Cohen, Sally S. 2001. *Championing Child Care.* New York: Columbia University Press.

Crane, Jonathan, and Mallory Barg. 2003. Do Early Childhood Intervention Programs Really Work? Coalition for Evidence-Based Policy. Unpublished manuscript, available at http://www.evidencebasedprograms.org/static/pdfs/Do%20Early%20Intervention%20Programs%20Really%20Work7.pdf.

Crary, David. 2006. "A New Labor Battle: Child-Care Workers Are Organizing, but Some States Resist." *Philadelphia Inquirer*, February 6, 2006, C03.

Dickens, William T., et al. 2006. *The Effects of Investing in Early Education on Economic Growth.* Washington, DC: Brookings Institute.

Dixon, Heather S. 2005. National Daycare: A Necessary Precursor to Gender Equality with Newfound Promise for Success. *Columbia Human Rights Law Review* 36: 561-661.

Ebeling, Ashlea. 2009. "The ABCs of Child Care Breaks." Forbes.com, March 18. http://www.forbes.com/2009/03/18/nanny-tax-credit-personal-finance-taxes-child-care-html (on file with the Harvard Law School Library).

Editorial. 2009. "Home Alone." *New York Times*, October 19, A30.

England, Paula, and Nancy Folbre. 1999. Who Should Pay for the Kids? *The ANNALS of the American Academy of Political and Social Science* 563: 194-207.

Falling Behind: Working Women in Germany Grapple with Limited Child-Care Options. 2007. Knowledge @ Wharton, March 28. http://knowledge.wharton.upenn.edu/createpdf.cfm?articleid=1694 (on file with the Harvard Law School Library).

Farrington, David P., and Brandon C. Welsh. 2007. *Saving Children from a Life of Crime: Early Risk Factors and Effective Interventions*. New York: Oxford University Press.

Fleron, Lou Jean, et al. 2006. "Buffalo Child Care Means Business" (slide show). Ithaca, NY: Cornell University, School of Industrial and Labor Relations. http://digitalcommons.ilr.cornell.edu/conference/4.

Flowers, R. Barri. 2002. *Kids Who Commit Adult Crimes: Serious Criminality by Juvenile Offenders*. London: Haworth.

Frank Porter Graham Child Development Center. 1974. *The Carolina Abecedarian Project*. Chapel Hill: University of North Carolina at Chapel Hill. http://www.fpg.unc.edu/~abc/assets/pdf/1974_abc_brochure.pdf.

Frank Porter Graham Child Development Center. 1999. *Early Learning, Later Success: The Abecedarian Study*. Chapel Hill: University of North Carolina at Chapel Hill. http://www.fpg.unc.edu/~abc/ells-04.pdf.

Gottfredson, Denise C., Gary T. Gottfredson, and Stephanie A. Weisman. 2001. The Timing of Delinquent Behavior and Its Implications for After-School Programs. *Criminology and Public Policy* 1: 61-86.

Goubau, Dominique. 2000. Joint Exercise of Parental Authority: The Quebec Civil Law Perspective. *Canadian Journal of Family Law* 17: 333-70.

Greenwood, Peter W. 2006. *Changing Lives: Delinquency Prevention as Crime-Control Policy*. Chicago: University of Chicago Press.

Grogan-Kaylor, Andrew, et al. 2008. Behaviors of Youth Involved in the Child Welfare System. *Child Abuse and Neglect* 32: 35-49.

Gunnarsson, Lars, et al. 1999. *Early Childhood Education and Care Policy in Sweden*. OECD Review Team: 30. http://www.oecd.org/dataoecd/48/17/2479039.pdf.

Haskins, Ron, and Hank Brown. 1989. "The Day-Care Reform Juggernaut." *National Review*, March 10, 40-41.

Hasselbrack, Anne. 2002. Watching Grassroots Grow in Louisiana: The Children's Initiatives. In *Juvenile Justice Today: Essays on Programs and Policies* 61 (American Correctional Association edition).

Hawkins, J. David, Richard F. Catalano, and Devon D. Brewer. 1995. Preventing Serious, Violent, and Chronic Juvenile Offending. In *A Sourcebook: Serious, Violent, and Chronic Juvenile Offenders*, edited by James C. Howell, Barry Krisberg, J. David Hawkins, and John J. Wilson, 47. Thousand Oaks, CA: Sage.

Heckman, James J. 2006. Skill Formation and the Economics of Investing in Disadvantaged Children. *Science* 312: 1900-1902.

Helburn, Suzanne W., and Barbara R. Bergmann. 2002. *America's Child Care Problem: The Way Out*. New York: Palgrave.

Hirsch, Barton J. 2005. *A Place to Call Home: After-School Programs for Urban Youth*. Washington, DC: American Psychological Association.

Hooton, Angela. 2002. From Welfare Recipient to Childcare Worker: Balancing Work and Family under TANF. *Texas Journal of Women and the Law* 12: 121-65.

Jenson, Jane, and Mariette Sineau. 2003. France: Reconciling Republican Equality with "Freedom of Choice." In *Who Cares? Women's Work, Childcare, and Welfare State Redesign*. Toronto: University of Toronto Press.

Juvenile Curfews and the Major Confusion over Minor Rights. 2005. *Harvard Law Review* 118: 2400-2421.

Kaminer, Debbie. 2007. The Child Care Crisis and the Work-Family Conflict: A Policy Rationale for Federal Legislation. *Berkeley Journal of Employment and Labor Law* 28: 495-540.

Knudsen, Eric I., James J. Heckman, Judy L. Cameron, and Jack P. Shonkoff. 2006. Economic, Neurobiological, and Behavioral Perspectives on Building America's Future Workforce. *Proceedings of the National Academy of Science of the United States of America* 103 (27): 10155-62.

Land, Kenneth C. 2009. The 2009 Foundation for Child Development Child and Youth Well-Being Index (CWI Report). Foundation for Child Development. http://www.fcdus.org/usr_doc/Final2009CWIReport.pdf.

Lipsey, M. W., and D. B. Wilson. 1998. Effective Intervention for Serious Juvenile Offenders. In *Serious and Violent Juvenile Defenders*, edited by R. Loeber and D. P. Farrington. Thousand Oaks, CA: Sage.

Lombardi, Joan. 2003. *Time to Care: Redesigning Child Care to Promote Education, Support Families, and Build Communities*. Philadelphia: Temple University Press.

Martin, Claude, and Blanche Le Bihan. 2009. Public Child Care and Preschools in France. In *Child Care and Preschool Development in Europe*. Chippenham, England: Palgrave Macmillan.

Mead, Sara. 2009. *Education Reform Starts Early: Lessons from New Jersey's PreK-3rd Reform Efforts*. Washington, DC: New America Foundation. http://www.newamerica.net/sites/newamerica.net/files/policydocs/Education%20Reform%20Starts%20Early_0.pdf.

Medina, M. Isabel. 1994. In Search of Quality Childcare: Closing the Immigration Gate to Childcare Workers. *Georgetown Immigration Law Journal* 8: 161-99.

Meyers, Marcia K., and Theresa Heintze. 1999. The Performance of the Child-Care Subsidy System. *Social Service Review* 73: 39-64.

Morgan, Kimberly. 2002. Does Anyone Have a "Libre Choix"? Subversive Liberalism and the Politics of French Child Care Policy. In *Child Care Policy at the Crossroads*. New York: Routledge.

Morgan, Kimberly J. 2006. *Working Mothers and the Welfare State*. Stanford, CA: Stanford University Press.

Morrissey, Taryn W., and Patti Banghart. 2007. *Family Child Care in the United States*. New York: National Center for Children in Poverty. http://www.nccp.org/publications/pub_720.html.

Nagle, Geoffrey A. 2009. The Economics of Infant Mental Health. In *Handbook of Infant Mental Health*, edited by Charles H. Zeanah Jr., 580. New York: Guilford Press.

O'Connor, Thomas G., and David B. Parfitt. 2009. Applying Research Findings on Early Experience to Infant Mental Health. In *Handbook of Infant Mental Health*, ed. Charles H. Zeanah Jr., 120. New York: Guilford Press.

Parker, Michael D. 1989. Vouchers for Day Care of Children: Evaluating a Model Program. *Child Welfare* 68: 633-42.

Parks, Greg. 2004. High/Scope Perry Preschool Project. *Juvenile Justice Bulletin* 4. Washington, DC: Office of Juvenile and Delinquency Prevention, U.S. Department of Justice. http://www.ncjrs.gov/pdffiles1/ojjdp/181725.pdf.

Peisner-Feinberg, E. S., et al. 1999. *The Children of the Cost, Quality, and Outcomes Study Go to School: Executive Summary*. Chapel Hill: University of North Carolina at Chapel Hill, Frank Porter Graham Child Development Center. http://www.fpg.unc.edu/ncedl/PDFs/CQO-es.pdf.

Pitegoff, Peter. 1993. Child Care Enterprise, Community Development, and Work. *George-town Law Journal* 81: 1897-1943.

Platt, Anthony M. 2009. *The Child Savers: The Invention of Delinquency.* 40th ed. Chicago: University of Chicago Press.

Posting of Lisa Guernsey to Early Ed Watch. December 8, 2009. http://earlyed.newamerica.net/blogposts/2009/breaking_down_the_walls_between_hhs_and_the_dept_of_ed-24871 (on file with the Harvard Law School Library).

Posting of Lisa Guernsey to Early Ed Watch. November 19, 2009. http://earlyed.newamerica.net/blogposts/2009/duncan_early_ed_can_get_schools_out_of_the_catch_up_business-18435 (on file with the Harvard Law School Library).

Privor, Brian. 1999. Dusk 'Til Dawn: Children's Rights and the Effectiveness of Juvenile Curfew Ordinances. *Boston University Law Review* 79: 415-92.

Ramey, Craig. 2000. Helping Children Get Started Right: The Benefits of Early Childhood Intervention. In *Helping Poor Kids Succeed: Welfare, Tax, and Early Intervention Policies,* edited by Karen Bogenschneider and Jessica Mills. Wisconsin Family Impact Seminar Briefing Report No. 14, 32 pages. Madison: University of Wisconsin Center for Excellence in Family Studies. http://www.familyimpactseminars.org/s_wifis14report.pdf.

Samansky, Allan J. 1996. Tax Policy and the Obligation to Support Children. *Ohio State Law Journal* 57: 329-80.

Satkowski, Christina. 2009. *The Next Step in Systems-Building: Early Childhood Advisory Councils and Federal Efforts to Promote Policy-Alignment in Early Childhood.* Washington, DC: New America Foundation. http://newamerica.net/sites/newamerica.net/files/policydocs/Early_Childhood_Advisory_Councils_Nov_09_0.pdf.

Schuler-Harms, Margarete. 2009. Money Matters: Experiments in Financing Public Child Care. *Child Care and Preschool Development in Europe.* Chippenham, England: Palgrave Macmillan.

Schweinhart, Lawrence J. 2005. *The High/Scope Perry Preschool Study through Age 40.* Ypsilanti, MI: High/Scope Educational Research Foundation. http://www.highscope.org/file/Research/PerryProject/3_specialsummary%20col%2006%2007.pdf.

Selmi, Michael, and Naomi Cahn. 2006. Women in the Workplace: Which Women, Which Agenda? *Duke Journal of Gender Law and Policy* 13: 7-30.

Shurtz, Nancy E. 1997. Gender Equity and Tax Policy: The Theory of "Taxing Men." *Southern California Review of Law and Women's Studies* 6: 485-532.

Smith, Peggie R. 2006. Laboring for Child Care: A Consideration of New Approaches to Represent Low-Income Service Workers. *University of Pennsylvania Journal of Labor and Employment Law* 8: 583-621.

Stewart, Anna, Michael Livingston, and Susan Dennison. 2008. Transitions and Turning Points: Examining the Links between Child Maltreatment and Juvenile Offending. *Child Abuse and Neglect* 32: 51-66.

Tanenhaus, David S. 2004. *Juvenile Justice in the Making.* New York: Oxford University Press.

Tietze, Wolfgang, and Debby Cryer. 1999. Current Trends in European Early Child Care and Education. *The ANNALS of the American Academy of Political and Social Science* 563: 175-93.

Tremblay, Richard E., and Wendy M. Craig. 1995. Developmental Crime Prevention. *Crime and Justice* 19: 151-236.

Trollinger, Tona. 1996. The Juvenile Curfew: Unconstitutional Imprisonment. *William and Mary Bill of Rights Journal* 4: 949-1003.

Ulrich, Katherine Elizabeth. 2002. Insuring Family Risks: Suggestions for a National Family Policy and Wage Replacement. *Yale Journal of Law and Feminism* 14: 1-68.

UNICEF Innocenti Research Centre. 2008. *The Child Care Transition* 4. http://www.unicefirc.org/publications/pdf/rc8_eng.pdf.

U.S. Bureau of Labor Statistics, U.S. Department of Labor. 2008. *Women in the Labor Force*, 13, tbl.5. http://www.bls.gov/cps/wlf-databook-2008.pdf.

U.S. Census Bureau, U.S. Department of Commerce. 2005. *Who's Minding the Kids? Child Care Arrangements: Spring 2005.* http://www.census.gov/population/www/socdemo/child/ppl-2005.html (scroll to PPL Table 6) (on file with the Harvard Law School Library).

Watson, Jane. 1995. Crime and Juvenile Delinquency Prevention Policy: Time for Early Childhood Intervention. *Georgetown Journal on Fighting Poverty* 2: 245-58.

Wax, Amy L. 2001. A Reciprocal Welfare Program. *Virginia Journal of Social Policy and the Law* 8: 477-516.

Wood, Cheri L. 1995. Childless Mothers? The New Catch-22: You Can't Have Your Kids and Work for Them Too. *Loyola of Los Angeles Law Review* 29: 383-428.

Yinlan, Xia. 2005. The Legal System of Guardianship over Minors in the People's Republic of China. *Family Law Quarterly* 39 (2): 477-88.

Yoshikawa, Hirokazu. 1995. Long-Term Effects of Early Childhood Programs on Social Outcomes and Delinquency. *Future of Children* 5: 51-75. http://www.princeton.edu/futureofchildren/publications/docs/05_03_02.pdf.

Zatz, Noah D. 2006a. Welfare to What? *Hastings Law Journal* 57: 1131-88.

Zatz, Noah D. 2006b. What Welfare Requires from Work. *University of California at Los Angeles Law Review* 54: 373-464.

Zigler, Edward F. 1989. Addressing the Nation's Child Care Crisis: The School of the Twenty-First Century. *American Journal of Orthopsychiatry* 59 (4): 484-91.

3

Challenging the Overuse of Foster Care and Disrupting the Path to Delinquency and Prison

LESLIE JOAN HARRIS

Foster care is supposed to be a temporary safe haven for abused and neglected children, a place where they are cared for while their parents solve the problems that led to their mistreatment. For many children, foster care undoubtedly serves this function well. However, thousands of children live in foster care for extended periods of time, many leaving care only when they become adults. Recent studies show that for many of these children, foster care is not a safe, nurturing place. Instead, being in care exposes these children to substantial risks of later juvenile delinquency and adult criminal arrest and conviction, as well as mental health problems, difficulties in school, poor employment prospects, poverty, and homelessness. Other studies also show that many children are placed in foster care unnecessarily, in the sense that they could safely remain in their parents' homes if appropriate services were provided to the parents. This evidence suggests that law and public policy should place greater emphasis on providing services to families and reducing the use of foster care. Ironically, reducing the use of foster care and focusing more on in-home services have been public policy goals in the United States for more than thirty years, and the roots of these policies go back more than a century. Despite this long consensus, the foster care system has been stubbornly resistant to change.

This chapter examines the problem of the overuse of foster care and argues that conventional reform proposals are unlikely to succeed, as they have not succeeded for a century. Borrowing from the work of French social historian and philosopher Michel Foucault, I suggest that the current foster care system may persist because it is performing other, covert functions very well. In particular, the system allows society to assert that it is protecting children from harm while refusing to provide substantial material support to poor parents. The system conforms to the more generally applicable policy of minimizing direct economic assistance to poor adults while allowing us to believe that poor children do not really suffer from this policy. I argue that turning this analytical lens on the actual functioning of the foster care system and its harmful effects on many children could provide new ways to argue for legal and policy reforms to the child welfare system that could reduce the unnecessary use of foster care and the consequences of that overuse for delinquency.

The chapter first reviews the recent research that demonstrates how harmful foster care is to many children. Next, I examine the history of child welfare interventions over the last century, showing that for many decades well-informed professionals have argued that the child protection system should leave children at home if possible, rather than removing them from their parents' custody. Despite this advocacy, hundreds of thousands of children have been and continue to be removed from their parents' homes and placed in foster care, and their parents have not received the services that might make removal unnecessary. Reform efforts have made small inroads on this reality. The third part of the chapter turns to Foucault's study of prisons and particularly his analysis of why prisons have continued to be the dominant mode of punishment, little changed for centuries, even though they have long been criticized for being ineffective (not reducing crime) and even harmful (producing recidivism). Foucault argues that when an institution persists despite its apparent failure to achieve its social purpose, it is in fact serving some other, unarticulated goals very well. In the final section of this paper, I use this analytical structure to reexamine the overuse of foster care and suggest how the insights that the analysis produces might be used to support more effective reform efforts.

I. Foster Care as a Precursor to Delinquency and Conviction of Adult Crime

A great deal of social science research shows that children who spend significant amounts of time in foster care are at increased risk for being found delinquent in juvenile court and convicted of crimes as adults (Bender 2010). Almost 20 percent of the U.S. prison population under the age of thirty and 25 percent of those with prior convictions are former foster children (Doyle 2008). A recent large-scale study of foster children, conducted by the Chapin Hall research center at the University of Chicago, explores this connection in detail. The Chapin Hall researchers compared data about youth who had been in foster care homes in several states in the Midwest to a very large control data set.

More than half the young people in the Chapin Hall study who had been in foster care had been arrested, over one-third had spent a night in jail, and one-third had been convicted of a crime (Courtney, Terao, and Bost 2005). For most offenses, the proportion of former foster care youth seventeen to eighteen years old committed offenses at twice or more the rate of the control group. The offenses considered were damaging property, stealing, going into a building to steal something, selling drugs, hurting someone badly enough for the person to need medical care, using or threatening to use a weapon, participating in a group fight, pulling a knife or gun on someone, and shooting or stabbing someone. For nineteen-year-olds, the Chapin Hall researchers found much smaller differences in offending, although youth who had been in foster care reported that they were significantly more likely to damage property, steal something worth more than fifty dollars, take part in a group fights, and pull a weapon on someone. More significantly, the nineteen-year-olds who had been in foster care faced much higher rates of arrest; 57 percent of the males reported that they had been arrested at least once, compared to 20 percent of the control group, and 36 percent reported having been arrested since age eighteen, compared to 2 percent of the control group. The percentage of female foster youth reporting that they had been arrested was not only higher than that of the female control group but also higher than that of the male control group (Cusick and Courtney 2007).

Other recent studies also find a strong correlation between foster care placement and later involvement with the juvenile justice and criminal systems. Researchers using child welfare and juvenile justice system data from Cook County, Illinois, between 1995 and 2000 found that children placed in foster homes or other substitute care for at least a year were twice as much at risk of becoming involved in the juvenile delinquency system as abused or neglected children left at home. For girls, being placed in just one out-of-home placement significantly increased the risk, while boys' risk did not rise until they experienced multiple placements (Ryan and Testa 2005).

However, the reasons why placement in foster care increases the risk of future involvement with the delinquent and criminal systems are not obvious. For example, it seems quite possible that the experience of being maltreated makes it more likely that children will engage in behavior that will bring them into conflict with the law as they grow older. MIT economics professor Joseph J. Doyle developed a method of analyzing foster care and criminal arrest data that teases out the relationship between foster care and later criminal involvement. He found that for a significant number of children, removal from home and placement in foster care in itself increases the risks of adjudication as a delinquent and conviction of crimes in adult court (Doyle 2008).

Doyle's study is limited to poor children between the ages of five and fifteen who live in the urban Chicago area. He focused on children whom he identified as being "on the margin" of placement, that is, ones about whom professional child welfare workers could reasonably disagree as to the need for placement in foster care (Doyle 2008). Some of the children in this marginal group had "strict" caseworkers who removed them to foster care, and others had more "lenient" workers who left them at home while working with their parents (Doyle 2008). Doyle concluded that children on the margin of placement had a much lower risk of criminal involvement if left at home. The children placed in foster care had a delinquency rate three times that of children left at home (Doyle 2007). They also had adult arrest, conviction, and imprisonment rates that were three times higher than the rates of children who had been left at home (Doyle 2008).

Doyle, the Chapin Hall project, and other researchers have also examined other ways in which former foster children differ from their peers in the general population, finding that they are much more likely to have the kind of health, education, and employment problems that are associated with an increased risk of involvement in the juvenile and criminal justice systems. By the time they turned twenty-one years old, nearly a quarter of the Chapin Hall foster care alumni had not obtained a high school diploma or a GED; they were more than twice as likely to lack either credential compared to similar young people in the general population. Only 30 percent had completed any college, compared to 53 percent of 21-year-olds in the general population. Just over half were currently working, compared with nearly two-thirds of 21-year-olds nationally (Courtney, Dworskey, and Pollack 2007). Doyle also found that children who were removed were less successful in the employment market; they worked 11 percent fewer quarters and earned $850 less than those who were left in their homes (Doyle 2007).

The findings from another large-scale study of former foster children from Oregon and Washington, conducted by the Casey Family Programs in Seattle, are similar. The proportion of Casey alumni who had a high school diploma or a GED was comparable to that of the general population (84.8 percent), but the alumni were much more likely to have only a GED—28.5 percent compared to 5 percent of the general population. While more than a quarter of the general population aged twenty to thirty-four had completed a bachelor's degree, only 1.8 percent of the foster care alumni had (Pecora et al.

2005). Not counting people who were not in the workforce, only 80 percent of the Casey foster care alumni aged twenty to thirty-four were employed compared to 95 percent in the general population. A third of the foster care alumni had household incomes at or below the poverty level, double the national average for people eighteen to thirty-four, and 22 percent experienced homelessness after leaving foster care (Pecora et al. 2005).

Perhaps the most striking information from the Casey study was the very high incidence of mental health problems among former foster children. Within the twelve months before the study was conducted, more than half the foster care alumni (54 percent) had had clinical levels of at least one mental health problem, and 20 percent had had three or more such problems. In contrast, less than a quarter of the general population had had mental health problems in the same time period. Twenty-five percent of the foster care alumni had been diagnosed with post-traumatic stress disorder within the previous twelve months, a rate twice as high as that of U.S. war veterans (Pecora et al. 2005).

The clear implication of all of this research is that efforts to keep children in their homes rather than removing them to foster care should pay off by generally improving the life prospects of abused and neglected children, as well as avoiding the costs of future lawbreaking (Pecora et al. 2005). Of course, federal and state child welfare policy has long recognized the importance of trying to keep maltreated children in their own homes by providing services to families. For three decades, federal and state laws have provided that children should not be removed from their parents' homes if possible and that child welfare agencies should make reasonable efforts to prevent the need to remove children and, if they are removed, to reunite them with their families (Adoption Assistance and Child Welfare Act of 1980). Moreover, leaving mistreated children with their families of origin if possible has been advocated by experts for much longer, as the next section outlines.

II. A Century of Calls for Leaving Children at Home

By the late nineteenth century, the desirability of raising children in their homes rather than in institutions was generally accepted (Breckenridge and Abbott 1912), and child welfare professionals have long recognized that keeping children at home if possible was better for them. For example, in 1909 Judge Julian Mack, one of the leaders of the juvenile court movement, argued that children should not be removed from home because their parents were too poor to care for them (Mack 1909). Simultaneously with the development of the first juvenile courts in the early 1900s, states developed mothers' aid programs that provided funds to enable poor children to remain in their (worthy) mothers' homes rather than being placed in poorhouses, orphanages, and other institutions (Kahn 1962). The first White House Conference on Children, convened in 1909, endorsed programs intended to keep children at home rather than remove them because of their parents' poverty (*Proceedings* 1909). The report of the conference proclaimed, "Home life is the highest and finest product of civilization," and "children should not be deprived of it except for urgent and compelling reasons" (*Proceedings* 1909, 5). However, mothers' aid programs were always limited and poorly funded, reflecting social ambivalence about providing cash assistance to the poor. Despite the expressed preference for leaving children at home, thousands of children continued to be placed in orphanages and other institutions (Grossberg 2002).

Throughout the twentieth century, the developing child welfare profession continued to emphasize the value of preserving children's families. In 1930 the Public Charities Association of Pennsylvania declared, "Every effort should be made to prevent the removal of children from their own homes with services which their own families may, with assistance, perform with better and long-lasting results" (Levine 1973, 19). Grace Abbott, an early social worker who led the United States Children's Bureau during the 1930s, made the same argument in *The Child and the State*, a seminal book that explores the obligation of the state to care for dependent children (Abbott 1938). The Great Depression of the 1930s completely overwhelmed states' modest efforts to support families through mothers' aid laws; in 1935 the Social Security Act created the Aid to Dependent Children program, which provided federal funds to enable impoverished mothers to keep their children at home with them (Witte 1963). In 1951 the American Humane Association recommended that every reasonable effort to protect a child in the parents' home should be made and that a child should be removed only if these efforts failed (American Humane Association 1951). Statements of good practices during the 1960s emphasized that when a child was taken into foster care, parents should be offered help to correct the problems that led to removal, and plans should be made to return the child promptly (Lewis 1964; Arnold 1960).

Despite this theoretical recognition of the value of leaving children at home and efforts to reunite them with their parents when they were removed, every year thousands of children were removed from home, first to institutions and then, as foster care replaced institutional care, to foster homes. In 1959, an estimated 254,000 children were in out-of-home care (Maas and Engler 1959), and ten years later 249,000 children were in foster families (White 1973). The estimates of the number of children in foster care in the mid-1970s ranged from two hundred thousand to five hundred thousand (Law Enforcement Assistance Administration 1976; Mnookin 1973; Davidson 1981).

While foster care was, in theory, temporary, a place for children to stay safely while their parents got their acts together, a 1959 article by Maas and Engler presented data showing that many children remained in foster care for very long periods of time, often until they reached the age of majority (Maas and Engler 1959). In the next decade and a half, other academic social workers replicated and expanded on their findings, and the term "foster care drift" became the shorthand designation for this phenomenon and its consequences (Emlen 1976). Social work researchers who studied the causes of foster care drift concluded that neither demographic factors, modes of entry into foster care, nor the reasons for placements accounted for much of the variance in how long children remained in foster care (Emlen 1976).

During the 1970s, a major social work research project set out to identify the causes of foster care drift and to develop steps for eliminating them. The project identified foster children considered unlikely to return home and assigned them caseworkers with reduced caseloads and training in assessing cases, obtaining and organizing legal evidence, participating in court hearings, and planning adoptions (Emlen 1976; Downs et al. 1978; Emlen 1977). The project succeeded in moving the great majority of these children into permanent homes, mostly by returning them to their parents (Downs et al. 1978; Emlen 1977). Similar results were achieved in other states that later replicated this program (Harris 1983).

During the same time that this research was laying the foundation for current social work practices, legal scholars were arguing that then-current law encouraged the child welfare system to intervene too easily into families in the name of child protection without requiring caseworkers to assess whether problems could be solved while children remained at home or to compare the alternative of staying at home to removal (Smith et al. 1980; Mnookin 1975; Wald 1975; Areen 1975). The academic lawyers also criticized the law for its inattention to what happened after a child was removed from home, saying that the failure to require planning and monitoring of cases contributed substantially to foster care drift (Wald 1976).

To solve these problems, and consistent with the recommendations of the social workers described above, the law professors argued that juvenile court laws should be revised to require child welfare agencies to prepare specific goal-oriented treatment plans in every case; that courts should regularly review progress toward achieving the goals; and that the plans should be modified as necessary, in terms of both the goals to be achieved and the means of achieving them. They also argued that the law should encourage termination of parental rights when it was clear that foster children could not return home within a reasonable time, thus freeing them to be placed in other permanent homes (Wald 1975; Wald 1976; Mnookin 1973).

These arguments substantially shaped major proposals to revise state juvenile codes (Law Enforcement Assistance Administration 1976; Office of Juvenile Justice and Delinquency Prevention 1980). The most influential proposal was the Institute of Judicial Administration–American Bar Association Standards Relating to Abuse and Neglect (IJA-ABA Joint Commission 1981).

The results of the social work foster care studies and the proposals of the legal academics pointed in the same direction, and they culminated in 1980 in Congress's enactment of the Adoption Assistance and Child Welfare Act. This act amended the federal statutes setting out the requirements states must satisfy to be eligible to receive federal foster care funds. Besides requiring case planning and periodic reviews, the act also required state child welfare agencies to provide preventive services to allow abused or neglected children to remain at home safely rather than be placed in foster care and, if removed, to allow them to be reunited with their parents. Juvenile courts were required to review cases to determine whether these "reasonable efforts" had been made (Adoption Assistance and Child Welfare Act of 1980).

However, these reforms did not succeed in reducing the number of children in foster care (Children's Bureau 1997). In 1980, the year when the federal reform legislation was enacted, 276,000 children were in foster care (Staff of H.R. Committee 2004). Five years later, the foster care population was the same, and by 1990 the population had mushroomed to 405,743 (Staff of H.R. Committee 2004). This failure to reduce the number of children in foster care, combined with criticism of the reasonable-efforts requirements in cases in which children returned to parents were seriously injured or killed (Gelles 1996), prompted the enactment of further reforms to the federal legislation, the Adoption and Safe Families Act of 1997 (ASFA).

ASFA requires that state law place more emphasis on child safety than the 1980 act did, and it requires states to have laws that encourage more rapid termination of parental rights when children have been in foster care for an extended period of time (ASFA §§ 101-103). However, ASFA retains the essential structure of the 1980 act and the emphasis on requiring efforts to avoid foster care placements in the first place and to reunify parents and children if a child is placed in foster care.

Since ASFA was enacted, the foster care population has remained high. At the end of fiscal year 2008, 463,000 children were in foster care in the United States (Administration for Children and Families 2009). While the number of children in care decreased from a high of 552,000 in 2000 (Administration for Children and Families 2006), the foster care population in 2008 exceeded that in 1995 and was one and two-thirds that of 1980, the year when the Adoption Assistance and Child Welfare Act was enacted (Staff of H.R. Committee 2004).

Historically, and still today, the failures of the child welfare system have been attributed mostly to lack of resources, including money for treatment services and sufficient numbers of well-trained caseworkers to implement the treatment ideals of the system (Rosenheim 1962; Keith-Lucas 1964; Empey 1979). Child welfare workers were often inexperienced, ill-trained, and poorly supervised (Polier 1941; Cheney 1966). Even though a worker might believe that the ideal solution to a problem was providing care for a child at home, he or she nevertheless might well employ foster care because that was all that was available (Child Welfare League of America 1969).

The Chapin Hall study reached similar conclusions. In a study of 480 parents receiving in-home family preservation services and 494 parents whose children were in foster care, the researchers reported that the caseworkers were generally young and inexperienced. Caseworkers serving families whose children were left at home with family preservation services were, on average, twenty-eight years old or younger, and their median experience in social work was 2.5 years. Caseworkers for families with children in foster care averaged about thirty years of age but had only 1.6 years of experience in social work (Courtney et al. 2004).

The researchers asked parents what services they needed and then asked the child welfare case managers what services they recommended for these parents and found significant disparities. Across the board, the parents reported higher needs for services than the case managers recommended for them. The discrepancy was particularly pronounced for concrete services such as employment assistance and help finding a place to live (Zinn and Courtney 2008; Courtney et al. 2004; Courtney et al. 2002). The parents also reported that their children needed more services than case managers recommended. "It is noteworthy that a large number of parents cited a need for services that are typically thought to be outside the mission of child welfare agencies, including educational services (48.1 percent of Ongoing Services and 61.7 percent of Safety Services parents) and after-school services (46 percent of Ongoing Services and 60.2 percent of Safe Services parents)" (Zinn and Courtney 2008, 8). Speculating on the reason for the differences, the researchers wrote,

> One possible explanation is that case managers responded to the questions concerning service needs with an eye toward the types of services they knew to be available. Alternatively, case managers may not have viewed these types of concrete services as relevant to the issues that lead to child welfare services involvement. (Zinn and Courtney 2008, 6-7)

Current reform proposals, like those in earlier years, typically recommend more and better-targeted resources for the child welfare system. Supporters of the 1980 Adoption Assistance and Child Welfare Act made such a recommendation, and in 2008 the Pew Charitable Trusts Commission on Children in Foster Care recommended that federal child welfare dollars, which go mostly to fund foster care, should be reallocated to provide much more money for preventive services (Pew Commission 2008). However, given the long history of an underfunded child welfare system and lack of funds for services to families, it seems unlikely that society will provide enough resources any time soon. Indeed, since the number of children and families who might be identified as in need of child welfare services is indeterminate, it may be that the system will by definition always be underfunded.

The practice of placing hundreds of thousands of children found to be abused or neglected out of their homes even when their immediate safety does not demand it has persisted for more than a century, despite repeated professional criticism. Efforts to reform the system, to make it function as it is supposed to function, have been made repeatedly without reducing the use of institutions and foster care. To explain the continued vitality of this system, despite its continuing failure to achieve its expressed goals, perhaps we should revise our interpretation of what is going on. As the French philosopher and social historian Michel Foucault observed of prisons, when an institution is criticized as failing in its primary mission (for prisons, reducing crime) and yet persists for many years, it is probably doing something very well, even if that something is not the expressed goal of the system (Foucault 1977). The next sections review Foucault's analysis and consider how it might be applied to the child welfare system.

III. Foucault on the Function of the Prison System

In *Discipline and Punish*, Foucault contrasts the dominant mode of punishment during the seventeenth century, torture and other forms of brutal corporal punishment, to the modern prison system. He argues that both kinds of punishment act on prisoners' bodies to induce docility and obedience, but that they operate by very different means. Torture terrorizes the convicts and the general population, demonstrating the overwhelming power of the sovereign (Foucault 1977). In contrast, prison controls offenders by subjecting them to constant surveillance and repetitive exercises. Prison enforces rules, as do other disciplinary institutions (such as schools, factories, and the military), by making people adhere to behavior norms down to small details. The legal processes that determine who will go to prison complement the reformative rationale of prison by seeking to identify the offenders who need to be reformed. The judge who decides whether to send someone to prison examines not merely the defendant's act but his or her very soul to determine how and why he or she deviates from the accepted norms. The person found guilty in this system is not simply an offender but a delinquent—one whose self does not conform to the norms and must, therefore, be reshaped, at least in theory (Foucault 1977).

However, Foucault observes, prisons were branded as failures almost from the time they were first established. Critics have always pointed out that prison does not reduce crime, that many prisoners are recidivists, and that prison is a school for crime. Foucault argues that these results are not surprising and that, indeed, prisons cannot help but create delinquents. He points to the conditions of prisoners' lives: while in prison they have no or useless work and are subject to violent and arbitrary constraints and to the corruption of the informer system, both of which induce anger, rage, and rebellion. When they leave prison, they are under constant police surveillance and cannot find work because of their criminal history, and their families are thrown into destitution (Foucault 1977).

As Foucault describes, the official response to this criticism of prisons was usually the same: reformers argued that prisons failed because the fundamental theories upon which the prison system was based were not fully and properly implemented. The solution was to reform prisons by reintroducing those principles, which were themselves not questioned (Foucault 1977).

To explain this adherence to a system that failed time after time and the failure to question its underlying premises, Foucault argues that the prison system in fact successfully carries out functions other than the elimination of crime. He says that prison should be understood as intended not to eliminate crime but to distinguish and distribute offenses; rather than rendering docile those who are liable to break the law, this form of punishment sets the limits of tolerated lawbreaking and creates a delinquent culture. This strategy allows the dominant group to manage and control illegal conduct and cabin it into forms that are more structured and constrained and, hence, less dangerous to the status quo than roving bands of beggars who may join forces to engage in looting and rioting (Foucault 1977).

> [I]t is possible to divert this self-absorbed delinquency to forms of illegality that are less dangerous: maintained by the pressure of controls on the fringes of society, reduced to precarious conditions of existence, lacking links with the population that would be able to sustain it . . . delinquents inevitably fell back on a localized criminality, limited in its power to attract popular support, politically harmless, and economically negligible. (Foucault 1977, 278)

While the modern criminal justice/prison system has shed some of the rehabilitative trappings that Foucault describes, its purpose is still said to be to reduce crime, and it is still criticized for failing to do so. The system continues to create a class of recidivist criminals who serve the same social functions that he describes. Of perhaps greater importance for the purposes of this chapter, Foucault's analytical perspective on the prison continues to ring true and can readily be adapted to other institutions of social control, including the child welfare/foster care system.

IV. The Overuse of Foster Care through Foucault's Lens

During the same time that prisons were being invented, the disciplinary practices that Foucault describes were also being extended to cover children of the poor, through institutions such as Houses of Refuge and reformatories and through the juvenile court (Foucault 1977; Platt 1969; Rothman 1971). The early-twentieth-century arguments that children should be kept in their parents' homes if possible, which are discussed above, were in fact criticisms of the overuse of these institutions (Mack 1909; *Proceedings* 1909; Kahn 1962). By the mid-twentieth century, foster care had replaced these institutions, but essentially the same criticisms attached to this new means of providing care to children who were removed from their parents' homes upon juvenile court findings of abuse or neglect.

As discussed earlier, critics have always argued that many children who are removed from their parents' homes to alternative care could safely remain at home, particularly if appropriate services were provided. The most high-profile reform proposals have not challenged the essential structure of the system, but rather have sought to refine it and bring it closer to its theoretical ideal (Adoption Assistance and Child Welfare Act of 1980; Adoption and Safe Families Act of 1997). However, the resources to keep children in their homes have not been forthcoming. According to the Pew Commission on Children in Foster Care, of the millions of children reported to child protection authorities, only 2.5 percent received any kind of preventive services, and only 60 percent of children with confirmed cases of abuse or neglect received services (Pew Commission 2008). Ninety percent of the federal funds spent on child welfare in 2007 supported children in foster care and children adopted from foster care, leaving only 10 percent available to the states to allocate for family services and support, including prevention and reunification services (Pew Commission 2008).

The child welfare/foster care system, then, may well be an institution that, like the prison, is doing something very well, something other than effectively addressing the problems of child abuse and neglect. I argue that the system may be serving two related purposes—feeding young people into the penal system and shoring up public policies that deny significant financial assistance to poor adults, including poor parents.

First, the child welfare system, particularly the overuse of foster care, channels thousands of young people into the juvenile justice and adult criminal systems. It can, therefore, be understood as part of the prison system and as serving the ends of that system by its impact on the children themselves.

However, children's behavior and character are not the primary focus of the child welfare system. Instead, the system primarily examines and acts on parents, parents who are found to be inadequate and who lose custody of their children, sometimes for only a short time and sometimes forever through termination of parental rights. The fundamental purpose of the system is supposed to be correcting the parents' inadequacies (and, more recently, identifying those parents who cannot be corrected and finding alternative permanent homes for their children) (Adoption Assistance and Child Welfare Act of 1980; Adoption and Safe Families Act of 1997; IJA-ABA Joint Commission 1981). Therefore, Foucault's lens must be turned on the system's treatment of parents, revealing a second function of the system.

The child welfare system acts mostly on very poor families (Guggenheim 2000). In 1994, social welfare scholar Duncan Lindsey estimated that 48 percent of children in foster care did not require it and that poverty was the greatest reason that children were removed from their parents' homes (Lindsey 1994). Most of the families in the Chapin Hall studies were desperately poor (Zinn and Courtney 2008; see also Courtney et al. 2004).

The families in the child welfare system are not only overwhelming poor; they are also disproportionately people of color (Roberts 2001; Needell, Brookhard, and Lee 2003). And families of color are more likely to experience foster care placement than are white families. An analysis of all the investigated reports of child abuse and neglect in the United States in which maltreatment was substantiated during 2005—more than 71,802 reports—found that African American children have a 44 percent higher chance of being placed in foster care than Caucasian children (The researchers controlled for child, caregiver, household, and abuse characteristics.) (Knott and Donovan 2010). A significantly higher percentage of the foster care alumni in both the Chapin Hall and Casey studies were African American than in the general population (Cusick and Courtney 2007; Pecora et al. 2005). While poverty can be causally linked to some kinds of child maltreatment, the second and third National Incidence Studies of Child Abuse and Neglect found no significant racial differences in the incidence of maltreatment of children (Miller 2009). This suggests that the second function of the child welfare and foster care system's approach to families is, then, a piece of the way in which poor people, especially poor people of color, are treated and have been treated throughout history.

Americans have always been deeply ambivalent about the poor, willing to help the "worthy poor," that is, those who cannot work, but not able-bodied people, whose poverty is often attributed to their own moral failings. This ambivalence has long manifested itself in public policy, particularly reluctance to provide even the worthy poor with financial and other material assistance much above subsistence level, lest they and others be deterred from working (Katz 1986; Trattner 1974). These attitudes continue to inform welfare policy today (Handler 2000). On the other hand, society also expresses deep concern for the welfare of children and the desire to protect them from harm.

The child welfare system's actual (as compared to rhetorical) preference for foster care over in-home services reinforces and supports these policies well. The poor adults, the parents, do not receive the publicly funded supports that would improve their lives, and children are protected from the immediate dangers in their parents' homes. Further, losing one's children can be seen as an additional adverse consequence of poverty, substance abuse, and the other conditions that underlie most allegations of child neglect. Parents whose children are in foster care supposedly have an even greater incentive to solve their own problems, for only by doing so can they regain the custody of their children.

This perspective on the overuse of foster care says more than "Here is another way in which the poor and people of color are mistreated." It requires us to confront the reality that current policies and practices that avoid providing substantial financial assistance to poor parents come at the cost of harm to many children and that they operate in ways that, on their face, appear, quite simply, to be racist. Facing this reality could prompt policy makers to look at proposals to reform the child welfare system and reduce the use of foster care in a new way. Reform proposals that assume the problem to be simply that not enough resources are provided for in-home services are not likely to change the system (although it is certainly worthwhile to continue to try to shift funds from paying for foster care to paying for services to parents). On the other hand, proposals that make it more difficult to remove children from their parents' homes in the first place or that directly acknowledge how poverty increases the risk of child maltreatment may be more effective in decreasing the number of children who wind up in the juvenile justice and adult criminal systems.

An example of laws that directly affect the ease with which children are placed in foster care are the statutes that define abuse and neglect for purposes of juvenile court jurisdiction and that govern when children may be removed from their parents' homes. Traditional juvenile court statutes define the criteria for jurisdiction very vaguely and broadly and allow removal when the judge finds this to be in the child's best interests (Katz et al. 1975). These statutes, which intentionally grant substantial discretion to judges, are also very vulnerable to the effects of unintentional racial and class prejudice. Legal reformers in the 1970s who developed the proposals that led to the 1980 federal Adoption Assistance and Child Welfare Act proposed not only case planning, reviews, and service provision. They also recommended that the legal standards for finding children to be maltreated and for removing them from their parents' care be significantly tightened, requiring findings of proof of specific kinds of serious harm before courts could take jurisdiction over children and allowing removal from the parents' homes only if necessary to protect the children's safety (Wald 1975; Wald 1976; IJA-ABA Joint Commission 1981).

These recommendations did not, however, find their way into the federal law, and they have generally not been widely accepted by state legislatures.

Instead, the argument that the changes would allow some children to "fall through the cracks" has often prevailed. The harm to children of being taken from their parents often does not play an important role in legislative decisions, any more than the racial and class disparities within the system do. If the specific information about the impact on children of extended stays in foster care and about the disproportionate impact on poor and minority families discussed in this chapter were highlighted for the legislatures, perhaps they would be more willing to make legal and policy changes that would limit the use of foster care, avoiding the unnecessary and destructive disruption of families.

V. Conclusion: The Imperative to Support Families to Protect Children

The recent empirical studies by the Chapin Hall and Casey Family researchers clarify why the overuse of foster care affects children so negatively, and Professor Doyle's study confirms that foster care itself can compound the harms caused by abuse and neglect. Yet in a real sense, this research simply reiterates the conclusions that child welfare experts have repeatedly reached for more than a century. From the earliest days of the juvenile court, unnecessary removal of poor children from their parents' homes has been criticized as harmful to the children and inconsistent with fundamental family values. Frustratingly, reforms to the child welfare system, intended to make it function more like it ideally should, have not reduced the use of foster care. From this experience we should learn that reforms that replicate longstanding approaches to the foster care problem are not likely to be effective. Instead, we need to look at the child welfare system from a new angle, one that reveals the limitations placed on it by policies that deny effective assistance to poor parents, particularly poor parents of color. Then we can challenge these limitations with legal and policy reforms based on supporting children's families. By supporting children within their families, we can help them grow into healthy, productive adults and decrease the risks that they will fall into the juvenile justice and adult criminal systems.

REFERENCES

Abbott, Grace. 1938. *The Child and the State*. Chicago: University of Chicago Press.
Administration for Children and Families, U.S. Department of Health and Human Services. 2006. *AFCARS Rep. 12, Final Estimates for FY 1998 through FY 2002*. http://www.acf.hhs.gov/programs/cb/stats_research/afcars/tar/report12.pdf.

Administration for Children and Families, U.S. Department of Health and Human Services. 2009. *Trends in Foster Care and Adoption.* http://www.acf.hhs.gov/programs/cb/stats_research/afcars/trends02-08.pdf.

Adoption and Safe Families Act of 1997. Public Law no. 105-89.

Adoption Assistance and Child Welfare Act of 1980. Public Law no. 96-272.

American Humane Association. 1951. *Standards for Child Protective Agencies.* Albany, NY: author.

Areen, Judith C. 1975. Intervention between Parent and Child: A Reappraisal of the State's Role in Child Neglect and Abuse Cases. *Georgetown Law Journal* 63: 887-937.

Arnold, Mildred. 1960. The Growth of Public Child Welfare Services. *Children* 7: 131-35.

Bender, Kimberly. 2010. Why Do Some Maltreated Youth Become Juvenile Offenders? A Call for Further Investigation and Adaptation of Youth Services. *Children and Youth Services Review* 32: 466-73.

Breckenridge, Sophisba P., and Edith Abbott. 1912. *The Delinquent Child and the Home.* New York: Russell Sage Foundation Charities Publication Committee.

Cheney, Kimberley B. 1966. Safeguarding Legal Rights in Providing Protective Services. *Children* 13: 86-92.

Child Welfare League of America. 1969. *The Need for Foster Care: An Incidence Study of Requests for Foster Care and Agency Response in Seven Metropolitan Areas.* New York: author.

Children's Bureau, U.S. Department of Health and Human Services. 1997. *National Study of Protective, Preventive, and Reunification Services Delivered to Children and Their Families.* Washington, DC: Government Printing Office. http://www.acf.hhs.gov/programs/cb/pubs/97natstudy/index.htm.

Courtney, Mark E., Amy Dworsky, and Harold Pollack. 2007. *When Should the State Cease Parenting? Evidence from the Midwest Study.* Chicago: Chapin Hall Center for Children at the University of Chicago. http://www.chapinhall.org.

Courtney, Mark E., Steven L. McMurtry, Noel Bost, Katrin Maldre, Peter Power, and Andrew Zinn. 2002. *An Evaluation of Safety Services in Milwaukee County.* Chicago: Chapin Hall Center for Children at the University of Chicago. http://www.chapinhall.org.

Courtney, Mark E., Steven L. McMurtry, Andrew Zinn, Peter Power, and Katrin Maldre. 2004. *An Evaluation of Ongoing Services in Milwaukee County: Profiles and Outcomes of Newly Opened Cases.* Chicago: Chapin Hall Center for Children at the University of Chicago. http://www.chapinhall.org.

Courtney, Mark E., Sherri Terao, and Noel Bost. 2005. *Midwest Evaluation of the Adult Functioning of Former Foster Youth.* Chicago: Chapin Hall Center for Children at the University of Chicago. http://www.chapinhall.org.

Cusick, Gretchen R., and Mark E. Courtney. 2007. *Offending During Late Adolescence: How Do Youth Aging Out of Care Compare with Their Peers?* Chicago: Chapin Hall Center for Children at the University of Chicago. http://www.chapinhall.org.

Davidson, Howard A. 1981. Periodic Judicial Review of Children in Foster Care: Issues Related to Effective Implementation. *Juvenile and Family Court Journal* 32: 61-69.

Downs, Glen, Susan Downs, Arthur Emlen, Janet Lahti, and Alec McKay. 1978. *Overcoming Barriers to Planning for Children in Foster Care.* Portand, OR: Regional Research Institute for Human Services, Portland State University.

Doyle, Joseph J., Jr. 2007. Child Protection and Child Outcomes: Measuring the Effects of Foster Care. *American Economics Review* 97: 1583–1610.

Doyle, Joseph J., Jr. 2008. Child Protection and Adult Crime: Using Investigator Assignment to Estimate Causal Effects of Foster Care. *Journal of Political Economy* 116: 746-70.

Emlen, Arthur. 1976. *Barriers to Planning for Children in Foster Care*. Portland, OR: Regional Research Institute for Human Services, Portland State University.

Emlen, Arthur. 1977. *The Oregon Project County by County: Outcomes of Permanency Planning for Children in Foster Care*. Portland, OR: Regional Research Institute for Human Services, Portland State University.

Empey, LaMar T. 1979. The Social Construction of Childhood and Juvenile Justice. In *The Future of Childhood and Juvenile Justice*, edited by LaMar T. Empey. Charlottesville: University Press of Virginia, pp. 138-74.

Foucault, Michel. 1977. *Discipline and Punish: The Birth of the Prison*. Alan Sheridan, trans. New York: Vintage Books.

Garrison, Marsha. 2005. Reforming Child Protection: A Public Health Perspective. *Virginia Journal of Social Policy and Law* 12: 590 – 637.

Gelles, Richard. 1996. *The Book of David: How Preserving Families Can Cost Children's Lives*. New York: Basic Books.

Grossberg, Michael. 2002. Changing Conceptions of Child Welfare in the United States, 1820-1935. In *A Century of Juvenile Justice*, edited by Margaret K. Rosenheim, Franklin E. Zimring, David S. Tanenhaus, and Bernardine Dohrn. Chicago: University of Chicago Press, pp. 3-41.

Guggenheim, Martin. 2000. Somebody's Children: Sustaining the Family's Place in Child Welfare Policy. *Harvard Law Review* 113: 1716-49.

Handler, Joel F. 2000. The Third Way or the Old Way? *University of Kansas Law Review* 48: 765-800.

Harris, Leslie J. 1983. The Utah Child Protection System: Analysis and Proposals for Change. *Utah Law Review* 1983: 1-97.

IJA-ABA Joint Commission on Juvenile Justice Standards. 1981. *Standards Relating to Abuse and Neglect*. Cambridge, MA: Ballinger.

Kahn, Alfred J. 1962. Court and Community. In *Justice for the Child*, edited by Margaret Keeney Rosenheim. New York: Free Press of Glencoe, pp. 217-34.

Katz, Michael B. 1986. *In the Shadow of the Poor House: A Social History of Welfare in America*. New York: Basic Books.

Katz, Sanford N., Ruth-Arlene W. Howe, and Melba McGrath. 1975. Child Neglect Laws in America. *Family Law Quarterly* 9: 1-372.

Keith-Lucas, Alan. 1964. Child Welfare Services Today. *The Annals* 355: 2-8.

Knott, Theresa, and Kirsten Donovan. 2010. Disproportionate Representation of African-American Children in Foster Care: Secondary Analysis of the National Child Abuse and Neglect Data System 2005. *Children and Youth Services Review* 32: 679-84.

Law Enforcement Assistance Administration, National Advisory Committee on Criminal Justice Standards and Goals. 1976. *Task Force on Juvenile Justice and Delinquency Prevention Report*. Washington, DC: Government Printing Office.

Lewis, Mary. 1964. Foster-Family Care: Has It Fulfilled Its Promise? *The Annals* 355: 31-41.

Levine, Richard Steven. 1973. Caveat Parents: A Demystification of the Child Protection System. *University of Pittsburgh Law Review* 35: 1, quoting Child Welfare Division, Public Charities Association of Pennsylvania. 1930. *Which Way?*

Lindsey, Duncan. 1994. *The Welfare of Children*. New York: Oxford University Press.

Maas, Henry H., and Richard E. Engler. 1959. *Children in Need of Parents*. New York: Columbia University Press.

Mack, Julian W. 1909. The Juvenile Court. *Harvard Law Review* 23: 104–22.

Miller, Oronde A. 2009. *Reducing Racial Disproportionality and Disparate Outcomes for Children and Families of Color in the Child Welfare System*. Seattle, WA: Casey Family Programs. http://www.casey.org.

Mnookin, Robert H. 1973. Foster Care: In Whose Best Interest? *Harvard Educational Review* 43: 599-683.

Mnookin, Robert H. 1975. Child Custody Adjudication: Judicial Functions in the Face of Indeterminacy. *Law and Contemporary Problems* 39: 226-93.

National Advisory Committee on Criminal Justice Standards and Goals. 1976. *Task Force on Juvenile Justice and Delinquency Prevention Report*. Washington, DC: Government Printing Office.

Needell, Barbara, M., Alan Brookhard, and Seon Lee. 2003. Black Children and Foster Care Placement in California. *Children and Youth Services Review* 25: 393-408.

Office of Juvenile Justice and Delinquency Prevention, U.S. Department of Justice. 1980. *Standards for the Administration of Juvenile Justice*. Washington, DC: Government Printing Office.

Pecora, Peter J., Ronald C. Kessler, Jason Williams, Kirk O'Brien, A. Chris Downs, Diana English, James White, Eva Hiripi, Catherine Roller White, Tamera Wiggins, and Kate Holmes. 2005. *Improving Family Foster Care: Findings from the Northwest Foster Care Alumni Study*. Seattle, WA: Casey Family Programs. http://www.casey.org.

Pew Commission on Children in Foster Care. 2008. *Time for Reform: Investing in Prevention: Keeping Children Safe at Home*. Washington, DC: author. http://www.pewtrusts.org.

Platt, Anthony M. 1969. *The Child Savers: The Invention of Delinquency*. Chicago: University of Chicago Press.

Polier, Justine Wise. 1941. *Everyone's Children, Nobody's Child*. New York: Scribner's.

Proceedings of the Conference on the Care of Dependent Children. 1909. Washington, DC: U.S. Government Printing Office.

Roberts, Dorothy. 2001. *Shattered Bonds: The Color of Child Welfare*. New York: Perseus Books.

Rosenheim, Margaret Keeney. 1962. Perennial Problems in the Juvenile Court. In *Justice for the Child*, edited by Margaret Keeney Rosenheim. New York: Free Press of Glencoe, pp. 1 – 16.

Rothman, David J. 1971. *The Discovery of the Asylum: Social Order and Disorder in the New Republic*. Boston: Little, Brown.

Ryan, Joseph P., and Mark F. Testa. 2005. Children Maltreatment and Juvenile Delinquency: Investigating the Role of Placement and Placement Instability. *Children and Youth Services Review* 27: 227.

Sheridan, William H., and Herbert Wilton Beaser. 1975. Model Family Court Act §2.

Smith, Charles P., David J. Berkman, and Warren M. Fraser. 1980. *A Preliminary National Assessment of Child Abuse and Neglect and the Juvenile Justice System: The Shadows of Distress*. Washington, DC: U.S. Department of Justice, Office of Juvenile Justice and Delinquency Prevention.

Staff of H.R. Committee on Ways and Means, 108th Congress. 2004. *2004 Green Book*. http://waysandmeans.house.gov/media/pdf/greenbook2003/Section11.pdf.

Trattner, Walter I. 1974. *From Poor Law to Welfare State: A History of Social Welfare in America*. New York: Free Press.

Wald, Michael S. 1975. State Intervention on Behalf of "Neglected" Children: A Search for Realistic Standards. *Stanford Law Review* 27: 985-1040.

Wald, Michael S. 1976. State Intervention on Behalf of "Neglected" Children: Standards for Removal of Children from Their Homes, Monitoring the Status of Children in Foster Care, and Termination of Parental Rights. *Stanford Law Review* 28: 623-706.

White, Sheldon H. 1973. *Federal Programs for Young Children: Review and Recommendations*. Washington, DC: U.S. Government Printing Office.

Witte, Edwin E. 1963. *The Development of the Social Security Act*. Madison: University of Wisconsin Press.

Zinn, Andrew E., and Mark E. Courtney. 2008. *Are Family Needs and Services Aligned? Evaluating the Bureau of Milwaukee Child Welfare*. Chicago: Chapin Hall Center for Children at the University of Chicago. http://www.chapinhall.org.

4

Preventing Incarceration through Special Education and Mental Health Collaboration for Students with Emotional and Behavioral Disorders

JOSEPH C. GAGNON AND BRIAN R. BARBER

J.D.S. is a thirteen-year-old who had difficulties with school attendance. In 2006 she was placed on probation for her truancy; over the next three years, J.D.S. continued to have attendance problems at school. Early in 2009, J.D.S. ran away from her foster home, was placed in a residential facility, and then ran away from the residential facility. Throughout this time, J.D.S. continued to have problems attending school. In May of 2009 J.D.S. was placed in the Department of Corrections (DOC). Following a status review hearing in August of that year, J.D.S. was ordered to remain in the DOC and complete a General Education Development (GED) program. The basis of the trial court's decision was that due to drug use, truancy, and running away from the foster home and residential facility, it was in J.D.S.'s best interests to be placed in the DOC. The attorney for J.D.S. argued, in part, that the DOC facility was not the least restrictive placement, and was not close to her home. Concerning the restrictiveness of the placement, the Indiana court of appeals concluded that the trial court did not abuse its discretion by continuing J.D.S.'s placement with the DOC (J.D.S. v. State of Indiana 2010).

Unfortunately the case of J.D.S. is not unique. Relying on the corrections system to serve as a de facto mental health system in place of more appropriate school– and community-based services is common (Grisso 2008). The U.S. House of Representatives Committee on Government Reform (2004) reported that in two-thirds of the states, youth with mental disorders are detained even though no criminal charges have been filed. The case of J.D.S. represents a distressing example of our failure to appropriately support youth with severe emotional and behavioral needs.

The unlawful reliance on the juvenile justice system to supplant appropriate community– and school-based treatment serves as but one indicator of the complex issues involved in the provision of appropriate educational and mental health supports for at-risk youth. Emotional and behavioral supports for youth are also hindered by inadequacies of the treatment that is provided. Approximately 20-38 percent of youth in public schools are in need of mental health interventions; yet less than one-third receive treatment (Zahner, Pawelkiewicz, DeFrancesco, and Adnopoz 1992). Psychologists, special educators, and general educators all view mental health services in their schools as ineffective (Repie 2005). In fact, less than half of students receiving treatment are provided with services considered by mental health experts to be adequate (Paternite 2005).

Despite concerns with quality of services, youth are substantially more likely to seek help when school-based services are available than when services are offered in the community (Slade 2002). The U.S. surgeon general considers schools to be an important setting for the potential recognition of mental disorders in children and adolescents (U.S. Department of Health and Human Services 1999). School-based mental health service delivery has received increased recognition within juvenile justice and mental health communities (The National Association of State Mental Health Program Directors and the Policymaker Partnership for Implementing IDEA 2002; Repie 2005). As education, mental health, and juvenile justice service systems look to comprehensive service delivery models that capitalize on the strengths inherent in each system, policies that have historically informed approaches to service provision have come under scrutiny. What is clear is that reactive and punitive approaches to dealing with youth mental disorders, such as expanding juvenile correctional facilities and "get tough" policies, are less effective and cost more than proactive approaches (Leone, Quinn, and Osher 2002). Moreover, there is widespread agreement that multiagency collaboration is essential to effectively serve youth with mental health needs and that failure to do so leads to a host of problems, including gaps in service, redundancy, and contradictory approaches to service (Pullman et al. 2010).

Youth Characteristics

Youth at risk for involvement with the juvenile corrections system present with a range of educational and mental health issues that affect the services they require. To understand the complicated needs of youth, we must first consider these characteristics, as well as common risk factors. For example, youth with the special education classification of emotionally disturbed (ED) are at increased risk for involvement in juvenile corrections. Twenty percent of youth with ED are arrested, detained, or on probation prior to exiting school (Snyder and Sickmund 2006). The special education classification of ED is based upon the following definitional assumptions or criteria:

(4)(i) *Emotional disturbance* means a condition exhibiting one or more of the following characteristics over a long period of time and to a marked degree that adversely affects a child's educational performance:

(A) An inability to learn that cannot be explained by intellectual, sensory, or health factors.

(B) An inability to build or maintain satisfactory interpersonal relationships with peers and teachers.

(C) Inappropriate types of behavior or feelings under normal circumstances.

(D) A general pervasive mood of unhappiness or depression.

(E) A tendency to develop physical symptoms or fears associated with personal or school problems.

(ii) Emotional disturbance includes schizophrenia. The term does not apply to children who are socially maladjusted, unless it is determined that they have an emotional disturbance under paragraph (c)(4)(i) of this section. (Individuals with Disabilities Education Improvement Act (IDEIA) 2006, 34 C.F.R.71. §, 300.8(c)(4)(i-ii))

The very nature of the ED classification includes student behavioral characteristics that affect student academic success. In fact, youth with ED are more likely to fail courses than nondisabled students (Landrum, Tankersley, and Kauffman 2003). It is not suprising, then, that approximately two-thirds of youth with ED exit school without a high school diploma (U.S. Department of Education 2009). Youth educational failure and dropping out are potential risk factors for law violations (Doren, Bullis, and Benz 1996).

In addition to problems in school, many youth with ED meet criteria for mental health and/or substance use disorders. For example, youth with ED are more likely to be depressed than nondisabled youth (Newcomer, Barenbaum, and Pearson 1995). Also, 45 percent of students classified with ED receive services for problems with drug abuse (Wagner and Cameto 2004). Moreover, student mental health characteristics (e.g., prior participation in therapy, prior use of psychotropic medication) are predictive of special education status (Krezmien, Mulcahy, and Leone 2008).

In contrast to special education criteria, identification of youth with a mental disorder is based on criteria set in the fourth edition of the Diagnostic and Statistical Manual of Mental Disorders (DSM IV-R) (American Psychiatric Association 1994). Researchers have determined that youth with diagnosed mental disorders are at an increased likelihood for involvement with, and repeated exposure to, the juvenile justice system. For example, Vander Stoep, Evens, and Taub (1997) reported that youth in community-based public mental health programs were almost three times more likely to be involved in the juvenile justice system compared to youth in the general population. Rosenblatt, Rosenblatt, and Biggs (2000) also reported that 20 percent of youth receiving mental health services had recent arrest records.

The link between youth mental disorder and risk for involvement in the juvenile justice system is further substantiated by research investigating the characteristics of youth who are already involved in the juvenile justice system. Studies of youth involved in juvenile corrections indicate that 50–70 percent had at least one psychiatric disorder (Skowyra and Cocozza 2006; Wasserman et al. 2005). By comparison, the prevalence rates of psychiatric disorders for youth in the general population are estimated at 15–25 percent (Kazdin 2000). Complicating these data is the fact that incarcerated youth often have more than one mental disorder. For example, in one study 80 percent of youth met criteria for more than one disorder while 60 percent of incarcerated youth met criteria for three or more mental disorders. In addition, 60 percent also had a substance use problem or disorder (Skowyra and Cocozza 2006).

Finally, factors exist that are common to at-risk youth, including experiences of abuse and neglect, and exposure to violence. Compared to youth without such experiences, abused youth are six to seven times more likely to be arrested (Brooks and Petit 1997). Youth with ED are particularly at risk due to the fact that nearly half of such youth have been abused or neglected (Oseroff, Oseroff, Westling, and Gessner 1999). The links between experiencing harm and perpetration of harm are also clear. Those who experienced traumatic life events are incarcerated at higher rates than youth without previous similar experiences. Roughly 50-70 percent of delinquent youth reported experiences of prior abuse (Evans, Alpers, Macari, and Mason 1996). Abram and colleagues (2004) reported that approximately 90 percent of youth involved in the juvenile justice system had witnessed or experienced prior violence.

When we examine students who are at the highest risk for involvement in the juvenile justice system, we are essentially talking about a group of youth whose risk factors include those associated with both mental disorders and educational disability, and who may also have other risk factors in their history. In light of their dismal long-term trajectories, as well as the high level of intensive supports that they need, effective and proactive services and support are essential. The remainder of this chapter addresses federal education policies and national mental health recommendations; policies and practices that are barriers to provision of appropriate school-based mental health supports; and recommendations for collaboration between special-education and mental-health professionals to effectively serve these troubled youth.

Federal Education Policies and National Mental Health Recommendations

Educational and mental health disabilities, as well as histories of school failure, clearly complicate the provision of preventive services for youth at highest risk for involvement in the juvenile justice system. Indeed, untreated and undertreated disorders underlie many of the academic and behavioral problems of youth and are associated with a cascade of negative consequences for individuals and families (Marsh 2004). In the 2000 report of the surgeon general on mental health, it was estimated that one in five children and adolescents experience signs and symptoms of a DSM-IV disorder during the course of a year, with about 5 percent experiencing impairment of functioning that qualifies as extreme. Youth experiencing undiagnosed academic and psychosocial problems may account for up to 40 percent of the school population (Adelman and Taylor 2006). Such figures reinforce the fact that a segment of students in dire need of services and supports are underidentified and inadequately served by school and mental healthcare systems.

The lack of attention to the education and mental health status of youth at risk for delinquency has been addressed in part by recent educational reform. The Individuals with Disabilities Education Improvement Act regulations (IDEIA 2006), as well as the No Child Left Behind Act of 2001 (NCLB) require that a high-quality education be provided to students with and without disabilities within public schools. Therefore, access to an appropriate education must include supports and services aimed at improving the symptoms associated with a student's disability, including those that are behavioral in nature. Learning-related support services also include mental health interventions (Kataoka, Rowan, and Hoagwood 2009). Additionally, IDEIA promotes interagency agreements for the coordination and delivery of services from other public agencies that have responsibility for paying for or providing needed services. Youth mental health services have been most substantially funded by IDEIA, with more than 60 percent of school districts taking advantage of this funding source (Foster et al. 2005).

Despite good intentions, the implementation of appropriate educational and mental health programming and supports for youth with emotional and behavioral disorders has been undermined by the seemingly conflicting goals of providing these services while emphasizing academic achievement. While these aims were not intended to be mutually exclusive, youth often do not receive the services that they require (Paternite 2005). It is estimated that between 5 and 9 percent of children fail to achieve due to emotional and behavioral issues (U.S. Department of Health and Human Services 1999). The majority of court-involved youth have experienced academic failure, school exclusion, and dropout (Christle, Jolivette, and Nelson 2005), sequelae that remain at odds with the emphasis in this legislation on ensuring high levels of academic achievement for all students.

Unfortunately, few studies examining IDEIA and NCLB have focused on youth with disabilities who may enter the juvenile justice system (Mears and Aron 2003). The President's Commission on Excellence in Special Education (2002) acknowledged these and other concerns, encouraging "state agencies with authority over the direction and expenditure of federal and state funds under IDEA and the No Child Left Behind Act to develop interagency agreements with juvenile corrections agencies, foster care and other relevant authorities to ensure continued alternative educational services" (id., 39).

Complexities of the provisions within the No Child Left Behind Act have also made it difficult for educators and mental health professionals to understand the legal and practical interface between the act and school mental health. While specific language exists regarding the need for school-based prevention services aimed at neglected, delinquent, or at-risk youth, the reach of these provisions has been modest and restricted mainly to discretionary grant programs that have recently seen reduced funding (Kataoka, Rowan, and Hoagwood 2009). However, a 2003 report by the New Freedom Commission on Mental Health highlighted the importance of early intervention and outlined recommendations for expanded screening and assessment, intervention, training, and financing of services. Significantly, one recommendation focuses on the improvement and expansion of school mental health programs as a means to provide adequate treatment to at-risk youth.

Despite the increased emphasis on school-based mental health, difficulties with collaboration remain. In a 2006 review of ninety-two evidence-based programs and practices for treating youth with emotional and behavioral problems, only fifteen were found to involve collaboration of both school and community mental health agencies (Kutash, Duchnowski, and Lynn 2006). In light of the critical importance of collaborative efforts to prevent youth involvement in the juvenile corrections system, it is important to consider policies and practices that inhibit collaboration and provision of appropriate school-based mental health services.

School-Level Policies and Practices That Inhibit Provision of Services

Researchers have asserted the importance of interventions within relevant contexts, such as schools, in order for services to effectively assist youth with problem behaviors and mental disorders (Repie 2005; Stormshak, Dishion, Light, and Yasui 2005). Several school-level policies and practices exist in both special education and mental health fields, however, that result in stalemate in attempts to provide appropriate evidence-based services to highly vulnerable youth (Kataoka, Rowan, and Hoagwood 2009). "A state's mental health program for children is often separate from that state's public education program. . . . [a]lthough they often serve many of the same children" (The National Association of State Mental Health Program Directors and the Policymaker Partnership for Implementing IDEA 2002, 6). Collaborative efforts are inhibited by differences in the perspectives of mental health and special education systems: special education professionals are concerned primarily with academic achievement, while mental health professionals focus on youth functioning both inside and outside of the classroom (Kutash, Duchnowski, and Lynn 2006).

To move the conversation forward and provide recommendations, we must first acknowledge several school-level barriers to the collaborative provision of mental health services. In the next sections, we discuss three policy barriers (criminalization of behavior under zero tolerance policies, resources, and provision of broad versus intensive interventions) and two practice barriers (personnel and family involvement).

Zero Tolerance Policies

Zachary, a first-grader at Downes Elementary School in Newark, Del., was suspended for carrying a camping utensil that contained a spoon, fork, bottle opener and knife to school. "I wasn't really trying to get in trouble," 6-year-old Zachary said. "I was just trying to eat lunch with it." (Cuomo, Clarke, and Netter 2009, 1)

There are numerous stories of the extreme application of zero tolerance policies in schools. While there is no single definition of zero tolerance (American Psychological Association 2008), it is clear that the initial focus of the policy—to provide swift and consistent consequences to school drug and weapons violations—has been extended to other behaviors and includes harsh punishments with little or no room for discretion (Skiba and Rausch 2006). For example, zero tolerance has expanded from mandatory consequences for bringing deadly weapons to school to talking back to teachers (Stinchcomb, Bazemore, and Riestenberg 2006). "Zero tolerance has become a one-size-fits-all solution to all the problems that schools confront. It has redefined students as criminals, with unfortunate consequences" (Martin 2001, 1).

Despite the widening use of zero tolerance policies, little research has evaluated the effectiveness of this approach to school discipline. Results of the few studies that have investigated the policy's impact have overwhelmingly indicated that it is an ineffective approach (American Psychological Association 2008). Moreover, school psychologists commonly report that zero tolerance policies are among the most ineffective for promoting positive youth behavior in schools (Sherer and Nickerson 2010).

Zero tolerance is part of a disturbing trend in which youth are placed in the custody of the juvenile justice system in order to receive mental health services that are not available in the community. In a study of a decade of data from 1985 to 1995, the researchers noted a 72 percent increase in the number of youth held in secure detention, and two-thirds of these youth were held for nonviolent offenses (Orlando 1999). Clearly, effective and proactive approaches are needed in schools to address the behavior of youth with emotional disturbances and mental disorders, rather than utilizing harsh, reactive punishments, including use of the juvenile justice system.

Resources

A second barrier to greater mental health intervention in schools is the difficulties associated with funding such supports. A lack of financial resources has been noted as the primary obstacle to implementing school-based mental health programs (Stephan et al. 2007). Complicating issues of funding is the pervasive view that mental health services in schools are a supplemental, rather than necessary, service (id.). The common use of IDEIA (2006) funding for mental health results in competition between programs explicitly designed to address academic achievement and those designed to address mental health needs (Kataoka, Rowan, and Hoagwood 2009). As Malti and Noam (2008) assert, the moment has come to develop renewed and cost-effective collaborative interventions that are appropriately funded and address student needs.

Broad-based versus Intensive Intervention

A third policy barrier to effective school-based mental health services is the need to supplement common broad-based interventions with more intensive interventions for at-risk and troubled youth. In a 2004 policy statement by the American Academy of Pediatrics, school-based prevention services are characterized within a three-tiered model of services and needs. *Universal prevention strategies* are not applied on the basis of the identification of individual risk; rather, outcomes of such programs are desirable for all involved youth. *Selective prevention strategies* target individuals or subgroups that share a significant elevated risk according to one or more factors, including imminent and/or lifetime risk. *Indicated prevention strategies* target treatment of youth with severe and chronic problems, such as those with special education classification or DSM-IV diagnosis (Weisz, Sandler, Durlak, and Anton 2005). While definitional criteria for each preventive tier have not been commonly accepted and model-specific revisions are commonplace (Kutash, Duchnowski, and Lynn 2006), the tiered approach has potential for coordinating the collaborative activities of educational and mental health professionals.

Broad-based, universal approaches to addressing youth problem behavior are often designed to create a positive climate for all youth in a school or classroom and promote social and academic growth (Gagnon and Leone 2001). However, researchers have typically noted only modest gains for interventions delivered in this fashion, in part because they lack the individualization necessary for subpopulations with more significant mental health and behavior problems (Hoagwood et al. 2007). Hence, there is a need to combine universal, selective, and indicated interventions in schools via collaborative efforts between mental health and educational professionals.

Collaborative efforts are particularly crucial for youth who require intensive (i.e., selective or indicated) interventions for both mental disorders and substance abuse problems. In general, substance abuse services are commonly lacking in schools (Repie 2005). Moreover, traditional approaches often separate mental health and drug abuse treatment (New Freedom Commission 2003). Development and implementation of interventions that include treatment for drug abuse, as needed, are more likely to be effective (Albus, Weist, and Perez-Smith 2004).

Personnel

In addition to these policy barriers, there are practice barriers to providing school-based mental health services. The complex nature of supports needed to promote school success for students with more serious emotional and behavioral problems can overwhelm the existing capacity of school personnel and resources (Fredericks 1994). A number of models exist for the provision of school-based mental health, ranging from a reliance on service implementation by trained psychologists to use of current school staff (e.g., teachers, counselors) to a combination of those approaches based on the severity of youth needs. Due to limited resources, a common approach is to rely on teachers and school counselors to provide mental health programs to students (Han and Weiss 2005). However, these professionals rarely possess adequate training to deliver mental health interventions with fidelity.

Lack of education, as well as a need for ongoing training for educators, is problematic (Weist 2005). Many teachers do not have even the most basic training and knowledge of proactive and effective behavioral interventions (Oliver and Reschly 2010). Further, educators commonly report that they are provided few, if any, professional development opportunities related to understanding and addressing student mental health needs (Repie 2005). It is not surprising, then, that a recent study found that 80 percent of school districts implemented a drug use prevention program, but only 14 percent used effective content and delivery methods (Ennett et al. 2003).

Family Involvement

A final challenge to effective prevention is family involvement. "Parents are a vital component of any plan to positively affect youth trajectory toward independence and self-sufficiency" (Gagnon and Richards 2008, 17). In fact, relationships between schools and families predict academic and mental health outcomes for students (Hoagwood et al. 2007). Unfortunately, of families that pursue community-based mental health treatment for their child, about half terminate treatment prematurely (Heatherfield and Clark 2004). School-based mental health services are one way to help engage parents, in comparison to clinic-based care, which may present transportation and fiscal difficulties (Evans, Axelrod, and Langberg 2004). School-based options for mental health treatment address the additional concern that youth are often served in placements several hours from their home or in out-of-state facilities (New Freedom Commission 2003).

Family involvement is particularly critical in light of the fact that family problems were one of the most frequent issues reported in a national survey of public schools (Foster et al. 2005). Parental involvement is needed not just for consent but as a part of youth mental health treatment (American Academy of Pediatrics 2004). However, schools' lack of parental engagement is often attributed to a lack of resources, as well as to the fact that school counselors and psychologists are "trained and operate from an individual model of development and service delivery, which rarely incorporates parents" (Stormshak, Dishion, Light, and Yasui 2005, 724). Additionally, changing public policies have reduced commitment to school-based mental health programs that include parental involvement as a critical component (id.).

Recommended Collaborative Practices of Special Education and Mental Health Systems

Historically, response to the public's concern with juvenile delinquency and violence has been to pass legislation promising stiffer penalties as well as harsher sentences for juvenile offenders (Leone, Quinn, and Osher 2002). Providing educational and other supports to youth and their families, however, is more effective and cost-effective than more traditional approaches such as incarceration (Larson and Turner 2002; Caldwell, Vitacco, and Van Rybroek 2006). Despite this knowledge, effective school-based programming for students with educational and mental health difficulties remains a challenge. For example, in a review of effective prevention programs for juvenile offenders, Greenwood asserts that "despite more than ten years of research on the nature and benefits of evidence-based programs, such programming is the exception rather than the rule. Only about 5 percent of youth who should be eligible for evidence-based programs participate in one" (2008, 202).

Effective deterrence of youth from initial contact with the juvenile justice system is attributable to the existence of communication, cooperation, and collaboration across the different systems focused on children and youth (Leone, Quinn, and Osher 2002). As early as 1974, the Juvenile Justice Delinquency Prevention Act encouraged coordination and collaboration of local service systems to improve juvenile delinquency prevention programming. Nation and colleagues (2003) identified the following six characteristics of effective coordination of school-based prevention programming:

1. uses a research-based risk– and protective-factor framework that involves families, peers, schools, and communities as partners to target multiple outcomes;
2. is long-term, age-specific, and culturally appropriate;
3. fosters development of individuals who are healthy and fully engaged through teaching them to apply social-emotional skills and ethical values in daily life;
4. aims to establish policies, institutional practices, and environmental supports that nurture optimal development;
5. selects, trains, and supports interpersonally skilled staff to implement programming effectively;
6. incorporates and adapts evidence-based programming to meet local community needs through strategic planning, ongoing evaluation, and continuous improvement.

These characteristics do not include all of the factors accounting for effective school-based prevention of youth delinquent behavior. However, they serve as guiding considerations for professionals contemplating the adoption of programs that require collaborative attention across educational and mental health perspectives. With these programmatic characteristics in mind, the following sections provide a review of some research-validated approaches to collaboration that have potential for reducing delinquency. To frame our discussion of programs and strategies, we rely on the tiered approach to service delivery that has been effectively adopted for providing school-based behavioral and mental health services (e.g., Interconnected Systems Model; see Adelman and Taylor 2006), addressing problems of behavioral adaptation (e.g., Positive Behavioral Intervention and Supports; see Sugai and Horner 2002), and identifying and preventing academic and behavioral difficulties of youth that are associated with school failure (e.g., Response to Intervention, see Fuchs and Fuchs 2006).

Universal Prevention Approaches and Programs

Numerous universally implemented school-based prevention approaches and programs have proven effective in preventing drug use, delinquency, antisocial behavior, and early school dropout (Gottfredson, Wilson, and Najaka 2002). Many of these involve broad instruction and intervention that target problematic or health risk behaviors (Flay 2002). However, recommendations to develop more integrated and comprehensive practices have emerged. Practically speaking, school-based preventive efforts that are capable of addressing multiple risk factors and behaviors have the potential to decrease the burden on schools, and consequently increase the potential for effective implementation (Botvin, Griffin, and Nichols 2006; Wilson, Gottfredson, and Najaka 2001).

Few reviews have been undertaken that focus on the effectiveness of school-based mental health programs that are universally applied. However, in one review, Wells, Barlow, and Stewart-Brown (2003) concluded that long-term interventions, including changes to school climate, were most successful (as opposed to class-based programs). Additionally, many effective programs involved an instructional focus on conflict resolution, promotion of prosocial skills, and/or the prevention of internalizing behavioral symptoms. Another meta-analytic review by Durlak and Wells (1997) reviewed 129 school-based primary preventive interventions aimed at behavioral and social aspects of mental health. Most studies showed a positive effect. Rones and Hoagwood (2000) identified a number of proven school– or class-wide approaches and programs targeting the prevention of emotional and behavioral symptoms or disorders. For example, the Promoting Alternative Thinking Strategies program (PATHS) (Greenberg, Kusche, Cook, and Quamma 1995) curriculum, which aims to increase emotional understanding, self-control, and interpersonal problem-solving skills, was effective in preventing youth emotional and behavioral problems. PATHS was also noted as an indicated intervention for preventing youth conduct problems.

Additionally, approaches that modified school policy, implemented class management strategies, developed curriculum changes, and facilitated parent-school communication were effective for reducing youth difficulties, as exemplified by Project ACHIEVE (Knoff and Batsche 1995). This program demonstrated reduction in disciplinary infractions and the number of referrals for special education. With regard to the goal of preventing conduct disorder, Rones and Hoagwood suggest that multilevel or system approaches overall were met with mixed effectiveness. However, positive outcomes were shown for the multicomponent intervention Linking the Interests of Families and Teachers (LIFT; Reid, Eddy, Fetrow, and Stoolmiller 1999); for the nonviolent conflict resolution program Resolving Conflicts Creatively (RCCP; Aber et al. 1998); and for single-component programs utilizing peer mediation and class management strategies, such as the Student-Mediated Conflict Resolution Program (Cunningham et al.

1998) and the classroom management–based Good Behavior Game (Kellam, Rebok, Iolongo, and Mayer 1994). Additional effects of specific programs for associated risk factors (e.g., substance abuse, depression) were also noted (Rones and Hoagwood 2000).

By and large, universal prevention programs are not of sufficient intensity or targeted specifically to risk factors to have a discernible impact for higher-risk youth (Weissberg, Kumpfer, and Seligman 2003). However, a number of comprehensive prevention programs that combine universal, selective, and indicated approaches into multicomponent, multiyear projects show positive effects for these high-risk subgroups (Catalano et al. 2002; Greenberg, Domitrovich, and Bumbarger 2001). As such, for youth with greater emotional and behavioral concerns (and thus increased risk for delinquency), universal strategies should be combined with more intensive programs and services that require greater collaboration on the part of educators with mental health professionals.

Selective Prevention Approaches and Programs

Selective prevention strategies target those youth with known, increased levels of risk. Typically, selective prevention approaches are characterized by smaller numbers of youth who are recruited to participate in the intervention, and require a larger number of skilled staff to work with youth and their families. Locating groups of high-risk youth with specific profiles for selective prevention programs remains a challenge; as a result, collaborative efforts necessarily include the identification and assessment of youth at risk for specified emotional and behavioral problems. While it is beyond the scope of this chapter to outline the numerous risk assessments incorporating educational and mental health input, it should be noted that recruitment to and evaluation of progress within selective programs should occur via an established team consisting of education and mental health personnel.

Selective intervention approaches include alternative and vocational education, which are based on the association between school failure and delinquency. Some school districts locate alternative programs in schools, while others operate within separate facilities. Day treatment models are one example in which students and families are provided with intensive mental health and special education services. Appropriate alternative programs are not custodial; rather, they include collaboration with regular schools to facilitate reintegration (Tobin and Sprague 1999). Characteristics of effective alternative programs include the following (Quinn, Osher, and Valore 1997):

- intensive individualized instruction in credit-earning coursework;
- continuation of special education services for students with IEPs;
- positive behavioral supports—including social skills and anger management/abatement—within a structured school environment;
- psychological and mental health consultation and counseling;
- active family involvement;
- transition services that support the return to regular school;
- community agency involvement (e.g., mental health programs, social services, law enforcement, juvenile justice);
- caring staff committed to building relationships with students;
- effective, engaging instructional techniques with curriculum demands that match each student's academic skills.

Alternative academic and vocational skills training has become an important facet of selective prevention programs for delinquency. However, a general lack of evaluation of the impact of such programs has persisted, despite the incorporation of such approaches by a majority of districts (Lehr, Moreau, Lange, and Lanners 2004).

School-based approaches to providing family therapy and skills training have also been identified as promising selective prevention strategies. Results of school family treatments have shown reductions in family dysfunction and delinquency (Henggeler and Borduin 1990). In a study that combined parent and youth training, results indicated that school-based parent behavioral training and youth social skills instruction were particularly effective for reducing disruptive behavior problems (Tremblay et al. 1992). The small, yet promising, literature base for school-based family therapy and skills training suggests that more research is warranted to evaluate this approach.

Evidence for effective selective prevention programming also exists. Durlak and Wells (1998) reviewed 130 controlled-outcome studies of programs targeting externalizing, internalizing, mixed symptom, academic achievement, and peer relations. Results of this and other reviews (e.g., Lipsey 2009; Wilson and Lipsey 2007) provide support for the applicability of behavioral and cognitive-behavioral strategies for reducing various forms of dysfunction in individually delivered and group formats; particularly strong effects were evident for externalizing behavior problems of youth.

Indicated Prevention Approaches and Programs

Effective indicated approaches for youth with serious emotional and behavioral problems are typically based on an ecological framework, with a focus on increasing intersystem collaboration and comprehensive service planning in multiple domains (Goldstrom et al. 2000). Intervention programs that integrate individual, parent, family, and community systems and that address the multiple determinants of delinquency have demonstrated effectiveness for reducing behavioral symptoms, criminal activity, and recidivism (Lipsey, Wilson, and Cothern 2000).

One approach, referred to as "systems of care" (Stroul and Friedman 1986), incorporates a comprehensive spectrum of mental health and other necessary services organized into a coordinated network for children with emotional and behavioral problems. Key components include intensive services within the home and community, which are considered and delivered in partnership between families and service providers. Importantly, the systems-of-care approach is distinguished from other ecological approaches by the coordination of activities at the systems level, such as through interagency agreements, information sharing, and multi-agency training. Although there are relatively few systematic efforts to evaluate the evidence basis for systems of care, informal evaluations suggest that the approach may be effective in achieving important system improvements, such as reducing use of residential and out-of-state placements, and in achieving improvements in functional behavior (U.S. Department of Health and Human Services 1999).

Integrated systems of care for children with severe emotional disturbance have historically been viewed as clinical interventions (Rosenblatt and Woodbridge 2003). However, systems-of-care principles have been applied within the continuum of services provided within education settings (Woodruff et al. 1999). In these settings, "systems of care" refers to those intensive services, such as special education and related long-term therapies, that are reserved for students with the most persistent and multifaceted emotional and behavioral impairment. Treatments are developed by a team of professionals in coordination with a youth's individual education plan (IEP) and designate equivalent responsibility and decision making to all agency representatives. Systems of care facilitate the identification and early referral of youth requiring services, increase school performance, reduce suspensions, improve school attendance, and decrease school mobility (Woodruff et al. 1999).

Another related approach for reducing juvenile delinquency is providing collaborative *wraparound services* (Leone, Quinn, and Osher 2002). The concept of wraparound servicing was developed in the 1980s as a means of maintaining youth with serious emotional and behavioral problems in their homes and communities (Farmer, Dorsey, and Mustillo 2004). By definition, wraparound service approaches attempt to redress the fragmentation of services that exists in the health and human services systems. In general, wraparound services maintain the following objectives: (a) identifying gaps in service delivery and assigning organizational responsibility for implementing services; (b) reducing barriers to obtaining services (e.g., streamlining application procedures, reducing geographical distance between provider and client, decreasing waiting periods for treatment); and (c) conserving institutional resources by sharing efforts across systems or by reducing unnecessary duplication of efforts (Rossman 2001).

The largest evidence base for the wraparound approach exists in the fields of children's mental health and juvenile justice. Results of nine studies indicate improvements on measures of emotional and behavioral health, family functioning (including decreases in out-of-home placements and episodes of running away), and a variety of educational outcomes (reduced expulsions, disciplinary actions, and dropping out) (Walker and Bruns 2007). Outcomes related to delinquency or police contact have also been found, with a number of studies reporting reductions or delays in incarceration, detention, and psychiatric hospitalization.

Several effective indicated programs have been developed that may be used in conjunction with, or as a component of, multisystemic approaches. For students with emotional and behavioral disorders, the Vanderbilt School-Based Counseling Program (Catron, Harris, and Weiss 1998) has shown important effects for improving youth levels of behavioral functioning, as well as for increasing service accessibility. The program provides students with services from trained, licensed mental health clinicians upon referral, including individual and group therapy, parent training and consultation, and case management (id.).

Other comprehensive indicated programs have been developed with education and mental health collaboration in mind. One example is the Family and Schools Together (FAST) Track program, a multicomponent, multiyear intervention consisting of home visitation, parent training, and case management activities in conjunction with social skills training and academic tutoring. Program effectiveness for multiple outcomes associated with delinquency reduction has been shown; specifically, participants displayed decreased conduct problems and reductions in the likelihood of referral for special education services (Conduct Problems Prevention Research Group 1999).

Although these approaches and programs are promising, research is sorely needed to evaluate their effectiveness at each tier, as well as the effectiveness of providing services to youth across multiple tiers. However, it is clear that school-based approaches and programs delivered collaboratively by educators and mental health professionals can potentially play an integral role in the reduction of youth delinquency.

Conclusion

Youth who are at risk for involvement with the juvenile justice system possess a complicated array of characteristics and risk factors. Regrettably, coordinated school-based services and supports provided by a team of concerned adults and professionals remain relatively rare. Rather, juvenile corrections has become the default system for youth with emotional and behavioral difficulties. Yet mental health research has identified multiple strategies and programs that have potential for school application (Ringeisen, Henderson, and Hoagwood 2003). Many of these focus on identified youth characteristics and the prevention or amelioration of risk factors that are associated with delinquency. If implemented with fidelity, lasting a sufficient duration, and set within school and other natural contexts, such approaches and programs can provide a positive and proactive alternative to incarceration.

Through effective collaborative efforts, schools, families, and communities can design and implement a continuum of services that include universal, selective, and indicated prevention and intervention for troubled youth. A coordinated and comprehensive approach has the potential to improve service delivery and working relationships between professionals, as well as avoid gaps in or duplication of services (Holden et al. 2003). Streamlined collaborative school-based services have tremendous potential to positively impact at-risk youth, their families, and communities, and reduce the unfortunate reliance on the juvenile justice system.

REFERENCES

Aber, J. L., S. M. Jones, J. L. Brown, N. Chaudry, and F. Samples. 1998. Resolving conflict creatively: Evaluating the developmental effects of school-based violence prevention program in neighborhood and classroom context. *Development and Psychopathology* 10: 187-213.

Abram, K. M., L. A. Teplin, D. R. Charles, S. L. Longworth, G. M. McClelland, and M. K. Dulcan. 2004. Posttraumatic stress disorder and trauma in youth in juvenile detention. *Archives of General Psychiatry* 61: 403-10.

Adelman, H. S., and L. Taylor. 2006. *The school leader's guide to student learning supports: New directions for addressing barriers to learning.* Thousand Oaks, CA: Corwin Press.

Albus, K. E., M. D. Weist, and A. M. Perez-Smith. 2004. Associations between youth risk behavior and exposure to violence: Implications for the provisions of mental health services in urban schools. *Behavior Modification* 28: 548-64.

American Academy of Pediatrics. 2004. Policy statement: Organizational principles to guide and define the child health care system and/or improve the health of all children. *Pediatrics* 113: 1839-45.

American Psychiatric Association. 1994. *Diagnostic and statistical manual of mental disorders* (4th ed.). Washington, DC: Author.

American Psychological Association Zero Tolerance Task Force. 2008. Are zero tolerance policies effective in the schools? An evidentiary review and recommendations. *American Psychologist* 63: 852-62.

Botvin, G. J., K. W. Griffin, and T. D. Nichols. 2006. Preventing youth violence and delinquency through a universal school-based prevention approach. *Prevention Science* 7: 403-8.

Brooks, T. R., and M. Petit. 1997. *Early intervention: Crafting a community response to child abuse and violence.* Washington, DC: Child Welfare League of America.

Caldwell, M. F., M. Vitacco, and G. J. Van Rybroek. 2006. Are violent delinquents worth treating? A cost-benefit analysis. *Journal of Research in Crime and Delinquency* 43: 148-68.

Catalano, R. F., M. L. Berglund, J. A. M. Ryan, H. S. Lonczak, and J. D. Hawkins. 2002. Positive youth development in the United States: Research findings on evaluations of positive youth development programs. *Prevention and Treatment* 5: 457–65.

Catron, T., V. S. Harris, and B. Weiss. 1998. Posttreatment results after 2 years of services in the Vanderbilt School-Based Counseling Project. In M. H. Epstein, K. Kutash, and A. Duchnowski (eds.), *Outcomes for children and youth with emotional and behavioral disorders and their families: Programs and evaluation best practices* (pp. 653-56). Austin, TX: PRO-ED.

Christle, C. A., K. Jolivette, and C. M. Nelson. 2005. Breaking the school to prison pipeline: Identifying school risk and protective factors for youth delinquency. *Exceptionality* 13: 69-88.

Conduct Problems Preventions Research Group. 1999. Initial impact of the FAST TRACK prevention trial for conduct problems: I. The high-risk sample. *Journal of Consulting and Clinical Psychology* 67: 631-47.

Cunningham, C. E., L. J. Cunningham, V. Martorelli, A. Tran, J. Young, and R. Zacharias. 1998. The effects of primary division, student-mediated conflict resolution programs on playground aggression. *Journal of Child Psychology and Psychiatry* 39: 653-62.

Cuomo, C., S. Clarke, and S. Netter. 2009. *Boy, 6, faces reform school for carrying camping utensil to school.* ABC News. http://abcnews.go.com/GMA/zachary-christie-suspended-bringing-camping-utensil-school/story?id=8812939.

Doren, B., M. Bullis, and M. Benz. 1996. Predicting arrest status of adolescents with disabilities in transition. *Journal of Special Education* 29: 363-80.

Durlak, J. A., and A. M. Wells. 1997. Primary prevention mental health programs for children and adolescents: A meta-analytic review. *American Journal of Community Psychology* 25: 115-52.

Durlak, J. A., and A. W. Wells. 1998. Evaluation of indicated preventive intervention (secondary prevention) mental health programs for children and adolescents. *American Journal of Community Psychology* 26: 775-802.

Ennett, S. T., C. L. Ringwalt, J. Thorne, L. A. Rohrbach, A. Vincus, A. Simons-Rudolph, and S. Jones. 2003. A comparison of current practice in school-based substance use prevention programs with meta-analysis findings. *Prevention Science* 4: 1-14.

Evans, S. W., J. Axelrod, and J. M. Langberg. 2004. Efficacy of school-based treatment program for middle school youth with ADHD: Pilot data. *Behavior Modification* 28: 528-47.

Evans, W., E. Alpers, D. Macari, and A. Mason. 1996. Suicide ideation, attempts, and abuse among gang and nongang delinquents. *Child and Adolescent Social Work Journal* 13: 115-26.

Farmer, E. M. Z., S. Dorsey, and S. A. Mustillo. 2004. Intensive home and community interventions. *Child and Adolescent Psychiatric Clinics of North America* 13: 857-84.

Flay, B. 2002. Positive youth development requires comprehensive health promotion programs. *American Journal of Health Behavior* 26: 407-24.

Foster, S., M. Rollefson, T. Doksum, D. Noonan, G. Robinson, and J. Teich. 2005. *School mental health services in the United States, 2002-2003.* Rockville, MD: Center for Mental Health Services, Substance Abuse and Mental Health Services Administration.

Fredericks, B. 1994. Integrated service systems for troubled youth. *Education and Treatment of Children* 17: 387-416.

Fuchs, D., and L. S. Fuchs. 2006. Introduction to response to intervention: What, why, and how valid is it? *Reading Research Quarterly* 41: 93-99.

Gagnon, J. C., and P. E. Leone. 2001. Alternative strategies for youth violence prevention. In R. J. Skiba and G. G. Noam (eds.), *New directions for youth development* (no. 92; Zero tolerance: Can suspension and expulsion keep schools safe?) (pp. 101-25). San Francisco, CA: Jossey-Bass.

Gagnon, J. C., and C. Richards. 2008. *Making the right turn: A guide about youth involved in the juvenile corrections system* (pp. 1-61). Washington, DC: National Collaborative on Workforce and Disability for Youth, Institute for Educational Leadership.

Goldstrom, I., F. Jaiquan, M. J. Henderson, A. Male, and R. W. Mandersheid. 2000. The availability of mental health services to young people in juvenile justice facilities: A national survey. In R. W. Mandersheid and M. J. Henderson (eds.), *Mental health, United States, 2000.* Washington, DC: Department of Health and Human Services, Substance Abuse and Mental Health Services Administration.

Gottfredson, D. C., D. B. Wilson, and S. S. Najaka. 2002. School-based crime prevention. In L. W. Sherman, D. P. Farrington, B. C. Welsh, and D. L. MacKenzie (eds.), *Evidence-based crime prevention.* London: Routledge.

Greenberg, M. T., C. E. Domitrovich, and B. Bumbarger. 2001. The prevention of mental disorders in school-aged children: Current state of the field. *Prevention and Treatment* 4: 1-63.

Greenberg, M. T., C. A. Kusche, E. T. Cook, and J. P. Quamma. 1995. Promoting emotional competence in school-aged children: The effects of the PATHS curriculum. *Developmental Psychopathology* 7: 117-36.

Greenwood, P. W. 2008. Prevention and intervention programs for juvenile offenders. *Future of Children* 18: 185-210.

Grisso, T. 2008. Adolescent offenders with mental disorders. *Future of Children* 18: 143-64.

Han, S. S., and B. Weiss. 2005. Sustainability of teacher implementation of school-based mental health programs. *Journal of Abnormal Child Psychology* 33: 665-79.

Heatherfield, L. T., and E. Clark. 2004. Shifting from categories to services: Comprehensive school-based mental health for children with emotional disturbance and social maladjustment. *Psychology in the Schools* 41: 911-20.

Henggeler, S. W., and D. M. Borduin. 1990. *Family therapy and beyond: A multisystemic approach to treating the behavior problems of children and adolescents*. Pacific Grove, CA: Brooks/Cole.

Hoagwood, K. E., S. S. Olin, B. D. Kerker, T. R. Kratochwill, M. Crowe, and N. Saka. 2007. Empirically based school interventions targeted at academic and mental health functioning. *Journal of Emotional and Behavioral Disorders* 15: 66-92.

Holden, E. W., R. L. Santiago, B. A. Manteuffel, R. L. Stephens, A. M. Brannan, R. Soler, Q. Liao, F. Brashears, and S. Zaro. 2003. Systems of care demonstration projects: Innovation, evaluation, and sustainability. In A. Pumariega and N. Winters (eds.), *The handbook of child and adolescent systems of care: The new community psychiatry* (pp. 432-58). San Francisco: Jossey-Bass.

Individuals with Disabilities Education Improvement Act. 2006. 34 CFR Parts 300 and 301.

J.D.S. v. State of Indiana. 2010. 71A04-0910-JV-613 (IN Ct. App. 2010).

Juvenile Justice Delinquency Prevention Act. 2003. P.L. 107-273.

Kataoka, S. H., B. Rowan, and K. E. Hoagwood. 2009. Bridging the divide: In search of common ground in mental health and education research and policy. *Psychiatric Services* 60: 1510-15.

Kazdin, A. 2000. Adolescent development, mental disorders, and decision making of delinquent youths (pp. 33-65), in T. Grisso and R. Schwartz. *Youth on trial: A developmental perspective on juvenile justice*. Chicago: University of Chicago Press.

Kellam, S., G. Rebok, N. Ialongo, and L. Mayer. 1994. The course and malleability of aggressive behavior from early first grade into middle school: Results of a developmental epidemiologically-based preventive trial. *Journal of Child Psychology, Psychiatry, and Allied Disciplines* 35: 259-81.

Knoff, H., and G. Batsche. 1995. Project ACHIEVE: Analyzing a school reform process for at-risk and underachieving students. *School Psychology Review* 24: 579-603.

Krezmien, M. P., C. A. Mulcahy, and P. E. Leone. 2008. Detained and committed youth: Examining differences in achievement, mental health needs, and special education status. *Education and Treatment of Children* 31: 445-64.

Kutash, K., A. J. Duchnowski, and N. Lynn. 2006. *School-based mental health: An empirical guide for decision-makers*. Tampa: University of South Florida, Louis de la Parte Florida Mental Health Institute.

Landrum, T. J., M. Tankersley, and J. M. Kauffman. 2003. What is special about special education for students with emotional and behavioral disorders? *Journal of Special Education* 37: 148-56.

Larson, K. A., and K. D. Turner. 2002. *Best practices for serving court-involved youth with learning, attention, and behavioral disabilities*. Washington, DC: U.S. Department of Education and U.S. Department of Justice.

Lehr, C. A., R. A. Moreau, C. M. Lange, and E. J. Lanners. 2004. *Alternative schools: Findings from a national survey of the states* (Research Report 2). Minneapolis: Alternative Schools Research Project, Institute on Community Integration, University of Minnesota. http://ici.umn.edu/alternativeschools/.

Leone, P., M. Quinn, and D. Osher. 2002. *Collaboration in the juvenile justice system and youth-serving agencies: Improving prevention, providing more efficient services, and reducing recidivism for youth with disabilities.* Washington, DC: American Institutes for Research.

Lipsey, M. W. 2009. The primary factors that characterize effective interventions with juvenile offenders: A meta-analytic overview. *Victims and Offenders* 4: 124-47.

Lipsey, M. W., D. B. Wilson, and L. Cothern. 2000. Effective interventions for serious juvenile offenders. *Juvenile Justice Bulletin.* Washington, DC: U.S. Department of Justice, Office of Justice Programs, Office of Juvenile Justice and Delinquency Prevention.

Malti, T., and G. G. Noam. 2008. The hidden crisis in mental health and education: The gap between student needs and existing supports. *New Directions for Youth Development* 120: 13-29.

Marsh, D. 2004. Serious emotional disturbance in children and adolescents: Opportunities and challenges for psychologists. *Professional Psychology: Research and Practice* 35: 443-48.

Martin, R. C. 2001. *Zero tolerance policy report.* Chicago: American Bar Association. http://www.abanet.org/crimjust/juvjus/zerotolreport.html.

Mears, D. P., and L. Y. Aron. 2003. *Addressing the needs of youth with disabilities in the juvenile justice system: The current state of knowledge.* Washington, DC: Urban Institute, Justice Policy Center.

Nation, M., C. Crusto, A. Wandersman, K. L. Kumpfer, D. Seybolt, E. Morrissey-Kane, and K. Davino. 2003. What works in prevention. *American Psychologist* 58: 449-56.

National Association of State Mental Health Program Directors and the Policymaker Partnership for Implementing IDEA Education. 2002. *Mental health, schools, and families working together for all children and youth: Toward a shared agenda.* Alexandria, VA: National Association of State Directors of Special Education.

New Freedom Commission on Mental Health. 2003. *Achieving the promise: Transforming mental health care in America. Final report.* Rockville, MD: U.S. Department of Health and Human Services.

Newcomer, P. L., E. Barenbaum, and N. Pearson. 1995. Depression and anxiety in children and adolescents with learning disabilities, conduct disorders, and no disabilities. *Journal of Emotional and Behavioral Disorders* 3: 27-40.

No Child Left Behind Act. Reauthorization of the Elementary and Secondary Education Act. 2001. Pub. L. No. 107-110, 2102(4).

Oliver, R. M., and D. J. Reschly. 2010. Special education teacher preparation in classroom management: Implications for students with emotional and behavioral disorders. *Behavioral Disorders* 35: 188-99.

Orlando, F. 1999. *Controlling the front gates: Effective admissions policies and practices.* Baltimore: Annie E. Casey Foundation.

Oseroff, A., C. E. Oseroff, D. Westling, and L. J. Gessner. 1999. Teachers' beliefs about maltreatment of students with emotional/behavioral disorders. *Behavioral Disorders* 24:197-209.

Paternite, C. E. 2005. School-based mental health programs and services: Overview and introduction to the special issue. *Journal of Abnormal Child Psychology* 33: 657-63.

President's Commission on Excellence in Special Education. 2002. *A new era: Revitalizing special education for children and their families.* Washington, DC: U.S. Department of Education, Office of Special Education and Rehabilitative Services.

Pullmann, M. D., J. Kerbs, N. Koroloff, E. Veach-White, R. Gaylor, and D. Sieler. 2010. Juvenile offenders with mental health needs: Reducing recidivism using wraparound. *Crime and Delinquency* 24: 375-97.

Quinn, M. M., D. Osher, and T. Valore. 1997. The positive education program in practice. *Reaching Today's Youth: The Community Circle of Caring Journal* 1: 58-62.

Reid, J., M. Eddy, R. Fetrow, and M. Stoolmiller. 1999. Description and immediate impacts of a preventive intervention for conduct problems. *American Journal of Community Psychology* 27: 483-517.

Repie, M. S. 2005. A school mental health issues survey from the perspective of regular and special education teachers, school counselors, and school psychologists. *Education and Treatment of Children* 28: 279-98.

Ringeisen, H., K. Henderson, and K. Hoagwood. 2003. Context matters: Schools and the "research to practice gap" in children's mental health. *School Psychology Review* 32: 153-68.

Rones, M., and K. Hoagwood. 2000. School-based mental health services: A research review. *Clinical Child and Family Psychology Review* 3: 223-41.

Rosenblatt, J. A., A. Rosenblatt, and E. E. Biggs. 2000. Criminal behavior and emotional disorder: Comparing youth served by the mental health and juvenile justice systems. *Journal of Behavioral Health Services and Research* 27: 227-37.

Rosenblatt, A., and M. W. Woodbridge. 2003. Deconstructing research on systems of care for youth with emotional and behavioral disorders: Frameworks for policy research. *Journal of Emotional and Behavioral Disorders* 11: 27-37.

Rossman, S. 2001. *From prison to home: The effect of incarceration and reentry on children, families, and communities.* Washington, DC: Urban Institute.

Sherer. Y. C., and A. B. Nickerson. 2010. Anti-bullying practices in American schools: Perspectives of school psychologists. *Psychology in the Schools* 47: 217-29.

Shufelt, J., and J. Cocozza. 2006. *Youth with mental health disorders in the juvenile justice system: Results from a multi-state prevalence study.* Delmar, NY: National Center for Mental Health and Juvenile Justice. http://www.ncmhjj.com/pdfs/publications/PrevalenceRPB.pdf.

Skiba, R. J., and M. K. Rausch. 2006. Zero tolerance, suspension, and expulsion: Questions of equity and effectiveness. In C. M. Evertson and C. S. Weinstein (eds.), *Handbook of classroom management: Research, practice, and contemporary issues* (pp. 1063-89). Mahwah, NJ: Erlbaum.

Skowyra, K., and J. J. Cocozza. 2006. A blueprint for change: Improving the system response to youth with mental health needs involved with the juvenile justice system. *Research and program brief.* National Center for Mental Health and Juvenile Justice. Delmar, NY: National Center for Mental Health and Juvenile Justice. http://www.ncmhjj.com/Blueprint/default.shtml.

Slade, E. P. 2002. Effects of school-based mental health programs on mental health service use by adolescents at school and in the community. *Mental Health Services Research* 4: 151-66.

Snyder, H. N., and M. Sickmund. 2006. *Juvenile offenders and victims: 2006 national report.* Washington, DC: U.S. Department of Justice, Office of Justice Programs, Office of Juvenile Justice and Delinquency Prevention.

Stephan, S. H., M. Weist, S. Kataoka, S. Adelsheim, and C. Mills. 2007. Transformation of children's mental health services: The role of school mental health. *Psychiatric Services* 58: 1330-38.

Stinchcomb, J. B., G. Bazemore, and N. Riestenberg. 2006. Beyond zero tolerance: Restoring justice in secondary schools. *Youth Violence and Juvenile Justice* 4: 123-47.

Stormshak, E. A., T. J. Dishion, J. Light, and M. Yasui. 2005. Implementing family-centered interventions within the public middle school: Linking service delivery to change in student problem behavior. *Journal of Abnormal Child Psychology* 33: 723-33.

Stroul, B., and R. Friedman. 1986. *A system of care for children and youth with severe emotional disturbances* (rev. ed.). Washington, DC: Georgetown University Child Development Center, National Technical Assistance Center for Children's Mental Health.

Sugai, G., and R. H. Horner. 2002. Introduction to the special series on positive behavior support in schools. *Journal of Emotional and Behavioral Disorders* 10: 130-35.

Tobin, T., and J. Sprague. 1999. Alternative education programs for at-risk youth: Issues, best practice, and recommendations. *Oregon School Study Council Bulletin* 42: 17-36.

Tremblay, R. E., B. Masse, D. Perron, M. LeBlanc, A. E. Schwartzman, and J. E. Ledingham. 1992. Early disruptive behavior, poor school achievement, delinquent behavior, and delinquent personality: Longitudinal analyses. *Journal of Consulting and Clinical Psychology* 60: 64-72.

U.S. Department of Education. 2009. 28th annual report to Congress on the implementation of the Individuals with Disabilities Education Act. Washington, DC: Author.

U. S. Department of Education Office of Special Education and Rehabilitative Services. 2002. *A new era: Revitalizing special education for children and their families.* Washington, DC: Author.

U. S. Department of Health and Human Services. 1999. *Mental health: A report of the surgeon general.* Rockville, MD: National Institute of Mental Health.

U.S. Department of Health and Human Services. 2000. *Report of the surgeon general's conference on children's mental health: A national action agenda.* Rockville, MD: National Institute of Mental Health.

U.S. House of Representatives Committee on Government Reform—Minority Staff Special Investigation Division. 2004. *Incarceration of youth who are waiting for community mental health services in the United States.* Washington, DC: Author.

Vander Stoep, A., C. C. Evens, and J. Taub. 1997. Risk of juvenile justice referral among children in a public mental health system. *Journal of Mental Health Administration* 24: 428-42.

Wagner, M., and R. Cameto. 2004. The characteristics, experiences, and outcomes of youth with emotional disturbances. *NLTS2 Data Brief* 3(2): 1-8.

Walker, J. S., and E. J. Bruns. 2007. *Wraparound: Key information, evidence, and endorsements.* Portland, OR: National Wraparound Initiative. http://www.nwi.pdx.edu/.

Wasserman, G. A., L. S. McReynolds, S. J. Ko, L. M. Katz, and J. R. Carpenter. 2005. Gender differences in psychiatric disorders at juvenile probation intake. *American Journal of Public Health* 95: 131-37.

Weissberg, R. P., K. L. Kumpfer, and M. E. Seligman. 2003. Prevention that works for children and youth: An introduction. *American Psychologist* 58: 425-32.

Weist, M. D. 2005. Fulfilling the promise of school-based mental health: Moving toward a public health promotion approach. *Journal of Abnormal Child Psychology* 33: 735-41.

Weisz, J. R., I. Sandler, J. Durlak, and B. Anton. 2005. Promoting and protecting youth mental health through evidence-based prevention and treatment. *American Psychologist* 60: 1578-85.

Wells, J., J. Barlow, and S. Stewart-Brown. 2003. A systematic review of universal approaches to mental health promotion in schools. *Health Education* 103: 197-220.

Wilson, D. B., D. C. Gottfredson, and S. S. Najaka. 2001. School-based prevention of problem behaviors: A meta-analysis. *Journal of Quantitative Criminology* 17: 247-72.

Wilson, D. B., and M. Lipsey. 2007. School-based interventions for aggressive and disruptive behavior: Update of a meta-analysis. *American Journal of Preventive Medicine* 33: 130-43.

Woodruff, D. W., D. Osher, C. C. Hoffman, A. Gruner, M. A. King, S. T. Snow, and J. C. McIntire. 1999. The role of education in a system of care: Effectively serving children with emotional or behavioral disorders. *Systems of care: Promising practices in children's mental health, 1998 Series, Volume III.* Washington, DC: Center for Effective Collaboration and Practice, American Institutes for Research.

Zahner, G. E., W. Pawelkiewicz, J. J. DeFrancesco, and J. Adnopoz. 1992. Children's mental health service needs and utilization patterns in an urban community: An epidemiological assessment. *Journal of the American Academy of Child and Adolescent Psychiatry* 31: 951-60.

5

Looking for Air

*Excavating Destructive Educational and Racial
Policies to Build Successful School Communities*

THERESA GLENNON

Americans invest public schools with their most fearsome anxieties and deepest longings for a better life. Our current theories of schooling reflect this great anxiety (Ravitch 2010). The 1960s and 1970s saw a focus on those whose educational opportunities had been denied or diminished by discriminatory policies, including racial segregation. By the 1980s, however, those who viewed the effects of this more inclusive vision of U.S. education as "dumbing down" the educational system demanded a "get tough" approach. Getting tough on education focused on standards, accountability based on standardized testing, and heightened consequences for misbehavior in school. At the same time, desegregation dropped off the national agenda, and racial justice concerns receded in importance (Urban and Wagoner 2009). The fallout of the get-tough approach is visible now in the high rates of students, disproportionately students of color, whose educational careers are derailed by harsh school discipline, high-stakes testing, and juvenile crime policies.

As a result, African American boys are trapped at the intersection of educational policies based on harsh judgments, exclusion, a narrow definition of educational success, and a view of racism that denies their lived experiences. This leads inexorably to their disproportionate representation in the juvenile justice system. It is time to reverse course. The federal government must take the lead in redefining educational policy to accord with child development theories, employ positive behavioral interventions that build communities of trust rather than climates of suspicion, and strive to overcome the twin barriers of structural and interactive racism (Lawrence 2006). Federal leadership is needed to revise those education policies, such as zero tolerance school discipline policies and federally inspired testing requirements, and fully employ statutes to prevent race discrimination.

The statistics are shocking: fewer than half of African American males successfully complete high school (Orfield et al. 2004); 19 percent are suspended each year (U.S. Department of Education, Office for Civil Rights 2006); and many others are held back from promotion to the next grade or are unable to pass the tests required for graduation (Losen 2004). In some states, students may be excluded from the regular school environment and sent to alternative schools for disruptive youth (Education Law Center 2010). These approaches to school discipline often lead to criminal sanctions as well.

This chapter focuses on those young African American males who are most affected by zero tolerance and high-stakes testing requirements. The chapter also investigates the federal government's role in public education and the education of African American boys. First, it examines federal zero tolerance policies and high-stakes testing under the No Child Left Behind Act of 2001 (NCLB) that advance a view of education fundamentally at odds with the teachings of child development theory. It also examines the widespread use of zero tolerance school discipline policies and high-stakes testing requirements for promotion and graduation implemented by many states and many local school districts. These policies have led to excessively high rates of school exclusions and overreliance on standardized test scores to determine school success or failure. They have had an especially harsh impact on African American boys.

Second, I examine the misguided direction in which the federal government has led us on the issue of race. It has narrowly defined racial equality as the absence of explicit racial classifications or discriminatory purpose and turned a blind eye to the devastating effects of racial disparities in the lives of its citizens. In so doing, the federal government has undermined and stigmatized efforts to address the structural, institutional, and interactive forms of racism that permeate the lives of racial and ethnic minorities, and in particular African American boys. It obscures the very racial stereotypes that may have made harsh school discipline and testing policies palatable to policymakers and the public.

This chapter critically examines three approaches to addressing the stark racial disparities in school discipline and high-stakes testing. Efforts to date have failed in part because they have not acknowledged the multilayered and everyday nature of racism. Because they have been enacted without an adequate understanding of racism, many of these strategies have served only to reinforce rather than eliminate negative racial and ethnic stereotypes regarding educational attainment and behavior. One approach involves challenges to school actions under the Equal Protection Clause of the Fourteenth

Amendment and judicial and administrative actions under the Civil Rights Act of 1964 (Title VI). The second focuses on federal statutory efforts to address racial disparities in the context of special education and juvenile justice. This includes provisions concerning the overrepresentation of minorities in special education found in the Individuals with Disabilities Education Act (IDEA) and the disproportionate minority contact provisions in the Juvenile Justice Delinquency Prevention Act (JJDPA). The final approach considered is a recent proposal to develop an "architecture of inclusion" to empower institutional citizens to address institutional practices that exclude or diminish some of those citizens on the basis of race, ethnicity, or gender (Sturm 2006).

The Harsh Impact of Zero Tolerance Discipline on the Education of African American Boys

The United States education system loses about 30 percent of its students before graduation (Orfield et al. 2004). Those who do not receive a high school diploma face significant barriers to employment, and their lifetime earnings fall well below those with more education. Lack of education is related to other problems as well, including a lower rate of employment, reduced overall health status, greater rates of incarceration, and shorter life span (NAACP 2005; powell 2008). On all of these measures, African American boys and men face the greatest obstacles.

One important reason for the public school system's failings towards African American boys is the destructive nature of our school discipline policies, often referred to as "zero tolerance." Zero tolerance includes "disciplinary philosophies and policies that are intended to deter disruptive behavior through the application of severe and certain punishments" (American Psychological Association 2006, 19). These policies have created high rates of suspension and expulsion, especially for African American boys. They have led to much closer cooperation between schools and criminal justice authorities, which increases students' involvement with juvenile justice authorities and their rates of incarceration.

Zero tolerance policies have been subject to criticism on a number of fronts. While originally intended only for very serious infractions, such as bringing guns to school, many states and local school districts have expanded their use of suspensions and expulsions to include minor infractions, such as bringing over-the-counter medication to school, talking back, or swearing. The policies undermine trust between school officials and students. They are also criticized for disrupting the education of students against whom they are used, and for too often involving the juvenile justice authorities in minor matters. The FBI itself has warned that harsh school discipline practices can create the anger that fuels more dangerous acts in the future (American Psychological Association 2006).

The use of the term "zero tolerance" in the school context began with local school district discipline policies that mandated suspension or expulsion for specific violations in response to concerns about drugs and gang-related activities (American Psychological Association 2006). Zero tolerance became federal policy with the passage of the Gun-Free Schools Act of 1994 (GFSA), which requires states, as a condition of receiving federal education funds, to expel for at least one year students who bring firearms to school. School district heads may exercise discretion to modify the expulsion for individual students. The statute also requires schools to report to law enforcement agencies students who bring firearms to school (GFSA 2003).

The GFSA focused solely on firearms, but many states and local school districts expanded the zero tolerance approach to include mandatory expulsion for weapons, possession of drugs or alcohol, fighting, or threats in the school environment. A Florida statute (2010) requires expulsion for students in possession of weapons or for students making "a threat or false report," while a Kentucky statute (2006) requires school boards to adopt polices requiring disciplinary actions, including expulsion from school, for possession/sale of drugs and assaults on students or teachers. Some state laws permit suspensions or expulsions for numerous categories of offenses, or leave it up to school districts to define those offenses themselves; Illinois (2010) lets school districts expel students "guilty of gross disobedience or misconduct," and New Jersey (2011) allows school districts to impose suspension or expulsion for a wide range of offenses, including assault, open defiance, continued and willful disobedience, and substantially damaging school property. Local school district policies differ widely in their application of mandatory exclusions (Fultz 2002). Some resulting horror stories have gained publicity, such as the teen expelled for talking on his cell phone to his mother, who was serving in the military in Iraq, and the ten-year-old girl expelled for giving her teacher a small knife her mother had mistakenly placed in her lunch to cut her apple (American Psychological Association 2006). Less visible is the daily stream of suspensions and expulsions, many for small misbehaviors.

This get-tough approach to school discipline results in a high number of suspensions and expulsions annually (Skiba and Peterson 1999). In the 2005-2006 school year, 3.3 million students received at least one suspension and ninety-seven thousand students were expelled. Minority students receive an inordinate number of these suspensions and expulsions. In the 2005-2006 school year, white students, who comprise 56 percent of the student population, received 39 percent of the suspensions and expulsions, while minority students, who make up 44 percent of the student population, received 61 percent of the suspensions and expulsions. Male students were also hard hit by suspensions and expulsions. While they constitute 51 percent of the student population, they received 68 percent of the suspensions and expulsions. African American male students, just under 9 percent of the student population, represented almost 24 percent of those receiving out-of-school suspensions and 27 percent of the students expelled (U.S. Department of Education, Office for Civil Rights 2006).

In addition to suspensions and expulsions, some states and school districts have developed alternative education programs for disruptive youth (AEDY). For example, Pennsylvania currently has almost thirty thousand students in 614 AEDYs across the state. Students may be sent to these programs with little or no due process, and the quality of education varies across providers. While they were originally designed to serve only the most disruptive students, AEDYs now include students who have committed minor violations of the school discipline code and those who are chronically truant. Truancy in particular is often a symptom of disability, or family or mental health problems, and should result in evaluation, not transfer to an alternative program (Education Law Center 2010).

Researchers and advocates have raised serious concerns about the segregation of special education and minority students from the regular school environment into AEDYs (Education Law Center 2010). Thirty-seven percent of the students attending these programs in Pennsylvania during the 2005-2006 school year were reported to be in need of special education. Almost 37 percent of the students in these programs were African American, more than twice their representation in the public school population. This data raises the concern that these disciplinary schools divert students who really need special education from the regular school environment, in contravention of their rights under the IDEA. They may also reflect racial bias in the disciplining of African American students (Education Law Center 2010).

These possibilities are especially disconcerting considering that the education provided in AEDYs is often of lower quality than is found in the regular public schools. In some programs, the school day is much shorter than in other public schools. Some programs lack academic rigor, have limited curricular offerings, and fail to employ effective, proven methods of pedagogy (Education Law Center 2010).

These statistics demonstrate that suspension or placement in alternative disciplinary school settings is a common experience of African American boys, nationally involving almost 20 percent of all African American male students per year. If they are not excluded themselves, their friends most likely are. Children are affected by suspensions of their friends and peers, and often not in the way that the school wishes. School discipline may unite the students against what they perceive to be the arbitrary use of authority, undermining trust between students and teachers.

Trust can be significantly undermined when students are aware of racial disparities in the application of school discipline. One study found that both white and black students believe that racism affects the application of school discipline. While white students perceived disciplinary disparities as unintentional or unconscious, students of color saw them as conscious and deliberate. African American students felt that lack of respect, differences in communication styles, teacher disinterest, and "being purposefully pushed to the edge where they were expected and encouraged to be hostile" were the primary causes of many disciplinary conflicts (Sheets 1996, 175). They viewed the rules as arbitrary, allowing teachers to remove students they did not like. The experiences that lead students to hold this view only serve to drive them further away, rather than providing a positive environment for learning (Sheets 1996).

The student view that racial disparities in school discipline are not justified is consistent with the research literature, which finds that African American students do not misbehave at higher rates than white students. Rather, African American students are punished for behavior that is less serious than the behavior for which white students are punished. Studies conducted over a twenty-year period show that African American students face more severe punishments for less serious violations. These studies are consistent with studies of racial disparities in the juvenile justice system, which demonstrate the same bias (American Psychological Association 2006).

Those who support zero tolerance policies argue that they are necessary to keep schools safe by excluding those who present a serious threat to the school environment. However, suspensions and expulsions are not limited to acts that endanger the school environment. Most suspensions are the result of minor school offenses such as talking back to teachers. Data collected by the Maryland State Department of Education for the 2006-2007 school year revealed that almost half of the out-of-school suspensions were ordered for acts such as cutting classes, tardiness, truancy, disrespect, insubordination, classroom disruption, and refusal to obey school policies (Maryland State Department of Education 2007).

Research reveals that high levels of suspensions and expulsions do not make the school environment safer. School districts vary widely in their reliance on suspensions and expulsions and the extent of the racial disparities in their application (Gordon et. al. 2000; Green 2000). Those schools that employ high levels of suspensions and expulsions are not safer than schools that have found other ways to deal with safety issues (Skiba 2000).

The evidence also undermines the claim that zero tolerance produces a better learning environment—in fact, higher rates of suspension correlate with less positive school climate (American Psychological Association 2006). A state's suspension ranking correlates negatively with its record on the National Assessment of Education Progress rankings in math, writing, and reading. Reliance on suspensions and expulsions undermines the school climate because of the conflictual student-school relationships they create (American Psychological Association 2006).

Further, suspensions and expulsions are quite destructive to the educational careers of those who receive these punishments (Schiraldi and Ziedenberg 2001; American Psychological Association 2006). These students fall behind in their studies and often have difficulty catching up, especially if their behavior problems are an expression of frustration due to undiagnosed learning disabilities. Unsupervised time during suspensions and expulsions increases susceptibility to criminal activity. Further, harsh discipline policies, strip searches, verbal abuse of students by school personnel, and overuse of juvenile confinement harms the mental health and well-being of students affected (Hyman and Snook 1999).

The high rate of suspensions and expulsions, along with the stark racial and ethnic disparities in their application, has garnered the attention of advocates and researchers. A number of organizations, including the American Bar Association (2001), American Psychological Association (2006), NAACP Legal Defense Fund (2005), and Justice Policy Institute (Schiraldi and Ziedenberg 2001), have published major reports detailing the harsh consequences of zero tolerance school discipline policies and the racial, ethnic, and gender disparities in their application. Scholars and student activists have analyzed the causes of racial and ethnic disparities in the application of zero tolerance policies (Skiba and Peterson 1999; Skiba et al. 2000). They have also provided evidence-based positive behavioral approaches to keeping students safe in school without imposing harsh consequences on students (Education Law Center 2010; Skiba and Sprague 2008). In response to these efforts, Florida has revised its school discipline statute to prevent "petty acts of misconduct and misdemeanors" from leading to student suspension and expulsion (Fla. Stat. 2010).

Despite the growing chorus of criticism and concrete proposals for reform, the federal government and most states have not grappled with the consequences of the zero tolerance policies: the large overall number of suspensions and expulsions, with their deleterious effects on the schooling of the students suspended or expelled; the dramatic gender imbalance in the application of these measures; and the stark racial and ethnic disparities in their use.

The Role of High-Stakes Testing under the No Child Left Behind Act

A second factor in the matrix that disproportionately impacts African American boys and triggers risk of involvement in the juvenile justice system is the implementation of testing regimes that punish those who fail. Testing implemented under NCLB is designed to accomplish the act's goal to encourage "excellence and equity" (Ryan 2004, 934). The philosophical underpinning for standardized testing as the primary method of evaluating the school learning environment and student learning is apparent in the NCLB statement of purpose, which is "to ensure that all children have a fair, equal, and significant opportunity to obtain a high-quality education and reach, at a minimum, proficiency on challenging state academic achievement standards and state academic assessments" (20 U.S.C. §6301). To the contrary, however, the NCLB undermines rather than advances the learning of many students of color.

NCLB is the federal government's latest version of Title I of the Elementary and Secondary Education Act of 1965 (ESEA), an act that was designed to direct federal education money to the poorest students. ESEA's statement of purpose in 1965 differs dramatically from the statement for NCLB. Rather than focusing on testing, it states,

> In recognition of the special educational needs of children of low-income families and the impact that concentrations of low-income families have on the ability of local educational agencies to support adequate educational programs, . . . [the policy] provide[s] financial assistance . . . to expand and improve their educational programs by various means . . . which contribute particularly to meeting the special education needs of educationally deprived children.

This emphasis on "special education needs" of students from low-income families, especially in areas in which low-income families are concentrated, continues to be supported by the research, which finds that student achievement is negatively affected by poverty, and that minority students are negatively affected by racial segregation in low-income neighborhoods. The challenges related to poverty, such as low birth weight, lead poisoning, malnutrition, reduced reading and parenting time, increased TV time, and student mobility caused by economic insecurity, all undermine student performance (Lawrence 2006). Despite high hopes that the ESEA would achieve its aspiration to meet students' special educational needs, it instead evolved into a remediation program focused on pulling students out of the regular classroom with little educational progress to show for it (Kelly 1998).

The 1994 Improving America's Schools Act shifted the program's focus to standards-based reform and set the stage for the NCLB, which prioritized standardized test results as the primary measure of schools. The NCLB is about teachers, testing, and accountability (Ryan 2004). It requires states to devise a plan to place "highly qualified" teachers in all schools. They must test reading and math annually in grades 3–8 and once more during grades 10–12, and test student knowledge of science at least three times (Ryan 2004). Schools must show annual yearly progress towards the goal of 100 percent student proficiency on the designated tests, and they must show such progress not only for their student population as a whole, but also for subgroups such as migrant or disabled students, English-language learners, students from all major racial and ethnic groups, and economically disadvantaged students (NCLB 2010).

States receiving NCLB funding may distribute the funds to schools within their state as needed, so not all schools within a state necessarily receive NCLB money. When a state receives funding under NCLB, accountability is nevertheless required for all schools within that state. However, stricter accountability measures are required for schools that are actually getting NCLB money, which is more than half of our nation's public schools. Accountability for schools that fail to meet annual yearly progress goals comes in the form of increasingly harsh "corrective actions," none of which includes extra funding (Ryan 2004). These sanctions include allowing student transfers to nonfailing public schools; preparing a two-year school improvement plan; using NCLB funds to tutor students in failing schools; restructuring through methods such as private management or converting to a charter school; or replacing school staff (Ratner 2007). These threats have not been effective in improving schools, although they reportedly undermine student and teacher morale (Ratner 2007). Many needed reforms are outside the authority of individual schools, extending to the myriad problems faced by children and schools in poor, largely minority neighborhoods that remain unaddressed by NCLB (Ratner 2007).

NCLB has provided an economic boost for the $500 million per year testing industry in elementary and secondary education (Toch 2006). Despite this large investment, researchers argue that state tests fail to properly measure student performance against state standards and that the tests mostly value low-level skills rather than high standards (Ravitch 2010; Toch 2006). Scholars have argued that the two most utilized and least expensive approaches to standardized tests are simply incapable of testing much of what we want students to learn (Kelly 1998; Ratner 2007). The testing companies caution publicly that their tests should not be the sole measure of success or failure (Ravitch 2010).

Even on the narrow skills measured by standardized tests, few important gains for students as a whole or low-income or minority students have appeared. While many states have announced major gains on their standardized tests, such gains are likely to result more from a lowering of state standards than from improved student performance. National Assessment of Educational Progress tests show that students' performance improved only slightly in math and remained flat in reading between 2002 and 2007 (U.S. Department of Education 2008). The racial gap in achievement on basic skills in reading and math remains large (Ratner 2007). Data from the Office for Civil Rights for the U.S. Department of Education (OCR) reveals that African American students appear in gifted and talented classes at just over one-half the rate of their representation in the public school population, they take AP courses at less than half the rate of white students, and they have little success on AP tests. They are overrepresented among students who must retake graduation tests to pass (U.S. Department of Education, Office of Civil Rights 2006). African American boys fare worse than African American girls on all of these measures.

Scholars have criticized the perverse incentives for school administrators and teachers established by high-stakes testing regimes like NCLB (Ryan 2004). Schools may use disciplinary measures and other methods to encourage low-performing students to exit their schools (Mintrop and Sunderman 2009). Charter schools may use entrance requirements like parent interviews and student essays to weed out students whom they believe will be low-performing (Ravitch 2010). Schools may employ strategies to shift students across different categories, such as disabled or English language learners, in order to make their annual yearly progress goals (Ravitch 2010).

Critics also argue that NCLB has distorted pedagogy in the classrooms of low-income and low-achieving students into "drill and kill" techniques that highlight rote memorization rather than critical thinking skills (Lawrence 2010; Nash 2002). Schools may neglect or deemphasize subjects like social studies, foreign languages, arts, and music that may be sources of great interest and engagement for students (Ratner 2007). This approach to education violates what we know about child development and children's needs as learners. Research shows that not only does the United States have a high dropout rate, but 40-60 percent of those students in attendance are chronically disengaged from their schools (Ratner 2007). In order for educators to promote student learning, students need to feel connected to their teachers, and schools need to be designed around children's learning needs, not the needs of standardized tests (Darling-Hammond 1997; Sizer and Sizer 1999).

A rich literature has developed about children's learning needs. It emphasizes that students learn in different ways, and their interests and talents vary widely (Levine 2002). Requiring a teacher to get students to repeat words in rapid-fire succession at the front of the room may be using an appropriate technique for some students, but it is likely to exclude others from success. Students learn best if they can connect new concepts or information to familiar concepts or experiences (Darling-Hammond 1997). Many students need to be actively involved in solving problems to be engaged in the learning process (Ratner 2007). Children's physical needs, when not addressed, may interfere with their ability to learn. For example, the pressure to achieve on standardized tests has led many schools to lengthen the school day or curtail gym and recess for children. Research shows, however, that direct attention is a limited resource, and that children need time to play in order to renew their ability to attend and focus on learning tasks (Barros et al. 2009). Students with better aerobic fitness perform better on standardized tests (Roberts et al. 2010).

While these reforms ignore the child development needs of all children, we cannot ignore the disproportionate effect they have on children of color, and in particular, African American boys. Professor Charles Lawrence points out that that while many schools have increasingly focused on teaching to standardized tests, the schools in which these methods predominate are populated by poor black students. NCLB encourages schools to adopt educational models that highlight rote memorization, not critical thinking skills (Lawrence 2006). Professor Lawrence concludes,

Not only do we teach children in different schools, separated by race, class, and how much money we spend; we also teach them differently. We offer different content, we speak to them differently, and we listen differently, too. We have different expectations, aspirations, and goals. We are educating them for different futures. We send them different messages about their value to us, to the world, and to themselves. (712-13)

High-stakes testing tells many children that they are academic failures. Even if they are making good progress, if they still have not mastered the tested subjects or do not perform well in timed test situations, they are labeled failures (Advancement Project 2010). These messages of failure can lead students who have been striving to succeed to disengage or drop out of school. Both of those outcomes put students at risk to enter the juvenile justice system.

School "Reforms" Ignore the Realities of Racism and Reinforce Their Effects

Zero tolerance policies have, to date, failed to address the severe racial disparities in the discipline of students. While the NCLB draws attention to racial disparities in achievement, it provides no explanation for them other than, perhaps, schools' unwillingness to do their job for their minority students. The act ignores the harm done to African American male students by structural, institutional, and interactive racism, racism that gets effectuated through zero tolerance and high-stakes testing policies. The NCLB

> achieves its greatest injury by erasing the history and conditions that have caused the achievement gap it ostensibly seeks to close. . . . To listen to the discourse of [NCLB] is to hear a story of failing schools without a history—a history of segregation, of inadequate funding, of white flight, of neglect, of eyes averted and uncaring while the savage inequalities of American education grew ever wider. (Lawrence 2006, 706)

The NCLB ignores the long history of oppression and segregation of African Americans, a history that resulted in the creation of highly segregated, low-income cities, neighborhoods, and schools. Students of color continue to face very high levels of segregation—segregation that is increasing rather than decreasing (Orfield and Lee 2005). The students in these schools face numerous hurdles in their educational careers—hurdles that are directly related to the history of segregation and white flight during the brief and limited era of desegregation, a middle-class flight that left many cities in devastating economic and social conditions (Orfield and Lee 2005). As a result of the historical and current conditions of racial inequality, 34 percent of African American children lived in poverty in 2007, compared to 11 percent of white children (Denavas-Walt et al. 2008). These pervasive conditions of inequality are so long-standing that we take them for granted, fail to take them into account in shaping educational policies, and ignore how deeply they inhabit the psyche of students who grow up under these conditions (powell 2008).

These aspects of structural racism in our society affect many students of color in all aspects of their lives, including their school lives (powell 2008). Their schools often have less funding available to them, and the long history of lower funding has left many with a deteriorating infrastructure. Schools with a predominantly minority student population may have a harder time recruiting and retaining highly qualified teachers. Recruitment may be especially difficult in schools subject to NCLB sanctions, which face the threat of removal of all school staff if scores do not meet the statute's unrealistic goals. Teachers may also be put off by the exclusive focus on improving test scores—a focus that may come at the expense of engaging in the activities with students that teachers find the most enjoyable and enriching for their students and themselves (Ravitch 2010).

Racism infects institutional practices within schools as well. Thirty-five years ago, a federal court judge recognized that institutional racism exists when "the standard operating procedures of an institution are prejudiced against, derogatory to, or unresponsive to the needs of a particular racial group" (*Hawkins v. Coleman* 1974, 1336). This insight now appears lost to the federal judiciary. Professor Haney Lopez argues that while it is unrecognized, racial discrimination leads institutions to enforce racial hierarchies through myriad methods (2000, 1811). High-stakes standardized testing graduation requirements, which predictably exclude more students of color from graduation than criteria that evaluate a student's entire academic record, serve as a powerful example of institutionalized racism.

In addition, African American students are harmed by interactive racism. Ideally, schools create safe and nurturing relationships that promote learning, development, and self-esteem. Yet, this essential relational basis for quality learning is all too often lacking. Professor Lawrence and many others have explored the role of unconscious racism, which creates cognitive distortions that reinforce racist beliefs (Lawrence 2006). This sets in place a spiraling process of interactive failures that has been described as "reciprocal distancing" (Larson and Irvine 1999; Maital 2000, 390). The theories of cognitive distortion and reciprocal distancing challenge the belief that behavior and ability are fixed characteristics within the individual. Instead, they point out how fundamentally subject to interpersonal interactions they are. Reciprocal distancing involves a series of "interactive failures" that occur between students and teachers. Initial failures in interaction lead to mutual feelings of failure, frustration, and disappointment and cause each to distance from the other. The child who feels hurt may withdraw or act out. The teacher, feeling angry or guilty, may then attribute the failure to the child. Negative interactions escalate, as both sides distance themselves even further and harden themselves against the other (Maital 2000).

In schools, teachers and school administrators caught in this negative cycle have the power to sanction and label students. Certain labels—incapable, uncooperative, delinquent, dangerous—may stay with and harm children subject to this type of stereotyping. Because of the reciprocal nature of the interactions and the distorted lens through which minority students' actions are seen, school officials usually feel fully justified in the assigning of these labels. This labeling, however, affects the hearts and behavior of the labeled students.

The combination of the racially disparate impact of suspensions and expulsions and high-stakes testing, together with structural, institutional, and interactive racism, severely harms African American boys and derails their future opportunities. We must do better.

Seeking Solutions to Racial Inequality in Schools and the Outcome of Schooling

This section examines three strategies to address the structural and interactive racism at work through policies such as zero tolerance and high-stakes testing to undermine the educational opportunities of African American boys and other students of color. One strategy looks to the Equal Protection Clause and Title VI. A second approach adopts race-conscious measures within specific pieces of legislation, such as the Disproportionate Minority Contact (DMC) requirement under the JJDPA and provisions in the IDEA, together with the racial-disparities requirements of NCLB. A third strategy envisions an "architecture of inclusion," a groundbreaking approach to addressing issues of race theorized by Professor Susan Sturm (2006).

The last thirty years of Supreme Court decisions have undermined the potential of the Equal Protection Clause to effectively address racial injustice and have transformed the Equal Protection Clause into a defense to block race-conscious remedies to segregation and the widespread inequality faced by African Americans (Karlan 2009). While many have read *Brown v. Board of Education* as condemning the invidious use of race to segregate black children from their white peers for the purpose of subordination, the Supreme Court has reinterpreted *Brown* and the Equal Protection Clause to mean that states may not use race for almost any purpose. The Supreme Court now finds that "all race-conscious government action, whether it serves to segregate or to integrate civic institutions, is equally suspect" (Karlan 2009, 1052).

In this era, African American school plaintiffs generally find that they may only prevail under the Equal Protection Clause if they can show that school officials employed an explicit racial classification or acted with a discriminatory purpose, exceedingly difficult burdens to surmount (Haney Lopez 2000). White plaintiffs who challenge explicitly racial policies designed to integrate public schools face no such burden; rather, school officials in those cases must prove that their race-conscious integration policies serve a compelling state purpose in the most narrowly tailored manner possible (*Parents Involved in Community Schools v. Seattle School District No. 1*, 2007). Redress of prior societal discrimination has been rejected as a compelling state purpose. This understanding of the workings of racial discrimination is "exactly backwards," since "[i]nstitutional racism easily occurs without conscious thought of race, and consciously considering race may stem from a desire to ameliorate rather than to perpetuate institutional racism" (Haney Lopez 2000, 1838). Institutions that seek to implement measures to eradicate racial discrimination find themselves more restricted than if they seek to remedy gender and disability discrimination, for which the Supreme Court allows governmental entities greater latitude.

Private litigants must also prove discriminatory intent in actions brought under Title VI. In *Alexander v. Sandoval*, the Supreme Court rejected lower court interpretations of the Title VI federal regulations permitting litigants to challenge policies and practices that result in racial disparities. This prevents most private individuals from bringing their claims of racially and ethnically disproportionate suspensions and expulsions or the negative impact of high-stakes testing directly to court, as it is extremely difficult to demonstrate discriminatory purpose in the adoption and implementation of these school policies. Absent an adequate understanding of racial discrimination, Supreme Court Equal Protection and Title VI jurisprudence now does more to damage the possibility of eradicating racial injustice than to further its demise.

Private individuals may continue to press claims that these policies have a disparately negative impact on the racial and ethnic groups to which they belong through administrative complaints to OCR. OCR is charged with implementing regulations promulgated under Title VI that prohibit recipients of federal funds from using "criteria or methods of administration *which have the effect of subjecting individuals to discrimination because of their race, color, or national origin, or have the effect of defeating or substantially impairing accomplishment of the objectives of the program* as respect individuals of a particular race, color, or national origin" (34 C.F.R. § 100.3(b)(2); italics added).

Courts have interpreted "disparate impact" analysis under Title VI regulations as requiring consideration of three issues. This analysis first considers whether a practice that appears to be neutral has a racially disproportionate adverse effect, and whether there is a causal link between the challenged practice and the identified disparate impact. Second, such disproportions are permissible only if the challenged practice is substantiated by "educational necessity," and the practice must be "demonstrably necessary" to meet an important education goal. Third, even if the practice is substantiated by educational necessity, it must be eliminated if "there exists a comparably effective alternative practice which would result in less disproportionality" (*Elston v. Talladega County Bd. of Educ.* 1993, 1412).

While the regulatory language under Title VI strongly supports eliminating barriers to success for racial and ethnic minorities, court challenges to school policies and practices in the areas of school discipline and high-stakes testing under a disparate-impact theory have brought very limited success. Courts have found that school-discipline and high-stakes testing policies are necessary to achieve important educational goals. Racial disparities, even those that thwart the educational aspirations of high levels of students of color, have been deemed acceptable to serve these important goals (Losen 2004).

Scholars have raised concern about whether the structure of legal doctrine under the disparate-impact standard is appropriate to the types of problems faced by African Americans. Professor Olatunde Johnson writes,

> The very questions posed by the Griggs approach—involving primarily an institution's justification for its practices—are ill-suited to examine the complex questions that underlie disparate impact cases, specifically the way in which government policies and practices (e.g., a decision to grant a permit to a polluting facility or to fund transportation services) interact with the structure of race in American society (e.g., residential segregation or racial disparities in poverty rates). (2007, 396)

In examining the judicial application of Title VI in the graduation testing context, Professor Johnson notes that while a court examining Texas's graduation test requirement expressed willingness to hold the state responsible for using an "educationally invalid test," it proved itself unwilling to require the state to develop an approach that took into account the unequal educational conditions minority students face (2007, 400).

The more nuanced analysis suggested by Professor Johnson may be available to those who seek redress from OCR rather than the court system. The Supreme Court's decision in *Alexander v. Sandoval* does not affect OCR's administrative handling of complaints and conduct of compliance reviews under Title VI. OCR has the authority to investigate and resolve complaints concerning racial and ethnic discrimination and is also entitled to initiate investigations under Title VI where it believes that a state or local school district is not complying with the disparate impact regulations. OCR should affirmatively enforce Title VI's prohibition on using criteria or methods of administration that "have the effect of defeating or substantially impairing accomplishment of the objectives of the program" for racial and ethnic groups to conduct compliance reviews of local school districts, and advocates should bring complaints about unequal benefits to OCR. Title VI requires governmental agencies and other recipients of federal funds to transform their programs to be "equally effective" at serving members of racial minority groups as they are at serving members of the majority group. Equal effectiveness is an affirmative description of the explicit regulatory mandate and should be the basis for determining whether programs such as zero tolerance or high-stakes testing are a success (Glennon 2002).

The equal-effectiveness standard can be the basis for directly challenging beliefs that inequalities are due to characteristics of the protected class rather than the result of structural racism, discriminatory institutional practices, or unequal conditions. In order to hold these programs accountable for failing to provide equally effective services, advocates need to highlight and call into question the long-accepted institutional practices and ingrained racial stereotypes that prevent programs from effectively meeting the learning needs of African American boys. They must also be prepared to successfully rebut arguments from schools that the services fail to be more effective because of some other factor outside the school's control, such as the characteristics of African American boys or their home lives. Equal effectiveness requires educational methods and their implementation that take account of the students and the challenges they actually face.

The OCR complaint and compliance review processes allow the use of various tools to enforce Title VI. Many of these processes are informal, such as providing technical assistance to state educational agencies and local school districts regarding policies and practices that have been shown to reduce racial and ethnic disparities. The OCR complaint and compliance review process may be an especially good forum in which to raise the equal effectiveness claim, since OCR employs a "partnership" approach to resolving complaints and conducting its compliance reviews. The partnership approach allows OCR to enter into agreements with states and local school districts to implement strategies to reduce racial disparities (Glennon 2002). These measures can include, for example, positive behavioral support programs and other measures to improve school climate and learning without the use of zero tolerance school discipline. These agreements can also include educational approaches that best address the structural-racism challenges many students of color face and train staff to avoid the downward spiral created by interactive racism. OCR can be the catalyst for the development of the "architecture of inclusion" described below.

The Title VI disparate impact regulations will be more effective if private plaintiffs are able to regain access to the courts to enforce them. Congress should reopen the courts to private parties under Title VI by overruling the Court's decision in *Sandoval*, as it has done in the past with other Supreme Court decisions that undermined civil rights statutes (Sullivan 2010; Suthammanont 2009). While the record of effectiveness of disparate impact theory in the courts is mixed, its availability opens the door to negotiation to address racial disparities.

A second strategy that has been tried in an attempt to address racial disparities in educational processes and outcomes incorporates race-conscious measures in legislation about specific programs. In addition to NCLB, two other education-related statutes—the IDEA and the JJDPA—incorporate explicit findings about racial disparities and require recipients of program funds to take explicit actions to alleviate these disparities. The IDEA and JJDPA require states to collect data by race and to take affirmative steps to reduce the disproportionate representation of minority youth in special education and residential juvenile facilities.

The IDEA includes requirements concerning minority overrepresentation in special education. Congress found that "[g]reater efforts are needed to prevent the intensification of problems connected with mislabeling and high dropout rates among minority children with disabilities" (IDEA 2010 §1401(c)(12)(A)). The IDEA requires states to monitor school districts for potential discrimination in identification of students as disabled, placement of students in educational settings, and suspensions and expulsions of children with disabilities. When states' indicators point to significant racial disproportionality in special education identification and placement, they must review and revise policies, procedures, and practices related to identification and placement. Any local educational agencies with significant disproportions must also publicly report on their activities (IDEA § 1418(d)). The U.S. Department of Education also sponsors technical assistance for states and local school districts seeking to reduce the racial and ethnic disproportionalities in special education identification and placement. After an initial spurt of activity under this provision, there appears to be little agency activity under or enforcement of this requirement.

The JJDPA requires states participating in the federal grant program to:

> address juvenile delinquency prevention efforts and system improvement efforts designed to reduce, without establishing or requiring numerical standards or quotas, the disproportionate number of juveniles members of minority groups, who come into contact with the juvenile justice system. (JJDPA § 5633(a)(22))

These efforts to reduce racial and ethnic disparities in confinement are a "core requirement" of the JJDPA. States that fail to make the required efforts to reduce disproportionate confinement are subject to a 20 percent reduction in their next annual formula grant and become ineligible to receive any further funds under the program unless they make a financial and substantive commitment to comply with the provision. These DMC regulations require "specific efforts to reduce the proportion of juveniles detained or confined" in secure facilities (28 C.F.R. 31.303(j)). States must provide detailed data on minority confinement rates and a complete assessment of disproportionate minority confinement, and they must specify a time-limited plan of action to reduce the disproportion. The Office of Juvenile Justice Delinquency and Prevention maintains an active DMC website that makes available federal requirements and research on the issue of disproportionate confinement.

The DMC regulations encourage close scrutiny of institutional practices to identify the workings of institutional and interactive racism without requiring plaintiffs to sue and meet difficult evidentiary burdens. They require states to correct racial disparities without forcing those affected to first prove that the racial disparities are caused by the juvenile justice system or permitting states to defend the disparities as an institutional necessity. States must take affirmative steps to reduce racial disparities in juvenile justice, steps that can cut across agency lines and force agencies to consider how apparently neutral factors, such as considering family structure as a part of the assessment of whether detention is necessary, may negatively affect racial minorities (Johnson 2007).

The IDEA and JJDPA requirements are stronger than the NCLB requirement for average yearly progress by specific groups, though it remains difficult to assess their impact. These statutory provisions create requirements for the collection and public dissemination of data and qualitative research on racial, ethnic, and gender disparities and federal oversight to ensure that states follow through on programmatic changes to alleviate any racial and ethnic disparities that are found. They can lead to the development of close institutional analyses that track the mundane, everyday workings of racism within educational and juvenile justice programs (Johnson 2007). They provide models for legislative advocacy to require data collection, program evaluation, and reform efforts regarding the racial, ethnic, and gender disparities in suspensions and expulsions and high-stakes testing. By focusing on the public dissemination of data and research, state and local-level evaluations of discriminatory practices, and the development and implementation of action plans, this type of statute may also open up new avenues for advocates to work with educators at the state and local level to reduce the excessive use of suspensions and expulsions and the harsh racial and ethnic disparities in their application.

These efforts are not without risk. They raise the possibility of the "perverse incentives" problem created by NCLB. In addition, separate requirements for disproportions in special education, test scores, and school discipline may divide up information and analysis and obscure the reasons for racial disparities that cut across these and other areas of concern. This may leave unaddressed the structural, institutional, and interactive forms of racism that pervade the lives of racial minority students. Legislation that targets minority overrepresentation in one specific area may have spillover effects on other areas. Thus, institutional practices need to be evaluated holistically for their racial, ethnic, and gender effects so that addressing one problem area, such as school exclusions, does not lead to increases in a different problem, such as the overuse of special education.

A third approach involves the development of an "architecture of inclusion" that seeks to achieve gender and racial equality in an institutional context through "institutional mindfulness" (Sturm 2006, 258). Professor Susan Sturm argues that the typical approach to issues of equity, which involves a task force report with little follow through, rarely leads to deep and long-lasting institutional change. She notes:

Those on the front line must figure out how to achieve inclusive institutions when the problems causing racial and gender under-participation are structural, and they must do this under conditions of considerable legal ambiguity. They have learned that studies alone do not produce significant change, nor does providing support or legal protection for individual women and people of color. Workplace equality is achieved by connecting inclusiveness to core institutional values and practices. This is a process of ongoing institutional change. It involves identifying the barriers to full participation and the pivot points for removing those barriers and increasing participation. Those involved in this work must be able to articulate why under-participation is a problem that warrants sustained public attention. They must also find ways to locate responsibility for achieving inclusiveness with those in a position to have an impact. (Sturm 2006, 249)

Sturm advocates the implementation of at least three ideas to advance institutional equity: a norm of institutional citizenship that supports all participants in achieving their potential and participating fully in the life of the institution; identifying "organizational catalysts" to trigger and follow through with change; and employing public or quasi-public "institutional intermediaries" to sustain and provide accountability for the change process (Sturm 2006).

The idea of institutional citizenship dramatically changes the role of all actors. Because institutional citizenship highlights the need to look at all institutional participants, this framework would include strategies that treat children, as well as teachers and administrators, as change agents. For example, strong improvements in school safety and climate have been achieved by putting students in charge of discipline through mediation and conflict resolution programs (Trevaskis et al. 2007). Engaging students in the process of identifying key educational goals and how they can be best achieved is an important change from the philosophy of NCLB, and certainly dramatically different than a zero tolerance policy that is based on excluding students rather than engaging them to improve the school environment.

The architecture-of-inclusion approach is also data driven. Social science data often reveals many levels at which racism creeps into the actions of individuals within an institutional context (Skiba et al. 2000). Institutional actors must be presented with data analyzing in detail the institutional processes that create racial disparities. This data will highlight that there is no single fix to the issue, but that institutional actors need to change their conduct across a wide range of practices. The data is used to instruct participants and motivate them to engage in needed change. Strategies to actually achieve change are taught by organizational catalysts who follow through to ensure that changes in practices small and large occur and are sustained. Researchers who have written extensively on the workings of racial exclusion and methods that achieve positive school environments without reliance on suspensions and expulsions can be an excellent source of information for schools. Pulling this research together in readily accessible forms is an appropriate role for the federal government. OCR can use its authority to enter into agreements with school districts to follow up and ensure that the targeted changes occur, and that they prove effective.

Professor Sturm's approach is especially beneficial to promote change at the school and school district levels, where there is a centralized institutional structure. Schools do control their use of discipline, placement in special education, and numerous other institutional practices that can be changed to stop feeding racial inequalities. Her method can lead schools and all stakeholders in the schools, including students, to examine the numerous ways in which race and gender are interwoven with institutional practices, the relationships within schools, and the interactions among school administrators, teachers, and students. However, her approach does not tackle some important structural impediments to racial equality. These include worsening resegregation, declining school financing, and the troubling relationship between education and the criminal justice system. These major structural problems need to be tackled at the federal and state levels; otherwise, addressing institutional and interactive racism may have a more limited effect.

The strategies of reinvigorating Title VI advocacy through OCR, enacting targeted legislation to create data and support for examining and eliminating racial disparities, developing an architecture of inclusion, and approaching racial inequities at the macro-structural level are ways to address the wrongs of racial discrimination in school discipline, high-stakes testing, and other education programs. They will only be effective, however, if used within a working conceptual framework that explains how racial discrimination insinuates itself into multiple decision points and experiences. Efforts to create change absent such understanding may, like NCLB, zero tolerances policies, and recent Supreme Court jurisprudence, undermine rather than create progress.

Students, and especially students of color, must be at the center of our vision for change, and they must be active participants in creating those changes. We must not permit legislators to base harsh legislation such as zero tolerance and NCLB on their unconscious and negative racial stereotypes of African American boys and other students of color. We need to envision schools as places that nurture rather than tear down their students; value students as active citizens rather than disparage them as obstacles to schools' ability to meet testing targets; excite more than evaluate students; unfold their strengths rather than trigger their weaknesses; and raise up rather than undermine their dreams. African American boys should not be the roadkill of educational reform; rather, they should be active citizens who tell us if our approaches are working.

REFERENCES

Advancement Project. 2010. *Test, Punish, and Push Out: How "Zero Tolerance" and High-Stakes Testing Funnel Youth into the School-to-Prison Pipeline.* . http://advancementproject.org/sites/default/files/publications/rev_fin.pdf.

American Bar Association. 2001. *ABA Juvenile Justice Policies: Zero Tolerance Policy Report.* http://www.abanet.org/crimjust/juvjus/zerotolreport.html.

American Psychological Association. 2006. *Are Zero Tolerance Policies Effective in the Schools? An Evidentiary Review and Recommendations.* A Report by the American Psychological Association Zero Tolerance Task Force, written by Russell Skiba, Cecil R. Reynolds, Sandra Graham, Peter Sheras, Jane Close Conoley, and Enedina Garcia-Vazquez. http://www.senate.state.tx.us/75r/Senate/commit/c530/handouts06/092006.c530.LevinM.1.pdf.

Barros, Romina M., Ellen J. Silver, and Ruth K. Stein. 2009. School Recess and Group Classroom Behavior. *Journal of Pediatrics* 123: 431-36.

Darling-Hammond, Linda. 1997. *The Right to Learn: A Blueprint for Creating Schools That Work.* San Francisco: Jossey-Bass.

Denavas-Walt, Carmen, Bernadette D. Proctor, and Jessica C. Smith. 2008. *Income, Poverty, and Health Insurance Coverage in the United States: 2007.* Washington, DC: U.S. Census Bureau, Current Population Reports: 60-235.

Education Law Center. 2010. Improving "Alternative Education for Disruptive Youth" in Pennsylvania. http://www.elc-pa.org/pubs/downloads2010/ELC_AHEdPA_FullReport.pdf.

Fultz, Allison. 2002. Comment: Making Kids Toe the Line in the Old Line State: The Disparate Application of Public School Discipline Policies in Maryland. *American University Journal of Gender, Social Policy, and Law* 11 (1): 175-209.

Gordon, Rebecca, Libero Della Piana, and Terry Keleher. 2000. Facing the Consequences: An Examination of Racial Discrimination in U.S. Public Schools. *ERASE Initiative: A Project for the Applied Research Center.* http://www.arc.org.

Green, Rick. 2000. "Punishment in School; Kicking Out the Problem." *Hartford Courant,* July 6.

Glennon, Theresa. 2002. Knocking against the Rocks: Evaluating Institutional Practices and the African American Boy. *Journal of Health Care Law & Policy* 10: 10-67.

Haney Lopez, Ian F. 2000. Institutional Racism: Judicial Conduct and a New Theory of Racial Discrimination. *Yale Law Journal* 109: 1721-1884.

Hyman, Irwin A., and Pamela A. Snook. 1999. *Dangerous Schools: What We Can Do about the Physical and Emotional Abuse of Our Children*. San Francisco: Jossey-Bass.

Johnson, Olutande C.A. 2007. Disparity Rules. *Columbia Law Review* 107: 374-425.

Karlan, Pamela. 2009. What Can Brown Do for You? Neutral Principles and the Struggle over the Equal Protection Clause. *Duke Law Journal* 58: 1049-68.

Kelly, Lisa. 1998. Yearning for Lake Woebegon: The Quest for the Best Test at the Expense of the Best Education. *University of Southern California Interdisciplinary Law Journal* 7: 41-77.

Larson, Joanne, and Patricia D. Irvine. 1999. "*We* Call Him Dr. King": Reciprocal Distancing in Urban Classrooms. *Language Arts* 76: 393-400.

Lawrence, Charles. 2006. Who Is the Child Left Behind? The Racial Meaning of the New School Reform. *Suffolk University Law Review* 39: 699-717.

Levine, Mel. 2002. *A Mind at a Time*. New York: Simon & Schuster.

Losen, Daniel. 2004. Challenging Racial Disparities: The Promise and Pitfalls of the No Child Left Behind Act's Race-Conscious Accountability. *Howard Law Journal* 47: 243-98.

Maital, Sharon. 2000. Reciprocal Distancing: A Systems Model of Interpersonal Processes in Cross-Cultural Consultation. *School Psychology Review* 29: 389-400.

Maryland State Department of Education. 2007. *Suspensions, Expulsions, and Health-Related Exclusions: Maryland Public Schools, 2006-2007*. http://marylandschools.org / NR/rdonlyres/BF1EED33-A890-434D-BFDD-07EA226A6F93/14968/susp07.pdf.

Mintrop, Heinrich, and Gail L. Sunderman. 2009. *Why High Stakes Accountability Sounds Good but Doesn't Work—and Why We Keep Doing It Anyway*. Los Angeles: Civil Rights Project/Proyecto Derecho Civiles.

NAACP Legal Defense and Education Fund. 2005. *Dismantling the School-to-Prison Pipeline*. http://www.naacpldf.org/content/pdf/pipeline/Dismantling_the_School_to_Prison_Pipeline.pdf.

Nash, David. 2002. Improving No Child Left Behind: Achieving Excellence and Equity in Partnership with the States. *Rutgers Law Review* 55: 239-70.

Orfield, Gary, and Chungmei Lee. 2005. *Why Segregation Matters: Poverty and Educational Inequality*. Cambridge: Civil Rights Project at Harvard University. http://www.civilrightsproject.ucla.edu/research/deseg/Why_Segreg_Matters.pdf.

Orfield, Gary, Daniel Losen, Christopher B. Swanson, and Johanna Wald. 2004. *Losing Our Future: How Minority Youth Are Being Left Behind by the Graduation Rate Crisis*. A Joint Release by the Civil Rights Project at Harvard University, the Urban Institute, Advocates for Children of New York, and the Civil Society Institute. http://www.civilrightsproject.ucla.edu/research/dropouts/LosingOurFuture.pdf.

powell, john. 2008. Structural Racism: Building upon the Insights of John Calmore. *North Carolina Law Review* 86: 791-816.

Ratner, Gershon. 2007. Why the No Child Left Behind Act Needs to be Reconstructed to Accomplish Its Goals and How to Do It. *University of the District of Columbia Law Review* 9: 1-51.

Ravitch, Diane. 2010. *The Death and Life of the Great American School System: How Testing and Choice Are Undermining Education*. New York: Perseus Books Group.

Roberts, Christian K., Benjamin Freed, and William J. McCarthy. 2010. Low Aerobic Fitness and Obesity Are Associated with Lower Standardized Test Scores in Children. *Journal of Pediatrics* 156: 711-18.

Ryan, James E. 2004. The Perverse Incentives of the No Child Left Behind Act. *New York University Law Review* 79: 932-89.

Schiraldi, Vincent, and Jason Ziedenberg. 2001. *Schools and Suspensions: Self-Reported Crime and the Growing Use of Suspensions.* Washington, DC: Justice Policy Institute. http://www.justicepolicy.org/sss/.

Sheets, Rosa Hernández. 1996. Urban Classroom Conflict: Student-Teacher Perception; Ethnic Integrity, Solidarity, and Resistance. *Urban Review* 28:165-83.

Sizer, Theodore R., and Nancy Faust Sizer. 1999. *The Students Are Watching: Schools and the Moral Contract.* Boston: Beacon Press.

Skiba, Russell. 2000. *Zero Tolerance, Zero Evidence: An Analysis of School Disciplinary Practice.* Indiana Education Policy Center Policy Research Report #SRS2. http://www.indiana.edu/~safeschl/ztze.pdf.

Skiba, Russell, Robert S. Michael, Abra C. Nardo, and Reece L. Peterson. 2000. *The Color of Discipline: Sources of Racial and Gender Disproportionality in School Punishment.* Indiana Education Policy Center Policy Research Report #SR51. http://www.indiana.edu/~safeschl/cod.pdf.

Skiba, Russell, and Reece L. Peterson. 1999. The Dark Side of Zero Tolerance: Can Punishment Lead to Safe Schools? *Phi Delta Kappan* 80 (5): 372-76, 380-81.

Skiba, Russell, and Jeffrey Sprague. 2008. Safety without Suspensions. *Educational Leadership* 66 (1): 38-43.

Sturm, Susan. 2006. The Architecture of Inclusion: Advancing Workplace Equity in Higher Education. *Harvard Journal of Law & Gender* 29: 247-344.

Sullivan, Charles R. 2010. Raising the Dead? The Lilly Ledbetter Fair Pay Act. *Tulane Law Review* 84: 499-563.

Suthammanont, Victor. 2009. Rebalancing the Scales: Restoring the Availability of Disparate Impact Causes of Action in Title VI Cases. *New York Law School Law Review* 54: 27-57.

Toch, Thomas. 2006. Margins of Error: The Education Testing Industry in the No Child Left Behind Era. *Education Sector Reports* 6: 1-23. http://www.educationsector.org/research/research_show.htm?doc_id=346734.

Trevaskis, David Keller, and Amy Niedzalkoski. 2007. Educating for Democracy in the 21st Century: Civic Learning and Project PEACE in Interesting Times. Annenburg Classroom. http://communities.annenbergclassroom.org/blogs/050606trevaskis/default.aspx.

Urban, Wayne, and Jennings Wagoner. 2009. *American Education: A History.* New York: Routledge.

U.S. Department of Education. 2008. *Mapping America's Educational Progress.* http://ed.gov/nclb/accountability/results/progress/index.html.

U.S. Department of Education, Office for Civil Rights, Case Processing Manual, 2010. http://www2.ed.gov/about/offices/list/ocr/docs/ocrcpm.html.

U.S. Department of Education, Office for Civil Rights, National Data Collection. 2006. *Projected Values for the Nation.* http://ocrdata.ed.gov/downloads/projections/2006/2006-nation-projection.xls.

TABLE OF CASES

Alexander v. Sandoval. 2001. 121 S.Ct. 1511.

Brown v. Board of Education. 1954. 347 U.S. 483.

Elston v. Talladega County Bd. of Educ. 1993. 997 F.2d 1394.

Hawkins v. Coleman. 1974. 376 F. Supp. 1330.

Horn v. Madison County Fiscal Court. 1994. 22 F.3d 653.

James v. Jones. 1993. 148 F.R.D. 196.

Parents Involved in Community Schools v. Seattle School District No. 1. 2007. 127 S.Ct. 2738.

Tejas v. Tex. Educ. Agency. 2000. 87 F.Supp. 2d 667.

TABLE OF STATUTES AND REGULATIONS

28 C.F.R. § 31.303(j).

34 C.F.R. §100.3.

Civil Rights Act of 1964. 2009. Title VI, 42 U.S.C. § 2000d.

Elementary and Secondary Act of 1965, Pub.L. 89-10, Section 901.

Fla. Stat. 2010. 1006.07(2)(k), 1006.13(1).

Gun-Free Schools Act. 2003. 20 U.S.C. § 7151 (2003).

Illinois School Code. 2010. 105 ILCS 5/10-22.6.

Improving America's Schools Act of 1994, Pub.L. 103-382.

Individuals with Disabilities Education Act. 2010. 20 U.S.C. §§ 1400(c)(12)(A), 1412(a) (24), 1418(d).

Juvenile Justice Delinquency Prevention Act. 2010. §§ 5601 et seq., 5633 (a)(22).

Ky. Rev. Stat. Ann. 2006. § 158.150 (2).

N.J. Stat. Ann. 2011. § 18A:37-2.

No Child Left Behind Act of 2001. 2010. 20 U.S.C. §§6301 et seq., 6311 (b)(2)(C)(vi), (vii).

Race, Gender, and Sexual Orientation

The Black Nationalist Cure to Disproportionate Minority Contact

KENNETH B. NUNN

It takes a village to raise a child.

—African proverb

"It takes a village to raise a child." On this we can all agree. But what happens to the children when a village has been destroyed? Or harmed? If it takes a village to raise a child, then children cannot be raised properly when there is no village to take care of them. Less drastically, if it is fair to suppose that a well-functioning village will produce high-functioning children, then a poorly functioning village will produce poorly functioning children. While children are extremely resilient, even a resilient child has little chance to make it to adulthood without proper attention and care.

In his best-selling book, *Outliers*, Malcolm Gladwell points out that success is not only the result of individual effort; it requires a supportive cultural foundation as well. According to Gladwell, "The culture we belong to and the legacies passed down by our forebears shape the patterns of our achievement in ways we cannot begin to imagine" (Gladwell 2008, 19). In other words, "it takes a village to raise a child."

To illustrate his point, Gladwell recounts an intriguing medical mystery surrounding health outcomes in the small town of Roseto, Pennsylvania. In the 1950s, prior to the introduction of cholesterol-lowering medication and widespread awareness of heart-healthy diets, doctors discovered that heart disease was nearly nonexistent in Roseto. Further investigation revealed that Rosetans had a remarkably good quality of life in general. According to sociologist John Bruhn, "There was no suicide, no alcoholism, no drug addiction, and very little crime. They didn't have anyone on welfare. Then we looked at peptic ulcers. They didn't have any of those either. These people were dying of old age. That's it" (Gladwell 2008, 18).

Careful research removed diet, exercise, genetic background, and environmental factors as explanations for the Rosetans' good fortune. In the end, the researchers concluded it was the unique social environment that the Rosetans had constructed for themselves that explained the health outcomes of the village—the way they communicated with each other, the way they shared, the respect they had for elders, and their commitment to civic involvement. Gladwell tells us that "[i]n transplanting the *paesani* culture of southern Italy to the hills of eastern Pennsylvania, the Rosetans had created a powerful, protective social structure capable of insulating them from the pressures of the modern world" (Gladwell 2008, 9).

Gladwell argued that if doctors truly wanted to understand why an individual was healthy, they

> had to look *beyond* the individual. They had to understand the culture he or she was part of, and who their friends and families were, and what town their families came from. They had to appreciate the idea that the values of the world we inhabit and the people we surround ourselves with have a profound effect on who we are. (Gladwell 2008, 10-11)

African Americans, Native Americans, Hispanics/Latinos, Native Hawaiians, and Asian Americans are disproportionately represented in the nation's juvenile justice infrastructure. They are referred to juvenile programs more frequently by social workers, they are arrested more frequently, they are charged with juvenile crimes more frequently, they are adjudicated more frequently, and they are more likely to be held in custody and referred to juvenile prisons and jails. The Department of Juvenile Justice refers to this phenomenon as "disproportionate minority contact" and in an effort to stop it has encouraged scholars, policymakers, NGOs, and public agencies to focus their attention on this issue. Since 1988, the department has instituted an array of programs, policies, recommendations, and funding opportunities seeking to reduce or end disproportionate minority contact, and an entire ecosystem of programs, grantees, and experts has been created to help end it.

In this chapter, I argue that these efforts may have some success, but ultimately they will miss the mark of ending disproportionate minority contact. For they treat symptoms, not the disease. I argue that what causes disproportionate minority contact is the social and political oppression of young people's communities. The very existence of disproportionate minority contact is evidence of that oppression and the reason why these communities cannot function as they should.

Unlike the Italian immigrants in Roseto, Pennsylvania, African Americans were not able to transport their culture intact across the Atlantic.

They were not able to maintain the bonds of family, traditional values, and social institutions essential to a happy and healthy community life. Certainly, Africans did not come across the Atlantic empty handed. They were able to preserve and maintain their culture in many forms, both obvious and obscure.[1] But African culture was never allowed to take root in the United States the way *paesani* culture did in eastern Pennsylvania. African culture was always under attack and under pressure. Due to African resilience and ingenuity, African culture *survived* in North America, but it could not *thrive*.

A well-functioning community has the ability to endure over time. It has the ability to replicate itself through succeeding generations by being able to feed, clothe, shelter, and provide other forms of material needs for its young. More importantly, a working community is able to socialize each generation so that it is equipped to fulfill desirable social roles. The larger community not only does not want to do this, but cannot. This socialization role includes giving children a positive self-image and high self-esteem.

Communities must be able to access the resources that allow this kind of socialization to occur. The problem that communities of color in a larger white-dominated society face is that they do not have access to the material, psychological, and sociocultural resources that their children need to thrive. Often, the adults in these communities are unable to provide supportive and protective environments for their children and their children must fend for themselves. Thus, children of oppressed communities are easy targets to be shunted into the juvenile justice system and victimized by the social control structure of the dominant society.

Viewing disproportionate minority contact through a Black nationalist lens can identify its true causes and suggest lasting solutions. In this chapter I first examine the contours of disproportionate minority contact by reviewing recent research on its frequency and causes. In part 2, I examine the link between it and oppression. I will argue that most of the effects of disproportionate minority contact are caused by oppression, either directly by the operation of juvenile justice institutions or indirectly by the disadvantages experienced by Black and other communities of color, which make their children less likely to avoid juvenile justice involvement. In part 3, I discuss the importance of culture to community well-being and viability. In part 4, I describe the Black nationalist norm of cultural autonomy. I argue that embracing this norm can lead to empowered communities that resist oppression and avoid the entrapment of their youth in the criminal justice system.

First, a note on terminology. In order to emphasize the cultural connectedness of all members of the African family, I intentionally use the word "African" throughout this chapter to refer to persons who are of African descent, whether they may reside on the continent or in the diaspora. When it is necessary to distinguish African people resident in the United States from African people elsewhere, I use the term "African American." "Black," when used, denotes racial and cultural identity rather than mere physical appearance and is, therefore, capitalized (Nunn 1993, 64 n.7).

I. Recent Research on Disproportionate Minority Contact

"Disproportionate minority contact" (or DMC) is the bureaucratic term used to refer to racial and ethnic disparities in the juvenile justice system. As described in the amended version of the Juvenile Justice and Delinquency Prevention Act (Public Law 93-415, 42 U.S.C. 5601 et seq.), DMC exists "if the proportion of a given minority group of youth who [came into contact with some aspect of the juvenile justice system] exceeded the proportion that group represented in the general population" (Hsia, Bridges, and McHale 2004, 11). Originally, the statutory concern was disproportionate minority *confinement*, but Congress extended the scope of the act to disproportionate minority contact after it became evident that children of color were disproportionately involved at every stage of the juvenile justice process.

About two-thirds of youth involved with the juvenile justice system are children of color. In 2006, youth from communities of color constituted 63 percent of the juveniles detained and 69 percent of those committed to secure juvenile correctional facilities (Sickmund, Sladky, and Kang 2008). These figures are almost double the percent of youth of color in the general population. African American youth are overrepresented to a greater degree than any other racial/ethnic category. African American youth constituted about 13 percent of the nation's juvenile population in 2006 (Puzzanchea, Sladky, and Kang 2009); however, they represented 30 percent of all juveniles arrested (Criminal Justice Information Services 2007), 42 percent of those who were detained, and 39 percent of those in residential placement (Sickmund, Sladky, and Kang 2008).

States that demonstrate DMC are required to take steps to reduce it in order to receive federal funding from the Office of Juvenile Justice and Delinquency Prevention (OJJDP) in the U.S. Department of Justice. In addition, research into disproportionate minority contact has been spearheaded by grants offered by the OJJDP. The OJJDP requires states seeking funding to first identify whether DMC is an issue in the state. Then, states must evaluate how white youth and youth of color are treated at discretionary stages in the juvenile justice system by conducting a state assessment (Hsia, Bridges, and McHale 2004). According to the OJJDP, "The focus of state assessments is to determine why DMC exists in order to address it successfully" (id.). To conduct an assessment, states are required to gather quantitative and qualitative data from a variety of sources, including tracking of case files, surveys, and interviews.

There are two general theories to explain DMC's prevalence (Moriearty 2008; Nunn 2002b). One theory supposes that children of color offend differently than white children (Moriearty 2008). Proponents of this theory argue that children of color are treated differently in the juvenile justice system because they offend more frequently and commit more serious crimes.[2] The other theory would allocate DMC to societal causes that affect both the opportunity to offend and the harshness of treatment (Moriearty 2008). The two theories do not differ significantly for my purpose here since most scholars who adhere to the view that children of color offend differently also credit that different offense pattern to societal factors (Sampson and Lauritsen 1997).

Evidence collected by the OJJDP suggests that societal factors do figure largely in the incidence of DMC. Review of state assessments nationally by OJJDP reveals several environmental factors that contribute to DMC. These factors can be organized into four key areas: (1) the juvenile justice system, (2) the educational system, (3) socioeconomic conditions, and (4) the family (Hsia, Bridges, and McHale 2004).

Factors contributing to DMC within the juvenile justice system itself include "racial stereotyping and cultural insensitivity," "lack of alternatives to detention and incarceration," "misuse of discretionary authority in implementing laws and policies," and "lack of culturally and linguistically appropriate services." Racial stereotyping and cultural insensitivity include both intentional and unintentional conduct by police, judges, and juvenile court workers. In the OJJDP survey, racial attitudes are specifically identified as "contributing to higher arrest rates, higher charging rates, and higher rates of detention and confinement" of youth of color. In addition, due to cultural insensitivity, "The demeanor and attitude of minority youth can contribute to negative treatment and more severe disposition relative to their offenses." Furthermore, alternative dispositions like treatment programs are used less frequently for youth of color due to the belief that they "cannot benefit from treatment programs" (Hsia, Bridges, and McHale 2004, 12).

The state assessments disclose that detention centers are often located in large urban areas, which also have significant African American and other communities of color. Given few alternatives to detention, "nearby detention centers become 'convenient' placements for urban minority youth." Discretion is often misused in ways that disadvantage youth of color. According to the OJJDP survey, "Five states observed that laws and policies that increase juvenile justice professionals' discretionary authority over youth contribute to harsher treatment of minority youth." Finally, the lack of culturally and linguistically appropriate services contributes to the non-English-speaking population's "misunderstanding of services and court processes and their inability to navigate the system successfully" (id.).

Deficiencies within the educational system also contribute to DMC. According to data collected by the OJJDP, educational failures contributing to early academic failure and early involvement in delinquency include "the lack of educational resources in schools in minority neighborhoods, the failure of schools to engage minority students and their families, the inability to prevent early and high rates of school dropout among minority students, and the concomitant failure of minority students and their families to participate fully in the educational system" (id.).

Socioeconomic conditions such as poverty, substance abuse, lack of job opportunities, high neighborhood crime rates, and lack of positive role models were identified as factors placing youth of color at higher risk for delinquent behaviors. High juvenile justice system involvement in some states was also asserted to be due to "concerted law enforcement targeting of high-crime areas" leading to higher numbers of arrests and formal processing for youth of color. Once involved in the juvenile justice system, youth of color were disadvantaged because their "communities have fewer service programs that function as alternatives to confinement and/or support positive youth development" (Hsia, Bridges, and McHale 2004, 13).

Family conditions were also identified as a contributing factor to DMC. Most youth in confinement "came from low-income, single-parent households (female-headed households, in particular) and households headed by adults with multiple low-paying jobs or unsteady employment" (id.). In addition, DMC was attributed to family poverty, family disintegration, "diminished traditional family values," parental substance abuse, and insufficient parental or adult supervision. Family dysfunction also leads to the inability to take advantage of opportunities through probation or alternative sentencing. "Given the multiple stressors and limitations experienced by many minority families, their relative inability to comply with the requirements of diversion programming is not surprising" (Hsia, Bridges, and McHale 2004, 13).

In sum, the existence of DMC can be traced to low economic and social status. DMC is the result of racial insensitivity, racial discrimination, lack of alternatives to incarceration for youth of color, and low expectations for youth of color. In addition, poor educational resources, underresourced communities, and dysfunctional families are contributing factors to DMC. None of these factors points to moral failing as a cause for the greater involvement of young people of color in the juvenile justice system, nor do they point to intellectual or cultural propensities for crime. Instead, they point to oppression.

II. Oppression and Disproportionate Minority Contact

Paulo Friere describes oppression chiefly as dehumanization, as "a *distortion* of the vocation of becoming more fully human" (Friere 1989, 28). He also defines oppression operationally as "encompassing any situation in which 'A' objectively exploits 'B' or hinders his pursuit of self-affirmation as a responsible person" (40). We can accept Friere's definition of oppression as dehumanization, and yet seek a more detailed operational definition than the one he proposes. Similar to Friere, Iris Marion Young defines oppression as an "institutional constraint on self-development" (Young 1990, 37). Operationally, she describes the contours of oppression as consisting of five "faces": exploitation, marginalization, powerlessness, cultural imperialism, and violence (37-40). Asa G. Hilliard gives a far more extensive outline of the operational processes that constitute oppression in action. According to Hilliard (1973), oppression has twelve dimensions: (1) differentiation (or "othering"); (2) defamation; (3) cultural genocide; (4) distortion of history; (5) deindividualization; (6) destabilization of leadership; (7) construction of supportive myths and ideology; (8) control of language and names; (9) control of information; (10) development of dependency; (11) miseducation; and (12) alienation.

Each of these definitions suggests that oppression is manifested internally and externally, both in the way that a community is treated and in the way that a community responds to that treatment. The juvenile justice system both *oppresses* communities of color and *produces effects of oppression* within those communities. These two distinct phenomena are examined further below.

Oppressive Characteristics of the Juvenile Justice System

The very existence of DMC is oppressive. DMC is the use of the coercive structure of the juvenile justice system as warranted by the characteristics of the group involved. The social policy concern surrounding DMC assumes that this disproportionate involvement is excessive and that it should not be necessary. In other words, using Young's terms above, DMC is a manifestation of the violent "face" of oppression. In order to oppress, an oppressor must establish coercive control over the oppressed. Historically, then, group oppression has always involved some form of coercive control, be it slavery, concentration camps, fortified villages, dungeons, prisons, or policing (Young 1990; Fanon 1963).

Another indicator of the oppressive character of the juvenile justice system in Young's terms is powerlessness. While communities of color are disproportionately affected by the criminal laws and juvenile justice policies, they do not make those laws or policies. As political minorities, they have little or no protection in the American political system, which has no minority rights, limits protection from discrimination, and allows moneyed interests excessive influence (Young 1990).

Finally, the oppressive character of the juvenile justice system in its external dimension manifests in the particular way that it operates. As evident in the OJJDP data on DMC, racial disparities are found at each stage of the juvenile justice system—intake, detention, petitioning, waiver, adjudication, and disposition (Nunn 2002a). The overrepresentation of African American youth in the juvenile justice system begins with the intake decision. While African American youth comprise only 22 percent of the U.S. population aged ten through seventeen in 2005, they accounted for 33 percent of the juveniles in that age group referred for prosecution. African American youth were also overrepresented in the number of arrests, at 30 percent of the total (Puzzanchera and Adams 2008).

The next stage of the juvenile justice process is the decision to detain. While only 33 percent of the referral population was African American, 42 percent of referred children who were detained were African American (id.). In comparison to the treatment afforded to white youths, the treatment of African American children is stark:

> While Black children are overrepresented among detainees in respect to their proportion of the referral population, white children are underrepresented. This pattern of disparity is repeated across all offense categories, but it is most extreme in drug cases. In drug offense cases, African

Americans amounted to 55 percent of those detained, but only 32 percent of the referral population. The disparate treatment of African American youth at the detention stage is pervasive and readily apparent. Even when charged with the same offense, African American youth are more likely to be detained pretrial than white youth. (Nunn 2002a, 684)

The charging decision takes place at the petitioning stage. While white youth are less likely to be petitioned (charged) than they are to be referred, African American youth are more likely to be petitioned than referred. In 2005, African American youths were involved in 33 percent of referrals and 37 percent of petitioned cases (Puzzanchera and Adams 2008). During the same year, white youth were involved in 64 percent of juvenile court referrals and 60 percent of petitioned cases (id.). African American youth are substantially more likely to be waived from juvenile court to adult court (id.). In 2005, over a third (39 percent) of waived cases involved African Americans, compared to 37 percent of petitioned cases (id.).

Racial disparities are also present at the disposition and confinement stages of the juvenile justice system. Disposition is akin to adult sentencing. It occurs when the judge determines whether to place the juvenile offender in secure confinement, on probation, or in some other alternative delinquency program. African American youth are more likely to be placed in residential placement facilities, and less likely to be placed on probation in comparison to similarly situated white youth. There are great disparities at the confinement stage, where the overwhelming majority of youth housed in secure residential placements are youth of color (Nunn 2002a, 686). In 2006, almost two-thirds of detained and committed youth were from communities of color (Sickmund et al. 2008). In 2006, over 39 percent of the juveniles in locked residential facilities were African American, three times the percentage of African American youth in the population (id.). As a result, "more African American youth are in secure residential placements than are juveniles from any other racial or ethnic group" (Nunn 2002a, 686).

These figures demonstrate the coercive impact of the juvenile justice system on particular individuals and their families. It is oppressive, because in comparison to white youth it is excessive. It is also unnecessary, if we believe the data the OJJDP has collected from state assessments. According to OJJDP data, disparities in the juvenile justice system exist due to racism, low expectations for children of color, and the failure to value children of color enough to allocate sufficient resources for alternatives to juvenile correction (Hsia, Bridges, and McHale 2004).

Vulnerabilities in African Diaspora Communities and Oppression

The view that the United States has currently entered a "postracial" phase of its history is currently in vogue. Those who hold this view claim that racism is no longer a factor in American life and the effects of discriminatory treatment are no longer present. However, the available evidence would seem to belie these claims. African communities in the United States suffer from the effects of oppression in many ways. The vast majority of African people continue to live on the bottom rungs of the economic ladder. They are disproportionately poor, poorly educated, locked out of wealth and political power, and vulnerable to economic downturns.

Hurricane Katrina disclosed to the world the precarious condition of African people in the richest country in the world. African descendents made up the vast majority of the population in the city of New Orleans—with a legacy of slavery, Jim Crow segregation, and the cultural refuge that New Orleans offered to Africans across the southern region of the United States (Nunn 2009). The poverty rate for Africans in New Orleans was over twice the national rate, and the bulk of those in poverty were in "deep poverty" with incomes that were less than one-half the official poverty rate (id.). In addition, New Orleans was highly segregated and the African population was forced into the least desirable areas of the city that were most vulnerable to flooding (id.). Due to poverty and lack of economic opportunity, most Africans did not own cars and were unable to evacuate the city without assistance. When the hurricane struck, the African communities in New Orleans were devastated and dispersed (id.).

The situation of African people in New Orleans is representative of the situation of Africans throughout the United States. As a whole, Africans are socially marginalized and mired in poverty. As the National Urban League publication, *The State of Black America,* observes, "Ironically, even as an African American man holds the highest office the country, African Americans remain twice as likely as whites to be unemployed, three times more likely to live in poverty and more than six times as likely to be incarcerated" (Wilson 2009, 15). The disparity in income between white workers and African workers remains stark. In fact, most of the poverty found in the African community is directly traceable to wage inequalities between African and white employees (Brown et al. 2003). Not only do Africans in America receive lower pay, but also they find it harder to obtain and keep employment than similarly situated whites (id.).

The economic condition of African people is not tied simply to income. The low wealth attainment of African families and communities, as a measure of material resources available to be exploited economically, limits their ability to wield economic and political power (Shapiro 2004). A 2010 study by the Brandeis University Institute on Assets and Social Policy found that African American assets trailed those of whites by ninety-five thousand dollars. On average, the study found, whites hold assets of one hundred thousand dollars, compared to only five thousand dollars for African Americans (McGreal 2010). A key source of wealth is ownership of property, especially houses. However, less than 50 percent of Black families own their homes, versus over 70 percent of whites (Shapiro 2004). One reason for the low rate of African home ownership is the fact that Africans are more than twice as likely to be denied mortgages and home improvement loans than are whites (Barr 2005). When Africans do own homes, they are generally worth less than homes owned by white Americans. According to the latest FHA statistics, homes owned by African descendents are valued, on average, at $42,800 less than homes owned by white Americans (Orozco and Tomarelli 2009).

Low income and low wealth attainment lead to other social and political consequences, as was demonstrated in New Orleans during Hurricane Katrina. Low income means trouble accessing housing, transportation, and health care. It means not being able to "buy" political clout by financially supporting candidates who support your issues (Jacobs and Skocpol 2005). It means not being able to control media outlets and not being able to produce media that is sympathetic to your views (Owens 2004). Recent research into the geography of race discloses that most hospital closings are in areas that affect African people the most, and that most new jobs are in areas that are beyond the reach of Africans who want to work (Brown et al. 2003).

These vulnerabilities of African communities are due to oppression. Because Africans were enslaved, they did not arrive in this country with economic resources and political clout. Although Africans were liberated after the Civil War, they were not empowered economically, and what limited advancement they made during Reconstruction was swiftly rolled back in the years that followed (Lui et al. 2006). Americans have never made good on the promise of "forty acres and a mule," and reparations for African victims of slavery and colonialism are not on the political agenda of any major party (Outterson 2009; Greene 2008). Although individual African descendents have gained some measure of personal success in the United States, it is the lack of collective wealth and power that prevents the resolution of the problems resulting from poor educational resources, underresourced communities, dysfunctional families, racial insensitivity, poverty, political powerlessness, etc. This lack of collective wealth and power is an artifact of the state of oppression that African people have endured historically and presently (Lui et al. 2006).

DMC and Oppression

As mentioned previously, "disproportionate minority contact" is the bureaucratic term used to describe the disparate numbers of African youth in the juvenile justice system. These disparate numbers are caused by a variety of interrelated factors clustered around the juvenile justice system, the educational system, socioeconomic conditions, and the family. In other words, DMC is an artifact of the oppressed condition of African people in the United States. The question is: why do we use this sterile bureaucratic language to refer to this obvious fact?

According to Asa Hilliard, one of the key determinants of oppression is the control of language and of names (Hilliard 1973). That is, the oppressor wants to control the language of the oppressed and to usurp completely the authority to name. To name is an exercise of power. It is part of the process of structuring one's own reality. To be deprived of the right to name things is to be disempowered. If you cannot name, then you are dependent on one who does name. This is why "names are one of the main vehicles for colonization" (id., 10).

According to Hilliard, the introduction of new names by the oppressor serves an ideological function. The purpose of using innocuous names for the effects and processes of domination is to decontextualize them and delink them from social and political reality. As a result, the new "context neutral" names of the oppressor do not provide any notion of cause and effect, and therefore do not assist efforts of liberation, that is, of eliminating the cause of oppression. Thus, "euphemisms must now become a means of escape from truth and responsibility" (Hilliard 1973, 10).

Hilliard notes that while it is easier to generate bureaucratic support for "a program to improve 'interpersonal communications' than to focus on problems associated with privilege or oppression" (Hilliard 1988, 39), relabeling problems related to oppression in euphemistic terms creates conceptual difficulties:

> [I]f we examine the activities [pursued under euphemistic] headings, there is the general absence of a historical and theoretical base, and the absence of valid remedial activities undertaken. In other words, a plan of remedial action should be based on some knowledge or theory as to what the problem is, how it came about, what maintains it, and how it can be changed. (Hilliard 1988, 39)

When we call the conditions of oppression that African children face "disproportionate minority contact," we obfuscate the cause of the phenomenon and thus hamper efforts to eliminate it. We must use the true name of what afflicts African children in the juvenile justice system and concentrate our efforts on eliminating the cultural and economic oppression that is the actual cause of DMC.

III. Culture and Community Viability

Culture, broadly speaking, may be the most important aspect of human existence. Culture holds a community together, gives it meaning, and assures its continuity.[3] Culture allows the establishment of mechanisms to enable mating, child raising, and the assignment of social roles for children, adults, and elders (Southern African Development Community 2000; Nunn 2006). Culture can enable economic activity, as when culture leads to the development of a particular cuisine, which then leads to opportunities to establish restaurants, restaurant supply firms, and farms (Frohnmayer 1993). Culture also supplies the most efficient tool to combat oppression (Cabral 1973a).

Amilcar Cabral (1973a; 1973b), Aime Cesaire (1976), Paulo Friere (1993), and others have theorized extensively on the use of culture as a tool to fight oppression. According to Cabral, "national liberation is necessarily an act of culture" (1973a, 43). Without the awareness on the part of the oppressed of their cultural unity, resistance to oppression is not possible (id.). This is true due to the very nature of culture. If culture is, at base, a means of organizing and managing a society, then for the society to be oppressed, its culture must be crushed or distorted enough to allow for external organization and management (Nunn 1997). This is why, in Cabral's terms, true liberation requires a cultural "return to the source" (Cabral 1973b, 63).

A "return to the source" assumes, of course, that there is a collective source to which one can return. In other words, a return to the source requires a viable group identity to be in place. Group identity is expressed through cultural means (Banks 2008; Cohen 1993; Frohnmayer 1993). Belongingness requires an identity to which to belong (Pierik 2004). There must be some aspect of being that is distinctive in terms of cultural expression for a group identity to exist, in terms of either language, art, religion, belief, worldview, or other social practices (Pierik 2004). To eliminate their oppression within the United States, Africans must resurrect and maintain their African culture (Hilliard 1999; Hilliard 1973). Doing so allows them to maintain a base that enables them to think, act, and create in their own interests (Hilliard 1995). They do not need to invent, borrow, or imitate someone else's culture, because they have one of their very own with its own rich traditions (id.).

Group identity is important in the DMC context because it provides a foundation for resolving the specific manifestations of oppression that African youth in the criminal justice system must face. There are a number of respects in which culture is particularly pertinent to the problems of oppression that result in DMC. These include providing a positive self-image for African youth, providing positive role models within the African community that African youth can seek to emulate, and allowing for the intergenerational transmission of values relevant to parenting and social behavior.

Culture and Self-Identity

Most psychologists agree that a positive self-image is necessary for well-being (Trzesniewski et al. 2006; Mruk 2006; Taylor et al. 2000). Criminologists have also observed that low self-esteem (lack of a positive self-image) can lead to involvement in criminal behavior (Schiele 1998; Yancy, Siegel, and McDaniel 2002). Research on minority participation in the juvenile justice system has listed low self-esteem as a potential cause of DMC (Poupart et al. 2005; Kakar 2006). Positive self-esteem comes from being immersed in a positive, loving environment that teaches you by the very way that you are treated that you are valuable (Mruk 2006). It is difficult to think you have no value when the world around you is telling you that you do.

Teaching African youth about African culture can reduce the incidence of low self-esteem (Schiele 1998; Henderson 2005). African youth can be inspired when they are made aware of the fact that they come from a vibrant culture and that they have individual worth and value within that culture (Hilliard 1995). African youth should know that they come from a people that built pyramids (Diop 1974), that created a computing device in prehistoric times to predict the phases of the moon (Finch 1998), and that discovered the invisible companion star of Sirius long before Western telescopes were available to confirm the discovery (Griaule and Dieterlen 1986). Young African women should know that in their culture women's work was valued long before Gloria Steinem and that African woman have been powerful leaders throughout the ages (Hudson-Weems 2004). In the hands of caring teachers, these facts can raise the self-esteem of African children and reduce their involvement in the juvenile justice system (Potts 2003).

Culture and Role Models

Children need role models (Pleiss and Feldhusen 1995). Role models, to be useful, must be attainable for the children. They must be people whom the children recognize as part of their reality, who tread a path that is open for them to follow (id.) (Anderson and Cavallaro 2002). A person who is viewed as remarkable, unique, or distant has no value as a role model. A vibrant, living community produces the best role models. The best role models are people a child can see in his or her daily life doing things that provide a positive impact on the community, and thus on the child him – or herself (Pleiss and Feldhusen 1995). A living community has a history and heritage. Role models may also be found in a community's heritage that children can emulate (Yancy et al. 2002). This is why cultures the world over have produced heroic myths (Pleiss and Feldhusen 1995). The hero is a role model for others to follow. African children should be aware that there are heroes (and "sheroes") in their culture as well (Hilliard 1995).

Culture creates the network of people who are available and appropriate to be role models for youth. Culture provides parents, older siblings, aunts, uncles, grandparents, teachers, local leaders, national leaders, and heroic figures for young people to emulate. One measure of a culture's health is the number and quality of role models it produces for its children (Anderson and Cavallaro 2002).

Culture and Values

As discussed above, environmental and family factors that lead to DMC include high neighborhood unemployment rates, high neighborhood crime rates, the prevalence of single-parent households, family disintegration, diminished family values, and insufficient adult supervision. Each of these factors is caused by a dysfunctional cultural environment and can be rectified by building a strong cultural base to support the community's children as they grow and mature (Hilliard 2000; Hilliard 2001). The main cause of these problems is a disrupted process of intergenerational transmission of values for living. How are young people to know how to conduct themselves in society if the values for doing so are not taught? Culture is the source of appropriate values, and a community that is immersed in its culture and following its cultural traditions has appropriate mechanisms for providing for the transmission of culture to succeeding generations (Hilliard 2001; Nobles 2008).

Intergenerational transmission of culture requires both a viable culture and a sufficient means of intergenerational communication (McGregor, Copestake, and Wood 2000). For juveniles, intergenerational communication requires both access to elders and opportunities for the elders to teach and direct (Fu-Kiau and Lukondo-Wamba 1988). These opportunities cannot be taken for granted, but must be organized in a cultural setting (Hilliard 2001). Without some sort of cultural base to support it, intergenerational communication cannot take place (id.). Using an example from their native Kongo, authors Fu-Kiau and Lukondo-Wamba describe the importance of the intergenerational transmission of culture through *Kindezi*, the Kongolese institution of babysitting:

> [G]reat attention is paid to whoever has a role to play in the life of a child—the human being with the quickest copying mind. This basic understanding that childhood is the foundation that determines the quality of a society is the main reason that prompted African communities to make *Kindezi* an art, or *kinkete*, to be learned by all their members. Thus, *Kindezi* is required in societies that want to prepare their members to become not only good fathers and mothers, but above all, people who care about life and who understand, both humanely and spiritually, the highly unshakable value of the human being that we all are. (Fu-Kiau and Lukondo-Wamba 1988, 5)

Culture, then, provides the mechanism for communication, and it also provides the content, consisting of social values, to be transmitted (Nobles 2008). If generations of children are growing up without the tools to succeed in life, then the culture of the community is broken. To raise children to be able to support themselves, to respect their parents and elders, and to be able to raise the next generation is a natural human activity. It has taken place for tens of thousands of years in every part of the globe where humans reside (Collard 2000). No culture is inherently dysfunctional. If a culture cannot meet basic human needs then the culture would cease to exist, since the functions of intergenerational transmission of culture are necessary for its continued existence (id.). African culture could not have survived over the centuries if it were inherently dysfunctional. If African culture is not functioning correctly in America's urban communities, it is because these communities are oppressed.

Reestablishing the values of African culture in African descendent communities in the United States is the way to eliminate societal factors such as the absence of family values, family disintegration, the high incidence of single-parent families, and the absence of proper adult guidance. Of course, reestablishing African cultural norms means little in a community that continues to be oppressed and that suffers enduring economic deprivation. The point is not that there is anything magical about African culture, but that its expression and fullness is an indication of a wholesome, vibrant community that is not oppressed (Hilliard 2001; Hilliard 2000). This is the type of community that will develop the high self-esteem, the supportive social networks, and the healthy attitudes that the residents of Roseta, Pennsylvania, imported from Italy (Gladwell 2008).

IV. Black Nationalism and Cultural Autonomy

Since the demise of the Garvey movement in the 1920s, integrationism has dominated African policy and perspectives both internally and externally (Martin 1982). African descendents within the United States, as well as white-dominated institutions in government, industry, and education, have embraced integrationist goals (Peller 1990). With the success of the NAACP program to dismantle Jim Crow through legal victories in the area of education, culminating in *Brown v. Board of Education,* the appropriateness of integrationist strategies to assure African success seemed certain (id.). However, the intervening years have provided sufficient reasons for at least some in the African community to question integration's utility as the universal solution for all that ails African people (Bell 2005).

Fifty-plus years after *Brown* it is clear that efforts to integrate American society have fallen short in many important respects (id.). African people remain marginalized and removed from the centers of power, even when they are not physically segregated from whites or excluded from white institutions (Brown et al. 2003; Martin 2004). While the integration that has taken place has opened up meaningful opportunities for certain African individuals, it has also encouraged a brain drain from the African community that has weakened African-controlled organizations, schools, and businesses (Johnson 1993; Martin 2004). Thus, integrationist policies are problematic in that they may permit marginalization of Africans (in the white community or in society as a whole) and the concomitant destruction of African cultural institutions (Peller 1990).

Black nationalism includes a range of political perspectives that encourage African independence and autonomy (Peller 1990; Harris 2001). Black nationalists argue that African identity is a reality that must be recognized and that this recognition includes the acknowledgment that African people may have specific interests and goals that are particular and unique to their conditions (Peller 1990). The existence of particular needs means that African societies must be organized in ways that allow those needs to be met, and it also requires institutions and organizations that African people control for that purpose (Harris 2001).

Cultural nationalists, in particular, argue that African people live in a cultural reality that is distinct from European culture and that African people must have cultural institutions that are autonomous and not subject to external control by Europeans or others (Harris 2001). Since African people live in an autonomous culture, they need all the attributes of culture that are necessary for the culture to be vibrant and alive. They need a culture that provides social roles for men, women, children, and elders, a culture that allows for the intergenerational transmission of values and that encourages the development of self-esteem and appropriate role models (Hilliard 2001). Using African culture as a base, Black nationalists believe Africans can build an infrastructure of businesses that can provide employment and economic opportunities for African community members (Blake 1969).

Building strong, autonomous African cultural institutions not only advances Black nationalist goals; it also helps to reduce the factors that lead to DMC. If DMC is the result of a dysfunctional African community, one that has been warped and distorted by the effects of oppression, then the restoration of African community life and institutions has to have a palliative effect. Thus policies and practices to reduce DMC should include proposals that are culturally based and that encourage autonomy and community control.

Conclusion

There is an old Chinese proverb that relates the story of a rich man who employed a poor man to carry him around all day, so he would not have to walk. One day the poor man became ill. He could barely carry the rich man on his rounds. The rich man expressed concern about the poor man's health. He asked him, "Is there something I can do to make you feel better." "Yes," the poor man replied. "You can get off of my back."

Mainstream policy prescriptions for the social, political, and economic disparities that African people face are a lot like the rich man's concern for the poor man in the Chinese proverb. Mainstream institutions focus on issues like the prevalence of teen pregnancy or AIDS in the African community, or issues like residential segregation or the disproportionate representation of Africans in prisons or jails. They miss the point that solutions require looking at true causes and not simply symptoms. Simply put, what causes African problems like disproportionate minority contact is oppression. Ending oppression in its economic, political, and social guises will end DMC.

NOTES

1. Many words (e.g., "gumbo") and commonplace cultural practices (e.g., jumping rope) in America trace their origin to African language and behaviors retained by enslaved Africans in the New World. See Joseph E. Holloway. 1991. *Africanisms in American Culture*. Bloomington: Indiana University Press.

2. In the OJJDP survey, a small number of states relied on this basis to explain the prevalence of DMC. According to the survey, "Three states identified the commission of more crime—and more serious crime—by minority youth as an important factor contributing to DMC. An assessment study in one of these states determined that between one-fourth and one-half of the racial disparity in confinement was due to racial differences in seriousness of the offenses and frequency of arrests."

3. Culture may be defined as that which is "the totality of a people's way of life, the whole complex of distinctive spiritual, material, intellectual and emotional features that characterize a society or social group, and includes not only arts and letters, but also modes of life, the fundamental rights of the human being, value systems, traditions and beliefs" (Southern African Development Community 2000).

REFERENCES

Anderson, Kristin J., and Donna Cavallaro. 2002. Parents or Pop Culture? Children's Heroes and Role Models. *Childhood Education* 78 (3): 161-69.

Banks, James A. 2008. Diversity, Group Identity, and Citizenship Education in a Global Age. *Educational Researcher* 37 (3): 129-39.

Barr, Michael S. 2005. Credit Where It Counts: The Community Reinvestment Act and Its Critics. *New York University Law Review* 80: 513-652.

Bell, Derrick. 2005. *Silent Covenants: Brown v. Board of Education and the Unfulfilled Hopes for Racial Reform*. New York: Oxford University Press.

Blake, J. Herman. 1969. Black Nationalism. *Annals of the American Academy of Political and Social Science* 382: 15-25.

Brown, Michael K., Martin Carnoy, Elliot Curry, Troy Duster, David B. Oppenheimer, Marjorie M. Schultz, and David Wellman. 2003. *White-Washing Race: The Myth of a Color-Blind Society*. Berkeley: University of California Press.

Cabral, Amilcar. 1973a. National Liberation and Culture. In African Information Service (ed.), *Return to the Source: Selected Speeches of Amilcar Cabral*. New York: Monthly Review Press.

Cabral, Amilcar. 1973b. Identity and Dignity in the Context of the National Liberation Struggle. In African Information Service (ed.), *Return to the Source: Selected Speeches of Amilcar Cabral*. New York: Monthly Review Press.

Césaire, Aimé. 1976. Culture and Colonization. In Aimé Césaire, *Oeuvres Complètes* (vol. 3). Paris: Éditions Désormeaux.

Cohen, Anthony P. 1993. Culture as Identity: An Anthropologist's View. *New Literary History* 24 (1): 195-209.

Collard, David. 2000. Generational Transfers and the Generational Bargain. *Journal of International Development* 12: 453-62.

Criminal Justice Information Services Division. 2007. *Crime in the United States, 2006*. Table 43.

Diop, Cheikh Anta. 1974. *The African Origin of Civilization: Myth or Reality?* New York: Lawrence Hill.

Fanon, Frantz. 1963. *The Wretched of the Earth.* New York: Grove Weidenfeld.

Finch, Charles S., III. 1998. *The Star of Deep Beginnings: The Genesis of African Science and Technology.* Atlanta: Khenti.

Friere, Paulo. 1989. *Pedagogy of the Oppressed.* New York: Continuum.

Frohnmayer, John. 1993. Should the United States Have a Cultural Policy? *Villanova Law Review* 38: 195–201.

Fu-Kiau, K. Kia Bunseki, and A. M. Lukondo-Wamba. 1988. *Kindezi: The Congo Art of Babysitting.* New York: Vantage Press.

Gladwell, Malcolm. 2008. *Outliers: The Story of Success.* New York: Little, Brown.

Greene, K. J. 2008. "Copynorms," Black Cultural Production, and the Debate over African American Reparations. *Cardozo Arts and Entertainment Law Journal* 25: 1179-1227.

Griaule, Marcel, and Germaine Dieterlen. 1986. *The Pale Fox.* Chino Valley, AZ: Continuum Foundation.

Harris, Jessica C. 2001. Revolutionary Black Nationalism: The Black Panther Party. *Journal of Negro History* 86 (3): 409-421.

Henderson, Shirley. 2005. A Time to Teach: Using Black History to Heal and Educate Children. *Ebony* (February).

Hilliard, Asa G., III. 2001. To Be an African Teacher. *Psych Discourse* 32 (8): 4-7. http://kintespace.com/kp_asao.html.

Hilliard, Asa G., III. 2000. *The State of African Education.* Paper presented in plenary session at the annual meeting of American Educational Research Association, New Orleans, LA (April). http://www.africawithin.com/hilliard/state_of_african_education.htm.

Hilliard, Asa G., III. 1999. What Do We Need to Know Now? "Race," Identity, Hegemony, and Education. *Rethinking Schools* 14 (2): 4-6. http://www.rethinkingschools.org/restrict.asp?path=archive/14_02/race142.shtml.

Hilliard, Asa G., III. 1995. The Maroon within Us: The Lessons of Africa for the Parenting and Education of African American Children. In Asa G. Hilliard III (ed.), *The Maroon Within Us: Selected Essays on African American Community Socialization,* pp. 50-70. Baltimore, MD: Black Classic Press.

Hilliard, Asa G., III. 1988. Conceptual Confusion and the Persistence of Group Oppression through Education. *Equity and Excellence in Education* 24 (1): 36-43.

Hilliard, Asa G., III. 1973. *Anatomy and Dynamics of Oppression.* Address to First National Conference on Human Relations in Education, Minneapolis, MN (June 26). Unpublished transcript on file with author.

Holloway, Joseph E. 1991. *Africanisms in American Culture.* Bloomington: Indiana University Press.

Hsia, Heidi M., George S. Bridges, and Rosalie McHale. 2004. *Disproportionate Minority Confinement: 2002 Update.* Washington, DC: U.S. Department of Justice, Office of Justice Programs, Office of Juvenile Justice and Delinquency Prevention.

Hudson-Weems, Clenora. 2004. *Africana Womanism: Reclaiming Ourselves.* Troy, MI: Bedford Publications.

Huizinga, David, Terence P. Thornberry, Kelly E. Knight, Peter J. Lovegrove, Rolf Loeber, Karl Hill, and David P. Farrington. 2007. *Disproportionate Minority Contact in the Juvenile Justice System: A Study of Differential Minority Arrest/Referral to Court in Three Cities.*

A Report to the Office of Juvenile Justice and Delinquency Prevention. Washington, DC: U.S. Department of Justice, Office of Justice Programs, Office of Juvenile Justice and Delinquency Prevention. http://www.ncjrs.gov/pdffiles1/ojjdp/grants/219743.pdf.

Jacobs, Lawrence R., and Theda Skocpol. 2005. American Democracy in an Era of Rising Inequality. In Lawrence R. Jacobs and Theda Skocpol (eds.), *Inequality and American Democracy*, pp. 1-18. New York: Russell Sage Foundation.

Johnson, Alex M., Jr. 1993. Bid Whist, Tonk, and *United States v. Fordice*: Why Integrationism Fails African-Americans Again. *California Law Review* 81: 1401-70.

Juvenile Justice Delinquency and Prevention Act, Public Law 93–415, 42 U.S.C. 5601 et seq.

Kakar, Suman. 2006. Understanding the Causes of Disproportionate Minority Contact: Results of Focus Group Discussions. *Journal of Criminal Justice* 34 (4): 369-81.

Lui, Meizhu, Barbara J. Robles, Betsy Leondar-Wright, Rose M. Brewer, and Rebecca Adamson. 2006. *The Color of Wealth: The Story Behind the U.S. Racial Wealth Divide*. New York: New Press.

Martin, Guy. 1982. Africa and the Ideology of Eurafrica: Neocolonialism or Pan-Africanism? *Journal of Modern African Studies* 20 (2): 221-38.

Martin, Waldo E., Jr. 2004. Through the Prism of Brown: Black Memory, Identity, and History. *Howard Law Review* 47: 851-62.

McGreal, Chris. 2010. "A $95,000 Question: Why Are Whites Five Times Richer Than Blacks in the US?" UK *Guardian*, May 17, 2010. http://www.guardian.co.uk/world/2010/may/17/white-people-95000-richer-black.

McGregor, J. Allister, James G. Copestake, and Geof D. Wood. 2000. The Inter-Generational Bargain: An Introduction. *Journal of International Development* 12: 447-51.

Moriearty, Perry L. 2008. Combating the Color-Coded Confinement of Kids: An Equal Protection Remedy. *New York Review of Law and Social Change* 32: 285-307.

Mruk, Christopher J. 2006. *Self-Esteem Research, Theory, and Practice: Towards a Positive Psychology of Self-Esteem*. New York: Springer.

Nobles, Wade W. 2008. *Per Âa* Asa Hilliard: The Great House of Black Light for Educational Excellence. *Review of Educational Research* 78 (3): 727-47.

Nunn, Kenneth B. 2009. "Still Up on the Roof": Race, Victimology, and the Response to Hurricane Katrina. In Jeremy I. Levitt and Matthew C. Whitaker, eds. *Hurricane Katrina: America's Unnatural Disaster*. 183-205. Lincoln: U. of Nebraska Press.

Nunn, Kenneth B. 2006. New Explorations in Culture and Crime: Definitions, Theory, Method. *Florida Journal of Law and Public Policy* 17: vii–xxiii.

Nunn, Kenneth B. 2002a. The Child as Other: Race and Differential Treatment in the Juvenile Justice System. *DePaul Law Review* 51: 679–714.

Nunn, Kenneth B. 2002b. Race, Crime, and the Pool of Surplus Criminality; or, Why the "War on Drugs" Was a "War on Blacks." *Journal of Gender, Race, and Justice* 6: 381–445.

Nunn, Kenneth B. 1997. Law as a Eurocentric Enterprise. *Law and Inequality* 15: 323–70.

Nunn, Kenneth B. 1993. Rights Held Hostage: Race, Ideology, and the Peremptory Challenge. *Harvard Civil Rights-Civil Liberties Law Review* 28: 63-118.

Office of Juvenile Justice and Delinquency Prevention. 2009. "Disproportionate Minority Contact." *In Focus* (October).

Orozco, Ana, and Robert Tomarelli. 2009. 2009 Equality Index. In Stephanie J. Jones (ed.), *The State of Black America 2009*, pp. 25-41. Washington, DC: National Urban League.

Outterson, Kevin. 2009. The End of Reparations Talk in an Obama World. *Kansas Law Review* 57: 935-48.

Owens, W. LaNelle. 2004. Inequities on the Air: The FCC Media Ownership Rules—Encouraging Economic Efficiency and Disregarding the Needs of Minorities. *Howard Law Journal* 47: 1037-71.

Peller, Gary. 1990. Race Consciousness. *Duke Law Journal* 1990: 758-847.

Pierik, Roland. 2004. Conceptualizing Cultural Groups and Cultural Difference: The Social Mechanism Approach. *Sage Publications* 4 (4): 523-44. http://www.rolandpierik.nl/theory/Downloads/Ethnicities.pdf.

Pleiss, Mary K., and John F. Feldhusen. 1995. Mentors, Role Models, and Heroes in the Lives of Gifted Children. *Educational Psychologist* 30 (3): 159-69.

Potts, Richard G. 2003. Emancipatory Education versus School-Based Prevention in African American Communities. *American Journal of Community Psychology* 31 (1-2): 173-83.

Poupart, John, John Redhorse, Melanie Peterson-Hickey, and Mary Martin. 2005. *Searching for Justice*. St. Paul, MN: American Indian Policy Center. http://www.airpi.org/research/SearchingforJustice/sjfindingscauses.htm.

Puzzanchera, C., and B. Adams. 2008. National Disproportionate Minority Contact Databook. Developed by the National Center for Juvenile Justice for the Office of Juvenile Justice and Delinquency Prevention. http://ojjdp.ncjrs.gov/ojstatbb/dmcdb/.

Puzzanchera, C., A. Sladky, and W. Kang. 2009. Easy Access to Juvenile Populations: 1990-2008. http://www.ojjdp.ncjrs.gov/ojstatbb/ezapop/.

Sampson, Robert J., and Janet L. Lauritsen 1997. Racial and Ethnic Disparities in Crime and Criminal Justice in the United States. *Crime and Justice* 21: 311-74.

Schiele, Jerome. 1998. Cultural Alignment of African American Youths and Violent Crime. *Journal of Human Behavior in the Social Environment* 1: 165-81.

Shapiro, Thomas M. 2004. *The Hidden Cost of Being African American: How Wealth Perpetuates Inequality*. New York: Oxford University Press.

Sickmund, Melissa, T. J. Sladky, and Wei Kang. 2008. Census of Juveniles in Residential Placement Databook. http://www.ojjdp.ncjrs.gov/ojstatbb/cjrp/.

Sickmund, M., T. J. Sladky, W. Kang, and C. Puzzanchera. 2008. "Easy Access to the Census of Juveniles in Residential Placement." http://ojjdp.ncjrs.gov/ojstatbb/ezacjrp/.

Southern African Development Community. 2000. *Protocol on Culture, Information, and Sport*, Art. 1(2). http:// www.sadc.int/index/browse/page/127.

Taylor, Shelley E., Margaret E. Kemeny, Geoffrey M. Reed, Julienne E. Bower, and Tara L. Gruenewald. 2000. Psychological Resources, Positive Illusions, and Health. *American Psychologist* 55 (1): 99-109.

Trzesniewski, Kali H., Terrie E. Moffitt, Richard W. Robins, Richie Poulton, and Avshalom Caspi. 2006. Low Self-Esteem during Adolescence Predicts Poor Health, Criminal Behavior, and Limited Economic Prospects during Adulthood. *Developmental Psychology* 42 (2): 381-90.

Wilson, Valerie Ralston. 2009. Introduction to the 2009 Equality Index. In Stephanie J. Jones (ed.), *The State of Black America 2009*, pp. 15-24. Washington, DC: National Urban League.

Yancy, Antronette K., Judith M. Seigel, and Kimberly L. McDaniel. 2002. Role Models, Ethnic Identity, and Health-Risk Behaviors in Urban Adolescents. *Archives of Pediatrics and Adolescent Medicine* 156: 55-61.

Young, Iris Marion. 1990. *Justice and the Politics of Difference*. Princeton, NJ: Princeton University Press.

7

Girl Matters

Unfinished Work

LAWANDA RAVOIRA AND VANESSA PATINO

Girls are victims of gender disparities that are pervasive through-out the juvenile justice system. Far too often girls are misunderstood, misla-beled, and inappropriately forced into a juvenile justice system unprepared to address their gender-specific needs. There is an urgent need to critically review the policies and processes that place girls at risk as well as the soci-etal practices that result in disparate treatment of girls (ABA and NBA 2001; Bloom, Owen, and Covington 2005).

The first national recognition of the need to provide gender-specific ser-vices in the juvenile justice system did not occur until 1992 with the reau-thorization of the Juvenile Justice and Delinquency Prevention Act of 1974 (42 U.S.C. 5601 223(8)(B)(i-ii)). This legislation required states to prepare an analysis and develop a plan for providing gender-specific services in the pre-vention and treatment of juvenile delinquency (Greene, Peters, and Associ-ates 1998). Despite the passage of this legislation, very few states have made the necessary policy and process changes, or funded their implementation, to promote a culture that is gender responsive and effectively addresses the multidimensional needs of girls and young women (Chesney-Lind et al. 2008; OJJDP 1998). This is especially troubling in light of the increasing numbers of girls entering the juvenile justice system and the seriousness of the circumstances that impact their daily lives.

This chapter reviews the issues facing girls and identifies what must be done to craft policies of prevention to address their needs in order to pre-vent their involvement with the juvenile justice system. The wisdom pro-vided through the life stories and voices of girls reminds us that there are simple steps we can take to affect girls' trajectories in more positive ways. The chapter therefore begins with two of their stories. They illustrate and bring to life much of the research, statistics, findings, and recommendations. We then identify girls' needs and pathways into the system, and the possibilities for prevention. We also explore girls' disparate treatment once they come in contact with the juvenile justice system. Finally, we make recommendations for changes in policies, processes, practices, and programming to improve outcomes for girls.

I. Understanding the Issues through the Life Stories of Incarcerated Girls

Gender inequity in the justice system is a common problem throughout the country and can result in devastating outcomes for girls and young women. The following stories, taken from interview transcripts with two young women incarcerated in a locked, razor-wire facility in a state system, provide a personal and sobering view of what happens to girls when we fail to intervene early in their lives.[1]

Tamela's Story

Tamela's story begins with her dad leaving when she was seven years old. She asked about him and her mother would never talk about what had happened, so "I just got frustrated and left the whole father thing alone." The "whole father thing" was that her father had molested her from age four to age seven, and was charged with sexual abuse. She never received any counseling or support.

Tamela's mom was in the military, and frequently Tamela stayed with relatives or acquaintances or was alone. By age eleven she started hanging out with older boys, and they "did things" to her, and she became sexually active very early. Before age twelve, she was placed in foster care because her mom had hit her. She lived with stranger after stranger, sleeping wherever there was space.

She started using marijuana at age twelve. From marijuana she progressed to using coke, prescription drugs, and crack. She ran away from foster care and began selling drugs to pay for places to stay. At fourteen, she was arrested for possession of drug paraphernalia. While on probation, she ran away and received a violation of probation.

The court sent her to a new program where she got in numerous fights. She was there for a year and a half and finally, by 2007, she went home to stay with her mother. "I tried to be good. I really tried to be good." She and her mother still had problems, and she continued to get in trouble. She is now in a residential commitment program for violation of probation, running away, and shoplifting. When asked what she wants to tell others so they can help girls, Tamela responded, "Tell adults to be there for them, what their parents couldn't, be somebody they didn't have. Be a friend, kids have no one to really talk to. That's where you can start to help us. Whether I am good or bad, I have no one, and I really try to be good but I always mess up."

When asked what she needs now, Tamela said, "I need to hear from successful people from where I was—that will motivate me. I need someone that has been through it . . . crack, doing anything for it, sleeping for it, men, women, for crack, it was my life. That will help me, knowing someone was successful. I need to know that someone like me has made it."

Maria's Story

Now seventeen, Maria identifies as biracial. At age ten, Maria and her two older brothers and young mother lived with her grandmother. There, they did not have much to eat, so she and her brothers then went to live with their aunt and her two young children.

One day her brother started touching her cousins. She did not know what to do. When recounting the incident, she softly said, "I was only ten." When the aunt came home, there was a lot of yelling and the police were called. "I prayed really hard and was hoping we would not be in trouble and that they would not take us from our grandmother." She and her brother were charged with lewd and lascivious behavior and placed in detention. She confessed to the charge in order to protect her brother, whose charges were dropped. Maria said, "I was smart then, too. I needed to protect my brother because he had been in trouble before."

From age ten to age thirteen, she went to court dates but received no counseling services. When she turned thirteen, the charges were reduced and she was placed on intensive supervision.

Then she began fighting in school. A year later, she was charged with battery for hitting the principal. She was sent to at least two alternative schools where she continued to fight, mainly with authority figures. At age fifteen, she and a principal got into a fight and she received a violation of parole charge.

At age sixteen, she took a girl's car, picked up friends and was driving around. The friends suggested robbing someone coming out of a store. She "went along" and stayed in the car while the robbery took place. When they were arrested, she was charged with having an alias, grand theft auto, grand theft, and robbery. She was placed in detention and was there for seven months. While in detention she "felt her life was over." She slept most of the time, wrote, and drew pictures. She was sent to another commitment program and within three weeks she fought with the program director. "I got tired of her calling the girls names—telling us that we don't do anything right, and she doesn't know why the judge keeps sending us to her program."

When describing what happened next, Maria explained, "afterwards I was put into a room for a long time, I prayed, I slept, I prayed I wasn't in that much trouble, that I wouldn't get arrested." She was arrested and sent back to detention for four months and later placed in a moderate-risk lock-up facility where she is currently getting B's in school. She hopes someday to go to college. She states that she always "messes up" and she doesn't want "to be bad again."

The stories of "Tamela" and "Maria" are, sadly, the stories of thousands of girls who suffered in silence as children. Their needs were ignored. These are the girls who are misunderstood and inappropriately labeled or, worse, who are simply invisible. When girls like Tamela and Maria do not receive the help they need to address the abuse and pain in their lives, the results can be tragic. Thus, it is critical to identify girls' risk factors and pathways and create structures that identify and support girls earlier to prevent their future involvement in the juvenile justice system.

II. Girls at Risk: Pathways into Juvenile Justice

In 1999, girls made up 27 percent of the 1.4 million arrests for youth under the age of eighteen. By 2008, girls constituted 30 percent of 1.3 million arrests (Federal Bureau of Investigation 2009). A one-day snapshot in 2006 revealed that 7,995 girls under age eighteen were committed to juvenile residential placements and an additional 4,458 girls were in detention across the United States (Sickmund, Sladky, and Kang 2008). Nationally, girls make up 15 percent of the incarcerated population, and in some states they constitute as much as 34 percent of the population (Sickmund, Sladky, and Kang 2008). Similar to their male counterparts, African American, American Indian, and Hispanic girls are incarcerated at higher rates than White girls. American Indian and African American girls are also sent to adult prisons at rates that are three to five times higher than those of White girls (Sickmund, Sladky, and Kang 2008). Regardless of offense type, there is cumulative disadvantage along the juvenile justice continuum from arrest to detention, judicial handling, commitment, and transfer to adult court for minority youth compared to White youth for similar offenses (Hartney and Silva 2007).

The Urban Justice Center reports that lesbian, gay, bisexual, transgender, and questioning (LGBTQ) youth comprise 4 to 10 percent of the juvenile justice population (Feinstein et al. 2001). Profound bias toward and damaging misconceptions of LGBTQ youth place them at risk of both being the victims of abuse and receiving additional charges while in residential facilities (Majd, Marksamer, and Reyes 2009). In addition to the risk factors for justice system involvement that impact LGBTQ youth in general, such as family rejection, school harassment, suicide risk, and high-risk sexual behaviors, lesbians and bisexual girls report higher rates of physical and sexual abuse than even their heterosexual female counterparts (Austin et al. 2008; Balsam et al. 2005; Saewyc et al. 2006). The juvenile justice system "routinely subjects LGBTQ youth to differential treatment, denies them appropriate services and fails to protect them from violence and harassment" (Estrada and Marksamer 2006, 415).

Girls' pathways into the juvenile justice system are different than boys'. Girls are arrested at younger ages, and many more come with histories of abuse, trauma, and victimization than their male counterparts. Twenty-five percent of girls in the system are ages fifteen and younger, compared to only 18 percent of boys (Sickmund, Sladky, and Kang 2008). Girls' rates for post-traumatic stress disorder, suicide attempts, and self-harming behavior are higher than boys' (Veysey 2003). In a comprehensive profile of 319 girls in juvenile justice programs across Florida, researchers learned that the following factors were contributing to girls' delinquency (Patino, Ravoira, and Wolf 2006): alcohol or drug abuse (46 percent); emotional and mental health factors, including depression, anger, and self-defeating behavior (79 percent); parental abuse (37 percent); girls committing offenses against family (61 percent); nonparental abuse (55 percent); both nonparental and parental abuse (25 percent); major illness (15 percent); history of pregnancy (35 percent); and having children (10 percent). In terms of educational risk factors, lack of interest in school/dropping out (54 percent) and extensive truancy (67 percent) contributed to girls' problem behaviors. Many of these girls' stories had a common theme: they were running away from an environment of abuse, violating curfew and terms of their probation because of dysfunction occurring in the home, and/or charged with assault due to family conflict (Patino, Ravoira, and Wolf 2006).

Abuse is a strong factor in the histories of girls in the juvenile justice system. The research shows that child victims of abuse were slightly more likely to be girls than boys and more at risk the younger they were (NCCD 2007). Children who are maltreated, compared to those who are not, were more likely to experience low academic performance (33 percent versus 23 percent), drug use (43 percent versus 32 percent), mental health problems (32 percent versus 18 percent) and, among females, teen pregnancy (52 percent versus 34 percent) (Smith and Thornberry 1995). In families where children are abused, there may be many complex interactions of individual, family, community, and societal factors that outweigh family and societal protective factors (Cicchetti and Carlson 1989; NCCD 2007). These may include high instances of parental substance abuse (CWLA 2001, 2004), intergenerational violence (Widom 1998), and domestic violence (Appel and Holden 1998; Edleson 1999).

Community factors such as poverty have been linked to child maltreatment and neglect (Sedlak and Broadhurst 1996; Black 2000; Lee and George 1999). Mothers who are abusive reported social isolation, fewer friends, and lower ratings of quality support received from friends (Bishop and Leadbeater 1999). Children of incarcerated parents are often in the child welfare system or residing with extended families where there is financial instability and instability in family relationships and structure (Garfinkel et al. 2007), as well as in school behavior and performance (Mumola 2000).

III. Prevention

Often, girls present with early risk factors in childhood that are ignored or not addressed in a comprehensive way. Tamela had been molested by her father starting at age four, but no one intervened until an incident in the home resulted in police intervention. Her story is the story of thousands of girls and young women who are spending their young lives in the juvenile justice system. Research and experience have clearly delineated the risk factors that can contribute to a host of negative outcomes, including juvenile justice system involvement. Yet, as a society we have not invested in front-end prevention and interventions but instead allow the issues to escalate and invest on the back end, at the cost of thirty-five to fifty thousand dollars for incarceration for one year (OPPAGA 2006). This does not include the cost of spending adolescence locked up and the added risks as a result of involvement in the system.

When prevention and early intervention services exist in local communities, they are often underfunded, fragmented, or operated independently, targeting a specific group of children and youth without recognizing the interrelated issues that result in violence and victimization of children. This targeting can also ignore the specific needs of girls and young women, youth with disabilities, and youth of color, as well as gay, lesbian, bisexual, transgender, and questioning youth. Children exposed to abuse and domestic violence need services that are developmentally appropriate and tailored to their age groups, gender, culture, and sexual orientation. Early intervention that incorporates developmentally appropriate services, including assessments, family counseling, individual counseling, and tutoring, could prevent the issues from becoming more entrenched, yet are often not available (ABA and NBA 2001).

Community-level risk factors (poverty, lack of access to education, and exposure to community violence) can be addressed through primary prevention efforts such as early childhood education programs (quality daycare and prekindergarten programs), which have been shown to improve outcomes for children and prevent girls from entering the juvenile justice system (Serna et al. 2002). Often, funding for these programs is not a priority. The literature on protective factors shows that school attachment (including teacher bonding and academic achievement) are stronger protective factors for girls than boys (Crosnoe, Erickson, and Dornbusch 2002), suggesting that supportive academic environments are key. School programs and environments that provide opportunities for catching up and creating healthy bonds with teachers and counselors can help reduce academic failure, one of the biggest predictors for girls' delinquency.

As girls get older, different risks and pathways are further compounded by inadequate and/or fragmented services and supports to meet treatment needs outside of, or before involvement with, the juvenile justice system. At age ten Maria was caught up in the child welfare and juvenile justice system with little support. Maria's mother had been a teenager when she was born, and we know that children of teen mothers are at high risk, yet there are limited programs promoting parent and child relationships accessible to the families that need them. Building these relationships is critical from an early age. Research shows the positive impact that parent-child attachment and bonding can have on children's health outcomes (Arbona and Power 2003), as well as success in school (Barber and Olsen 1997). And for girls, whose relationships are central in their lives, opportunities to build healthy relationships from early childhood to adolescence for Maria, her young mother, and her caretaker (her grandmother) were important. Maria is also at risk of teen pregnancy, family conflict that puts her at risk for running away, and charges associated with fighting with family members. Few resources and less concerted effort are made toward identifying, coordinating, and intervening with girls who are in crisis. Maria was not provided with counseling while she was going to court. While Tamela was on probation, no one intervened regarding her substance abuse and homelessness.

The implications of girls' risk and protective factors suggest community models of prevention that serve multiple purposes, including community prevention for the general population, targeted prevention for girls at risk, and specialized intervention and services for the girls and their families where problems are already present. A common theme echoed from parents is that "there was no one to help, nowhere to go," so they resort to calling the police to get help for their daughters who are out of control. This frustration with lack of services is echoed by judges who often incarcerate girls presenting with status offenses because that is the only way to get them services (OPPAGA 2003; Ravoira 2009).

There are system-level and individual-level interventions and supports that can address at-risk girls' needs through gender-responsive, culturally competent prevention services. Early identification is critical. If more girls had the opportunity to talk with a trusted school counselor/mentor and had access to timely information/available and relevant community services (domestic violence shelter, runaway shelters), community treatment (mental health screening and treatment), safe outlets, after-school programs, and health clinics, we would be doing a better job to ensure girls a safety net.

For girls with more intense needs, access to specialized mental health services to address emotional factors and substance use—including addiction and substance abuse, depression, trauma, physical, emotional, and/or sexual abuse, neglect, and family and domestic violence—are needed. Research supports the benefit of access to comprehensive health assessments and care, including comprehensive gynecological services (Acoca 2004). Girls need someone to talk to who can help guide them to establish safety for themselves and with others, recognize healthy and unhealthy relationships, and deal with depression and other common mental health problems (Chesney-Lind et al. 2008).

In addition to supporting girls, we must intervene with their families as well as other support systems and structures to build on strengths that exist at home and in the community. This includes counseling, parent support groups, transportation, quality daycare, adequate and safe supervision, and legal services. Greater effort is needed to change abusive and negative behaviors of adult family members and caretakers who victimize and sexually abuse children. More research, resources, and policies are needed to strengthen fractured families and prevent child maltreatment.

Funding for training regarding gender-responsive approaches and implications for practice is essential. Practitioners who come in contact with girls and families (counselors, law enforcement, and child welfare social workers) need training to recognize the signs of abuse and trauma, unsafe environments, depression, family conflict, and commercial sexual exploitation. Training is needed to understand adolescent female development in order to know how to approach difficult and complex issues, as well as the importance of significant relationships in girls' lives.

For girls who are arrested for status offenses, particularly runaways, probation officers and juvenile diversion program caseworkers must advocate on behalf of girls in their care, demanding changes to probation requirements that take into consideration the lives of girls. For instance, when Tamela violated probation, more attention should have been paid to her motivations for running away and to developing safety plans since she had been showing these patterns for years. Political support for true diversion programs to prevent girls from being committed for less serious offenses is essential. Further, social workers and probation officers have important insights and may provide meaningful contributions regarding the challenges they experience with girls and families as well as the injustices they see. These notes from the field must make it into policy considerations. At minimum, these are ways in which prevention policies and practices can be responsive before girls become entrenched in a system not designed to address their needs.

IV. Disparate Treatment in the Juvenile Justice System

Prevention is particularly critical for girls because once they come in contact with the existing juvenile justice system, they confront systemic policies and practices that result in unequal and harsh treatment of girls and young women. These policies and practices include labeling family disputes as domestic violence, subjecting girls to police practices specific to the enforcement of domestic violence laws; disproportionate charging with status offenses; disparities in the use of contempt of court proceedings and violation of probation; overuse of commitments to detention and residential confinement; and abuse inside of institutions.

There is a growing misperception that girls are becoming more violent. Recent data shows that arrests for aggravated assault and simple assault charges have narrowed between girls and boys, suggesting that more girls are fighting. Between 1999 and 2008, juvenile arrests for aggravated assault decreased more for males than for females (22 percent versus 17 percent). During the same period, juvenile male arrests for simple assault declined 6 percent while female arrests increased 12 percent (Puzzanchera 2009). Most importantly, however, the ratio of arrests for simple assault to arrests for aggravated assault is far higher for girls than boys, indicating that girls engage in less serious violence, while boys are more likely to use weapons and physically inflict more injury on victims (Zahn et al. 2008). It is also important to note who girls are fighting with and what their motivations are. Research suggests that girls are likely to fight with family members, and often this occurs in the context of being victimized, whereas boys are more likely to engage in fighting with friends or strangers (Brown 1998; Belknap, Holsinger, and Dunn 1997; Bloom et al. 2002; Sherman 2005; Zahn et al. 2008).

Recent research demonstrates that the perception that girls are becoming more violent may actually be the result of a change in societal responses and police practices, rather than a significant change in girls' behaviors (Sherman 1999; Lederman et al. 2004; Acoca and NCCD 2000; Bloom, Owen, and Covington 2005). Most noteworthy is the shift toward labeling girls' family conflicts as domestic violence offenses (Chesney-Lind 2001). Mandatory arrest policies associated with domestic violence statutes require police to make an arrest when there is a preponderance of evidence that hitting has taken place (Zahn et al. 2008; Sherman 2009). In many situations when police are called to the home to address a family dispute, mutual hitting is taking place and it is difficult to determine who is the aggressor and who is the victim. Police are faced with making a decision in a volatile situation. Numerous factors impact the decision on who will be arrested. In some instances, the adolescent girl "keeps arguing" or younger siblings are in the house. If the adult is arrested, there is no place to take the other children, and thus it is more expedient to arrest the adolescent female (Zahn et al. 2008; Gaarder, Rodriguez, and Zatz 2004). A review of these discretionary decisions and the labeling of family disputes as domestic violence is critical to curtailing the flow of girls into the justice system. What is needed is a review of the policies specific to domestic violence to distinguish between what is domestic violence and what constitutes a family dispute (Ravoira 2009). Family disputes between caretaker and child or between siblings need to be addressed differently than domestic violence (partner abuse). This is of particular concern in light of the reports from girls who are charged with domestic violence that indicate that some of the altercations are in response to fighting back against an abuser who is living in the home.[2] We recognize that distinguishing child abuse, domestic violence, and family disputes where there is physical and relational aggression is a challenging task for law enforcement. It is important that child abuse allegations are taken seriously and that law enforcement receive training and use discretion as to the type of charge (if any) when there are family disputes between children and their parents/guardians that are confrontational.

A second bias within the juvenile justice system with respect to girls is the disproportionate charging of girls with status offenses. Status offenses criminalize behavior that would be legal for an adult but that are not legal for a minor, such as truancy, running away from home, and curfew violations. Discretionary decisions by police, judges, and probation officers in response to girls who commit status offenses add to the disturbing increase in girls' involvement in the justice system (ABA and NBA 2001). Nationally, girls are disproportionately charged with status offenses. In 2008, 10 percent of the arrests for girls were for running away as compared to 3 percent for boys (FBI 2009). In addition, the reasons why girls run away are critical to understanding their victimization, as they frequently are fleeing an environment of abuse or family dysfunction (Stiffman 1989; Ravoira and Cherry 1992). In a study of runaway behavior, girls were found to be two to four times more likely to report running away from home before the age of sixteen if they were abused, as compared to girls who had not been maltreated (Andres-Lemay, Jamieson, and MacMillan 2005). Child abuse, according to all available indicators, is higher among runaway girls, as is pending or current parenthood. Additionally, substance use is higher among runaway youth (Kempf-Leonard and Johansson 2007).

Girls who are in need of counseling and other support services instead are ushered into the delinquency system. According to Francine Sherman, director of the Juvenile Rights Advocacy Project at Boston College Law School, girls arrive in the juvenile justice system often through paths marked by sexual and physical abuse, mental illness, substance abuse, family disconnection, and special education. They are disproportionately involved in the justice system as status offenders, are exploited by "pimps," are recruited into prostitution for survival, and often violate terms of probation and parole (Sherman 1999).

A third area of gender differentiation within the juvenile justice system is the high rate of girls who are detained for probation and parole violations (54 percent of girls versus 19 percent of boys) (Sherman 2005). The use of contempt proceedings and probation and parole violations makes it more likely that, without committing another crime, girls will be placed in detention or a residential commitment program. The practice of bootstrapping (charging girls with a delinquent offense for violation of a court order) is applied disproportionately to girls and results in severe and unjust treatment, especially of girls charged with status offenses (ABA and NBA 2001; Child Welfare League 2004).

A fourth gendered pattern in the system is that despite committing less serious offenses than boys, girls are more likely to be detained or committed to a residential commitment facility, and they are also more likely to be sent back to detention or residential commitment following discharge (ABA and NBA 2001). Of the 13,943 girls who were incarcerated in a 2006 one-day census snapshot, 14 percent had committed a status offense as their most serious offense, 21 percent had committed technical violations, including violation of probation, and the majority had committed misdemeanor offenses (Sickmund, Sladky, and Kang 2008). In four of the Annie E. Casey Juvenile Detention Alternative Initiative study sites, although girls comprised only 14 percent of the total detention population, 30 percent of them returned to detention within one year. Among those, 53 percent of the girls as compared with 41 percent of the boys who returned to detention within one year did so for probation or technical violations (Sherman 2005). According to Washoe County Department of Juvenile Services (one of the JDAI project sites) most girls in detention were not a threat to society, but were detained because they were a "threat to themselves" (Annie E. Casey 2008). This is of significant concern because girls' rates of recidivism are lower than those of boys and girls generally do not pose a serious public safety threat (ABA and NBA 2001).

Finally, of grave concern is the treatment of girls once they are detained and incarcerated (keeping in mind that they are sent to detention or residential facilities for less serious offenses more often than are boys). The rate of abuse for girls inside facilities is significant. Based on the Survey of Youth in Residential Placement (SYRP) and the first National Survey of Youth in Custody by the Bureau of Justice Statistics, preliminary data show that 5 percent of females reported being the victim of sexual assault while in custody (Sedlak 2008; Beck, Guerino, and Harrison 2010). Youth with sexual victimization histories were twice as likely to report being assaulted while in custody inside a facility (24 percent versus 10 percent). Most of those reporting sexual assault had been victimized multiple times (Krisberg 2009; Beck, Guerino, and Harrison 2010). Since 1998, the U.S. Justice Department has sued nine states and two territories alleging abuse, inadequate mental and medical care, and dangerous use of restraints in youth facilities (US DOJ 2010).

The impact of abuse inside institutions, coupled with past life experiences, puts girls at heightened risk for self-harming and high-risk behaviors (Hennessey et al. 2004). When trauma and/or victimization are unaddressed, we can expect that girls will be unable to effectively cope with stress or anger. These emotions manifest in behaviors that staff inside juvenile justice facilities refer to as "acting out," "drama," or "lashing out." Girls may be unintentionally further victimized or retraumatized when staff seek to control the acting-out behaviors because they do not understand the seriousness of the girls' trauma and untreated histories of victimization that are driving their behaviors (Ford et al. 2007; Hennessey et al. 2004).

Further, once girls enter the system, there is a lack of systemic interventions to prevent girls from going deeper into the system. Until staff are empowered to think critically about the long-term implications of their decisions to arrest girls in the first place, violate girls on probation, hold girls in contempt, charge girls an additional offense for fighting in a program, or write girls up for less serious infractions, girls will continue to be at a disadvantage. Agencies have not made it a priority to examine the impact of their program philosophies and policies on the girls in their care. When juvenile justice professionals (law enforcement, probation officers, judges, direct care workers, counselors, and program administrators) are not trained to take into account the power and importance of relationships in the lives of girls and young women, they continue to create a system that sets girls up for failure (Maniglia 1996).

The consequences for girls who are arrested, detained, and committed to a residential commitment facility can have serious long-term consequences. Girls who could have their lives turned around get trapped in a downward spiral, cycling in and out of multiple residential lock-up facilities. The lack of gender-responsive prevention, early intervention, and treatment services at the community level results in far too many girls in need of these services spending years of their adolescence incarcerated. We continue to miss opportunities to appropriately identify, divert, and connect girls with the appropriate resources to treat the root causes of their behaviors. At best, the current response is developmentally inappropriate; at worst, girls are further victimized and traumatized (Acoca 2000).

V. Recommendations and Models for Change
Using the Wisdom of Girls

One powerful insight into what is needed to serve girls can be found in listening to what girls themselves have to say. The NCCD Center for Girls and Young Women conducted individual interviews and focus groups in group homes, residential commitment facilities, and a detention center from 2006 to 2009 as part of the Justice for Girls: State of Florida initiative spearheaded by Children's Campaign, Inc. (Ravoira 2009). Responses fell into three distinct categories that focus on prevention and intervention services, family-focused interventions, and systemic reform. This is what girls have to say about these three areas.[3]

Community-Based Prevention and Intervention Services

- "Girls need mentors who won't give up on them."
- "Regardless of your situation, you need at least one person to believe in you."
- "I don't want to be a statistic (AIDS/HIV, Pregnant). We need sex education that is real. In fifth grade, I was a target. Men would talk to me and want to make me their girlfriend."
- "We need an opportunity to stay busy: church, sports, volunteering, somewhere to belong."
- "Girls need support groups. Create support groups for girls that cater to girls who have made the wrong decisions and those going through similar things. It is easier when you are with girls who are going through the same things."
- "Make a 'chat-line' for girls to talk to other girls who are not in the neighborhood. This will help us to meet girls who can talk about positive things."
- "Increase the awareness of programs that are available. We don't know where to go for help."

Family-Focused Services

- "Family counseling, I believe that's where every problem has started and that instead of punishing me every time, we could resolve the issues with a more positive alternative."
- "Find ways to get parents involved like a mother/daughter quality time."
- "Family counseling, talking and meetings."

Needed Policy and Systems Reform

- "Truancy laws are wrong."
- "Being searched all the time is wrong. I hate to be touched."
- "Let us complete probation and then start over with a clean slate."
- "If you would give me a second chance by taking me off probation, I promise you won't see me again."
- "I don't know why you made jails."
- "Shoving someone in jail all the time isn't always the best option."

The girls' responses both challenge us to continue to question current policies and practices and provide a clear direction for the development of programs and services. Programs and initiatives should be based on research, practical experience, feedback from community stakeholders, juvenile justice professionals, and, most importantly, the courageous voices of girls and young women.

Promising Models to Affect Change

There are examples of community responses and programs that illustrate the essential principles and practices needed for working with girls. These approaches offer a comprehensive continuum of services through community-based models. Further, they exemplify the many levels of prevention and intervention, including approaches to reduce risks in the general population, among girls identified as at risk, and among girls and families where problems have surfaced. The approaches are grounded in research and in the wisdom of girls. This section identifies several prevention efforts that are aligned with the implications previously reviewed in this chapter for preventing and reducing further delinquency of girls. These approaches demonstrate how communities can invest in prevention, provide holistic, gender-responsive services, and connect girls with treatment needs to community resources.

The Justice for Girls: Duval County Initiative is an example of how one North Florida community is tackling the issues facing girls. A Leadership Council comprised of community leaders representing business, philanthropy, research, education, volunteerism, and human rights was convened to serve as the coordinating body of this initiative. The role of the Leadership Council was to learn about the issues, provide pragmatic recommendations for change, and assume the strategic leadership role for advancing the goals and objectives of the initiative. To obtain stakeholder input regarding priorities for systemic change, focus groups and individual interviews were facilitated by NCCD with service providers, law enforcement, assistant state attorneys, public defenders, judges, school personnel, child welfare, juvenile justice, parents, and justice-involved girls.

After a twelve-month intensive review of the national, state, and local data as well as input from diverse stakeholders, the Leadership Council published *Justice for Girls: Duval County Blueprint for Action* (Ravoira 2009). The report outlined a two-pronged strategic direction for systemic change that entailed an advocacy strategy and the development of a local continuum of gender-responsive services.

The advocacy platform includes promoting legislative and policy changes regarding overuse of violation of probation/nonlaw violations; misapplication of domestic violence statutes; overuse of detention; review of "charges caught" inside poorly functioning residential facilities; and a protocol for staff training. The local continuum of care section outlines specific programming initiatives to reduce out of school suspensions, expand diversion options, and reform the local secure residential facility (Ravoira 2009).

The county initiative also identified elementary school–based intervention as a priority area for effecting change, fueled by the finding that 845 girls had been suspended from their elementary schools in the previous school year (Ravoira, Patino, and Rose 2008). To address overuse of suspension and to prevent juvenile justice involvement, efforts are underway to identify and provide services to girls who are presenting with behavior issues and at the same time to change school structures, policies, and practices, including staff training, so as to improve the response to girls who are displaying challenging behaviors. The model addresses the three prevention levels by having staff on-site at targeted schools to train staff on strategies to deescalate girls' behaviors, provide crisis intervention, assess and divert girls who have received a referral for suspension to better understand the motivations driving behavior, connect girls with developmentally appropriate resources, and, if more intense needs are identified, provide family interventions, connect with services, provide mentors, and establish longer-term monitoring. We suggest that this type of model can be replicated in other elementary and middle schools and tailored to meet the needs of girls and staff across many jurisdictions.

Another prevention approach, the PACE Center for Girls, is a gender-responsive prevention and early intervention program serving at-risk girls ages twelve to eighteen in day treatment centers across Florida. Academic difficulties have been noted as a very significant risk factor related to girls' delinquent behaviors. PACE is a promising model that addresses this relationship in a holistic manner by incorporating multiple developmental domains of adolescence in its interventions, as opposed to focusing solely on academic and behavioral challenges. These domains include the physical, emotional, intellectual, sexual, spiritual, and relational.

The gender-responsive environment is the context in which PACE interventions are provided, and nine Values and Guiding Principles are integrated into daily practice. These include Honor the Female Spirit, Focus on Strengths, Act with Integrity and Positive Intent, Embrace Growth and Change, Value the Wisdom of Time, Exhibit Courage, Seek Excellence, Create Partnerships, and Invest in the Future. Within this environment, academic and social service interventions are individualized for each girl. PACE's interventions include academic advising, individualized academic plans, counseling, care management, and the Spirited Girls! Life Skills development curriculum. The PACE model targets risk and protective factors identified through research to increase or decrease the likelihood of delinquency among girls. These include poor academic performance, relationships, sexual activity, substance use, stressors, aggression, and career/future outlook. PACE's interventions seek to increase girls' knowledge and skills so that girls can demonstrate improved outcomes in these areas (PACE 2010; Graziano and Patino 2010).

These programs for girls teach us that the time to intervene in girls' lives is early, and intensively, with comprehensive gender-responsive interventions that will address their multiple needs. The available research and experience underscore that many young women in the justice system need treatment to address their histories of trauma, abuse, and victimization.

VI. Unfinished Work: Recommendations for Meaningful Change in Policies, Processes, Practices, and Programming

The NCCD Center for Girls and Young Women urges states and local jurisdictions to make a commitment to overhauling current policies, processes, and practices that result in disparate treatment of girls and young women. The following tactical strategies are recommended as critical to bringing about meaningful reform.

1. Advocate for passage of legislation requiring gender-responsive services for girls.
2. Identify and reexamine state statutes, policies, procedures, and practices that shepherd girls into the system or result in disparate treatment of girls (i.e., overuse of commitment for less serious offenses; labeling of family disputes and changes in police practices specific to the enforcement of domestic violence laws; criminalizing of status offenses; disparities in the use of contempt of court proceedings and violation of probation; overuse of commitments to detention and residential confinement; abuse inside of institutions; and lack of training for juvenile justice professionals).
3. Create a high-level prevention task force charged with identifying strategies and services designed to keep girls out of the system. Include juvenile justice professionals (district attorney, law enforcement, public defender, judges, politicians, prevention, diversion, probation, parole, detention,

residential service providers) and stakeholders from other systems that touch girls' lives (education, mental health, child welfare, medical, faith community, community-based programs, business, politicians) and justice-involved girls and family members.

4. Determine points in the judicial process where girls could be diverted prior to formal intake into the system and develop strategies to divert girls whenever possible.

5. Provide alternatives to secure detention for those girls who do not pose a public safety or flight risk, including such options as home detention, use of electronic monitoring, or referral to community-based services.

6. Develop and adequately fund community-based diversion and intervention options that are gender responsive.

7. Invest in community-based services to address family conflict and domestic violence, including evidenced-based models such as Functional Family Therapy (Alexander et al. 1998), Multidimensional Treatment Foster Care (Chamberlain and Mihalic 1998), and Multisystemic Therapy (Henggeler et al. 1998).

8. Require gender-specific training for all justice professionals, including judges, state attorneys, police, school resource officers, as well as service providers.

As a nation we have failed to effectively address the needs of girls. We have stood by as the population of justice-involved girls continues to grow. They are younger, their offenses are less serious and often related to family issues, and they have greater mental health needs than their male counterparts. The current system is not designed with these differences in mind. Policymakers have not invested in community-based, gender-responsive prevention, intervention, and diversion programs that research and experience show us turn girls' lives around and are cost effective.

Our continued inaction results in tragic and unacceptable outcomes for the health and well-being of girls and young women. When girls' issues are left untreated, they are vulnerable to poor outcomes as they enter womanhood, including poor physical and mental health, substance abuse and dependence, increased likelihood of arrests and criminal activity, domestic violence, and parenting challenges (Hipwell and Loeber 2006). Changing how we respond to girls and young women is not an option. It is vital to the health and well-being of our states and our local communities and to the next generation of children. We must create a system that will stop asking girls what is wrong with them but instead start with the question, "What do we need to do to help you?"

NOTES

1. Names were changed to protect the confidentiality of the girls who shared their stories.
2. Reports from girls in a Fort Myers detention center.
3. Quotations taken from transcripts from individual interviews with girls in residential commitment, focus groups with girls in community-based nonresidential programs, and group sessions with girls in detention

REFERENCES

Acoca, Leslie. 2004. Are Those Cookies for Me or My Baby? Understanding Detained and Incarcerated Teen Mothers and Their Children. *Juvenile and Family Court Journal* 55: 65-80.

Acoca, Leslie, and National Council on Crime and Delinquency. 2000. *Educate or Incarcerate: Girls in the Florida and Duval County Juvenile Justice Systems.* Oakland, CA: National Council on Crime and Delinquency.

Alexander, James, Cole Barton, Donald Gordon, Jennifer Grotpeter, Kjell Hansson, Rich Harrison, et al. 1998. *Blueprints for Violence Prevention, Book Three: Functional Family Therapy.* Boulder, CO: Center for the Study and Prevention of Violence.

American Bar Association (ABA) and National Bar Association (NBA). 2001. *Justice by Gender: The Lack of Appropriate Prevention, Diversion, and Treatment Alternatives for Girls in the Juvenile Justice System.* Washington, DC: ABA and NBA.

Andres-Lemay, V. Joy, Ellen Jamieson, and Harriet L. MacMillan. 2005. Child Abuse, Psychiatric Disorder, and Running Away in a Community Sample of Women. *Canadian Journal of Psychiatry* 50: 684-89.

Annie E. Casey Foundation. 2008. Sustained and Deliberate Focus on Girls Realizes Impressive Results. *JDAI Electronic Newsletter.* http://www.aecf.org/MajorInitiatives/ JuvenileDetentionAlternativesInitiative/Resources/May08newsletter/FeatureStory1. aspx.

Annie E. Casey Foundation. 2003. *The Unsolved Challenge of System Reform: The Condition of the Frontline Human Services Workforce.* Baltimore, MD: AECF.

Appel, Anne E., and George W. Holden. 1998. Co-occurring Spouse and Child Abuse: Implications for CPS Practice. *APSAC Advisor,* 11-14.

Arbona, Consuelo, and Thomas G. Power. 2003. Parental Attachment, Self-Esteem, and Antisocial Behaviors among African American, European American, and Mexican American Adolescents. *Journal of Counseling Psychology* 50: 40-51.

Austin, S. Bryn, Hee-Jin Jun, Benita Jackson, Donna Spiegelman, Jane Rich-Edwards, Heather Corliss, and Rosalin J. Wright. 2008. Disparities in Child Abuse Victimization in Lesbian, Bisexual, and Heterosexual Women in the Nurses' Health Study II. *Journal of Women's Health* 17: 597-606.

Balsam, Kimberly F., Esther Rothblum, and Theodore P. Beauchaine. 2005. Victimization over the Lifespan: Comparison of Lesbian, Gay, Bisexual, and Heterosexual Siblings. *Journal of Consulting and Clinical Psychology* 73: 477– 87.

Barber, Brian K., and Joseph A. Olsen. 1997. Socialization in Context: Connection, Regulation, and Autonomy in the Family, School, and Neighborhood, and with Peers. *Journal of Adolescent Research* 12: 287–315.

Barnickol, Laura. 2000. The Disparate Treatment of Males and Females. *Journal of Law and Policy* 2: 435.

Beck, Alan, Paul Guerino, and Paige Harrison. 2010. *Sexual Victimization in Juvenile Facilities Reported by Youth, 2008-2009.* Washington, DC: Bureau of Justice Assistance. http://bjs.ojp.usdoj.gov/content/pub/pdf/svjfry09.pdf.

Belknap, Joanne, Kristi Holsinger, and Melissa Dunn. 1997. Understanding Incarcerated Girls: The Results of a Focus Group Study. *Prison Journal* 77: 381-404.

Bishop, Sandra, and Bonnie Leadbeater. 1999. Maternal Social Support Patterns and Child Maltreatment: Comparison of Maltreating and Nonmaltreating Mothers. American Journal of Orthopsychiatry 69: 172-81.

Black, Maureen. 2000. The Roots of Child Neglect. In R.M. Reece (ed.),*Treatment of Child Abuse: Common Mental Health, Medical, and Legal Practitioners.* Baltimore, MD: Johns Hopkins University Press.

Bloom, Barbara, Barbara Owen, and Stephanie Covington. 2005. *Gender Strategies for Women Offenders: Research, Practice, and Guiding Principles for Women Offenders.* Washington, DC: U.S. Department of Justice, National Institute of Corrections.

Bloom, Barbara, Barbara Owen, Elizabeth Deschenes, and Jill Rosenbaum. 2002. Improving Juvenile Justice for Females: A Statewide Assessment in California. *Crime and Delinquency* 48 (4): 526-52.

Brown, Lynn. 1998. *Raising Their Voices: The Politics of Girls' Anger.* Cambridge, MA: Harvard University Press.

Chamberlain, Patricia, and Sharon F. Mihalic. 1998. Multidimensional Treatment Foster Care. In D. S. Elliott (series ed.), *Book Eight: Blueprints for Violence Prevention.* Boulder: Institute of Behavioral Science, University of Colorado at Boulder.

Chesney-Lind, Meda. 2001. Are Girls Closing the Gender Gap in Violence? *Criminal Justice Magazine* 16: 1.

Chesney-Lind, Meda, Merry Morash and Tia Stevens. 2008. Girls' Troubles, Girls' Delinquency, and Gender-Responsive Programming: A Review. *Australian and New Zealand Journal of Criminology* 41: 162-89.

Child Welfare League of America. 2004. Girls in the Juvenile Justice System. http://www.cwl.org.

Child Welfare League of America. 2001. *Alcohol, Other Drugs, and Child Welfare.* Washington, DC: Child Welfare League of America.

Cicchetti, Dante, and Vicki Carlson, eds. 1989. *Child Maltreatment: Theory and Research on the Causes and Consequences of Child Abuse and Neglect.* New York: Cambridge University Press.

Crosnoe, Robert, Kristin G. Erickson, and Sanford M. Dornbusch. 2002. Protective Functions of Family Relationships and School Factors on the Deviant Behavior of Adolescent Boys and Girls: Reducing the Impact of Risky Friendships. *Youth and Society* 33: 515-44.

Edleson, Jeffrey L. 1999. The Overlap between Child Maltreatment and Woman Battering. *Violence against Women* 5:134-54.

Estrada, Rudy, and Jody Marksamer. 2006. The Legal Rights of LGBT Youth in State Custody: What Child Welfare and Juvenile Justice Professionals Need to Know. *Child Welfare* 85:171-94.

Federal Bureau of Investigation. 2009. Uniform Crime Reports for the United States: 2009. Table 33, Ten-Year Arrest Trends by Sex, 1999-2008. Washington, DC: U.S. Government Printing Office. http://www.fbi.gov/ucr/cius2008/data/table_33.html.

Feinstein, Randi, Andrea Greenblatt, Lauren Hass, Sally Kohn, and Julianne Rana. 2001. *Justice for All? A Report on Lesbian, Gay, Bisexual, and Transgendered Youth in the New York Juvenile Justice System*. New York: Urban Justice Center. http://www.urbanjustice. org/pdf/publications/lesbianandgay/justiceforallreport.pdf.

Ford, Julian D., John F. Chapman, Josephine Hawke, and David Albert. 2007. *Trauma among Youth in the Juvenile Justice System: Critical Issues and New Directions*. National Center for Mental Health and Juvenile Justice Research Brief, Department of Health and Human Services.

Gaarder, Emily, Nancy Rodriguez, and Marjorie S. Zatz. 2004. Criers, Liars, and Manipulators: Probation Officers' Views of Girls. *Justice Quarterly* 21:547-78.

Garfinkel, Irwin, Amanda Geller, and Carey Cooper. 2007. *Parental Incarceration in Fragile Families: Summary of Three Year Findings*. Unpublished report to the Annie E. Casey Foundation.

Gilligan, Carol. 1982. *In a Different Voice*. Cambridge, MA: Harvard University Press.

Graziano, Juliette N., and Vanessa Patino. 2010. Unpublished. *Theoretical and Empirical Foundation of the PACE Model*. Jacksonville, FL: NCCD Center for Girls and Young Women.

Greene, Peters, and Associates. 1998. *Guiding Principles for Promising Female Programs: An Inventory of Best Practices*. Washington, DC: United States Department of Justice, Office of Juvenile Justice and Delinquency Prevention.

Hartney, Christopher, and Fabiana Silva. 2007. *And Justice for Some: Differential Treatment of Youth of Color in the Justice System*. Oakland, CA: National Council on Crime and Delinquency.

Henggeler, Scott W., Sonja K. Schoenwald, Charles M. Borduin, Melissa D. Rowland, and Phillippe B. Cunningham. 1998. *Multisystemic Treatment of Antisocial Behavior in Children and Adolescents*. New York: Guilford Press.

Hennessey, Marianne, Julian Ford, Karen Mahoney, Susan Ko, and Christine Siegfried. 2004. *Trauma among Girls in the Juvenile Justice System*. National Center for Child Traumatic Stress. Los Angeles, CA: National Child Traumatic Stress Network. http://www. nctsnet.org/nctsn_assets/pdfs/edu_materials/trauma_among_girls_in_jjsys.pdf.

Hipwell, Alison, and Rolf Loeber. 2006. Do We Know Which Interventions Are Effective for Disruptive and Delinquent Girls? *Clinical Child and Family Psychology Review* 9 (3/4): 221-55.

Kempf-Leonard, Kimberly, and Pauline Johansson. 2007. Gender and Runaways: Risk Factors, Delinquency, and Juvenile Justice Experiences. *Youth Violence and Juvenile Justice* 5: 308-27.

Krisberg, Barry. 2009. *Special Report: Breaking the Cycle of Abuse in Juvenile Facilities*. Oakland, CA: National Council on Crime and Delinquency.

Lederman, Cindy S., Gayle A. Dakof, Maria A. Larrea, and Li Hua. 2004. Characteristics of Adolescent Females in Juvenile Detention. *International Journal of Law and Psychiatry* 27: 321–37.

Lee, Bong J., and Robert M. George. 1999. Poverty, Early Childbearing, and Child Maltreatment: A Multinomial Analysis. *Children and Youth Services Review* 21: 755– 80.

Majd, Katayoon, Jody Marksamer, and Carolyn Reyes. 2009. *Hidden Injustice: Lesbian, Gay, Bisexual, and Transgender Youth in Juvenile Courts.* San Francisco: The Equity Project.

Maniglia, Rebecca. 1996. New Directions for Young Women in the Juvenile Justice System. *Reclaiming Children and Youth: Journal of Emotional and Behavioral Problems* 5 (2): 96-101.

Mumola, Christopher J. 2000. *Incarcerated Parents and Their Children.* Washington, DC: U.S. Department of Justice. http://www.ojp.usdoj.gov/bjs/pub/pdf/iptc.pdf.

National Council on Crime and Delinquency. 2007. *Outcome Evaluation of Parents Anonymous.* Oakland, CA: National Council on Crime and Delinquency.

Office of Juvenile Justice and Delinquency Prevention. 1998. *Juvenile Female Offenders: A Status of the States Report.* Washington, DC: Office of Juvenile Justice and Delinquency Prevention, U.S. Department of Justice.

Office of Program Policy and Government Accountability (OPPAGA). 2006. *Effective Community Programs Reduce Commitment of Girls to Residential Programs.* Report no. 06-13. Tallahassee, FL: OPPAGA. www.oppaga.stat.fl.us/mnoitorDocs/Repports/pdf/0613rpt.pdf.

Office of Program Policy and Government Accountability (OPPAGA). 2005. *Qualifications, Screening, Salaries, and Training Affect Quality and Turnover of Juvenile Justice Employees.* Report no. 5-46. Tallahassee, FL: OPPAGA. http://www.oppaga.state.fl.us/reports/pdf/0546rpt.pdf

Office of Program Policy and Government Accountability (OPPAGA). 2003. More Youth Are Admitted for Less Serious Offenses, in Part to Meet Treatment Needs. Report no. 03-76. Tallahassee, FL: OPPAGA. http://www.oppaga.state.fl.us/reports/pdf/0376rpt.pdf.

PACE. 2010. PACE Center for Girls website. www.pacecenter.org.

Patino, Vanessa, Lawanda Ravoira, and Angela Wolf. 2006. *A Rallying Cry for Change: Charting a New Direction in the State of Florida's Response to Girls in Juvenile Justice.* Oakland, CA: National Council on Crime and Delinquency.

Puzzanchera, Charles. 2009. Juvenile Arrests, 2008. *Juvenile Justice Bulletin.* Washington, DC: Office of Justice Programs. http://www.ncjrs.gov/pdffiles1/ojjdp/228479.pdf.

Ravoira, Lawanda. 2009. Justice for Girls: Blueprint for Action. Tallahassee, FL: Children's Campaign. http://www.justiceforallgirls.org/advocacy/Bluprnto109.pdf

Ravoira, Lawanda, and Andrew L. Cherry Jr. 1992. *Social Bonds and Teen Pregnancy.* Westport, CT: Praeger.

Ravoira, Lawanda, Vanessa Patino, and Bonnie Rose. 2008. Unpublished. Justice for Girls: Briefing Paper #1; Profile of Duval County Girls and Young Women in or at Risk of Entering the Juvenile Justice System. Jacksonville, FL: NCCD Center for Girls and Young Women.

Saewyc, Elizabeth M., Carol L. Skay, Sandra L. Pettingell, Elizabeth A. Reis, Linda Bearinger, Michael Resnick, et al. 2006. Hazards of Stigma: The Sexual and Physical Abuse of Gay, Lesbian, and Bisexual Adolescents in the United States and Canada. *Child Welfare* 85: 195-213.

Sedlak, Andrea. 2008. *Introduction to the Survey of Youth in Residential Placement*. Washington, DC: U.S. Department of Justice, Office of Juvenile Justice and Delinquency Prevention.

Sedlak, Andrea J., and Diane D. Broadhurst. 1996. *The Third National Incidence Study of Child Abuse and Neglect (NIS-3)*. Washington, DC: U.S. Department of Health and Human Services.

Serna, Loretta, Elizabeth Nielsen, Katina Lambros, and Steven Forness. 2002. Prevention with Children at Risk for Emotional or Behavioral Disorders: Data on a Universal Intervention for Head Start Classrooms. *Behavioral Disorders* 26: 70-84.

Sherman, Francine. 2009. Reframing the Response: Girls in the Juvenile Justice System and Domestic Violence. *Juvenile and Family Justice Today* 18 (1): 16-20.

Sherman, Francine. 2005. *Pathways to Juvenile Detention Reform—Detention Reform and Girls: Challenges and Solutions*. Baltimore, MD: Annie E. Casey Foundation. http://www.aecf.org/upload/publicationfiles/jdai_pathways_girls.pdf.

Sherman, Francine. 1999. The Juvenile Rights Advocacy Project: Representing Girls in Context. *Juvenile Justice Journal* 6 (1). Washington, DC: Office of Justice Programs, U.S. Department of Justice, Office of Juvenile Justice and Delinquency Prevention.

Sickmund, Melissa, T. J. Sladky, and Wei Kang. 2008. Census of Juveniles in Residential Placement Databook. http://www.ojjdp.ncjrs.gov/ojstatbb/cjrp/.

Smith, Carolyn, and Terence P. Thornberry. 1995. The Relationship between Childhood Maltreatment and Adolescent Involvement in Delinquency and Drug Use. *Criminology* 33: 451-81.

Stiffman, Arlene R. 1989. Physical and Sexual Abuse in Runaway Youth. *Child Abuse & Neglect* 13: 417–26.

United States Department of Justice (US DOJ). 2010. Civil Rights of Institutionalized Persons Act (CRIPPA). *Complaints Filed in US District Court*. http://www.justice.gov/crt/split/findsettle.php#Complaints.

Veysey, Bonita. 2003. Adolescent Girls with Mental Health Disorders Involved in the Juvenile Justice System. *National Center for Mental Health and Juvenile Justice Research and Program Brief*. Policy Research Associates, NY. http://www.ncmhjj.com/pdfs/Adol_girls.pdf.

Widom, Cathy. 1998. The Cycle of Violence. *Science*. 14: 160-66.

Zahn, Margaret, Susan Brumbaugh, Darrell Steffensmeier, Barry Feld, Merry Morash, Meda Chesney-Lind, Jody Miller, Allison Payne, Denise Gottfredson, and Candace Kruttschnitt. U.S. Department of Justice: Girl Study Group. 2008. *Understanding and Responding to Girls' Delinquency: Violence by Teenage Girls; Trends and Context*. Washington, DC: OJJDP, Office of Justice Programs.

—————————————————————————————— 8 ——

Supporting Queer Youth

SARAH VALENTINE

Queer youth[1] cross all racial, ethnic, gender, religious, and class backgrounds. They are children forced from a very young age to cope with environments where victimization and harassment are normative (Ryan 2003). Their sexuality and gender identity often mark them as alien to their families and to society at large. Being perceived as queer sets them apart and makes them targets for neglect, rejection, bullying, and abuse at home and school. This increased risk of victimization compared to their heterosexual peers means queer youth suffer higher rates of homelessness, substance abuse, depression, suicide attempts, and sexual victimization (Rew et al. 2005) and thus increases their risk of involvement with the child welfare and juvenile justice systems.

The political minefield that is child and adolescent sexuality is rapidly expanding as children and adolescents are recognizing and acting on their sexuality at ever earlier ages (Savin-Williams 2005). Children who do not conform to social expectations of gender are also either self-identifying or being identified at much younger ages. Because society uses gender nonconformity as a marker by which to identify and target queer children, this segment of the queer youth population is especially imperiled. The risk of harm is exacerbated by the pathologizing of gender nonconformity through the fairly recent creation of "gender identity disorder" (Valentine 2008), a disorder that is often used by parents seeking treatment for their children to prevent them from becoming queer (Fedders 2006). Thus, gender-nonconforming youth,[2] perhaps even more than children who are seen as lesbian, gay, or bisexual, may be at increased risk for rejection by society (Greytak et al. 2009; Marksamer 2008; Ryan 2003). This is exemplified by studies indicating that gender-non-conforming homeless youth are more likely than others to be discriminated against by shelter workers, social service personnel, and the police—all of which increases their risk of arrest (Marksamer 2008; Ray 2006).

Another particularly vulnerable subset of the queer child population is queer youth of color. Youth of color are overrepresented in the juvenile justice system and queer youth of color, like all queer children, are likely to face homophobia within their families and ethnic communities (Reck 2009; Ryan 2003; Gipson 2002). Being identified as queer can place youth of color at risk for losing the connection to the only community that affirms their cultural or racial identity. Confronting the racism in mainstream society as well as any culture– or religion-based homophobia that may exist in their families and communities leaves this group of children highly vulnerable to becoming involved with the child welfare or juvenile justice system.

Because homophobia and heterosexism[3] are pervasive across social institutions, the effect of violence and discrimination against queer youth is similar and self-perpetuating, regardless of where it occurs. Youth in conflict with their family often end up in the child welfare system, in the juvenile justice system, or on the street. A child forced from school because of violence and abuse will face similar consequences without supportive family. Sexuality or gender identification becomes yet one more stressor, like poverty, racism, or family dysfunction, that propels children away from their families and communities and into state care.

Queer youth are far more likely to be detained pending trial than their heterosexual peers (Majd et al. 2009). Once in the child welfare or juvenile justice system, sexual minority youth often face longer stays and revolving placements because they lack supportive parents, or they face continued trouble in schools. A dearth of queer-friendly placements heightens the risk that sexual-minority youth will run from dangerous or unwelcoming out-of-home placements and shelters. When living on the street, queer youth are more likely to come into contact with police, which heightens the likelihood of arrest and further involvement with the legal system.

If we are to reduce the high rates of queer youth entanglement with the juvenile justice system, it is necessary to reduce the violence and discrimination they face either inside or outside of the system. If we are to address what is a pervasive problem, a public health framework for prevention must be adopted. This chapter outlines a public health approach to violence and examines the socially supported discrimination confronting queer youth in community institutions. Next, it describes similarities between the movement to ensure the safety of queer children and the intimate-partner-violence movement, which has adopted similar macro-level prevention strategies. The chapter also delineates three strategies that can be integrated into community institutions to protect queer youth and reduce their chances of extensive involvement in the juvenile justice or child welfare systems. The chapter concludes with a short discussion of various techniques that can aid advocates in implementing these strategies.

A Public Health Approach to Violence against Queer Youth

Because the violence queer children face is an aggressive reinforcement of society's devaluation of their individualized existence, neither a purely criminal justice approach nor a strategy that primarily focuses on repairing individual family relationships is sufficient. A criminal justice framework is useful for addressing stranger violence but is inherently limited in its ability to address interpersonal violence that occurs in private settings or among those who know each other well (Moore 1995). In addition, while there are therapeutic approaches that can assist in reuniting queer youth with their families, without community norms that recognize and support sexual and gender identity difference in children, those programs will remain underutilized. Although both the criminal justice system and family therapy have a role in reducing violence against queer youth, a broader community-based strategy is necessary to challenge the prejudice that promotes this violence. If the community environment can be changed to one that affirmatively provides safety and support for sexual minority youth, family and peer norms of violence and prejudice against these children will also shift.

A public health approach to violence is more empirical, proactive, and pragmatic than a purely criminal justice approach. It is based on the assumption that violence is a learned behavior that can be disrupted with targeted intervention that changes attitudes and behavior (Mercy et al. 1993). Heavily influenced by health sciences, it relies on research and data collection during both the earlier stages of defining the problem and identifying risk factors and the later stages of developing and evaluating prevention strategies (Mercy et al. 1993). Prevention efforts are "coordinated actions" that seek to prevent "predictable problems" while promoting "existing states of health and healthy functioning" and desired "potentialities in individuals and groups in their physical and sociocultural settings" (Bloom 1996, 2). Such "coordinated actions" to prevent the well-documented "predictable problems" driving queer youth into the juvenile justice system are what must be implemented to steer this population toward a healthy and safe adulthood.

A successful violence prevention program requires strategies for individual and community education as well as broad-based coalition building to support the adoption of policies that change social and organizational practices (Cohen and Swift 1999). While it must include the ability to effectively respond to individual events (tertiary intervention), successful prevention programs generally target specific at-risk populations and the community in which those populations reside. Advocates and policymakers have recognized the effectiveness of developing evidence-based interdisciplinary strategies to address complex social problems and have embraced this model to improve foster care (Duquette et al. 1997), combat youth violence (Prothrow-Stith 2004), reduce child abuse (Duquette 2007; Janus and Polachek 2009), and address intimate partner violence (Wolfe and Jaffe 1999; Parks et al. 2007). Such an approach is also appropriate to combat the discrimination and violence that face children society perceives as queer.

Recognizing and Diagnosing the Problem

The first step to ending the discrimination and violence against queer youth is to recognize the pervasiveness of the problem and the social structures that facilitate it. While societal attitudes toward adult sexuality may be shifting toward tolerance, the same cannot be said for attitudes on children's sexuality or gender differences. Judges continue to identify heterosexual modeling as socially important enough to allow discriminatory treatment of gays and lesbians (*Hernandez v. Robles* 2006; *Lofton v. Secretary of the Department of Children and Family Services* 2004; Robson 2001). Parental support for a child's gender nonconformity can result in a loss of custody or in a finding of neglect (*Smith v. Smith* 2007). Gays and lesbians are forbidden from acting as foster or adoptive parents in some states even as the need for foster parents and adoption increases (*Lofton* 2004; Arkansas Foster Care and Adoption Act of 2008). States continue to punish queer sexuality among teens more severely than heterosexual teen sexual conduct, often labeling queer youth who engage in consensual sex as sex offenders and sexual predators (*Higdon* 2008).

Such legally countenanced discrimination is a misguided and futile attempt to control child and adolescent sexuality. It encourages the social acceptance of homophobia and violence against children by naming their identity as unacceptable and potentially illegal. The long and ugly history of criminalizing and persecuting gay and lesbian behavior in the United States is reflected in our families, our schools, and our child welfare systems. Thus it is not surprising that queer youth can experience crushing levels of discrimination and violence both at home and in the community (Valentine 2008). The social effects of this are dramatic and well documented. Sexual-minority youth are overrepresented in the child welfare system (Sullivan et al. 2001) and the juvenile detention system (Irvine 2010) and are consistently estimated to constitute between 20 and 30 percent of the youth homeless population (Rew et al. 2001; Van Leeuwen et al. 2006; National Alliance to End Homelessness 2008).

It is doubtful that many would argue that the child welfare or juvenile justice systems are healthy places for any child. However, for a queer child the environments of these systems are extremely dangerous and work against the chance for positive outcomes from placement. If part of the mission of the child welfare and juvenile justice systems is to safeguard a child and to provide services that will minimize the potential for further state involvement, in the case of queer youth the systems are actually counterproductive.

The high rate of queer youth homelessness is caused in part by the negative treatment this population receives in out-of-home care (McHaelen et al. 2006; Ray 2006). One study found that 78 percent of queer youth were removed or ran away from their placements as a result of hostility toward their sexual orientation or gender identity (McHaelen et al. 2006). Homeless queer youth experience higher rates of substance abuse, sexually transmitted diseases, sexual victimization, and depression than do heterosexual homeless youth (Van Leeuwen et al. 2006). They are also at comparatively higher risk than the general adolescent population for being either victims or perpetrators of physical violence (id.). Each of these factors increases the likelihood that a child will either come into contact with or move deeper into the juvenile justice system, a system that is astonishingly maladapted to meeting their needs.

Unlike adults, once in the custody of the state children can be held in seemingly never-ending, vaguely defined, therapeutic confinement. This is especially true if their behavior fails to meet heteronormative behavioral standards of judges, foster families, probation officers, group home officials, or detention facility personnel. The child welfare system commonly considers gender nonconformity transgressive behavior that must be modified. Transgender youth in state care are often refused gender-appropriate clothing and access to supportive mental health or medical care (Majd et al. 2009). A youth's refusal to alter his or her appearance to comply with cultural expectations of gender is seen as a refusal to conform, to follow rules, or to become rehabilitated—all of which lead to punishments such as revocation of privileges and extensions of placements (Majd et al. 2009; Marksamer 2008; Tarzwell 2006).

Queer youth are also seen almost entirely through a lens of predatory sexuality. Thus they are often punished more severely for age-appropriate behaviors such as holding hands, dating, or other expressions of affection (Majd et al. 2009; Curtin 2002). They are routinely labeled as sex offenders, not because of any overtly aggressive behavior on their part but solely because of the perception of their sexuality (Majd et al. 2009; Valentine 2008).

It is also common for judges and detention facility administrators to demand that queer youth be isolated or sent to more heavily supervised facilities for their own protection. Isolating or segregating queer youth reduces their ability to access services, partake in education and training, or develop supportive relationships, all of which are necessary for a successful return to society. Queer youth experience being segregated as a form of punishment, regardless of the intention behind the practice (Majd et al. 2009). In 2006 a federal district court agreed, finding the practice of isolating queer youth to be inherently punitive and an unacceptable correctional practice for juveniles (*R.G. v. Kollor* 2006).

While individual foster families are considered optimal placements for children in state custody, they are not without significant danger to queer youth. Cultural or religious conflict with foster families or with residential placement staff is not uncommon. Such conflicts can result in a range of negative consequences, from rejection to attempts to forcibly convert the child to heterosexuality or to enforce gender conformity. Queer youth are the specific targets of conservative Christian groups who claim that reparative therapy can "cure" homosexuality or prevent "prehomosexuality" (Valentine 2008), and it is not unusual for foster families or residential placement facilities to pressure queer youth into this or similar therapy, directly undermining their sense of self (Gilliam 2004; see also *Bellmore v. United Methodist Children's Home of North Georgia* 2002).

Even if religious placements do not actively attempt to "change" queer youth, their actions cause harm. By implying that queer sexuality is bad, by firing queer adults, or by rejecting queer youth once their difference comes to light, they remove any chance for sexual-minority youth to envision themselves as safe and healthy adults (Gilliam 2004). Unfortunately, non-religious group homes and state-run facilities are also problematic and are rarely prepared to address the needs of queer youth. It is well established that queer youth in these facilities are at heightened risk of attack, and, in a surreal catch twenty-two, they are often punished with extended placements or moves to more secure detention when they complain or fight back to protect themselves (see, e.g., Marksamer 2008).

While not all queer children become victims, by their very nature the juvenile justice and child welfare systems are populated by overwhelmed, stressed, angry, and often dangerous children and adults. A child perceived as different, as isolated, as "queer," is likely to become a target and driven deeper into despair and to homelessness or further into the juvenile justice system. In order to counter this potentially negative spiral, programs and policies that protect, support, and nurture this population must be developed. Systemic institutional change has been proven effective at reducing homophobia and heterosexism faced by queer youth (Szalacha 2003). By supporting these children, allowing them to strengthen and build on their own inner resiliency, and by reconnecting them to their communities safely, we can begin to reduce the chances that they will enter the juvenile justice system.

Fortunately, there is a burgeoning collection of social science data on queer children with which to work. Child welfare organizations and advocacy groups have begun to use this data to design and evaluate successful strategies to support and protect queer youth (Hooks Wayman 2009; New England Network for Child, Youth, and Family Services 2007; Wilber and Marksamer 2006; Szalacha 2003). The social science data and established programs are the foundations on which local advocates can build successful frameworks for reducing violence against queer youth in their home communities. Moreover, the domestic– or intimate-partner-violence movement can provide queer youth advocates with something of a blueprint for developing these programs.

The Intimate-Partner-Violence Movement

The movement to address intimate partner violence (IPV) has had to confront issues of privacy, cultural diversity, and sexuality and can provide guidance for advocates for sexual minority youth. In addition, the IPV movement has recognized the importance of prevention programs targeting domestic and family violence (Wolfe and Jaffe 1999; Jenkins and Parmer Davidson 2001; Parks et al. 2007) and adolescent dating violence (Smith and Donnelly 2001). The programs developed to address these issues have much to offer those seeking to support queer youth.

While theorists are moving toward an integrated approach to explaining interpersonal violence (Jenkins and Parmer Davidson 2001), it is clear that like violence against queer youth, IPV takes place in a sociocultural environment that contributes to its extensiveness. Parks, Cohen, and Kravitz-Wirtz (2007) identify several specific norms that perpetuate this environment in the United States. These are the traditional gender roles that promote domination, control, and the objectification and oppression of women; the valuing of power and of maintaining control over others; the valuing of violence in which aggression is tolerated and blame is attributed to the victim; and the valuing of privacy, where norms associated with individual and family privacy are considered sacrosanct and silence and secrecy is fostered (id.). Smith and Donnelly suggest that similar social norms contribute to adolescent dating violence (2001). These are also the norms linked to the violent suppression of homosexuality (Dowd 2008, 22-23; Mayes 2001; Arriola 1998), a suppression that often begins in childhood with violence against queer youth.

Beyond the norms giving rise to both IPV and violence against queer youth, the movements to eradicate both have additional similarities. The intimate-partner-violence movement has struggled with issues of heterosexism and homophobia (Robson 1990; Knauer 1999) and denunciation by religious conservatives. It was not so long ago that political opposition to domestic violence legislation, funding for shelters, and other strategies designed to address the issue were seen as a radical attack on the traditional family (Ammons 1999; Colker 2006). These arguments are eerily similar to those now used to challenge programs for queer youth (Hirschfeld 2001; Valentine 2008). Finally, the IPV movement has had to confront issues of race, class, and culture in order to successfully serve a broad spectrum of victims, issues that also impact the provision of services to queer youth.

Recognizing the similarities between intimate partner violence and violence against queer youth provides guidance for those seeking to support and protect queer youth. It allows us to move forward faster by not reinventing the (entire) wheel and avoiding some of the mistakes made by those struggling to protect battered women. Understanding the similarities also allows for linkages among advocacy groups working to eradicate all forms of interpersonal violence, linkages that will strengthen community responses to violence based on traditional reactions to gender and sexual difference.

Community-Based Prevention Strategies to Support and Protect Queer Youth

Because violence directed at queer youth is supported by cultural norms, it is important that prevention strategies be directed at educating those who work with children and youth. This would include reforming college and graduate-level education but would also include the provision of additional education and training to those already working with children. However, education is by nature a long-term strategy. Thus, two additional approaches are necessary. The first of these is to create safe and supportive spaces for sexual minority youth within community institutions. Such spaces are necessary because attempts to change institutional environments often encounter significant opposition, and support and protection must be provided in the interim. Finally, it is also essential to specifically prohibit harassment and discrimination on the basis of sexual orientation and gender identity. Enumerated policies prohibiting harassment and discrimination on the basis of perceived sexual orientation or gender identity are necessary in order to confront the bias that creates the need for safe and supportive spaces in the first place and in order to reinforce the education and training provided to those who work with children.

Education and Training

Raising awareness of the underlying conditions that foster violence and the impact unchecked violence has on individuals and communities is an essential part of the spectrum of prevention. While it will be necessary to develop programs to educate children and families about sexual–minority youth, this cannot be done until the adults who work with children are themselves educated about the issues affecting this population (Szalacha 2003; Smith and Donnelly 2001). Education provides these professionals, regardless of their own sexual identity, with the tools to effect change within their individual institutions and to successfully advocate for change across their communities.

The IPV movement successfully changed the education and training provided to teachers, social workers, and health care personnel (Trubek and Farnham 2000). Today these professionals are unlikely to graduate without being introduced to the impact domestic violence has on their client populations as well as being provided skills to recognize and address it. Recognizing the importance of educating those most likely to see and intervene in the lives of battered women, IPV advocates also established a sustained curriculum of continuing education programs for criminal justice and legal professionals (Parker 2007, 298). This targeted education of community professionals was necessary before the development of successful strategies of prevention directed at individual abusers could occur. Educating those who work with children about the violence and prejudice facing queer youth is similarly necessary (Martin et al. 2009; McHaelen et al. 2006).

Unfortunately, while the benefits of providing services to adolescents in a culturally competent manner are well documented, higher education programs in social work and education fail to teach the skills necessary for the competent provision of services to queer youth (Martin et al. 2009; GLSEN and Harris Interactive 2008). One study found coverage of queer children lacking even in courses specifically devoted to child welfare and development (Martin et al. 2009). Thus it is unsurprising that most of those who work with children, either in child welfare institutions or in education, at best feel unprepared to work with queer youth and at worst are oblivious to their needs (Wornoff et al. 2006; GLSEN and Harris Interactive 2008; Irvine 2010).

However, the structures necessary to facilitate the provision of this education already exist. Most states require mandatory education levels for educators, those who administer youth facilities or child welfare programs, and social workers. Many states also require some form of continuing education for those who work with children in either an educational or a child welfare capacity. These requirements provide an opportunity to educate teachers, foster parents, social workers, and family counselors on the complex realities of working with queer youth.

Along with the existing structures within institutional systems that encourage or mandate training, advocates for youth have additional support when advocating for this type of education and training for staff. All major educational, mental, and physical health professional organizations have amended their ethical guidelines to require that queer children be treated in a safe, supportive, and affirming manner (see, e.g., American Academy of Pediatrics 2004; National Association of Social Workers 2008). There are also established guidelines and training programs on which to draw. The National Association of Social Workers, among others, has created curricula specifically aimed at educating social workers and other child welfare practitioners to better serve and respond to the needs of queer youth (*Moving the Margins* 2009; McHaelen et al. 2006), and there are similar programs for educational and legal professionals. Several states, such as California, Connecticut, Illinois, Michigan, New York, Utah, and Virginia, require some or all of their child welfare professionals be trained to work with queer youth and have developed programs easily adopted by other jurisdictions.

Nevertheless, even as the ability for advocates to successfully argue for the need to educate child welfare professionals about queer youth grows, additional strategies are necessary. Education and training take time to filter into the community, and protection must be provided to this population now. Therefore, along with providing education and training, we must take additional steps to protect those children currently facing violence and discrimination by instituting programs to ensure their safety.

Providing Safe Spaces and Supportive Services

Another part of the strategy to limit the dangers facing queer youth is the development of safe spaces and supportive services within community institutions. Like domestic violence shelters, safe spaces for queer youth allow them to escape abuse, access queer-positive services and information, and reclaim their dignity. Such programs do not have to be elaborate or costly. The mere presence of supportive adults within an institution can strengthen a child's ability to overcome stigma (Gastic and Johnson 2009) and reduces victimization (Goodenow et al. 2006). In schools, student-organized Gay/Straight Alliances (GSAs) are a structurally simple but highly effective source of support for queer youth. While sometimes opposed by conservative parents or community groups, GSAs provide a large measure of safety and acceptance regardless of whether an individual child actually joins (Goodenow et al. 2006). Similar to the presence of supportive adults, these groups can have a large impact on reducing queer youth alienation without requiring extensive institutional infrastructure.

Several states and localities have developed queer-friendly spaces for homeless youth or those in out-of-home care. Like domestic violence shelters, these programs provide a variety of services specifically supporting queer youth, including substance-abuse and safe-sex counseling, job training, mental health services, and family reunification counseling (Hooks Wayman 2009). Programs like Green Chimneys and the Ali Forney Center in New York, the Ruth Ellis Center in Detroit, and the Waltham House in Massachusetts are designed specifically to provide supportive and affirming services to queer youth. While the numbers of these facilities are growing, they are unable to meet the demand for their services.

Thus, while the development of supportive facilities may be politically or economically difficult, some queer-friendly space must be provided in all child welfare programs or juvenile justice facilities. Again this may be, at least initially, as simple as supportive staff or staff who are openly queer. Like the presence of GSAs in schools, open and supportive staff provide indicia of acceptance for vulnerable teens. Child welfare staff and youth in care routinely note the importance of an accepting atmosphere in helping queer youth feel safe in state care (Nolan 2006; Ragg et al. 2006). Other indicia of support such as posters providing queer-positive information or details of antidiscrimination policies are simple techniques many state agencies now use to create a safer and more secure environment for sexual-minority youth in their care.

The development of education programs and safe and supportive space for sexual-minority youth, while important, will have only limited effect without challenges to the homophobic and heterosexists norms that perpetuate the violence they face. As domestic violence shelters alone cannot reduce intimate partner violence, safe and supportive spaces for queer youth are only one part of a strategy to reduce the violence against them. The adoption of antiharassment and antidiscrimination policies is necessary to establish that institutions will not tolerate oppressive behavior based on negative perceptions of sexual orientation or gender identity.

Antiharassment and Antidiscrimination Policies

The enactment of queer-specific antiharassment and antidiscrimination polices is the most contentious of the strategies discussed here, but it is essential to the success of any prevention program seeking to reduce violence and discrimination against queer youth. The adoption of policies that specifically include sexual orientation and gender identity as protected categories ensures that queer youth are treated with safety and respect. Such policies increase the likelihood that adults within the institution will confront and intervene in antiqueer behavior and provide protection for those adults who wish to openly support sexual-minority youth. Specifically prohibiting antiqueer behavior fosters an environment in which violence and aggression is reframed as negative, regardless of the victim. As the United States Supreme Court has stated when discussing the importance of antidiscrimination laws, because it establishes clear expectations for compliance, enumeration is what makes "the duty not to discriminate concrete" (*Romer v. Evans* 1996, 628).

Although similar, antiharassment and antidiscrimination policies target different populations. Antiharassment policies are generally aimed at stopping peer aggression in schools or other settings. Antiqueer harassment is rampant in the education system and is linked to poor academic performance, exclusion from school activities, a lack of positive psychological development, and dropping out (Murdoch and Bolch 2005; Szalacha 2003). Policies prohibiting peer harassment, when coupled with an expectation of enforcement and compliance, can significantly reduce the level of peer harassment faced by queer youth (Szalacha 2003). A recent survey indicates that a majority of school principals recognize that it is important to include sexual orientation and gender identity in their antiharassment policies (GLSEN and Harris Interactive 2008). Less than a third of those schools with existing policies indicated they faced parental or community objections when enumerated policies were adopted (id.), and most principals believe that a majority of students, teachers, and school administrators would support efforts to address issues of school safety for queer youth and their families (id.).

However, while antiharassment policies are necessary, they must be written carefully to avoid unintended consequences similar to those created by the mandatory arrest policies now recognized by many in the IPV movement as antithetical to violence reduction. Thus advocates for queer youth must avoid lobbying for zero tolerance policies, which merely criminalize youth behavior and exempt administrators from positively engaging with issues of adolescent sexuality. Zero tolerance policies have not been shown to reduce aggressive behavior and, echoing the unintended consequences of mandatory arrest policies, may actually increase rates of misbehavior (American Psychological Association 2008). Advocates must argue for more nuanced and flexible policies that, while protecting queer youth, do not unnecessarily distance aggressive youth from the redemptive qualities of education and engagement.

Antidiscrimination policies are also essential in protecting queer youth in state custody. Such policies prohibit discrimination by state employees and may, depending on their breadth, prohibit discrimination by those who contract with the state to care for children, such as foster parents or organizations maintaining group homes or other residential facilities. Several jurisdictions have instituted policies prohibiting discrimination on the basis of sexual orientation, although fewer also prohibit discrimination on the basis of gender identity. A smaller number of states and cities specifically protect queer youth.

California is the only state that has adopted comprehensive protections for queer youth in foster care, known as the Foster Care Non-Discrimination Act. Connecticut has a policy whose purpose is to ensure that queer children and adolescents under the guardianship of the Department of Children and Families receive nondiscriminatory, safe, affirming, and nondetrimental services (Estrada and Marksamer 2006). New York has recently adopted and published queer-friendly policies that provide for staff training, established reporting and enforcement guidelines that are provided to youth in their care, and also established a committee to respond to requests or complaints from youth in placement (Majd et al. 2009). Unfortunately, the New York policy does not apply to contract agencies or to homeless shelters for teens and young adults, which severely limits its effectiveness. New York, like most states, contracts with private organizations to provide large portions of the services provided to children and adolescents. If outside organizations operating residential facilities or shelters are not required to operate in a nondiscriminatory manner, it is likely that queer youth will be discriminated against if placed there.

Implementation

Establishing policies to protect and support queer youth can be difficult because of institutional reluctance to be involved in the potentially explosive issue of child and youth sexuality. This is not unlike the initial resistance faced by those seeking to establish shelters and protection for battered women. However, advocates have a range of tools with which to build systemic support for queer youth. There is the depth of social science data, which both documents the critical need for prevention and evaluates a number of the programs developed to address the issue. There are also a number of successful programs, which can be easily adapted by local communities.

In addition, if faced with institutional reluctance, there are a series of successful lawsuits by queer youth harmed in schools and in state care that can be used to persuade institutional leaders of the economic as well as moral reasoning for providing such training (see, e.g., *Nabozny* 1996; *Henkle* 2001; *R.G.* 2006; *Rodriguez* 2006). These cases and others like them have persuaded school boards and state agencies around the country of the importance of training personnel to care properly for all children in their custody. While litigation is by nature a limited strategy, its effects can be far-reaching. Educating school administrators, state officials, and child welfare organizations about institutional liability for failure to protect queer youth can create unexpected support from institutional leaders.

Finally, even though it may take effort, creative negotiations pursued in a good-faith attempt to find common ground can result in significant successes for queer youth. Martha Minow has described this process as "convergence" and offers as an example the successful negotiations between the city of San Francisco and the Roman Catholic Archdiocese over the provision of spousal benefits for domestic partners (Minow 2008). One example of convergence in negotiations directly benefiting queer youth is provided by the year-long process to adopt a safe schools policy in Modesto, California (Doty 2001). There, guided by the principles of public engagement and alternative dispute resolution, a heavily divided community was able to move past overheated rhetoric and religious animosity to adopt a school safety policy that specifically references sexual orientation and allows the establishment of queer-friendly school programs. To ensure successful implementation of the antiharassment policies and other programs for gay and lesbian students, it was necessary to garner support from all stakeholders in the community, including those representing religious and politically conservative viewpoints (id.). The process would probably not have been undertaken without the school board recognizing its legal liability to protect queer youth, but it would not have been successful without the extensive outreach to and education of numerous community stakeholders.

Even when convergence is not immediately possible, good faith compromise while all sides continue to work towards convergence can overcome political gulfs around sexuality. Thus, where antidiscrimination policies cannot be immediately adopted, education and training of those who work with children, along with the provision of safe and supportive spaces for queer youth, can significantly reduce the violence and discrimination they face. Safer community institutions for queer youth will significantly reduce their overrepresentation in the child welfare and juvenile justice systems and reduce their numbers in the youth homeless populations. Safer communities for queer youth will provide this population of children a better chance at a stable and healthy future.

With a concerted effort, advocates for battered women established a community prevention framework to challenge the norms that support intimate partner violence. A similar framework—one that seeks to educate those who work with children, create safe and supportive spaces for queer youth, and prohibit violence and discrimination on the basis of sexual and gender identity—should be adopted to protect children perceived as being sexually different. The sociological research, successfully evaluated programs, articulated guidelines, and litigation on which to build better futures for queer youth already exist. All that is necessary is for advocates for these children to press forward.

NOTES

1. Queer or sexual-minority youth are minors who either self-identify as, or are perceived as and targeted for being, lesbian, gay, bisexual, transgender, or gender nonconforming. Child welfare professionals are beginning to understand that it is the perception of difference by others that puts a child at risk, not the child's personal identification. For example, the city of New York recently issued a policy directive to its child protective workers warning them that it is the caretaker's perception of a child being LGBTQ that places the child at risk of maltreatment, regardless of how the child identifies. City of New York, Administration of Children's Services, Division of Child Protection. 2009. *Assessing Safety of LGBTQ Children and Youth*. New York: author.

2. Because children are punished for how they are perceived, the term "gender nonconformity" will generally be used rather than "transgender," even though both terms extensively overlap (see Fedders 2006 and Ryan 2003). The term "transgender" will be used in discussions of youth who are actively seeking services (such as medical assistance) to establish a specific identity.

3. Heterosexism is defined as an "overt or tacit bias against non-heterosexuals based on a belief in the superiority or, sometimes, the omnipresence of heterosexuality. Heterosexism is a broader term than homophobia in that it need not imply the fear and loathing the latter term suggests. Heterosexism can describe seemingly benign [but harmful] behavior based on the assumption that heterosexuality is the norm" (Hirschfeld 2001, 617-18).

REFERENCES

American Academy of Pediatrics, B. Frankowski. 2004. Guidance for the clinician in rendering pediatric care: Sexual orientation and adolescents. *Pediatrics* 113 (6): 1827-32.

American Psychological Association, Zero Tolerance Task Force. 2008. Are zero tolerance policies effective in schools? An evidentiary review and recommendations. *American Psychologist* 63 (9): 852-62.

Ammons, L. 1999. What's god got to do with it? Church and state collaboration in the subordination of women and domestic violence. *Rutgers Law Review* 51: 1207-88.

Arkansas Foster Care and Adoption Act of 2008, AR St § 9-8-304.

Arriola, E. R. 1998. The penalties for puppy love: Institutionalized violence against lesbian, gay, bisexual, and transgendered youth. *Journal of Gender, Race, and Justice* 1: 429-70.

Bellmore v. United Methodist Children's Home of North Georgia. 2002. Complaint available at http://www.lambdalegal.org/our-work/in-court/complaints/bellmore-v-united-methodist.html.

Bloom, M. 1996. *Primary Prevention Practices.* Thousand Oaks, CA: Sage Publications.

Cohen, L., and S. Swift. 1999. The spectrum of prevention: Developing a comprehensive approach to injury prevention. *Injury Prevention* 5 (3): 203-7.

Colker, R. 2006. Marriage mimicry: The law of domestic violence. *William and Mary Law Review* 47: 1841-85.

Curtin, M. 2002. Lesbian and bisexual girls in the juvenile justice system. *Child and Adolescent Social Work Journal* 19 (4): 285-301.

Doty, D. S. 2001. Finding a third way: The use of public engagement and ADR to bring school communities together for the safety of gay students. *Hastings Women's Law Journal* 12: 39-94.

Dowd, N. E. 2008. Masculinities and feminist legal theory. *Wisconsin Journal of Law, Gender & Society* 23: 201-46.

Duquette, D. 2007. Looking ahead: A personal vision of the future of child welfare law. *University of Michigan Journal of Law Reform* 41: 317-57.

Duquette, D. N., S. K. Danziger, J. M. Abbey, and K. S. Seefelt. 1997. We know better than we do: A policy framework for child welfare reform. *University of Michigan Journal of Law Reform* 31: 93-157.

Estrada, R., and J. Marksamer. 2006. Lesbian, gay, bisexual, and transgender young people in state custody: Making the child welfare and juvenile justice systems safe for all youth through litigation, advocacy, and education. *Temple Law Review* 79: 415-38.

Fedders, B. 2006. Coming out for kids: Recognizing and respecting LGBTQ youth. *Nevada Law Journal* 6: 774-804.

Gastic, B., and D. Johnson. 2009. Teacher-mentors and the educational resilience of sexual minority youth. *Journal of Gay and Lesbian Social Services* 21: 219-31.

Gilliam, J. W. 2004. Toward providing a welcoming home for all: Enacting a new approach to address the longstanding problems lesbian, gay, bisexual, and transgender youth face in the foster care system. *Loyola of Los Angeles Law Review* 37: 1037-63.

Gipson, L. M. 2002. Poverty, race, and LGBT youth. *Poverty and Race* 11 (2): 1-11.

GLSEN and Harris Interactive. 2008. *The Principal's Perspective: School Safety, Bullying, and Harassment; A Survey of Public School Principals.* New York: GLSEN.

Goodenow, C., L. Szalacha, and K. Westheimer. 2006. School support groups, other school factors, and the safety of sexual minority adolescents. *Psychology in the Schools* 43 (5): 573-89.

Greytak, E. A., J. G. Kosciw, and E. M. Diaz. 2009. *Harsh Realities: The Experiences of Transgender Youth in Our Nation's Schools.* New York: GLSEN.

Henkle v. Gregory. 2001. 150 F. Supp.2d 1067.

Hernandez v. Robles. 2006. 855 N.E.2d 1.

Higdon, M. J. 2008. Queer teens and legislative bullies: The cruel and invidious discrimination behind heterosexist statutory rape laws. *University of California at Davis Law Review* 42: 195-253.

Hirschfeld, S. 2001. Moving beyond the safety zone: A staff development approach to anti-heterosexist education. *Fordham Urban Law Journal* 29: 611-34.

Hooks Wayman, R. 2009. Homeless queer youth: National perspectives on research, best practices, and evidence-based interventions *Seattle Journal for Social Justice* 7: 587-623.

Irvine, A. 2010. "We've had three of them": Addressing the invisibility of lesbian, gay, bisexual, and gender nonconforming youth in the juvenile justice system. *Columbia Journal of Gender and Law* 19 (3): 675-701.

Janus, E. S., and E. A. Polachek. 2009. A crooked picture: Reframing the problem of child sexual abuse. *William Mitchell Law Review* 36: 142-68.

Jenkins, P., and B. Parmer Davidson. 2001. *Stopping Domestic Violence: How a Community Can Prevent Spousal Abuse.* New York: Kluwer Academic.

Knauer, N. J. 1999. Same-sex domestic violence: Claiming a domestic sphere while risking negative stereotypes. *Temple Political and Civil Rights Law Review* 8: 325-50.

Lofton v. Secretary of the Department of Children and Family Services. 2004. 358 F.3d 804.

Majd, K., J. Marksamer, and C. Reyes. 2009. *Hidden Injustice: Lesbian, Gay, Bisexual, and Transgender Youth in Juvenile Courts.* Legal Services for Children, National Juvenile Defenders Center, and National Center for Lesbian Rights.

Marksamer, J. 2008. And by the way do you know he thinks he's a girl? The failures of law, policy, and legal representation for transgender youth in juvenile delinquency courts. *Sexual Research and Social Policy* 5 (1): 72-92.

Martin, J. I., L. Messinger, R. Kull, J. Homes, F. Bermudez, and S. Sommer. 2009. *Council on Social Work Education-Lambda Legal Study of LGBT Issues in Social Work.* Alexandria VA: Council on Social Work Education.

Mayes, T. A. 2001. Confronting same-sex, student-to-student sexual harassment: Recommendations for educators and policy makers. *Fordham Urban Law Journal* 29: 641-83.

McHaelen, R., R. Wornoff, and G. Mallon. 2006. Bridges, barriers, and boundaries: A model curriculum for training youth service professionals to provide culturally competent service for sexual and gender-minority youth in care. *Child Welfare* 85 (2): 407-36.

Mercy, J., M. Rosenberg, K. Powell, C. Broome, and W. Roper. 1993. Public health policy for preventing violence. *Health Affairs* 12 (4): 7-29.

Minow, M. 2008. Is pluralism an ideal or a compromise? An essay for Carol Weisbrod. *Connecticut Law Review* 40: 1287-1313.

Moore, M. H. 1995. Public health and criminal justice approaches to prevention. *Crime and Justice* 19: 237-62.

Moving the Margins: Training Curriculum for Child Welfare Services with Lesbian, Gay, Bisexual, Transgender, and Questioning (LGBTQ) Youth in Out-of-Home Care. 2009. National Association of Social Workers and Lambda Legal Defense and Education Fund.

Murdoch, T., and M. Bolch. 2005. Risk and protective factors for poor school adjustment in lesbian, gay, and bisexual (lgb) high school youth: Variable and person-centered analyses. *Psychology in the Schools* 42 (2): 159-72.

Nabozny v. Podlesny. 1996. 92 F.3d 446.

National Alliance to End Homelessness. 2008. *Incidence and Vulnerability of LGBTQ Homeless Youth*. Washington, DC: author.

National Association of Social Workers. 2008. *Code of Ethics*. Washington, DC: author.

New England Network for Child, Youth, and Family Services. 2007. *Reach Out: Enhancing Services to Out-of-Home Gay, Lesbian, Bisexual, Transgender, Queer, and Questioning Youth, Evaluation 2004-2006*. Burlington, VT: author.

Nolan, T. 2006. Outcomes for a transitional living program serving LGBTQ youth in New York City. *Child Welfare* 85 (2): 385-406.

Parker, H. 2007. Access denied: The disconnect between statutory and actual access to child support for civil protection order petitioners. *University of Cincinnati Law Review* 76: 271-98.

Parks, L. F., L. Cohen, and N. Kravitz-Wirth. 2007. *Poised for Prevention: Advancing Promising Approaches to Primary Prevention of Intimate Partner Violence*. Oakland, CA: Prevention Institute.

Peters, A. J. 2003. Isolation or inclusion: Creating safe spaces for lesbian and gay youth. *Families in Society* 84 (3): 331–37.

Prothrow-Stith, D. 2004. Strengthening the collaboration between public health and criminal justice to prevent violence. *Journal of Law, Medicine, and Ethics* 32: 82-89.

R.G. v. Koller. 2006. 415 F. Supp.2d 1129.

Ragg, D. M., D. Patrick, and M. Ziefert. 2006. Slamming the closet door: Working with gay and lesbian youth in care. *Child Welfare* 85 (2): 243-65.

Ray, N. 2006. *Lesbian, Gay, Bisexual, and Transgender Youth: An Epidemic of Homelessness*. New York: National Gay and Lesbian Task Force Policy Institute and the National Coalition for the Homeless.

Reck, J. 2009. Homeless gay and transgender youth of color in San Francisco: "No one likes street kids"—even in the Castro. *Journal of LGBT Youth* 6: 223-42.

Rew, L., M. Taylor-Seehafer, N. Thomas, and R. Yockey. 2001. Correlates of resilience in homeless adolescents. *Journal of Nursing Scholarship* 33 (1): 37-38.

Rew, Lynn, T. A. Whittaker, M. A. Taylor-Seehafer, and L. R. Smith. 2005. Sexual health risks and protective resources in gay, lesbian, bisexual, and heterosexual homeless youth. *Journal for Specialists in Pediatric Nursing* 10 (1): 11-19.

Robson, R. 2001. Our children: Kids of queer parents and kids who are queer; Looking at sexual minority rights from a different perspective. *Albany Law Review* 64: 915-48.

Robson, R. 1990. Lavender bruises: Intra-lesbian violence, law, and lesbian legal theory. *Golden Gate University Law Review* 20: 567-91.

Rodriguez v. Johnson. 2006. No. 06 CV 00214 (S.D. N.Y. Nov. 9, 2006) (stipulated order of settlement settling a claim against the New York State Office of Children and Family Services for discriminatory treatment of transgender youth while in state custody).

Romer v. Evans. 1996. 517 U.S. 620.

Rosenwald, M. 2009. A glimpse within: An exploratory study of child welfare agencies' practices with LGBTQ youth. *Journal of Gay & Lesbian Social Services* 21: 343-56.

Ryan, C. 2003. Lesbian, gay, bisexual, and transgender youth: Health concerns, services, and care. *Clinical Research and Regulatory Affairs* 20 (2): 137-58.

Savin-Williams, R. 2005. *The New Gay Teenager.* Cambridge, MA: Harvard University Press.

Smith, D. M., and J. Donnelly. 2001. Adolescent dating violence: A multi-systemic approach of enhancing awareness in educators, parents, and society. *Journal of Prevention and Intervention in the Community* 21 (1): 53–64.

Smith v. Smith, No. 05 JE 42, 2007 WL 901599 (Ohio App. Mar. 23, 2007), appeal denied, 873 N.E.2d 1315 (Ohio 2007).

Sullivan, C., S. Sommer, and J. Moff. 2001. *Youth in the Margins: A Report on the Unmet Needs of Lesbian, Gay, Bisexual, and Transgender Adolescents in Foster Care.* New York: Lambda Legal Defense and Education Fund.

Szalacha, L. A. 2003. Safer sexual diversity climates: Lessons learned from an evaluation of Massachusetts safe schools program for gay and lesbian students. *American Journal of Education* 110 (1): 58-88.

Tarzwell, S. 2006. The gender lines are marked with razor wire: Addressing state prison policies and practices for the management of transgender prisoners. *Columbia Human Rights Law Review* 38: 167-219.

Trubek, L., and J. Farnham. 2000. Social justice collaboratives: Multidisciplinary practices for people. *Clinical Law Review* 7: 227-72.

Valentine, S. E. 2008. Traditional advocacy for nontraditional youth: Rethinking best interest for the queer child. *Michigan State Law Review* 2008 (4): 1053-1113.

Van Leeuwen, J., et al. 2006. Lesbian, gay, bisexual homeless youth: An eight-city public health perspective. *Child Welfare* 85 (2): 151-70.

Wilber, S., C. Ryan, and J. Marksamer. 2006. *CWLA Best Practices Guidelines: Serving LGBT Youth in Out-of-Home Care.* Washington, DC: Child Welfare League of America.

Wolfe, D. A., and P. G. Jaffe. 1999. Emerging strategies in the prevention of domestic violence. *Future Child* 9 (3): 133-44.

Wornoff, R., R. Estrada, and S. Sommer. 2006. *Out of the Margins: A Report on the Regional Listening Forums Highlighting the Experiences of Lesbian, Gay, Bisexual, Transgender, and Questioning Youth in Care.* Washington, DC: Child Welfare League of America.

III

Legal Socialization and Policing

9

Deterring Serious and Chronic Offenders

Research Findings and Policy Thoughts
from the Pathways to Desistance Study

THOMAS A. LOUGHRAN, ALEX R. PIQUERO,
JEFFREY FAGAN, AND EDWARD P. MULVEY

Introduction

Deterrence, as traditionally hypothesized, is based upon the logic that criminal sanctions that are certain, severe, and swift will work to increase perceived sanction risk and cost, and in turn reduce criminal activity (Beccaria 1764; Zimring and Hawkins 1973; Andenaes 1974). Offenders' perceptions of certainty and severity are closely linked to economic and criminological theories of rational choice. A rational would-be offender will engage in crimes that are attractive because the expected rewards will exceed the expected costs (Becker 1968; Cornish and Clarke 1986). The expected costs of crime can be operationalized as an individual's perception of the severity of any sanctions, weighted by the perceived risk of detection. Thus, if this expected cost of crime can be made large enough to exceed any potential rewards, increasing an individual's perception of either costs or risks (or both) will cause him or her to see a decision to engage in crime as no longer rational. Simply put, the individual will be deterred from committing the crime.

There is a substantial body of empirical research testing theoretical and perceptual deterrence theory, dealing mainly with samples of adults, nonoffenders, or primarily nonserious offenders (Grasmick and Bursik 1990; Nagin 1998; Nagin and Paternoster 1993; Nagin and Pogarsky 2001, 2003; Piquero and Tibbetts 1996). This literature demonstrates an important, albeit often weak, relation between sanction-threat perceptions and criminal activity: what people think about the likelihood of getting caught and the likely sanction is related to level of criminal activity. However, an important limitation on this literature is that there is a lack of research attention to active and serious offenders, the precise group for whom studies of deterrence are ultimately most relevant (Apospori and Paternoster 1992; Decker et al. 1993; Piquero and Rengert 1999). The dearth of findings among serious offending adolescents presents a particularly important limitation, given the high level of involvement of this group in crime and the developmental deficits that may affect their cognition and decision-making ability with respect to crime (Steinberg and Scott 2003). Accordingly, a critical meta-policy question is whether or not more seriously or chronically offending adolescents consider and respond to sanction threats in their decision making and, by extension, whether they can actually be deterred at all (cf. Fagan and Piquero 2007).

This chapter reviews recent evidence from the Pathways to Desistance Study about deterrence (hereafter called "the Pathways study"). This study is a multisite, longitudinal sample of over thirteen hundred adolescent felony offenders that includes regular interviews with these adolescents as they moved from adolescence into early adulthood. The Pathways study addresses the issue of perceptions of deterrence directly and illuminates the mechanisms of deterrence for serious offenders. In this chapter, we provide a brief overview of current evidence on the role of deterrence and perceptions developed to date from the Pathways study. We consider possible policy implications and outline avenues for future research and policy development.

The chapter unfolds in five sections. First, we provide a brief summary of the Pathways to Desistance Study. Second, we review empirical evidence that demonstrates the rationality of high-risk adolescents (many of whom are now young adults) regarding involvement in crime. We show that offenders do consider rational-choice perceptions in their offending decisions, and can even be subclassified according to observed heterogeneity in their perceptions of risk and costs. Third, we discuss the elasticity and malleability of these perceptions, and whether adolescent offenders act differently when they change risk and cost perceptions. Fourth, we discuss extensions of findings to policy efforts aimed at maximizing deterrence among this group of offenders. Finally, we conclude with a discussion of future directions for theory and research.

The Pathways to Desistance Study

The Pathways to Desistance Study is an ongoing, multisite, longitudinal investigation of the transition from adolescence to young adulthood in serious adolescent offenders. Participants are adolescents who were adjudicated delinquent in juvenile court or found guilty in criminal court of a serious offense (almost entirely felony offenses) in either Maricopa County, Arizona, or Philadelphia, Pennsylvania. These youth were ages fourteen to seventeen at the start of the study. A total of 1,354 adolescents were enrolled, representing approximately one in three adolescents adjudicated on the enumerated charges in each locale during the recruitment period (November 2000 through January 2003). The study sample is mostly non-white (44.6 percent African American, 30.2 percent Hispanic) and male (86.4 percent).

Interviews were initially conducted with the adolescents at seven consecutive six-month periods, followed by yearly interviews thereafter. Information on the rationale and overall design of the study can be found in Mulvey et al. (2004), while details of the procedures for recruitment, a description of the full sample, and other aspects of the study methods are discussed in Schubert et al. (2004). In addition to findings on deterrence, the study has also produced research on other legal issues, including institutional placement and service provision (Loughran et al. 2009; Mulvey et al. 2007), community reentry (Chung et al. 2007; Steinberg et al. 2004), transfer to adult court (Schubert et al., 2010; Loughran et al., 2010), and legal socialization (Piquero et al. 2005; Fagan and Piquero 2007), as well as other, extralegal areas, such as patterns of offending (Mulvey et al. 2010), the effects of treatment for drug use/abuse (Chassin et al. 2010; Losoya et al. 2008), and acculturation and illegal activities (Knight et al. 2009). A full list of study measures and publications can be found at http://www.pathwaysstudy.pitt.edu/.

The Pathways measures of illegal behavior are based on both individual self-reported offenses and official arrest records that are measured longitudinally. The Pathways data also include rich longitudinal self-reported measures of individual perceptions of the risks, costs, and rewards of crime. Prior empirical evidence on deterrence suggests that offending involves both personal and social rewards and that punishment associated with offending may have distinct social and personal costs, may emanate from both formal and informal sources of social control, and are perhaps capable of changing within individuals over time (Williams and Hawkins 1986; Nagin 1998). As a result, indices of risks, costs, and rewards used in this study address the adolescent's perceived likelihood of detection and punishment for any of several types of offenses (Nagin and Paternoster 1994). This wealth of observation on both offending and perceptions presents a unique opportunity to study multiple deterrence-related questions in an offender-based sample.

Do Offenders Consider the Costs and Benefits of Crime in the Decision to Offend?

Beyond simply forming perceptions of certainty and severity of sanctions and rewards of crime, individuals will be deterred only if they actively and dynamically *consider and weigh* these perceptions when contemplating crime decisions. A first question is thus whether perceptions of risks and costs to offending even matter to active offenders. Furthermore, if these perceptions are actively considered by serious offenders, is there heterogeneity in these perceptions that may permit an assessment of individual variability in propensity to be deterred? In other words, are there differences within the offender population such that some of these individuals are more/less sensitive to the costs/benefits of criminal offending?

Fagan and Piquero (2007) consider the role of rational-choice perceptions—including risk, reward, and social and personal costs—in explaining individual offending trajectories in the Pathways data. They find evidence that rational-choice perceptual measures are associated with differences in offending trajectories and desistance. Specifically, when punishment risks and costs were salient in individuals, crime rates tended to be lower over time—both risk perceptions and evaluations of experienced punishment compete with perceived and experienced rewards of crime to influence individual offending trajectories. Fagan and Piquero argue that these factors work through the mechanism of legal socialization, that is, the internalization of legal rules and norms that regulate social and antisocial behaviors, to directly influence offending decisions. They also argue, however, that both mental health and developmental maturity moderate the effects of perceived crime risks and costs on criminal offending, indicating that the costs/benefits-to-crime relationship is not entirely general and may be shifted by other individual characteristics.

These results establish a necessary baseline for showing that even the most serious offenders can be deterred under certain conditions—specifically that, at least for some, rational-choice perceptions associated with the costs/benefits of offending do play some role in offender decision-making processes. Yet, it appears that, even within this class of serious and more seasoned offenders, there is variability in amenability to deterrence. Some of this variability might be attributable, as Fagan and Piquero point out, to developmental differences among these adolescents—some individuals may simply be older or more mature, and thus factors like costs and risk mean more to them in real terms. Alternatively, it is possible there may be other sources of variability in this group that are related to more stable individual differences.

Loughran, Piquero, Fagan, and Mulvey (in press) extend the reasoning of Fagan and Piquero (2007) by directly exploring heterogeneity in perceptions of risks, costs, and rewards to crime among the Pathways sample. They show that perceptions may evolve over time differentially among adolescent offenders. Important and *identifiable* differences in the sample based on offending perceptions suggest that amenability to deterrence varies widely among this group. Loughran et al. (in press) conclude that accumulated offending experience provides a simple way to decompose the sample and define very different groups of offenders in terms of their rational-choice perceptions. Specifically, they identified a group of high-rate offenders who display lower perceived risks of detection and punishment for crime and also higher perceived rewards from crime. Alternately, they found a group of low-rate offenders who report higher perceived risk and lower perceived reward regarding offending. Finally, they identified a third group of medium-rate offenders, whose perceptions of risk and reward fell in between those of the first two groups. Furthermore, these differences seem to be stable over time—the average levels of risk and reward perceptions between the three offending types identified did not converge after thirty-six months. The differences were robust to age or maturity effects that otherwise might have influenced group composition.

In arguing the importance of these findings, Loughran et al. advance the notion of *differential deterrence,* a term they intend to refer to the significant amount of heterogeneity that exists across serious juvenile offenders with respect to their decision-making calculus, perceptions of rational-choice components, and involvement in criminal activity. Loughran et al. demonstrate heterogeneity in the mechanisms of deterrence among serious adolescent offenders and conclude that some active offenders may be more deterrable than others, in that different groups of offenders may react and adjust their sanction-threat perceptions in significantly different ways. This underscores the notion that some serious offenders may be sensitive to changes in criminal justice efforts aimed at making crime less beneficial and more costly, while the signals of increased risk and cost may be missed by others.

This set of results opens the door to several other questions regarding deterrability: are these perceptions dynamic and thus changing over time in response to offending and its consequences, or are these perceptions static and thus largely insensitive to change and updating within individuals? Does the makeup of cost/benefit perceptions matter to some offenders more than others, and does this vary by individual characteristics and/or over time? Can influencing or changing perceptions actually affect offending behavior for such a serious group of offending adolescents, or do they ultimately not matter in the decision to offend? These results led us to the next set of studies, which ask the following question: if perceptions of risk change over time, how are these changes operationalized into decisions to commit or avoid crime, and how do these patterns vary among this group over time?

How Are Changes in Risk Operationalized among Offenders?

According to the original rational-choice model outlined by Becker (1968), if prospective criminals do weigh sanction and reward perceptions, they can be deterred by (a) increasing the costs to committing crimes, (b) decreasing the benefits to committing crimes, or (c) increasing the probability of detection, i.e., risk. The last of these mechanisms relies primarily on using arrest or the threat of arrest to deter individuals from committing crimes. However, arresting an individual will only deter him or her if two things ultimately happen. The risk perception of detection must *increase* in response to an arrest, and this increase in risk perception must lead to a *reduction* in the probability of reoffending. Both of these linkages must be active in order for deterrence to operate as hypothesized (Pogarsky et al. 2004). By examining both linkages among juveniles in the deep end of the system, we can essentially ask if these types of juveniles are in fact "deterrable" by this mechanism.

Anwar and Loughran (2011) explore the first of these two linkages in the Pathways data: do adolescent felony offenders update their subjective beliefs about certainty risk perceptions as they accumulate additional information about both offending and arrests, including undetected offenses? Their model to test this hypothesis is based on the concept of Bayesian learning theory, which predicts that previously held subjective beliefs will be adjusted, or updated, in response to newly observed information, known as empirical signals (in this case the ratio of number of arrests to self-reported crimes).

First, it is possible that an individual could lower his or her threat perception, rather than raise it, as the result of an arrest. Pogarsky and Piquero (2003) advanced the term "reset" to indicate the within-individual response of a lowered threat perception in response to being punished for an illegal act. Resetting is the process by which individuals revert their sanction-threat perceptions back to some level in response to the sanction as opposed to increasing their sanction-threat perception—as deterrence theory would anticipate. An individual who experiences punishment may reset his or her view of the punishment as a chance event that is unlikely to happen again—especially so soon after the offense that led to the punishment experience.

For individuals who are resetting, then, not only would an arrest not have a deterrent effect, but to the contrary it would encourage offending.

The analyses conducted by Anwar and Loughran (2011) demonstrated that, as is the case with nonoffenders (Pogarsky et al. 2004; Lochner 2007; Matsueda et al. 2006), individuals in the Pathways sample *do* tend to upwardly adjust their risk perceptions, by about 5 percent per arrest on average. This is a necessary condition for deterrence. However, when offending is undetected or avoids a legal reaction, individuals actually lower their perceptions of risk. This evidence suggests both symmetry in offenders' updating processes and a general fluidity in sanction-threat perceptions.

Anwar and Loughran show two other interesting, and policy-relevant, extensions to this basic updating process. The first is an "experience effect." Specifically, as predicted by Bayesian learning theory, individuals who are far along in their criminal careers might become quite certain about what their true arrest rate is and will therefore no longer update their risk perceptions based on their new experiences. These individuals may be "maxed-out" on information, and consequently, arresting them has no effect on their subsequent risk perceptions because they are quite certain in their perception already. This implies there is no longer a deterrent effect to arrests, at least in the sense of increasing sanction-risk perceptions to crime. In such instances where experience trumps new information, sanction threats may be only able to influence certain subgroups of the offender population (see also Parker and Grasmick 1979; Pogarsky 2002). The balance of this population might then be "undeterrable."

Anwar and Loughran show evidence that confirms such an experience effect. First, the weight placed on the prior belief is significantly greater for more experienced offenders. Also, the effect of an arrest on updated perceptions is significantly weaker for experienced offenders. Both results suggest that for those offenders further along in their criminal careers, arrests have a weaker perceptual deterrent effect, and, by extension, arrests early on in an individual's criminal career, versus those later on, may produce a greater deterrent effect. This highlights an interesting but understudied issue in criminological research: the relationship between accumulated offending experience and sanction-threat perceptions (Horney and Marshall 1992).

The second extension suggested by Anwar and Loughran (2011) concerns the observation that the risk-updating process may be crime specific. In this view, experiencing an arrest for one type of crime appears to affect only perceptions for that certain crime, rather than all crime-risk perceptions, at least at the level of income-generating (e.g., stealing) versus aggressive (e.g., assault) crimes. The policy relevance of this possibility seems clear. If risk-perception updating is crime specific, then police crackdowns on one type of crime are unlikely to have a deterrent effect on other crimes, and may even potentially encourage other crimes if police shift limited resources away from detecting certain crimes or by inducing a substitution effect (Nagin 1998). However, if risk perceptions are not crime specific, then cracking down on a specific crime will have a global deterrent effect. At least for the adolescents in the Pathways study, crime-specific updating implies that policies targeting specific types of offending may be more effective at deterring individuals from engaging in them than general polices aimed at overall crime reduction. If a police force has limited resources and it decides to target a specific crime, it will probably have to shift its focus away from other crimes, which may result in a reduction, among offenders, regarding the sanction risks for those other crimes. The results of Anwar and Loughran's analysis imply that individuals may respond to this by substituting out of the crime that police are targeting into other crimes with lower risks.

As mentioned earlier, the fact that individuals update their subjective risk perceptions in response to arrest is a necessary condition for deterrence. Yet observation of this connection between arrest and risk perception may ultimately be insufficient to finish that job if these changes in risk perceptions do not result in changes in offending behavior. Therefore, we ask whether changes in risk perceptions are associated with subsequent changes in behavior among serious offending juveniles, and if so, how do these changes manifest across different levels of risk perceptions?

There is a substantial body of evidence that has repeatedly demonstrated a small but significant "certainty effect," that is, a negative association between perceived certainty of detection and crime (Paternoster 1987; Nagin 1998). Again, however, much of these findings are derived from samples of nonoffenders, and the effects tend not to be large (Pratt and Cullen 2005). Therefore, it is uncertain whether there is a deterrent effect from increased risk perceptions among more seasoned adolescent felony offenders. Even if such risk-certainty deterrent effects do exist, it remains unknown whether the effect is constant across the risk spectrum or if there is a "tipping point" threshold above which changes in risk deter but below which they do not.

To examine these possibilities, Loughran, Pogarsky, Piquero, and Paternoster (2010) investigated the presence and salience of a "certainty" effect among the serious offenders in the Pathways study. While these investigators found strong evidence of a negative association between risk and self-reported offending, they also uncovered some important features of the *func-*

tional form of this relationship, i.e., its shape along different points of the risk continuum. The first point made is that there is strong evidence of nonlinearity in the risk-offending relationship. Linearity implies that increases in the perception of risk would be associated with similar decreases in reported offending regardless of the individual's prior risk perception—for instance, a 10 percent increase in risk from 10 percent to 20 percent would have the same magnitude in reduction of offending as a change from, say, 50 percent to 60 percent or 80 percent to 90 percent. Their analyses indicate that this is not the case.

Instead, Loughran et al. (2010a) find that, while increases in risk for those individuals in the midrange of the risk continuum (i.e., 30 percent–90 percent) are associated with a linear decline in the likelihood of offending, the probability of offending for individuals in the lower end of the risk continuum (i.e., < 30 percent) is relatively insensitive to sanction risk. Among this group, Loughran et al. (2010a) find no evidence of any certainty effect at all, i.e., increases in sanction risk were *not* associated with a reduction in offending. There appears to be a "tipping effect," or detection-probability threshold, that must be reached before any deterrent effect can be realized. Individual offenders deem law enforcement capabilities and sanction-threat perceptions to, in fact, be credible only when they are above that threshold. By extension, those offenders who do not deem such threats credible in the first place are unlikely to be deterred by greater sanction risks. Additionally, the analysis reveals that for very high-risk individuals (i.e., > 90 percent), the rate of decline in offending likelihood increases dramatically with changes in risk. Such "overweighting," or treating high probabilities as certainty, is again inconsistent with a linear risk-offending relationship, and it suggests that policies aimed at such high perceived-risk individuals are perhaps inefficient or unnecessary. Figure 9.1 summarizes the relationship between levels of perceived risk and potential deterrent effects for these different risk-based classes of offenders.

Lessons for Theory and Policy

These results have interesting implications for both theory and policy, and suggest the potential to reframe traditional models of rational choice. The standard economic model of crime generally assumes that offenders use a linear function to weigh the risk, benefit, and cost of involvement in crime. But substantial theoretical and empirical work in behavioral decision theory has repeatedly shown that individuals not only often deviate from rational

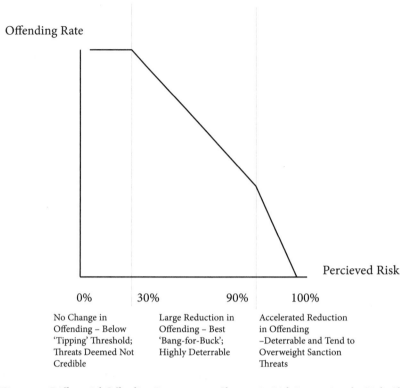

Figure 9.1. Differential Offending Responses to Changes in Risk Perceptions by Risk-Class (as adapted from Loughran, Pogarsky, Piquero and Paternoster, 2010)

behavior but also tend to do so in *predictable* ways. This seems true of the serious offenders in the Pathways group as well.

Given this, other theoretical approaches need to be integrated into work aimed at elucidating the mechanisms of deterrence. Loughran et al. (2010a) propose the use of Prospect Theory (Kahneman and Tversky 1979) as an alternative descriptive theory to traditional rational-choice theory when discussing deterrence. Furthermore, Loughran et al. advocate more rigorous consideration of other components of behavioral decision theory to advance the theoretical and empirical study of deterrence and offender decision making. For example, traditional rational-choice theory assumes, among other things, that individuals have well-defined preferences for benefit-cost components of crime, and *discount*, or devalue, future consequences of crime, by a fixed rate (see Nagin and Pogarsky 2004). However, results from research in behavioral decision theory show that this is not always that case, by revealing instances in which individuals may have a nonconstant, or hyperbolic, discount rate (O'Donoghue and Rabin 2000), where they tend to act impulsively and greatly (and irrationally) devalue the future when rewards to crime are more immediate, and other individuals may have a negative discount rate (Loewenstein 1987), in which outcomes in the future actually loom larger than those in the present. Those with a negative discount rate for punishment, for instance, would be more deterred by punishment that occurs in the future (since the pain of anticipation would itself act as a deterrent)—a notion that is contrary to the traditional belief that celerity of punishment is a mechanism of deterrence.

There are also important policy considerations for law enforcement and efforts aimed at deterring serious crime among older adolescents such as the Pathways group (Loughran et al. 2010a). First, sanction threats should be credible and well communicated. Absent credibility, the value of such threats will be negligible. Second, while some offenders are deterrable, and some are not deterrable, a large group of serious adolescent offenders will be conditionally deterrable, according to the manner in which sanction risks are expressed and conveyed. Thus, this group should be the focus of targeted enforcement policies that are different from the measures used with other groups, since the leverage for deterrence in this group is greatest. Identification of these offenders—those whose crime decisions can be changed as they still are considering future offending—should be a strategic element of law enforcement strategy. "Absolute deterrence" aimed at all offenders, including those with higher perceived risk, may be inefficient (Loughran et al. 2010a). For example, there may be little to gain by targeting individuals who already perceive a very high probability of detection, as the marginal deterrent effect for these individuals may be quite small and require a large amount of resources from the criminal justice system.

These analyses of the Pathways study data also show that there is considerable uncertainty, or *ambiguity*, in offender risk perceptions. Loughran, Paternoster, Piquero, and Pogarsky (2010b) investigate not only whether *average* risk perceptions deter would-be offenders but also whether the *variability*, or degree of uncertainty, of such perceptions matters as well. This concept is again taken from the literature on behavioral decision theory, where an important distinction is made between *risk*, or probabilities known to decision makers, and *uncertainty*, where such risks are unknown and are formed subjectively. This literature has shown that individuals tend to prefer known gambles over more uncertain ones, even for similarly valued outcomes (Camerer and Weber 1992). The extension to deterrence and criminal decision making, where detection probabilities are rarely known to potential offenders and are thus subjective, is straightforward.

As theorized by both Sherman (1990) and Nagin (1998), uncertainty in perceptions of detection probabilities may actually enhance the deterrent effect of increases in perceived certainty. According to Sherman (1990), this is the case because, while the overall mean detection level may be low, creating uncertainty about specific detection probabilities with respect to certain areas, crime types, or other factors may generate a larger deterrent risk of getting caught as compared to a constant, low rate of detection. Loughran et al. (2010b) tested this idea in the Pathways data by examining the role of ambiguity in offender risk perceptions and its relation to the certainty effect. Uncertainty for each individual was characterized as the amount of variability in each individual's crime-specific risk perceptions. These results show that for income-generating crimes, the deterrent effect of offender risk perceptions was actually *enhanced* for individuals who reported larger uncertainty in their perceptions near the lower end of the risk continuum. This result is consistent with Sherman's (1990) hypothesis, as well as the concept of "ambiguity aversion" in decision theory (e.g., Camerer and Weber 1992). While there was a slight increase in the magnitude of the deterrent effect of risk for aggressive crimes, the effect was not nearly as large, nor was the difference statistically significant.

The policy implications of these findings are both considerable and controversial. When the amount of uncertainty about the rate of detection is increased, the deterrent effect of potential detection increased dramatically. This finding argues for the introduction of randomization into policy surveillance and patrol, changes that do not necessarily require any additional law enforcement resources. For example, police could rotate their enforcement across both offenses and places so that the risk of punishment is far more unpredictable than it normally would be to active offenders (see, e.g., Harcourt and Meares 2010). Thus, with the same amount of resources, a modification of police practice to increase uncertainty could enhance overall deterrence.

The findings from the Minneapolis Hot Spots Experiment, in which police officers were rotated throughout the city at various hot spots of crime and for certain lengths of duration (Koper 1995), provide relevant data to illustrate this point. Koper examined whether stronger dosages (in terms of longer instances) of police presence produced greater deterrence and if so, whether there was an optimal length for police presence at hot spots. Findings indicated that for police stops, the ideal dosage for police presence was about ten to fifteen minutes, and that longer presences had diminishing effects. The policy implication from this finding is that police can maximize deterrence at hot spots by making proactive, short-duration stops on a random, intermittent basis, thereby making offenders continually guess where the police will be, how long they will be there, and where they may be going next. Although data on deterrence perceptions were not collected among would-be offenders, the random nature of police presence creates a widespread sense of the "Sword of Damocles," wherein sanction-threat certainty is heightened because of a would-be offender not knowing where or when the sword might fall.

Future Directions

As a whole, the results emerging from analyses done so far on data from the Pathways to Desistance study paint a rich picture of how we may begin to think of deterring serious adolescent offenders. But this picture is still incomplete. On one hand, the results discussed here suggest the possibility of effective deterrence for a subgroup of these offenders. Many of these serious offenders contemplate and weigh risk, cost, and rewards when deciding to engage in offending. They tend to adjust these perceptions according to recent sanction experience and react to these changes in ways that reflect deterrence. However, what is known about their sanction-threat perceptions and how it relates to subsequent offending decisions still only explains a small portion of the totality of their decision-making process. We are still uncertain about why some individuals in this group desist while others persist, and why some similarly situated individuals seem to be deterrable while others are not.

We can identify some extensions of these results to inform both theory and policy and provide some clarity regarding this last question. One issue is why some offenders appear to change their perceptions while others do not. For instance, while the results from Anwar and Loughran (2011) show that, on average, offenders in the Pathways sample update their risk beliefs, there is much variability in the level of updating that individuals are doing—some update risk perceptions dramatically, while others update very little or not at all. Because experience can only explain part of this incongruity, it appears important to achieve better understanding of individual-level factors that are associated with willingness and/or ability to revise perceptions, particularly if such factors are identifiable and relevant legal factors. For example, if different mental health diagnoses are associated with an inability or unwillingness to adjust one's perceptions, as results from Fagan and Piquero (2007) may suggest, then interventions aimed at stressing consideration of cost/risk in these individuals may prove beneficial.

Second, most of the research presented here is aimed at understanding perceived risks and, to a lesser extent, costs of offending. Yet, it is clear even from the results here and elsewhere that reward perceptions, in particular perceptions of personal rewards on top of monetary ones, are important factors in decisions to offend (Fagan and Piquero 2007). In fact, a recent meta-analysis of the relationship between perceived benefits and criminal offending showed that rewards are strongly related (and in the expected direction) to criminal offending across a range of offenders, offenses, and types of rewards measured (Baker and Piquero 2010). Deterrence based on rational choice assumes that individuals will be less likely to commit crime if expected costs are increased, but what if for some offenders, expected rewards are perceived to be so large that, even if their costs and risks can be increased, they are insufficient to exceed weighted benefits? Understanding the reward structure of offending and how serious and chronic offenders internalize these benefits needs to be elevated on the agenda of research in criminal decision making, especially if there are policies that can be adopted and subsequently designed to somehow diminish possible rewards.

This logic is similar to "supply-side" theories of economics, which encourage examining alternatives to simply stimulating demand for goods and services. In short, at the foundation of the deterrence framework, with its focus on the costs of crime, criminal justice policy has largely followed suit and focused most policy efforts at increasing the certainty and severity of punishment. However, as research convincingly shows, perceived *benefits* matter as well—and may matter more—to offending decisions. This implies that criminal justice policies should strongly consider efforts aimed at reducing the benefits associated with crime as offenders appear to be susceptible to those types of rational-choice considerations.

Third, with respect to adolescents, their maturity and development (particularly the interaction between maturity and risk perception) must be taken into account when considering their amenability to deterrence via sanction risks and costs. While many of the effects of deterrence for juveniles will come from what happens to them in institutional care, it is also important to note that there are other components to the perception of risk, cost, and reward, including peer and neighborhood concerns. For example, peers' offending and the consequences of offending may influence individual sanction-threat perceptions and behavior (Stafford and Warr 1993; Paternoster and Piquero 1995; Piquero and Paternoster 1998), and neighborhoods may also be influential in individual perception formation as some neighborhoods, as a result of their crime experiences, may help form individual attitudes (cf. Anderson 1999; Fagan and Wilkinson 1998). At a minimum, deterrence theory and research will need greater integration with other domains of adolescent and young adult development.

Finally, the results thus far from the Pathways study provide very strong evidence for a theoretical refinement of traditional rational-choice theory, which assumes that actors are rational in their decision making. While few would agree that any single individual is always perfectly rational in his or her decision making, rational-choice theory is generally preferred as an imperfect, but suitable, option to the nihilistic alternative that no individual is rational and thus offending decisions are arbitrary. However, this chapter begins to show that the integration of concepts from behavioral economics and behavioral decision theory, which predict ways in which individuals deviate from rational behavior, can be quite productive in explaining anomalies in rational choice. Furthermore, concepts that are part of these theories, for instance, "tipping effects" and "ambiguity," are not merely theoretical constructs but, rather, are often useful concepts for informing justice policy. It seems clear that the continued integration of concepts from decision theory and behavioral economics can both refine traditional rational-choice theories and push forward the understanding of deterrence in new and strategic directions. The Pathways research suggests that offenders are indeed susceptible to sanction threats; they are more deterrable than previous conceptions make them out to be, and public policy efforts may be able to influence offender decision-making processes.

REFERENCES

Andenaes, Johannes. 1974. *Punishment and Deterrence.* Ann Arbor: University of Michigan Press.

Anderson, Elijah. 1999. *Code of the Streets: Decency, Violence, and the Moral Life of the Inner City.* New York: Norton.

Anwar, Shamena, and Thomas A. Loughran. 2011. Testing a Bayesian Learning Theory of Deterrence among Serious Juvenile Offenders. *Criminology,* forthcoming.

Apospori, E., G. P. Alpert, and R. Paternoster. 1992. The Effect of Involvement with the Criminal Justice System: A Neglected Dimension of the Relationship between Experience and Perceptions. *Justice Quarterly* 9: 379-92.

Baker, Thomas, and Alex R. Piquero. 2010. Assessing the Perceived Benefits–Criminal Offending Relationship. *Journal of Criminal Justice* 38: 981-87.

Beccaria, Cesare. (1764) 1985. *On Crimes and Punishments.* New York: Macmillan.

Becker, Gary. 1968. Crime and Punishment: An Economic Approach. *The Journal of Political Economy* 76: 169-217.

Camerer, Colin, and Martin Weber. 1992. Recent Developments in Modeling Preferences: Uncertainty and Ambiguity. *Journal of Risk and Uncertainty* 5: 325-70.

Chassin, Laurie, Julia Dmitrieva, Kathryn Modecki, Laurence Steinberg, Elizabeth Cauffman, Alex R. Piquero, George P. Knight, and Sandra H. Losoya. 2010. Does Adolescent Alcohol and Marijuana Use Predict Suppressed Growth in Psychosocial Maturity among Male Juvenile Offenders? *Psychology of Addictive Behaviors* 24: 48-60.

Chung, He Len L., Carol A. Schubert, and Edward P. Mulvey. 2007. An Empirical Portrait of Community Reentry among Serious Juvenile Offenders in Two Metropolitan Cities. *Criminal Justice and Behavior* 34 (11): 1402-26.

Clarke, R. V., and D. B. Cornish. 1985. Modeling Offenders' Decisions: A Framework for Research and Policy. In M. Tonry and N. Morris, eds., *Crime and Justice: An Annual Review of Research*, vol. 24: 145-85. Chicago: University of Chicago Press.

Cornish, Derek B., and Ronald V. Clarke. 1986. *The Reasoning Criminal: Rational Choice Perspectives on Offending.* New York: Springer-Verlag.

Decker, S., R. Wright, and R. Logie. 1993. Perceptual Deterrence among Active Residential Burglars: A Research Note. *Criminology* 31: 135-47.

Fagan, J., and A. R. Piquero. 2007. Rational Choice and Developmental Influences on Recidivism among Adolescent Felony Offenders. *Journal of Empirical Legal Studies* 4: 715–48.

Fagan, Jeffrey, and Deanna L. Wilkinson. 1998. Guns, Youth Violence, and Social Identity. In M. Tonry and M. H. Moore, eds., *Crime and Justice: Annual Review of Research,* vol. 24: 105-88. Chicago: University of Chicago Press.

Grasmick, H. G., and R. J. Bursik Jr. 1990. Conscience, Significant Others, and Rational Choice: Extending the Deterrence Model. *Law and Society Review* 24: 837–61.

Harcourt, Bernard E., and Tracey L. Meares. 2010. Randomization and the Fourth Amendment. *Yale Law School Working Paper.*

Horney, Julie, and Ineke Haen Marshall. 1992. Risk Perceptions among Serious Offenders: The Role of Crime and Punishment. *Criminology* 30: 575-92.

Kahneman, Daniel, and Amos Tversky. 1979. Prospect Theory: An Analysis of Decisions under Risk. *Econometrica* 47: 313-27.

Knight, George P., Delfino Vargas-Chanes, Sandra Losoya, Sonia Cota-Robles, Laurie Chassin, and J. M. Lee. 2009. Acculturation and Enculturation Trajectories among Mexican American Adolescent Offenders. *Journal of Research on Adolescence* 19 (4): 625-53.

Koper, Christopher S. 1995. Just Enough Police Presence: Reducing Crime and Disorderly Behavior by Optimizing Patrol Time in Crime Hot Spots. *Justice Quarterly* 12: 649-72.

Lochner, Lance. 2007. Individual Perceptions of the Criminal Justice System. *American Economic Review* 97: 444-60.

Loewenstein, George. 1987. Anticipation and the Valuation of Delayed Consumption. *Economic Journal* 97: 666-84.

Losoya, Sandra H., George P. Knight, Laurie Chassin, Michelle Little, Delfino Vargas-Chanes, Anne Mauricio, and Alex R. Piquero. 2008. Trajectories of Acculturation and Enculturation in Relation to Binge Drinking and Marijuana Use in a Sample of Mexican-American Serious Juvenile Offenders. *Journal of Drug Issues* 38: 171-98.

Loughran, Thomas A., Edward P. Mulvey, Carol A. Schubert, Laurie Chassin, Laurence Steinberg, Alex R. Piquero, Sonia Cota-Robles, Jeffrey Fagan, Elizabeth Cauffman, and Sandra H. Losoya. 2010. Differential Effects of Adult Court Transfer on Juvenile Offender Recidivism. *Law and Human Behavior* 34: 476-88.

Loughran, Thomas A., Edward P. Mulvey, Carol A. Schubert, Jeffrey Fagan, Alex R. Piquero, and Sandra H. Losoya. 2009. Estimating a Dose-Response Relationship between Length of Stay and Future Recidivism in Serious Juvenile Offenders. *Criminology* 47: 699-740.

Loughran, Thomas A., Raymond Paternoster, Alex R. Piquero and Greg Pogarsky. 2010. On Ambiguity in Perceptions of Risk: Implications for Criminal Decision-Making and Deterrence. *University of Maryland Working Paper.*

Loughran, Thomas A., Alex R. Piquero, Jeffrey Fagan, and Edward P. Mulvey. In press. Differential Deterrence: Studying Heterogeneity and Changes in Perceptual Deterrence among Serious Youthful Offenders. *Crime and Delinquency*, forthcoming.

Loughran, Thomas A., Greg Pogarsky, Alex R. Piquero, and Raymond Paternoster. 2010. Reassessing the Certainty Effect in Deterrence Theory Using Insight from Prospect Theory. *University of Maryland Working Paper.*

Matsueda, Ross L., Derek A. Kreager, and David Huizinga. 2006. Deterring Delinquents: A Rational Choice Model of Theft and Violence. *American Sociological Review* 71: 95-122.

Mulvey, E., C. Schubert, and He Len Chung. 2007. Service Use after Court Involvement in a Sample of Serious Adolescent Offenders. *Children and Youth Services Review* 29: 518-44.

Mulvey, Edward P., Laurence Steinberg, Jeffrey Fagan, Elizabeth Cauffman, Alex R. Piquero, Laurie Chassin, George P. Knight, Robert Brame, Carol Schubert, Thomas Hecker, and Sandra H. Losoya. 2004. Theory and Research on Desistance from Antisocial Activity among Serious Juvenile Offenders. *Youth Violence and Juvenile Justice* 2: 213-36.

Mulvey, Edward P., Laurence Steinberg, Alex R. Piquero, Mitch Besana, Jeffrey Fagan, Carol A. Schubert, and Elizabeth Cauffman. 2010. Longitudinal Offending Trajectories among Serious Adolescent Offenders. *Development and Psychopathology* 22: 453-75.

Nagin, Daniel S. 1998. Criminal Deterrence Research at the Outset of the Twenty-First Century. In Michael Tonry, ed., *Crime and Justice: A Review of Research*, vol. 23: 1-42. Chicago: University of Chicago Press.

Nagin, Daniel S., and Raymond Paternoster. 1993. Enduring Individual Differences and Rational Choice Theories of Crime. *Law and Society Review* 27: 467-98.

Nagin, Daniel S., and Raymond Paternoster. 1994. Personal Capital and Social Control: The Deterrence Implications of a Theory of Individual Differences in Criminal Offending. *Criminology* 32: 581-606.

Nagin, Daniel S., and Greg Pogarsky. 2001. Integrating Celerity, Impulsivity, and Extralegal Sanction Threats into a Model of General Deterrence: Theory and Evidence. *Criminology* 39: 404-30.

Nagin, Daniel S., and Greg Pogarsky. 2004. Time and Punishment: Delayed Consequences and Criminal Behavior. *Journal of Quantitative Criminology* 20: 295-317.

Nagin, Daniel S., and Greg Pogarsky. 2003. An Experimental Investigation of Deterrence: Cheating, Self-Serving Bias, and Impulsivity. *Criminology* 41: 167-94.

O'Donoghue, Ted, and Matthew Rabin. 2000. The Economics of Immediate Gratification. *Journal of Behavioral Decision Making* 13: 233-50.

Parker, Jerry, and Harold Grasmick. 1979. Linking Actual and Perceived Certainty and Severity of Punishment. *Criminology* 17: 366-79.

Paternoster, Raymond. 1987. The Deterrent Effect of the Perceived Certainty and Severity of Punishment: A Review of the Evidence and Issues. *Justice Quarterly* 4: 173.

Paternoster, Raymond, and Alex R. Piquero. 1995. Reconceptualizing Deterrence: An Empirical Test of Personal and Vicarious Experiences. *Journal of Research in Crime and Delinquency* 32 (3): 251-86.

Piquero, Alex R., Jeffrey Fagan, Edward P. Mulvey, Laurence Steinberg, and Candice Odgers. 2005. Developmental Trajectories of Legal Socialization among Serious Adolescent Offenders. *Journal of Criminal Law and Criminology* 96 (1): 267-98.

Piquero, A. R., and R. Paternoster. 1998. An Application of Stafford and Warr's Reconceptualization of Deterrence to Drinking and Driving. *Journal of Research in Crime and Delinquency* 35: 3-39.

Piquero, A. R., and G. Pogarsky. 2002. Beyond Stafford and Warr's Reconceptualization of Deterrence: Personal and Vicarious Experiences, Impulsivity, and Offending Behavior. *Journal of Research in Crime and Delinquency* 39 (2): 153-86.

Piquero, A. R., and G. F. Rengert. 1999. Studying Deterrence with Active Residential Burglars. *Justice Quarterly* 16: 451-71.

Piquero, A. R., and S. Tibbetts. 1996. Specifying the Direct and Indirect Effects of Low Self-Control and Situational Factors in Offenders' Decision Making: Toward a More Complete Model of Rational Offending. *Justice Quarterly* 13: 481-510.

Pogarsky, Greg. 2002. Identifying Deterrable Offenders: Implications for Deterrence Research. *Justice Quarterly* 19: 431-52.

Pogarsky, Greg, and Alex R. Piquero. 2003. Can Punishment Encourage Offending? Investigating the "Resetting" Effect. *Journal of Research in Crime and Delinquency* 40: 95-120.

Pogarsky, Greg, Alex R. Piquero, and Raymond Paternoster. 2004. Modeling Change in Perceptions about Sanction Threats: The Neglected Linkage in Deterrence Theory. *Journal of Quantitative Criminology* 20: 343-69.

Pratt, Travis C., and Francis T. Cullen. 2005. Assessing Macro-Level Predictors and Theories of Crime: A Meta-Analysis. In Michael Tonry, ed., *Crime and Justice: A Review of Research,* vol. 32: 373-450. Chicago: University of Chicago Press.

Schubert, Carol A., Edward P. Mulvey, Thomas A. Loughran, Jeffrey Fagan, Laurie Chassin, Alex R. Piquero, Sandra Losoya, Laurence Steinberg, and Elizabeth Cauffman.2010. Predicting Outcomes for Transferred Youth. *Law and Human Behavior* 34: 460-75.

Schubert, Carol A., Edward P. Mulvey, Laurence Steinberg, Elizabeth Cauffman, Sandra H. Losoya, Thomas Hecker, Laurie Chassin, and George P. Knight. 2004. Operational Lessons from the Pathways to Desistance Project. *Youth Violence and Juvenile Justice* 2: 237–55.

Sherman, Lawrence W. 1990. Police Crackdowns: Initial and Residual Deterrence. In Michael Tonry and Norval Morris, eds., *Crime and Justice: An Annual Review of Research,* vol. 12: 1-48. Chicago: University of Chicago Press.

Stafford, Mark, and Mark Warr. 1993. A Reconceptualization of General and Specific Deterrence. *Journal of Research in Crime and Delinquency* 30: 123-35.

Steinberg, L., H. Chung, and M. Little. 2004. Reentry of Young Offenders from the Justice System: A Developmental Perspective. *Youth Violence and Juvenile Justice* 1: 21-38.

Steinberg, L. D., and E. S. Scott. 2003. Less Guilty by Reason of Adolescence: Developmental Immaturity, Diminished Responsibility, and the Juvenile Death Penalty. *American Psychologist* 58: 1009-18.

Williams, Kirk, and Richard Hawkins. 1986. Perceptual Research on General Deterrence: A Critical Review. *Law & Society Review* 20: 545-72.

Zimring, Franklin E., and Gordon Hawkins. 1973. *Deterrence: The Legal Threat in Crime Control.* Chicago: University of Chicago Press.

10

"I Want to Talk to My Mom"

The Role of Parents in Police
Interrogation of Juveniles

STEPHEN M. REBA, RANDEE J. WALDMAN,
AND BARBARA BENNETT WOODHOUSE

I. Introduction

Throughout childhood, a parent is the most important person in a child's life. A parent is tasked with teaching, disciplining, nurturing, and protecting her minor child. In essence, a parent is expected to mold the child into a civic-minded adult. When a child first encounters the juvenile justice system and is being questioned by the police about his involvement in an offense, a parent's role becomes muddled. Many states give a parent the right to be present while her child is being questioned. Some even mandate such participation. However, the ground rules for police interaction with parents during interrogations of juveniles remain ambiguous. Because of a parent's instincts and duties as truth seeker and disciplinarian, the parent can be turned from the child's nurturer, protector, and greatest ally to the child's most dangerous enemy.

A. John's Case

Fifteen-year-old John was arrested while riding his brother's scooter around the corner from his house. He was taken to police headquarters and placed in an interrogation room. When police began the interrogation process, one officer delivered John his *Miranda* rights as follows:

OFFICER: I've got to read this to you, okay? I have the right to remain silent [sic]. Okay, that means you don't have to say anything. Anything I say can be used against you in court [sic]. You have the right to an attorney for advice before I ask you any questions and have him with you during questioning. If you can't afford an attorney, one will be appointed for you before any questioning, if you wish. If you decide to answer questions now without an attorney, you'll still be allowed to stop answering at any time, if you request to be allowed to talk to an attorney. You have the right to have your parent or guardian present during questioning, if you wish. Okay, do you understand all those things I've just read to you?

JOHN: Yeah. Yes, sir.

OFFICER: Do you understand?

JOHN: Yeah.

OFFICER: Do you wish to talk to me now?

JOHN: I want my Mom. I want to talk to my Mom.

The officer then said, "I guess that's it" and left the room.

About twenty minutes later, the officer returned with John's cellular phone and asked him if he wanted to call his mother. After handing John his phone, the officer exited the interrogation room, shutting the door behind him. John called his mother, told her where he was, and asked that she come help him. Approximately fifty minutes later, John's mother arrived at the police station. The officer did not repeat John's *Miranda* warnings to her or advise her of John's right to a lawyer or indicate that John's statements to his mother could be used against him in a court of law. An officer simply led his mother to the interrogation room for a conversation with her son. As the officer was leaving the room, he said, "Your mom's here; she's going to talk with you for a minute." The officer then shut the door, leaving John and his mother alone.

John's mother scolded him. At times, she screamed, frustrated that her son had gotten into trouble. However, her main objective in the conversation was to learn from John what had happened, so she could counsel him, as a parent, about his situation. Responding to his mother's inquiries, John explained what had happened. After ten minutes, the same officer who had brought John's mother into the room knocked on the interrogation room door, opening the closed door and saying, "Sorry to interrupt." As soon as they heard the knock, John and his mother ceased their conversation and turned their attention to the interrupting officer's concerns. Throughout the time John and his mother spent together in the interrogation room, all the actions of the police officers conveyed that the conversation between John and his mother was private.

In fact, the police had been videotaping this entire sequence through a hidden camera, including John's phone call to his mother and their entire conversation in the interrogation room. John was charged with involvement in three armed robberies, two involving pizza delivery men and one involving a cab driver, and tried as an adult, under the state's automatic transfer statute. The hidden camera footage that captured the conversation between mother and child was played for the jury once during trial. While the footage did not contain a confession, it did contain an admission by John, in response to his mother's questioning, that he was not at home when he had told her he would be. It also showed a mother angrily berating her son, apparently questioning his innocence. Upon the jury's request, the footage was replayed twice during a ten-hour deliberation. Although John staunchly maintained his innocence, the jury did not believe him or his key witness, his mother, and ultimately convicted him of two counts of armed robbery. Although no one was injured in the robberies and less than forty dollars was taken, John was sentenced to twenty years. Twelve of those years are to be served confined in the state prison without the possibility of parole, and the remaining eight years will be served on probation.

B. Framing the Issues in Prevention Policy Context

The scenario presented above reads like a bizarre hypothetical, but it is all too real. John's case is an actual case from the files of Emory University's Barton Child Law and Policy Center. Like so many other juveniles' cases that pass below the radar screen, John's case raises numerous fundamental questions of both law and policy. Those questions include Fourth Amendment search and seizure, Fifth Amendment self-incrimination, Sixth Amendment ineffective assistance of counsel, Fourteenth Amendment Due Process and Eighth Amendment excessive punishment issues. In addition to the obvious criminal procedure issues, John's case poses questions located at the intersection of juvenile justice, child development, and constitutional doctrines of family privacy and parental authority. Is it constitutional for police secretly to videotape a child's meeting with his parent who has been called to advise him? Even if it is not unconstitutional, is it sound policy to trick a parent into gathering evidence for the prosecution when she believes she is giving tough love and parental guidance in a confidential setting?

Rather than focusing on all the issues presented in John's case, we wish to focus attention on the issues raised by the involvement of parents in the interrogation of youth and their implications for delinquency prevention. In juvenile justice, the focus is not exclusively on obtaining a conviction and incarcerating the offender. Prevention of delinquency and rehabilitation of youthful offenders are also important policy values (Bilchik this volume;

Slobogin and Fondacaro 2009). Parents are the first line of defense in turning troubled adolescents around and getting them back on track. Driving a wedge between child and parent at this critical moment, we will argue, is not only a violation of constitutionally protected family rights; it is also bad public policy.

In this chapter we will first describe how a project designed to provoke systemic change through appellate advocacy led us to take John's case. Next, we will explore the state and federal laws and constitutional principles protecting the parent-child relationship and recognizing the parent's role in guiding her minor child. We will then review current research on child development and the role of the parent in delinquency prevention and rehabilitation. Finally, we will explore three policy options for parental involvement in the interrogation process: (1) to maintain the status quo—which would allow use of the juvenile's conversations with parents to gather evidence to make a criminal case, as is routinely done with juveniles' interactions with peers and cell mates; (2) to keep parents out of the interrogation process entirely; or (3) to involve parents in the interrogation process, but with protections in place such as confidentiality of parent-child communications, a cooling-off period, and adequate time to consult.

II. How John's Case Came to the Appeal for Youth Project

Appeal for Youth is an Equal Justice Works project housed at the Barton Juvenile Defender Clinic. The project seeks systemic reform in Georgia through the holistic appellate representation of youthful offenders in the state's juvenile and criminal justice systems. By increasing the number of appeals from adjudications of delinquency, the project hopes to end the unwritten policies and practices that result in youths being committed to juvenile detention facilities. Similarly, by providing postconviction representation to youths who were tried and convicted as adults, the project aims to decrease the number of youthful offenders who languish in Georgia's prisons.

Appeal for Youth was founded by Stephen Reba, formerly a staff attorney for the Supreme Court of Georgia's Committee on Justice for Children. Reba, working with Randee Waldman, director of the Barton Juvenile Defender Clinic, joined Barton's team as the Ford and Harrison Equal Justice Works Fellow to spearhead this project. The project's involvement with John's case began with a call to the Barton Juvenile Defender Clinic in August 2009. John had lost his direct appeal in Georgia's intermediate appellate court. A panel of three Georgia court of appeals judges affirmed the trial court's admission of the DVD showing the conversations between John and his mother. John's appointed appellate counsel had argued that the recording violated John's Fourth Amendment rights. In response to this argument, two judges found that John had no reasonable expectation of privacy in the conversation with his mother in the interrogation room. The third judge, however, disagreed but voted to affirm the conviction and sentence on other grounds. According to this third judge,

> [T]he police should not be allowed, through the use of a hidden camera and without notice to the juvenile or his parent, to secretly invade the privacy of the parent-child encounter which our law authorizes and makes an integral part of the interview with a juvenile suspect. . . . Therefore, just as we would not countenance the recording of a conversation between a defendant and his attorney, we should not permit the recording of a conversation of a juvenile defendant and his parent in this context.[1]

After the Supreme Court of Georgia denied certiorari, John's right to counsel reached an end and John's mother contacted the appellate project at the clinic. John's incarceration had been particularly hard on his family. The family had already suffered dislocation and loss during the aftermath of Hurricane Katrina, when it was forced to move to Atlanta from New Orleans' Ninth Ward. The oldest of three children in a single-parent family, John had shared in caring for his severely disabled sister. Since his absence, John's mother has had to shoulder the entire burden, placing financial and emotional stress on an already impoverished family. Bitterest of all for John's mother was the knowledge that she had tried to save her son, by counseling him in a moment of crisis, only to have the state use John's trust in his mother to convict him of a crime. After speaking with John's mother, Reba agreed to meet with John and consider taking the case.

When Reba visited John in prison, he saw a nineteen-year-old struggling to adapt to his surroundings. In detention since he was fifteen, at seventeen, John had been forced to leave the juvenile detention center for the state prison system. For two years, older and larger inmates had bullied and provoked John into fights. He had been frequently injured and had spent a significant amount of time on restriction and in solitary. He still maintained his innocence of the charges against him, but he was no longer a child. Hope had drained from John, leaving mostly anger. The small fifteen-year-old boy from the interrogation room video was gone.

Since John's direct appeals had been exhausted, the next step was a state habeas corpus petition. Waldman and Reba saw a strong claim for ineffective assistance of counsel and pressing that claim would entail consideration of the constitutionality of the procedures used in John's interrogation. By drawing upon interdisciplinary, evidence-based practices as well as constitutional principles, the appeals process might promote not only individual justice but systemic change. It might help to shift interrogation practices involving Georgia youth suspected of crimes away from a single-minded focus on building a case for the prosecution and towards a model that values delinquency prevention and rehabilitation as the first and best option for troubled youth. Since the case involved issues at the intersection of juvenile justice, child development, and constitutional doctrines of family privacy, Reba and Waldman asked Barbara Woodhouse, who is codirector of Barton Center and an expert on the Constitution and the family, to collaborate on research and strategy.

III. The Legal and Constitutional Analysis

A. Constitutional Background

In this section we will argue that use by the police of a hidden video camera to eavesdrop on a mother counseling her child in a moment of crisis, without any notice to either the parent or the child that the conversation was being taped and would be used against the child at trial, violates fundamental constitutional values of family privacy and parental rights. These values are recognized in both the Georgia constitution and the Constitution of the United States.[2] As Justice O'Connor explained in *Troxel v. Granville,* "the interest of parents in the care, custody, and control of their children is perhaps the oldest of the fundamental liberty interests recognized by this Court."[3] This principle of family privacy and autonomy was established more than eighty-five years ago, in *Meyer v. Nebraska,* and has been repeatedly reaffirmed in a wide range of situations. As the Supreme Court established in *Prince v. Massachusetts,* "It is cardinal with us that the custody, care and nurture of the child reside first in the parents, whose primary function and freedom include preparation for obligations the state can neither supply nor hinder."[4]

The Supreme Court of the state of Georgia, like virtually every state in the union, recognizes these rights as a matter of state constitutional law as well as federal constitutional law.[5] The parent's role as guardian and counselor to the child is deeply rooted in history and tradition, and the relationship has merited special protection against intrusion by the state in a wide range of situations. As the Supreme Court has stressed, it is "plain beyond the need for multiple citation" that a natural parent's "desire for and right to 'the companionship, care, custody, and management of his or her children' is an interest far more precious than any property right."[6] These doctrines of family privacy and parental liberty implicate values that reach far beyond the rights of the individual parent and the individual child and are deemed necessary to ordered liberty in a free society. Parents' rights to bring up their children have been identified as the most fundamental of liberties, "essential to the orderly pursuit of happiness by free men."[7]

Under our system of laws, parents charged with the task of nurturing and educating the next generation of citizens need the liberty and authority to do this job effectively. Parents play a central role in counseling their children in many contexts and their consent is necessary in many situations before a child's decision can be given legal effect. For example, the Georgia parental notification statute requires a minor to consult with her parent or seek a judicial bypass before obtaining an abortion. Underage marriage, driving permits, quitting high school, and even body piercing require parental permission.[8] These laws are predicated on the crucial role parents play in the socialization of their children and in guiding children as they mature.

It is true that parental rights do not appear in the text of the Constitution. But, while there are dissenters who question the pedigree of parental rights, even the dissenters recognize that these rights merit special protection when presented as hybrid claims coupled with rights that are expressly enumerated in the Bill of Rights.[9] Fourth, Fifth, and Sixth Amendment rights are as old as the Constitution itself, and they protect juveniles as well as adults against self-incrimination and searches or seizures that invade protected zones of privacy, and entitle juveniles to representation and confidentiality in communications with counsel.[10]

If anything, juveniles are more in need of such protections than adults. The purpose of reading a suspect his *Miranda* rights is to insure that they are understood and that the suspect has an opportunity to invoke them. Research shows that, even when given an accurate reading of their *Miranda* rights, many juveniles do not fully comprehend the meaning of the words (Grisso 1980; Beyer 2000). Research further shows that juveniles are especially vulnerable to police pressure, increasing the likelihood that they will provide a false confession (Birckhead 2008; Scott-Hayward 2007; Beyer 2000). Parental advice and counsel in the context of interrogation of a juvenile should be given heightened protection, since it may be essential to protecting the child's explicitly enumerated constitutional rights. In fact, there are many examples of laws that do just that.

B. Laws Mandating Parental Notice and Opportunity for Consultation

One of the most difficult challenges a parent faces is a teenager who is suspected of engaging in unlawful behavior. Many times, it is the parent who succeeds in bringing home to the child the gravity of the situation and the importance of telling the parent the unvarnished truth. Without this frank exchange, the constitutionally protected authority and duties of the parent are an illusion. Georgia law, like that of many jurisdictions, recognizes the importance of the parent's role as a counselor to and guardian of the child who is suspected of violations of criminal laws. In considering whether a juvenile has validly waived his or her *Miranda* rights, an important factor is whether the child has been permitted to consult with a parent.[11]

Both federal and state laws are clear that, had John invoked his right to speak with an attorney, interrogation would have ceased and the conversations between the child and his counsel would have been privileged and confidential.[12] In the case of a juvenile, it is often the parent who functions as the child's counselor. Currently, federal law requires that, when a juvenile is suspected of a felony, the state must make a good faith effort to locate his parents or guardian before beginning questioning.[13]

There is support in state as well as federal law for the principle that, when a juvenile invokes his right to consult with his parent, their station house conversation is entitled to special protection. Under Georgia law, for example, counsel must be provided for a child not represented by the child's parent, guardian, or custodian. A parent may serve as her child's representative, instead of an attorney, if the parent so desires.[14] When John asked specifically for his mother instead of an attorney, John's private conversations with his mother in the interrogation room should have been considered tantamount to consultation with an attorney.[15]

We would argue that it was a violation of John's rights for the trial judge to allow the jury to view the privileged conversation. Additionally, the officers used John's mother in a manner that was contrary to his interests, in violation of John's rights. For instance, upon interrupting the private conversation between John and his mother for a second time, the officers resumed their interrogation of John. They did not explain John's *Miranda* rights to his mother, nor did they give her time to consult with a lawyer or consider John's full range of options. Instead, the officers used John's mother against him, in an attempt to elicit incriminating statements and build a case for criminal prosecution.

The Court of Appeals for the Ninth Circuit, in *U.S. v. Wendy G.*, construing federal laws on parent involvement, explains the commonsense reasoning for clear and protective rules about parental involvement, including a rule that the parent be provided with information about the child's rights under *Miranda*:

> We have explained that "children need parental involvement during interrogation" and that the purpose of § 5033 is to provide "meaningful protection" of juveniles by facilitating such involvement. . . . [W]e have been guided by common sense and the evident purpose of the parental notification requirement in interpreting the provision. In Doe IV, we addressed, for the first time, whether § 5033 requires that parents be notified of the juvenile's rights in prejudicial proceedings, such as pre-interrogation *Miranda* rights. In addressing this question, we reasoned that the statute's requirement of immediate parental notification must have a purpose, and that failing to include *Miranda* information would undermine the value of such a requirement. Elaborating on the purpose of the notification, we noted longstanding judicial recognition that children need parental involvement during interrogation.[16]

Judge Paez, writing for a three-judge panel, rejected the argument that the government's failure to advise a juvenile's mother of her child's *Miranda* rights prior to interrogation was a harmless error because the mother had no right to advise the juvenile to remain silent. The court reasoned that "the requirement that parents be advised of their arrested child's rights surely is not for the purpose of imparting general information in the abstract. Congress obviously intended that parents be informed of their children's rights so that they can assist their children in a meaningful way."[17] The court held that the requirement that parents be notified when a child is taken into custody would be completely meaningless if those same parents did not have the right to advise and counsel their children before police questioning. This is especially so in a case like John's, in which the juvenile clearly rejected the option of speaking with the police officer and instead asked to speak with his parent. In such a situation, communications between parent and child, like communications between lawyer and client, should be protected by rules of confidentiality.

Misuse by law enforcement of the child's trust in his or her parent stands in stark contrast to the respect traditionally accorded to parents as guardians of the child's welfare. The facts of John's case highlight the dangers of this approach. After being given a *Miranda* warning (albeit a garbled one) and asked if he wanted to talk with the police, the juvenile did not agree to talk with the police. Instead, he stated, "I want my Mom. I want to talk to my Mom." The officers correctly treated this as an invocation of his *Miranda* rights but did not immediately contact his mother. They waited twenty minutes before returning to the interrogation room and giving him a cell phone and instructing him to call his mother. Then they taped their entire interaction. Neither the child nor his mother knew that their conversation was being videotaped. In effect, bringing the mother to the police station became a strategy to gather evidence. It is one thing for the police to use such a strategy with a cell mate or another teenaged peer suspected of involvement in the crime. The parent-child relationship, however, has constitutional dimensions, and the state has a profound stake in protecting the privacy of the family and the role of parents as counselors to their children. John was denied this right to family privacy, as it has evolved under the Due Process Clauses of both the federal and state constitutions, when the police videotaped the private conversation between John and his mother and when the trial court allowed the conversation to be seen by the jury at John's trial.

IV. The Role of the Parent in Delinquency Prevention and Rehabilitation

Protection of parental authority and family privacy are grounded in science as well as in law. The social science literature has long recognized the critical role of the parent in delinquency prevention and rehabilitation. As early as 1958, social control theorists posited that parents influence their child's delinquency through the *direct control* of behavior via supervision and punishment, *internalized control* through the creation of a child's conscience, and *indirect control* through the amount of affectional identification the child has with parents. Later theorists suggest similarly that the most important family factor in controlling delinquency is the intimacy of communication between parent and child. In fact, this form of control was seen as significantly more effective than physical control (parental presence) because opportunities for delinquency are ample and it is only natural that parents cannot always be there to monitor their children. Whether parental controls are direct or indirect, authorities are unanimous that parental controls play a significant role in delinquency prevention (Greenwood 2008; Cernkovich and Giordano 1987; Demuth and Brown 2004; Wells and Rankin 1988). It is no surprise that a juvenile like John would ask to speak to his mother before asking to speak with a lawyer.

Research on risk and protective factors reinforces the importance of communication with an engaged and trusted parent. Social scientists have identified multiple risk factors for delinquency, including child abuse and neglect, single-parent households, low levels of parental involvement, high level of conflict, hostility, and aggression in the family, parental criminality, inadequate parental supervision, early parental loss, emotional deprivation, poor family management practices, child maltreatment, and parent-child separation (Henggeler and Bourduin 1990; Heilbrun et al. 2005). As these factors make clear, the lack of parental engagement plays a critical role in elevating the risk of juvenile crime. While single mothers were more effective than single fathers at exerting direct and indirect controls, "[p]arental closeness coupled with involvement, supervision, and monitoring, attenuate the effect of living in a single-parent (or step) family on delinquency" (Demuth and Brown 2004, 78). Not only theory but also logic and experience have long suggested that positive engagement of the parent can reduce risks of offending, promote rehabilitation, and reduce rates of recidivism (Garbarino 1999, 184).

These theories about the influence of parents have been empirically tested. During the first decade of this century, for the first time, researchers have documented a set of delinquency intervention strategies that have high success rates when measured in real-world situations. A consensus has developed among experts that family-based delinquency-prevention programs are effective at reducing juvenile offending and recidivism (Greenwood 2008). The most successful programs are programs that emphasize family interactions in order to provide skills to the adults who are in the best position to supervise and train the child. Effective programs not only redirect juveniles away from wasted lives of delinquency and crime but can also save tax dollars.

Two specific programs that show the best results for youth on probation are Functional Family Therapy (FFT) and Multisystemic Therapy (MST). FFT improves family functioning by "increasing problem-solving skills, enhancing emotional connections, and strengthening parents' ability to provide appropriate structure, guidance, and limits for their children" (Greenwood 2008, 198). FFT is effective towards a wide range of problem youth, and the evidence of its success has accumulated over thirty years of clinical research (Sexton and Alexander 2003). Functional Family Therapy has been used both as an intervention program, with youth at risk of offending, and as a prevention program, with youth who have already offended. FFT emphasizes the importance of respecting all family members on their own terms as they experience the intervention. It involves trained therapists in working closely with the youth and his parent or parents in building upon family strengths or protective factors while addressing family deficits or risk factors. Positive parenting skills and supportive communication are important protective factors. FFT motivates families by helping them build on family members' unique strengths in ways that enhance self-respect. FFT reduces recidivism and the onset of offending between 25 and 60 percent more effectively than juvenile justice approaches that do not integrate parents in treatment. FFT costs between seven hundred and one thousand dollars per family compared to costs of six thousand dollars for detention and fifteen thousand dollars for residential treatment (Sexton and Alexander 2000).

Similarly, MST focuses on helping parents deal effectively with their child's behavior, and has proven effective in reducing rearrest rates and out-of-home placements for a variety of problem youths. MST is an intensive program that uses a home-based intervention grounded on the theory that problem behaviors require interventions in real-life settings where the problems occur. It adopts Urie Bronfenbrenner's ecological model of child development, placing individuals in the context of family and social systems (Fondacaro and Fasig 2006; Henggeler and Borduin 1990). As with FFT, the parent is an integral part of the intervention. Parents are "enlisted to teach cognitive behavioral change strategies to youth (e.g., to reduce anxiety, develop self-management plan for substance use) and are critical to restructuring family relations in ways that decrease youth antisocial behaviour and support prosocial youth activities" (Henggeler and Schaeffer 2010). Like FFT, MST has been proven over many decades to be extremely cost effective and efficacious at preventing delinquency and reducing recidivism, when compared to other programs that do not include parental engagement. Continuing effects are seen as long as fourteen years after the intervention (Henggeler and Schaeffer. 2010).

If policymakers care about increasing public safety and reducing the social costs and incidence of juvenile offending, then programs such as FFT and MST are by far the most effective approaches (Sexton and Alexander 2000). Numerous studies show that get-tough approaches like trying children as adults and sentencing them to long terms of incarceration, as happened with John, undermine long-term interests in public safety while costing millions of unnecessary dollars (Slobogin and Fondacaro 2009; Greenwood 2008). From a policy perspective, the tactics used in John's case—using his trust in his mother to trick him into talking—add little or nothing of value to the investigation. On the other hand, the long-term social costs of police practices that undermine trust and communication between parent and child are extremely high.

V. Three Approaches to Parental Involvement in Interrogation

In this section we will discuss three potential approaches to parental involvement in the interrogation process. While recognizing the important role played by the advice and counsel of parents, we cast a critical eye on the assumption that the mere presence of the parent is sufficient to protect the child's rights. We propose policies to protect the confidentiality of parent-child communications and to mitigate risks that a distraught or unsophisticated parent may make an uninformed decision to effect a waiver of the child's *Miranda* rights.

A. The Status Quo: Totality of the Circumstances or Per Se Rule Requiring Parental Presence

Current law is a patchwork of policies. In the majority of states, including Georgia, courts look to a totality of circumstances test to determine if a juvenile has validly waived her *Miranda* rights (Feld 2006). This approach was adopted by the United States Supreme Court in *Fare v. Michael C.*[18] Among the factors to be considered in the totality of circumstances test is whether the juvenile has had the opportunity to consult with her parent. In addition, approximately twelve states have a per se rule requiring the presence of a parent or other "interested adult" during interrogation. Some scholars have recommended that this rule be mandated nationwide (McGuire 2000; Drizin and Colgan 2004; Feld 2006).

Neither the totality of circumstances rule nor the per se rule requiring an adult's presence serves to meet the needs of juveniles during the interrogation process. First, in those jurisdictions that use a totality of circumstances approach, the mere presence of a parent often seems to offset other factors, such as age or IQ, which would otherwise lead a court to a finding that the child has not knowingly and intelligently waived her rights (Farber 2004). In essence, then, the presence of a parent apparently serves as a per se rule in favor of a valid waiver despite the child's own lack of comprehension.

Another purpose of *Miranda* is prevention of coercion. Theoretically, the presence of an interested adult, like the presence of an attorney, protects the child from the coercive atmosphere of a police interrogation. For this to be true, though, the interested adult would need to understand the protections afforded by *Miranda* and the consequences of waiving those protections and would need to have the assertiveness to resist police pressures. Unfortunately, however, parents do not always have sufficient information or capacity to act in their child's best interest in the interrogation room. The guidance of even the most caring parent, as essential as it is to children's development, may not be an adequate substitute for advice of counsel in an adversarial situation (Drizin and Colgan 2004; Grisso and Ring 1979). Research has shown that a significant number of adults do not understand the *Miranda* warnings. In one study, only 42.3 percent of adults studied demonstrated an adequate understanding of each of the four *Miranda* warnings when asked to paraphrase each warning and 23.1 percent of adults received scores of zero in comprehension of at least one of the four warnings (Grisso 1980).

Perhaps most importantly, neither the totality of circumstances nor the per se approach protects a juvenile from the emotional response of her parent. When called to a police station, parents often fail to understand the consequences for their child of introducing the parental role as disciplinarian into the interrogation room. As we saw with John's mother, the initial reaction from a parent is an instinctual one of anger and frustration at the child's being in trouble and a desire to get the child to tell the truth. Parents may be ignorant of the long-term consequences from such a reaction (Kaban and Toby 1999; Grisso and Ring 1979).

Empirical research has supported the anecdotal observation that parents may be unable to protect a juvenile during police encounters (Grisso and Ring 1979). Surveyed parents reported a belief that their role was to pressure their children to cooperate with police. These parents appeared to be motivated by a stance that emphasized respect for authority and acceptance of responsibility for wrongdoing. They believed, often incorrectly, that a child who confesses will be treated more leniently. Furthermore, in the almost four hundred juvenile interrogations examined in the study, 70 to 80 percent of parents offered no advice to their children, apparently paralyzed or intimidated by the situation. When parental advice was given, parents were far more likely to advise their children to waive their rights than to assert them.

As a result, rather than assisting his child to understand and exercise her rights, a parent often serves to aid the police in their interrogation. The parent may even be drawn into "double teaming," in essence acting as a partner to the interrogating officer and adding pressure to an already coercive situation. The risks of overwhelming the child into falsely confessing or waiving her rights to counsel can be heightened rather than mitigated by the presence of a parent when the parent's anger and fear are misused by the interrogator to pressure the child (Farber 2004).

B. Exclude Parents

Given the problems posed by the presence of parents, it can be argued that the complete exclusion of parents from the interrogation process does more to protect children than the status quo. However, as discussed throughout this chapter, there are a number of valid reasons for the inclusion of parents in the interrogation process. First, the exclusion of parents at a time of crisis in the child's life, as we have shown, runs counter to a long line of cases supporting the constitutional rights of parents and children and the importance of parental involvement in children's lives. A rule preventing the parent from communicating with the child taken into police custody strikes judges and lay persons alike as fundamentally un-American. On a more pragmatic note, despite the shortcomings noted above, adults *are* more capable of understanding *Miranda* warnings than many juveniles, who need the assistance of a trusted adult in comprehending them. Finally, the presence of a parent can stabilize the child and offer reassurance, avoiding false confessions and other such miscarriages of the fact-finding process.

The interrogation process is an inherently coercive one. This environment is even more coercive in the case of juveniles (Scott-Hayward 2007). As the Supreme Court has held, "[i]f counsel was not present for some permissible reason when an admission was obtained, the greatest care must be taken to assure that the admission was voluntary, in the sense not only that it was not coerced or suggested but also that it was not the product of ignorance of rights or of adolescent fantasy, fright or despair."[19] Absent the presence of counsel, a parent is in the best position to further these interests in fairness and in accuracy.

C. Enhanced Protections for Parental Involvement

It is our position that the interrogation situation triggers a shared right of children and parents to confidential communication. While we believe parents should participate at the time of an interrogation, we also believe that additional protections must be put in place to allow for meaningful involvement of parents in the interrogation process. The steps we propose are as follows:

- When a child is brought into the interrogation room, the parent should be contacted immediately. It should not be necessary for the child explicitly to request to talk with the parent.

- Once the parent arrives, the police should advise the parent of the child's rights under *Miranda* before the parent meets with the child. This contact with the parent should not be used as an opportunity to interrogate the parent.
- The child and parent should be given a minimum of thirty to sixty minutes to consult in private without audio or video taping or eavesdropping. This will give the parent enough time to get over the initial shock, process what has occurred, find out from the child what has transpired, and begin to think clearly about next steps. This conversation should be privileged to the same degree as an attorney-client communication.
- Once the initial thirty-to-sixty-minute parent-child conversation has taken place, the police may begin the interrogation by advising the child and parent of the *Miranda* rights in language that is understandable to the child. The child must decide whether to waive her Miranda rights, with opportunity to consult (again confidentially) with the parent.
- If the child decides to talk with the police, the parent should leave the room to avoid any residual chance of double teaming by the parent.

These procedures focus on a particular moment in a police investigation of the minor suspect. Our proposals have strong foundations in constitutional law. The Bill of Rights recognizes that every suspect deserves due process. The Fifth Amendment addresses the evil of coercive interrogations and the risks of false or inaccurate statements. The Fourth Amendment protects the suspect from improper state intrusion on her constitutional privacy interests. The Sixth Amendment guarantees that the suspect will have access to counsel. Young suspects are, if anything, more subject to coercion and invasions of privacy, and more in need of informed advice than adults.

Beyond these constitutional considerations, these procedures recognize the importance of parents in the broader realm of delinquency prevention. It is easy, in the heat of the moment, for police and even for parents to lose sight of the multiple prevention values inherent in the juvenile justice process. The research on delinquency prevention shows that parents have a uniquely important role to play in deterring youth crime and reducing recidivism. But we must remember that programs like FFT and MST are effective precisely because they build on the child's trust in her parent and in the parent's credibility in demanding respect and obedience from his child. As a matter of policy, we must not permit interrogation practices that violate the confidentiality of this critically important parent-child encounter or manipulate parents in a moment of crisis into betraying their children. We should support parents and not set them up for failure in their roles as advisor and protector.

In light of the studies on parental participation in interrogations, we should assure that parents have the time, the privacy, and the necessary information about their children's rights to function effectively in their role as advisors. We should avoid pitting parents against children or manipulating parents into unwittingly harming their children. Whether the interrogation results in a delinquency petition, a criminal indictment, or realization that the young suspect is innocent, the parent and child are still parent and child the morning after. The family is our strongest weapon in reduction and prevention of delinquency and it makes no sense to sabotage the parent-child relationship in the name of public safety. We believe the procedures we propose do not unduly hamper police interrogations. They advance the state's interest in accurate fact-finding, the child's interests in due process, and the shared interest of children, parents, and society in the integrity of the parent-child relationship.[20]

VI. Conclusion

When a juvenile becomes a suspect, there are many important values implicated in what happens next. Due process, as represented by the *Miranda* warnings, is one of these values. Parental rights and family autonomy, as represented by Supreme Court doctrines, are another. Prevention, rehabilitation, and reduction of recidivism are also key values that must be taken into account in structuring ground rules for interrogation. Research and evaluation of evidence-based programs to reduce delinquency confirm our intuition that parents can play a crucial role in juvenile delinquency prevention and in rehabilitation of juvenile offenders. A single-minded focus on building a case against a juvenile suspected of criminal activity can lead to interrogation practices that compromise the parent-child relationship and interfere with broader goals of public safety and crime prevention and reduction. In our view, giving the parent time and privacy to consult with and advise the child before an interrogation begins strikes the appropriate balance both as a matter of juvenile justice policy and as a matter of constitutional law. The practices we have outlined, while they impose some restrictions on timing of an interrogation, are likely to lead to more accurate investigations, fairer outcomes, and fewer children lost to their families and to society in the criminal justice system.

1. *Dickerson v. State.* 2008. 666 S.E.2d43, 48 (Barnes, C.J., special concurrence).
2. *Clark v. Wade.* 2001. 273 Ga. 587, 589; *Meyer v. Nebraska.* 1923. 262 U.S. 390.
3. *Troxel v. Granville.* 2000. 530 U.S. 57, 65 (plurality opinion of Justice O'Connor).
4. *Prince v. Massachusetts.* 1944. 321 U.S. 158, 164.
5. The Supreme Court of Georgia has stated, "There can scarcely be imagined a more fundamental and fiercely guarded right than the right of a natural parent to its offspring." *Nix v. Dept. Human Resources.* 1976. 236 Ga. 794.
6. Among the numerous cases that establish the importance of parental rights are *Troxel v. Granville.* 2000. 530 U.S. 57, 65; *Santosky v. Kramer.* 1982. 455 U.S. 745, 759; *Quilloin v. Walcott.* 1978. 434 U.S. 246, 255; *Cleveland Board of Educ. v. LaFleur.* 1974. 414 U.S. 632, 639-40; *Stanley v. Illinois.* 1972. 405 U.S. 645, 651-52; *Prince v. Massachusetts.* 1944. 321 U.S. 158, 166; *Pierce v. Society of Sisters.* 1925. 268 U.S. 510, 534-35; and *Meyer v. Nebraska.* 1923. 262 U.S. 390, 399.
7. *Meyer,* 262 U.S. 390 at 399.
8. See *Planned Parenthood of Atlanta v. Harris.* 1987. 670 F. Supp. 971 (Georgia parental notification act requires child to consult with parent or to seek a judicial bypass before obtaining an abortion); O.C.G.A. §16-5-71.1 (parental consent needed for body piercing). For a list of state statutes that require parental consent to minor's actions, see *Brief of Juvenile Law Center, Children and Family Justice Center, Center on Children and Families, Child Welfare League of America, Children's Defense Fund, Children's Law Center of Los Angeles, National Association of Counsel for Children, and 45 Other Organizations, as Amici Curiae in Support of Respondent, Roper v. Simmons,* 543 U.S. 551 (2005), 2004 WL 1660637 (U.S., Jun. 19, 2004).
9. *Employment Division v. Smith.* 1990. 494 U.S. 872, 881 (Scalia, J.) (commenting that religion clause claims coupled with parental rights claims carry greater weight).
10. *In re Gault.* 1967. 387 U.S. 1.
11. *Riley v. State.* 1976. 237 Ga. 124, 128.
12. The recent case of *Berghuis v. Thompkins* 130 S. Ct 2250 (2010) holds that merely remaining silent is not enough to invoke *Miranda* rights. However, John declined to speak with the officers and affirmatively asked to speak with his mother.
13. The Federal Juvenile Delinquency Act, 18 USC § 5033, provides that
    > [w]henever a juvenile is taken into custody for an alleged act of juvenile delinquency, the arresting officer shall immediately advise such juvenile of his legal rights, in language comprehensive [sic] to a juvenile, and shall immediately notify the Attorney General and the juvenile's parents, guardian, or custodian of such custody. The arresting officer shall also notify the parents, guardian, or custodian of the rights of the juvenile and of the nature of the alleged offense.
14. O.C.G.A. § 15-11-6(b) ("Counsel must be provided for a child not represented by the child's parent, guardian, or custodian.").
15. The Supreme Court, in *Fare v. Michael C.,* 442 U.S. 707 (1979), rejected the notion that a suspect who asked to speak with his parole officer rather than a lawyer had an expectation of privacy. Expectations of confidentiality in discussion with a parent are grounded, as we have discussed, in doctrines of family privacy and parental rights that distinguish the relationship of parolee-parole office and parent-child.
16. *U.S. v. Wendy G.* 2001. 255 F.3d 761, 766 (internal quotations and citations omitted).

17. Ibid.

18. *Fare v. Michael C.* 1979. 442 U.S. 707.

19. *In re Gault.* 1967. 387 U.S. 1, 55.

20. Much has been written about the interrogation of juveniles and, while we do not discuss them here, we endorse additional protections for assuring fairness, such as videotaping of all police interrogations of juveniles (Drizin and Colgon 2004) and providing parent and child with an attorney to assist in the decision about waiver (Birckhead 2008).

REFERENCES

Beyer, Marty. 2000. Immaturity, Culpability, and Competency in Juveniles: A Study of 17 Cases. *Criminal Justice* 15: 27-35.

Bilchik, Shay. 2011. Redefining the Footprint of Juvenile Justice, in *Justice for Kids: Keeping Kids Out of the Juvenile Justice System*, ed. Nancy E. Dowd. New York: New York University Press.

Birckhead, Tamar R. 2008. The Age of the Child: Interrogating Juveniles after *Roper v. Simmons. Washington and Lee Law Review* 65: 385-450.

Cernkovich, Steven A., and Peggy C. Giordano. 1987. Family Relationships and Delinquency. *Criminology* 25: 295-322.

Demuth, Stephen, and Susan L. Brown. 2004. Family Structure, Family Processes, and Adolescent Delinquency: The Significance of Parental Absence versus Parental Gender. *Journal of Research in Crime and Delinquency* 41: 58-81.

Drizin, Steven A., and Beth A. Colgan. 2004. Tales from the Juvenile Confession Front: A Guide to How Standard Police Interrogation Tactics Can Produce Coerced and False Confessions from Juvenile Suspects. In *Interrogations, Confessions, and Entrapment,* ed. G. Daniel Lassiter. 153-55. New York: Springer Science & Business Media.

Farber, Hillary B. 2004. The Role of the Parent/Guardian in Juvenile Interrogations: Friend or Foe? *American Criminal Law Rev*iew 41: 1277-1312.

Feld, Barry C. 2006. Juveniles' Competence to Exercise Miranda Rights: An Empirical Study of Policy and Practice. *Minnesota Law Review* 91: 26-100.

Fondacaro, Mark R., and Lauren G. Fasig. 2006. Judging Juvenile Responsibility: A Social Ecological Perspective. In *Handbook of Children, Culture, and Violence*, ed. Nancy E. Dowd et al. 355-73. Thousand Oaks, CA: Sage.

Garbarino, James. 1999. *Lost Boys: Why Our Sons Turn Violent and How We Can Save Them.* New York: Simon & Schuster.

Greenwood, Peter. 2008. Prevention and Intervention Programs for Juvenile Offenders. *Future of Children* 18: 185-210.

Grisso, Thomas. 1980. Juveniles' Capacities to Waive Miranda Rights: An Empirical Analysis. *Cal. L. Rev.* 68: 1134-66.

Grisso, Thomas, and Melissa Ring. 1979. Parents' Attitudes toward Juveniles' Rights in Interrogation. *Criminal Justice and Behavior* 6: 211-26.

Heilbrun, Kirk, et al. 2005. *Juvenile Delinquency: Prevention, Assessment, and Intervention.* New York: Oxford University Press.

Henggeler, Scott W., and Charles M. Bourduin. 1990. *Family Therapy and Beyond: A Multisystemic Approach to Treating Behavior Problems of Children and Adolescents.* Pacific Grove, CA: Brooks/Cole Publishing.

Henggeler, Scott W., and Cindy M. Schaeffer. 2010. Treating Serious Emotional and Behavioral Problems Using Multisystemic Therapy. *Australian and New Zealand Journal of Family therapy* 31(2): 149-64.

Herrenkhol, Todd I., Eugene Maguin, Karl G. Hill, J. David Hawkins, Robert D. Abbot, and Richard F. Catalano. 2000. Developmental Risk Factors for Youth Violence. *Journal of Adolescent Health* 26: 178-86.

Kaban, Barbara, and Ann E. Toby. 1999. When Police Question Children: Are Protections Adequate? *Jouranl of the Center for Children and the Courts* 1: 151-60.

Lassiter, G. Daniel, ed. 2004. *Interrogations, Confessions, and Entrapment.* Athens: Ohio University.

McGuire, Robert E. 2000. A Proposal to Strengthen Juvenile Miranda Rights: Requiring Parental Presence in Custodial Interrogations. *Vanderbilt Law Review* 53: 1355-88.

Scott-Hayward, Christine S. 2007. Explaining Juvenile False Confessions: Adolescent Development and Police Interrogation. *Law and Psychology Review* 31: 53-76.

Sexton, Thomas L., and James F. Alexander. 2003. Functional Family Therapy: A Mature Clinical Model for Working with At-Risk Adolescents and Their Families. In *Handbook of Family Therapy: The Science and Practice of Working with Families and Couples*, ed. Thomas L. Sexton et al. New York: Brunner-Routledge. 323-48.

Sexton, Thomas L., and James F. Alexander. 2000. Functional Family Therapy. *Juvenile Justice Bulletin* 6: 1-8.

Sexton, Thomas L., Gerald R. Weeks, and Michael S. Robbins. 2003. *Handbook of Family Therapy: The Science and Practice of Working with Families and Couples.* New York: Brunner-Routledge.

Slobogin, Christopher, and Mark R. Fondacaro. 2009. Juvenile Justice: The Fourth Option. *Iowa Law Review* 95: 1-62.

Wells, Edward L., and Joseph H. Rankin. 1988. Direct Parental Controls and Delinquency. *Criminology* 26: 263-85.

Model Programs

Moving beyond Exclusion

Integrating Restorative Practices and Impacting School Culture in Denver Public Schools

THALIA N. C. GONZÁLEZ AND
BENJAMIN CAIRNS

Introduction

The practice of restorative justice within schools has emerged as an alternative model to traditional punitive and adversarial processes (Cox 1995; Cameron and Thorsborne 2001). Educators, policy makers, practitioners, and academics have identified restorative justice as both a theoretical and a practical framework by which to develop more balanced responses to occurrences of school-based misbehavior (Braithwaite 2002; Karp and Breslin 2001; Morrison 2001). In contrast to the retributive emphasis of traditional policies, such as zero tolerance, restorative approaches to school discipline focus on repairing the harm, engaging victims, establishing accountability, developing a community, and preventing future actions (Bazemore 1999; Bazemore 2001; Van Ness and Strong 2001). In this context, restorative justice converts the response to misbehavior from one of punishment or zero tolerance to interventions that accentuate accountability, fairness, and situational responses to unique events and individuals.

More specifically, in contrast to the emphasis of traditional punitive responses on uniformity, isolation, and, often, expulsion or suspension, restorative justice adamantly affirms that a wrong was done, acknowledges the resulting harm, and then promotes acceptance of the wrongdoing (Payne, Gottfredson, and Gottfredson 2003; Wenzel, Okimoto, Feather, and Platow 2008). Therefore, school-based restorative justice is characterized by its focus on relational rehabilitation (Karp and Breslin 2001). This approach is ultimately concerned with changing behaviors, promoting healthy school communities, and impacting larger issues of school safety, high dropout rates, and low graduation rates (Balfanz and Letgers 2004; Morrison, Blood, and

Thorsborne 2005). Although there have been a number of international studies emphasizing the effectiveness of restorative justice programs in schools, there continues to be a need for adoption and evaluation of school-based restorative justice programs within the United States.

The purpose of this chapter is to explore the potential of restorative justice to improve school safety, promote student performance, and increase student engagement without a disproportionate reliance on suspensions and expulsions. In doing so, this chapter will draw upon the experience of the restorative justice program at North High School in Denver, Colorado, as a case study of restorative justice with broader implications for more holistic educational reform. While the findings are preliminary, they are suggestive of promising alternatives to traditional punitive and exclusionary discipline practices in schools (Morrison, Blood, and Thorsborne 2005).

Understanding Restorative Justice

Restorative justice can be defined as a principle-based method of responding to harmful behavior (Morrison 2007). It includes processes that seek to achieve justice by repairing harms (Bazemore and Walgrave 1999; Van Ness and Strong 2001). The practice of restorative justice therefore challenges underlying assumptions of retributive forms of justice and places emphasis on healing over punishment (Braithwaite 2002; Braithwaite and Strang 2001). While the practice can involve punishment of the offender, it promotes more constructive forms of accountability as alternatives to the mere infliction of suffering (Wenzel, Okimoto, Feather, and Platow 2008). For example, after students fight at North High School (the focus of this study), they are given the chance to sit down with the other student and their parents or guardians in order to explore why they fought, what harm they did, and how that harm can be repaired. This process and its contractual outcomes often occur in lieu of suspensions, expulsions, referrals to law enforcement, or court citations.

Restorative justice is marked by three principles: (1) reparation of harm, (2) stakeholder involvement, and (3) transformation (Stinchcomb, Bazemore, and Riestenberg 2006). The first principle establishes the set of outcomes for the restorative practice and concentrates on repairing the harm. The second principle seeks to maximize involvement from all affected stakeholders, including the offender, the victim, their supporters, and the community as a whole. The third principle focuses on empowering individuals and building community capacity (Van Ness and Strong 2001). Through this lens, restorative justice focuses on addressing basic social and emotional needs of individuals and communities (Bazemore 1992; Zehr 2002). These interrelated principles also suggest independent goals and priorities. The first principle focuses on rebuilding and strengthening relationships (Zehr 2002). The second principle promotes ownership over the conflict and those harmed (Zehr 2002). The third principle represents a less direct role for traditional punitive justice systems through the engagement and empowerment of individuals and communities (Stinchcomb, Bazemore, and Riestenberg 2006).

Restorative justice offers all participants who are affected by the harmful behavior an opportunity to participate in a multifaceted dialogue that builds understanding and promotes social engagement. Accordingly, it is not a singular program or process, but rather a concept based on a core set of principles that are interrelated and mutually reinforcing (Braithwaite 1999). This multilevel approach is critical, for example, when considering the complex problems of school violence and discipline. As Skiba and Noam (2001) conclude, efforts must address a variety of levels and include universal interventions that teach all students alternatives to violence, procedures to identify and reintegrate students who may be at risk for violence, and interventions specifically designed for students already exhibiting disruptive or aggressive behavior. Furthermore, these strategies are consistent with theories of responsive regulation based on restorative justice (Braithwaite 2002). Central to the restorative practice is the maintenance of individuals' dignity and sense of self-worth (Morrison, Blood, and Thorsborne 2005). Therefore, the goal of restorative justice is to harness the capacity to strengthen internal sanctioning systems through building a community of accountability and responsibility. This creates a collective understanding of what happened and how people were affected, and then determines the appropriate responses to repair the harm (Morrison, Blood, and Thorsborne 2005).

Restorative Justice in Schools

The first documented use of restorative justice in schools occurred in the early 1990s with initiatives in Australia led by Margaret Thorsborne in response to issues raised by a serious assault after a school dance (Cameron and Thorsborne 2001). Since that time, school-based restorative justice programs have been studied in New Zealand, Canada, England, Wales, and the United States (Calhoun 2000; Stinchcomb, Bazemore, and Riestenberg 2006; Youth Justice Board 2004). As restorative justice models have evolved within schools, it is clear that they contribute to the aims of education by emphasizing accountability, restitution, and restoration of community. In other words, the primary function of the process is to reintegrate the offender as a productive member of the school community, rather than further exiling the student and thereby increasing the potential for separation, resentment, and recidivism. Schools, in contrast to the legal system, provide a unique context in which the injury to the community is clearly defined and restitution can be formulated. In schools, it is easier to identify members of the community who can play a positive role in the restorative justice process. Additionally, schools, unlike the legal system, have the capacity and knowledge to implement strategies that are long-term and sustainable.

The practice of restorative justice in schools has changed in response to the institutional framework of education (Morrison 2007). A significant development in the field was a movement beyond the conferencing model, as adopted from the criminal and juvenile justice systems, and the establishment of a continuum of restorative approaches. For example, Wachtel and McCold (2001) promoted the continuum model, which ranged from the informal to the formal. Movement along the continuum involved more people, planning, time, and structure in dealing with offenses to ensure the highest level of impact on the offender (Wachtel and McCold 2001). These practices include affective statements, questions, informal conferences, large-group circles, and formal conferences.

Hopkins (2004) defined a whole-school approach to restorative justice in terms of a framework that responded to the diverse needs of an individual school. In a whole-school approach, restorative practices include, but are not limited to, restorative inquiry, mediation, community conferences, small-group conferences, problem-solving circles, and family conferences. The whole-school approach is grounded in a shared set of values, respect, openness, empowerment, inclusion, tolerance, integrity, and congruence (Hopkins 2004). From these values, participants learn the skills of remaining impartial and nonjudgmental, respecting the perspectives of all involved, developing rapport, actively and empathically listening, creatively questioning, becoming empowered, and exercising compassion and patience (Hopkins 2004). Together these skills and values seek to involve the school community in the restorative process in order to collectively address the needs and obligations of the entire school.

Thorsborne and Vinegrad also envisioned a continuum of restorative practices as including both proactive and reactive processes (Morrison 2007). They distinguish between two types of conference models: the proactive model, which functions to enhance teaching and learning; and the reactive model, which responds to harm and wrongdoing (Morrison 2007). The proactive classroom conference focuses on supporting learning outcomes, setting boundaries, and developing relationships (Morrison 2007). These processes link curriculum, pedagogy, and behavior management. The reactive classroom conference provides an interpersonal and disciplinary link in the classroom (Morrison 2007).

It is important to understand that the implementation of restorative practice in every school will be different. Some schools will turn to restorative practices to address high suspension or expulsion rates (Riestenberg 2003; Morrison 2003; Stinchcomb, Bazemore, and Riestenberg 2006; IIRP 2009). Other schools will implement restorative practices to address issues of school safety or disrespectful relationships and behaviors (Stinchcomb, Bazemore, and Riestenberg 2006; Morrison 2003; IIRP 2009; Christensen 2009) or to improve academic success and student performance (Morrison, Blood, and Thorsborne 2005; Morrison 2007; Jennings, Gover, and Hitchcock 2008). As Blood and Thorsborne (2006) note in *Overcoming Resistance to Whole-School Uptake of Restorative Practices*, for implementation of restorative practice to be successful there must be a shift in value placement on developing relationships and connectedness across the school community rather than promoting exclusion and separation from the school community. The central point for school communities to recognize is that cultural change does not happen quickly and a long-term sustainable approach must be taken. Schools should envision a three– to five-year implementation plan that focuses on five key areas; first, gaining commitment from the school community, a process that requires establishing the reasons for implementation, as well as buy-in from key members of the school community; second, developing a clear institutional vision with short-, medium-, and long-term goals; third, establishing responsive and effective practice; fourth, developing policies that align with restorative practice to transition into a whole-school approach rather than a program-based model; fifth, investing in an ongoing system of growth and development for all members of the school community (Morrison, Blood, and Thorsborne 2005). Ultimately, in the context of sustaining school-wide behavioral change, it is important for schools to recognize that the implementation of restorative practice is not simply a case of overlaying the justice model of conferencing and achieving sustained outcomes (Morrison, Blood, and Thorsborne 2005). Unlike criminal justice settings, where victims and offenders may not see each other again, members of a school community often see each other the next day. As a consequence, minor incidents can quickly escalate if not addressed fully. Thus, restorative practices must be clearly embedded in the culture of the school for successful and sustained implementation to occur.

Punitive Discipline Policies in Schools

School communities, comprised of students, parents, teachers, and administrators, have long been viewed as fulfilling important roles in affirming norms and other positive social values that impact student engagement (Suvall 2009). The aim of restorative practices in schools is, therefore, to create a context in which students accept responsibility for their actions and develop stronger relationships within the school community (Morrison, Blood, and Thorsborne 2005). Unlike the simplicity of punitive models for regulating schools, such as zero tolerance policies, restorative practice approaches school-based offenses as complex behaviors. Given the inclusionary nature of restorative justice, a commitment is developed to the school as a community (Stinchcomb, Bazemore, and Riestenberg 2006). School-based restorative practice also has the capacity to build social and emotional capital through challenging students in the context of social and emotional learning (Morrison, Blood, and Thorsborne 2005). Reflecting on the initial work in Australian schools, Cameron and Thorsborne suggest that restorative practice should focus attention on relationships among all members of a school community (Cameron and Thorsborne 2001). Furthermore, their work proposes that restorative justice teaches participants the value of achieving positive outcomes through relationships (Cameron and Thorsborne 2001). By implementing restorative justice practices, schools can become institutions that develop the genuine and positive relationships essential to developing social capital (Payne, Gottfredson, and Gottfredson 2003; Morrison, Blood, and Thorsborne 2005).

The explicit concentration of restorative practice on relationships presents a positive alternative to exclusionary-based policies addressing student misconduct (Braithwaite 2002; Forgays and DeMilio 2005; Morrison, Blood, and Thorsborne 2005). Not only does exclusion, through suspension and expulsion, deprive students of educational opportunities but also it fails to make schools safer places for other students (Advancement Project 2005; Stinchcomb, Bazemore, and Riestenberg 2006; Suvall 2009). Exclusion and harsh discipline also have negative effects on the offending student, which increase the likelihood of future disciplinary problems. Furthermore, a focus on exclusion from the school community interferes with student academic achievement, further fueling negative attitudes and leading to increased dropout rates (Balfanz 2007). As researchers have consistently emphasized (Balfanz 2007; Balfanz, Herzog, and Mac Iver 2007; Balfanz, Fox, Bridgeland, and McNaught 2008), understanding the dropout problem in a school community is an important first step in developing and implementing plans to reduce the number of dropouts and increase the graduation rate. While many of the factors leading to student disengagement are not school related, the behavioral indicators of student disengagement, such as poor attendance and suspensions, manifest themselves directly at school. As Mac Iver and Mac Iver summarize in *Beyond the Indicators: An Integrated School-Level Approach to Dropout Prevention* (2009), the important research-based "early warning indicators" for student dropout include receiving an unsatisfactory behavior grade or suspension at the middle school level or suspension in the ninth grade. In fact, the best demographic indicator of a student who will face suspension or expulsion is not the behavior of the student but whether the student has been suspended before. Furthermore, Balfanz and Legters (2004) observed that many high schools in the United States could be considered "dropout factories" due to the fact that fewer than 50 percent of ninth graders completed the twelfth grade. Additionally, these schools consistently had daily attendance rates below 80 percent (Balfanz and Legters 2004). For example, data collected in five Colorado districts with high numbers of dropouts (Denver Public Schools, Jefferson County Public Schools, Aurora Public Schools, Adams 12 Five Star District, and Pueblo City Schools) shows that students who dropped out were roughly twice, and sometimes nearly three times, as likely to have been suspended at least once over the four-year period 2003-2004 to 2006-2007 (Mac Iver, Balfanz, and Byrnes 2009). In fact, analysis of the 2006-2007 dropouts in the Denver Public Schools indicated that 10 percent had been suspended at least once during the two-year period 2005-2007, compared to 6 percent of graduates (Mac Iver, Balfanz, and Byrnes 2009).

Restorative practice in schools also offers a proactive alternative to reactive zero tolerance policies. Emerging in the late 1980s, zero tolerance policies became widespread in the early 1990s (Skiba and Peterson 1999; Advancement Project 2010). As in the criminal context, the mandatory punishments of zero tolerance policies are designed to be highly punitive in order to send a strong deterrent message (Skiba and Noam 2001; Skiba and Peterson 1999; Hirschfeld 2008). Under school zero tolerance policies, students are suspended or expelled for a single occurrence of certain specified conduct (Advancement Project 2010). Zero tolerance policies include a range of behaviors, such as violence, bullying, threatening, use of profanity, alcohol or tobacco consumption, and other offenses (Stinchcomb, Bazemore, and Riestenberg 2006; Suvall 2009; Advancement Project 2010). "Three strikes" laws in Colorado allow teachers to permanently remove students from their classrooms if they are disruptive more than three times in one year, and another law mandates expulsion if a student is suspended three times during a school year for causing a "material and substantial disruption" (Advancement Project 2010; Colo. Rev. Stat. § 22-32-109.1 (2)(a)(II) 2008; Colo. Rev. Stat. § 22-33-106 (1)(c.5)(II) 2008). Zero tolerance policies reflect an approach to discipline that mirrors the criminal justice system (Skiba and Noam 2001; Suvall 2009). Unfortunately, this approach does not create safer school environments. In 2006, a task force of the American Psychological Association published an evidentiary review of studies over the preceding ten years evaluating the impact of zero tolerance policies. They found that zero tolerance did not improve school safety (APA Zero Tolerance Task Force 2006). Additionally, the study concluded that schools with higher suspensions and expulsions due to the presence of zero tolerance policies had less satisfactory ratings of school climate (APA Zero Tolerance Task Force 2006). The study also found that out-of-school suspensions and expulsions did not reduce the likelihood of future student misconduct (APA Zero Tolerance Task Force 2006).

Implementation of restorative practice, rather than punitive policies in schools, also presents a clear model for addressing the school-to-prison pipeline. A result of a movement in the 1980s to implement increased punitive policies in schools and the criminal justice system, the school-to-prison pipeline refers to school-discipline and criminal-justice policies that promote the removal of students from schools and speed up their entry into the juvenile– and criminal-justice systems (Siman 2005; Smith 2009; Advancement Project 2010). The continuum of entry points into the pipeline leading to prison range from early school-based behavior problems that result in suspensions, expulsions, or Disciplinary Alternative Education Program placements to more serious law breaking and probation violations that involve the juvenile justice system and, ultimately, criminal prosecution and incarceration by the adult penal system (Lewis 2009). In 2003, the House of Delegates of the American Bar Association, in recognition of the American Bar Association's extensive reporting on the racially disparate impacts of punitive discipline, voted to adopt the recommendation of its Commission on Youth at Risk, urging schools and courts to reduce criminalization of truancy, disability-related behavior, and other school-related conduct (American Bar Association 2003). In 2005, the Advancement Project's report, *Education on Lockdown: The Schoolhouse to Jailhouse Track,* examined the role of police in three school districts—Denver, Chicago, and Palm Beach County—and concluded that schools continued to inappropriately adopt law enforcement strategies leading students unnecessarily into the juvenile or criminal justice system (Advancement Project 2005). Similarly, the 2010 Texas Appleseed report, *Texas' School-to-Prison Pipeline: The Path from Lockout to Dropout*, showed that the 1995 reforms and zero tolerance school discipline policies had a major, deleterious impact on the rate of school dropouts and juvenile involvement with the criminal justice system. The report found that more than a third of Texas public school students dropped out in 2005-2006, one in three juveniles sent to the Texas Youth Commission were school dropouts, and more than 80 percent of Texas prison inmates are dropouts (Appleseed 2010). During 2008-2009, discretionary expulsions made up 71 percent of all expulsions statewide.

The transformation of educational systems associated with punitive discipline to systems associated with restorative justice is critical to improving student performance, impacting the school-to-prison pipeline, and creating safer school communities. Research clearly shows that students feel more connected to schools when they perceive their teachers to have high expectations for good behavior, demonstrate that they care, and implement discipline fairly and tolerantly (McNeely, Nonnemaker, and Blum 2002).

Restorative Justice Program at North High School

The Restorative Justice Program at North High School represents one example of a school-based disciplinary practice that has adopted alternative processes to build a safer school culture, reduce suspensions and referrals to law enforcement, and impact educational performance. To a large degree, the experience of North High School with restorative justice practice cannot be captured by quantitative data alone. Many of the individual participants, including students, parents, teachers, and administrators, shared numerous stories of transformational experiences as part of the restorative justice program. The case study *infra* represents one example of the multifaceted Restorative Justice Program at North High School.

Background

In 2006, Denver Public Schools approached the Colorado Department of Education with a proposal to institute a formal, school-based restorative justice program in response to increasing school suspensions and expulsions. For example, from 2000 to 2005, the number of out-of-school suspensions in the district rose from 9,846 to 13,487 (Baker 2007). The rise in suspensions was also coupled with a 71 percent increase in referrals to law enforcement (Baker 2007). Given this alarming trend, Denver Public Schools proposed the implementation of a restorative justice program to reduce its reliance on suspensions, expulsions, and referrals to law enforcement (Baker 2007). Subsequent to an assessment of these findings, the Colorado Department of Education awarded Denver Public Schools a three hundred thousand dollar grant for Expelled and At Risk Student Service Programs. The purpose of the grant was to support the district's efforts to engage in an educational trans-formation by reducing suspensions, expulsions, and tickets by 20 percent per year at North High School and its feeder middle schools, Horace Mann, Lake, and Skinner (Baker 2007).

North High School is one of Denver's oldest comprehensive high schools and historically has a reputation for violence, gang activity, and truancy (stu-dent interviews November 13, 2009). North High School's demographics are similar to those of many struggling urban schools across the country. The current enrollment at North High School is 961 students (Denver Public Schools 2009). Students qualifying for free and reduced lunches constitute 74 percent of the student body, and 93 percent of the students are minori-ties (Denver Public Schools 2009; Baker 2008). On the basis of issues related to violence, gang activity, truancy, dropouts, and poor student performance, North High School was selected as a pilot site for a formal restorative justice program.

Program Development and Implementation

The 2006 Colorado Department of Education grant provided for place-ment of a full-time Restorative Justice Coordinator at North High School to implement restorative justice practices. On the basis of positive initial results, the Colorado Department of Education expanded the grant to include a second high school and its feeder middle schools in early 2007. The Colorado Department of Education grant provided full funding for the 2006-2009 school years. Currently there are seven schools utilizing Colo-rado Department of Education grant funds to employ Restorative Justice Coordinators.

Consistent with findings by Karp and Breslin (2001) that school-based restorative justice program implementation requires adaptation to specific school culture, the North High School program utilizes diverse restorative methods (see also McNeely, Nonnemaker, and Blum 2002). Specifically, the North High School program focuses on developing a whole-school approach to restorative justice. Since its inception, the North High School program has been developed and implemented by a full-time Restorative Justice Coordinator who works collaboratively with the assistant principal, the student advisor or dean, and the school-based resource officer. North High School attributes the success of the Restorative Justice Program as a whole-school model to the close and interconnected relationships between the Restorative Justice Coordinator and school administrators (D. Fuentes, personal correspondence January 11, 2010). Since its creation, the goal of the Restorative Justice Program has been to provide a multilevel alternative to punitive discipline policies and practices in order to promote a healthy school community, positively impact school safety, and improve academic success.

Restorative Practices

While initial research on the Restorative Justice Program at North High School outlined a one-dimensional model for the program, the Restorative Justice Program now uses a continuum model, which includes formal and informal restorative practices (Jennings, Gover, and Hitchcock 2008). These practices include mediations, conferences, and circles. Each of these practices emphasizes key restorative principles of identifying harm, establishing responsibility, and developing a remedy. The aim of the Restorative Justice Program is to develop relationships among affected parties, including students, parents, teachers, administrators, and the community. This goal is consistent with Bazemore and Umbreit's (2001) balanced restorative justice model, which encourages integration of victims, offenders, and the school community.

The Restorative Justice Coordinator utilizes specific questions to establish a framework for each of the restorative practices used. These questions are as follows.

1. What happened?
2. What are the effects?
3. Who is responsible? What part of this problem are you responsible for?
4. How will the situation be repaired?

Restorative mediations are used when both parties bear equal responsibility for an incident, for example, when a fight occurs. The restorative mediation is structured in a manner that allows facilitated dialogue, where each party takes turns answering basic restorative questions until an agreement is reached. Consistent with underlying assumptions of restorative practice, the role of the Restorative Justice Coordinator is to remain neutral.

Restorative conferences are similar to mediations but occur when there is not an equally shared responsibility between parties, for example, when bullying occurs. During a restorative conference, the Restorative Justice Coordinator focuses on correcting an imbalance of power between parties and on creating a structure to protect the victim. Additionally, the Restorative Justice Coordinator is responsible for balancing the needs of the victim and the offender.

Restorative circles, characterized as group conferences in other research, are used for incidents among multiple parties. At North High School a restorative circle is similar to a restorative mediation, in that each party takes turns answering basic restorative questions. In contrast to a two-party restorative mediation, the participants are arranged in nonadversarial positions, and each answers the questions in the order in which he or she is sitting. Restorative circles at North High School are also structured to include members of the school community who are indirectly impacted by an incident or behavior. Restorative circles are most commonly used in classrooms to support learning outcomes, set boundaries, and develop positive relationships. The restorative circles are linked to curriculum, pedagogy, and behavior management. Additionally, restorative circles are used in circumstances when six or more students are involved.

Outcomes

Typical outcomes of the Restorative Justice Program include personal apologies, public apologies, agreements to be polite, reestablished friendship, agreements to show mutual respect, agreements to address conflicts in private, and community service. After each restorative mediation, conference, or circle, the Restorative Justice Coordinator follows up with all parties to ensure that the restorative agreement or outcome is being met. As programmatic evaluations indicate, Restorative Justice Program participants exhibit an 80 percent satisfaction rate (Baker 2007; Baker 2008). Additionally, results show that over 75 percent of participants feel that the agreements are followed completely (Baker 2007; Baker 2008). Moreover, 85 percent of all participants felt satisfied with the outcome of the process (Baker 2007; Baker 2008).

During its first two years, the Restorative Justice Program at North High School conducted an estimated 120 formal restorative mediations, conferences, and circles per academic year. During the 2008-2009 school year, the program conducted 199 formal cases. Fifty-seven of these cases were in lieu of suspension (Baker 2009). The Restorative Justice Program also reduced out-of-school suspensions by 39 percent, referrals to law enforcement by 15 percent, and expulsions by 82 percent by the end of the 2007-2008 school year (Baker 2008). In 2009, a student and faculty focus group conducted at North High School found strong support for the Restorative Justice Program and emphasized its positive impact on school culture (Baker 2009).

The North High School discipline team has also begun collecting data on school fights. During the 2007-2008 school year, the first year of the data collection, there were thirty-six "official" fights. During the 2008-2009 school year, twenty-four fights occurred, and in the fall of 2009, only seven fights occurred (D. Fuentes, personal correspondence January 11, 2010). The discipline team attributes this significant decrease in the severity and violence of fights to the use of restorative practices (D. Fuentes, personal correspondence January 11, 2010). The discipline team at North High School strongly believes that the adoption of a whole school approach to restorative practices will produce a continued drop in violent and antisocial forms of conflict management among students. There are many signs that this is already happening, such as students requesting mediation prior to a discipline incident (D. Fuentes, personal correspondence January 11, 2010). Additionally, one North High School security guard estimated that he and the dean conducted one hundred informal conferences in the fall of 2009 (C. Adams, personal correspondence January 8, 2009). Since these restorative practices occur prior to an incident becoming a formal discipline matter, and are preventative in nature, it is difficult to quantitatively identify their impact within the annual Denver Public Schools disciplinary program reports.

While the findings from North High School are preliminary, they suggest that implementation of restorative justice practice has begun to have whole-school impact. Evidence of a reduction in school suspensions, referrals to law enforcement, and expulsions, as well as the emerging trend of self-referrals to the Restorative Justice Program prior to engagement with formal discipline measures, clearly indicates positive long-term changes within the institution. Given the difficulty in assessing the transformative nature of school-based restorative practice through quantitative data alone, the following case study illustrates how the North High School program provides an individualized response to student misbehavior, supports uninterrupted academic experience, promotes school safety, and decreases student contact with the juvenile justice system.

Case Study

Incident

Jose entered North High School during the fall of 2006, the same year the Restorative Justice Program was formally launched. His brother Pedro entered the following year. While Jose and Pedro were not formally part of a gang, they associated with North Denver, or the "North Side." This association meant that while Jose and Pedro were affiliated with many gang members and had many friends who were active gang members, they did not consider themselves gang members. Their involvement was characterized by high levels of fighting if they felt like the "North Side" was disrespected, but did not involve specific fights over turf, tagging, or gang-specific criminal behavior. Like many students at North High School, they struggled academically and fell into the overaged/undercredited category.

In the fall of 2008, Jose and Pedro, along with their friend Joe, were referred to the Restorative Justice Program to address a disciplinary matter. Prior to 2008 each student had had limited contact with punitive school discipline processes. During a lunchtime basketball game, Jose and another young man, Tony, began exchanging words. After the game ended Jose felt like Tony was "muggin'" him. In a later restorative conference Jose defined "muggin'" to mean a look intended to threaten, intimidate, or challenge. Jose refused to look away and the students began to exchange further verbal threats. Tony was from East Denver, and the verbal exchange quickly escalated to include gang-related language. After the exchange, Jose felt disrespected and decided he could not allow this incident to go unaddressed. He located his brother Pedro and friend Joe, and they began looking for Tony. They found Tony sitting in his math class and entered the classroom. All three students then challenged Tony to a fight and threatened him with violence. The teacher called both school security and the school resource officer to remove the students from the classroom. School security brought Tony to the dean's office. Tony broke down sobbing in the dean's office. He thought the incident had ended with the few words at the basketball court, and felt very threatened by Jose, Pedro, and Joe. Additionally, Tony expressed concerns to the dean that he would be threatened or harmed by other "North Siders." He talked of leaving school and getting gang members he knew from East Denver to fight Jose, Joe, and Pedro.

Restorative Intervention

After meeting with Tony, the dean and the school-based resource officer decided that the incident might be more effectively addressed through the use of restorative practices, rather than punitive measures. Under the North High School student discipline policy, the incident, which began as an exchange of words and escalated to bullying and serious threats, was punishable by a court citation and a five-day out-of-school suspension. Prior to moving forward with a restorative solution, the Restorative Justice Coordinator held a brief meeting with Tony to determine if he was willing to participate in a restorative conference, before presenting this alternative process to the other students. In the meeting, the Restorative Justice Coordinator presented Tony with punitive and restorative options, and specifically asked him what would help him feel the safest at school. The options were (1) the three students would be charged in juvenile court and suspended for five days or (2) all four students would engage in a restorative conference with the intention of reaching an agreement focused on repairing the harm of the incident and preventing future incidents. Initially Tony was angry and humiliated, and not interested in a restorative solution, but ultimately he decided to engage in a restorative conference. He stated safety at school as his primary reason for engaging in the restorative conference. Although the school-based resource officer decided that it was important to issue a court citation, he and the Restorative Justice Coordinator agreed that they would communicate the outcome of the restorative process to the juvenile court. At the same time, the dean opted to hold the students' suspensions and await the outcome of the conference.

Once Tony made his decision, the Restorative Justice Coordinator met with him and the other students separately. He explained the basic process of the restorative conference, rules for the restorative conference, and possible outcomes, including what would happen if they were not able to reach a restorative outcome. Once all the students understood what was going to happen and what was expected of them, Jose, Pedro, and Joe were sent home for the rest of the day and Tony returned to class.

The restorative conference took place the following morning. The Restorative Justice Coordinator established the following "rules" for the conference: the students were not to interrupt each other; they were to speak respectfully; and what was said in the conference was to remain confidential. Once the participants agreed to participate, the Restorative Justice Coordinator explained the four questions that were to guide the restorative conference:

1. What happened?
2. What are the effects on you, the other people involved, your families, and the school?
3. What part of this incident are you responsible for?
4. How do we repair the harm or fix the situation?

Jose began with his answers and was followed by Tony. Joe and Pedro responded after Tony spoke. Initially the meeting was very tense. As Jose described the incident, he attempted to justify the threats of violence made against Tony. He also admitted that going to the room with two friends was unfair. When Tony told his side of the story, he expressed fear and concern for his safety at North High School. He told Jose he did not have an issue with him, regretted escalating their exchange of words, and said he was not someone who looked for fights. When the Restorative Justice Coordinator asked Pedro and Joe to respond to the questions, they both commented on how they realized that they were acting like bullies and how stupid it was to threaten Tony over something so trivial. During the conference Tony transitioned away from the role of a victim and acknowledged that he escalated the incident by "talking trash" and "muggin'" Jose.

Jose, Pedro, and Joe apologized to Tony for intimidating him. At the end of the conference the Restorative Justice Coordinator and the students drafted a restorative contract that stated how they would repair the harm or "fix" the situation. The restorative contract was focused on addressing issues of fear and school safety. It established a plan to speak with each other in a calm and private way to resolve any future incidents. It also required that all students tell their friends that the situation was fixed so that future conflicts would be avoided. Lastly, Jose decided that he would apologize to the class he interrupted, and acknowledged publicly that he should not have bullied Tony with his two friends. The students shook hands and went to class.

Subsequent to the restorative conference, the Restorative Justice Coordinator informed the juvenile court about the outcomes after observing that the terms of the agreement had been met. The juvenile court recommended that the students receive unsupervised diversion and required them to meet for six weeks with the Restorative Justice Coordinator to work on practicing nonviolent conflict resolution.

The agreement was honored throughout the school year. In fact, at the end of the year Tony thought Jose disrespected him in the bathroom.

Tony immediately met with the Restorative Justice Coordinator and requested that a restorative conference be facilitated with Jose. They held a restorative conference and quickly solved the issue. During the restorative conference Jose indicated he was glad that Tony requested a restorative conference, rather than escalating an unnecessary confrontation. Tony remained friendly with the other students the rest of the year. Since the initial restorative conference, all of the students involved have either utilized restorative principles or the North High School Restorative Justice Program to manage conflict.

Outcomes

Joe has not engaged in any further incidents or become further involved with the juvenile justice system. He has received all of his credits and anticipates graduating in May 2011.

Jose has also avoided further interaction with the juvenile justice system. Despite the fact that he continues to associate with a gang lifestyle, he has not been in a fight or altercation at North High School that warranted disciplinary action. Twice he has been involved in incidents that could have escalated to a fight, but both times he worked with the Restorative Justice Coordinator to avoid escalated conflicts. Jose has mediated several conflicts among his friends, indicating that his goal has been to maintain a peaceful school. He anticipates graduation upon completion of the 2010 fall semester.

Pedro continues to utilize informal and formal restorative justice processes to deescalate conflict. Early in the fall of 2009 he and another student planned to fight after school. Instead of fighting, he sought out the other student and engaged in an informal restorative conference before any school administrators were involved. In interviews, he stated that it is just easier to handle things the restorative way.

Tony has since transferred from North High School. He was involved in an incident at his new school and asked the administration for restorative justice. The administration contacted the North High School Restorative Justice Coordinator and reached a restorative solution to the situation.

Findings

As the case study shows, the use of restorative justice can positively impact issues of school safety, decrease contact with the juvenile justice system, and promote academic achievement.

While the case study is not meant to prove that school-based restorative justice programs automatically lead to desirable outcomes, it presents valuable insight into the potential impact of formal and informal restorative processes. Given this, several preliminary conclusions are warranted.

First, this case study affirms the conclusion that alternative discipline processes can promote student safety (Morrison 2003). For example, Tony was aware of Jose's gang connections and felt scared that Jose would ultimately follow through on the threats he made in the classroom. His initial response to involve gang members he knew to ensure his safety could have led to a dramatically different outcome than outlined in the case study. Additionally, suspending or expelling Jose, Pedro, and Joe would not have made Tony feel safer coming to school. In fact, implementing punitive measures against Jose, Pedro, and Joe would have probably led them to retaliate against Tony in a more violent manner. Moreover, a harsher outcome from the juvenile court would not have made Tony feel safer at school. It was only through the restorative conference and agreement that Tony's concerns regarding safety were alleviated.

Second, this case study confirms the conclusion that alternative discipline processes can decrease student contact with the juvenile justice system, thus impacting the school-to-prison pipeline (Siman 2005). In fact, data collected during the fall 2009 semester shows that the school-based resource officer has issued a significantly lower number of citations (eleven citations in the fall of 2009 compared to eighty in the previous school year). The discipline team at North High School attributes this decrease in citations to the effectiveness of the restorative justice program in achieving a safe school climate (D. Fuentes, personal correspondence January 11, 2010). Furthermore, neither Tony, Pedro, Jose, nor Joe has increased his gang involvement as a result of this incident.

Third, this case study supports the conclusion that alternative discipline processes promote uninterrupted academic experiences (Mac Iver, Balfanz, and Byrnes 2009). For example, Jose, Pedro, and Joe only missed two class periods, rather than five full academic days. Additionally, Tony did not miss school due to feeling unsafe or threatened. As noted in the 2009 report *Advancing the "Colorado Graduates" Agenda: Understanding the Dropout Problem and Mobilizing to Meet the Graduation Challenge*, schools must adopt goals and strategies for dropout prevention, such as reducing absences and suspensions (Mac Iver, Balfanz, and Byrnes 2009).

Fourth, this case study suggests that an effective restorative justice program requires widespread commitment to the restorative philosophy from the school (Morrison, Blood, and Thorsborne 2005). Not only was a full-time Restorative Justice Coordinator critical in facilitating the restorative conference and providing necessary followup, but without the support of the school-based resource officer and the dean, the students involved could have faced punitive processes leading to disengagement with the school community, increased violence, and interaction with the juvenile justice system. As Morrison, Blood, and Thorsborne indicate, it is critical for school officials to believe in restorative justice and its ability to resolve the situation more effectively than punitive measures (2005). Without commitment to restorative justice from all stakeholders in the North High School community, it is likely that the results of the incident would have been significantly different.

Conclusion

The practice of restorative justice empowers individuals and communities through building healthy relationships. In the context of schools, these practices seek to empower students, parents, teachers, administrators, and community members. Unlike punitive models for regulating schools, restorative justice practice provides school communities with the flexibility to address, confront, and resolve conflicts. In particular, restorative justice practice offers students the chance to voice their opinions and accept responsibility for their actions, while simultaneously allowing administrators to retain the necessary authority to maintain safe schools. While there is no single answer to school discipline, studies of school-based restorative justice programs reveal positive impacts for students.

The results found in this study of the North High School Restorative Justice Program are valuable, despite their limitations. The data collected at North High School confirms that when schools adopt alternative processes to address discipline, they can build a safer school culture, reduce entry into the school-to-prison pipeline, and positively impact educational performance. Finally, it is important to note that school-based restorative justice practice cannot be assessed by quantitative data alone. One comment from student interviews at North High School qualitatively captures the potential for change: "Back in the day there was a lot of beef [conflict], and now everyone is all homies with each other." Changing school culture is critical, and as the data collected from North High School reflects, restorative justice is both a prevention and an intervention strategy to address conflict before it escalates, and to deal with conflict after it occurs.

REFERENCES

Advancement Project. 2005. *Education on Lockdown: The Schoolhouse to Jailhouse Track*. Washington, DC: Advancement Project. http://www.advancementproject.org/digital-library/publications/education-on-lockdown-the-schoolhouse-to-jailhouse-track.

Advancement Project. 2010. *Test, Punish, and Push Out: How Zero Tolerance and High-Stakes Testing Funnel Youth into the School to Prison Pipeline*. Washington, DC: Advancement Project. http://www.advancementproject.org/digital-library/publications/test-punish-and-push-out-how-zero-tolerance-and-high-stakes-testing-fu.

American Bar Association. 2003. *Commission on Youth at Risk, Commission on Homelessness and Poverty, Report to the House of Delegates, Recommendation 118B*. old.cleweb.org/latest/ABA.118B.RighttoRemaininSchool.pdf.

American Psychological Association Zero Tolerance Task Force. 2006. Are Zero Tolerance Policies Effective in the Schools? An Evidentiary Review and Recommendations. *American Psychologist* 63 (9): 852-62.

Baker, M. 2007. *Denver Public Schools Restorative Justice Project*. Denver, CO: Outcomes.

Baker, M. 2008. *North High School Restorative Justice Project*. Denver, CO: Outcomes.

Baker, M. 2009. *DPS Restorative Justice Project: North High School*. Denver, CO: Outcomes.

Balfanz, R. 2007. *What Your Community Can Do to End Its Dropout Crisis: Learning from Research and Practice*. Baltimore, MD: Center for Social Organization of Schools.

Balfanz, R., J. Fox, J. Bridgeland, and M. McNaught. 2008. *Grad Nation: A Guidebook to Help Communities Tackle the Dropout Crisis*. Washington, DC: America's Promise Alliance. http://www.every1graduates.org/PDFs/GradNation_Guidebook_Final.pdf.

Balfanz, R., L. Herzog, and D. J. Mac Iver. 2007. Preventing Student Disengagement and Keeping Students on the Graduation Path in Urban Middle-Grades Schools: Early Identification and Effective Interventions. *Educational Psychologist* 42 (4): 223-35.

Balfanz, R., and N. Legters. 2004. *Locating the Dropout Crisis* (CRESPAR Report #70). Baltimore, MD: Center for Research on the Education of Students Placed at Risk.

Bazemore, G. 1992. On Mission Statements and Reform in Juvenile Justice: The Case of the "Balanced Approach." *Federal Probation* 56: 64-70.

Bazemore, G. 1999. The Fork in the Road to Juvenile Court Reform. *Annals of the American Academy of Political Social Science* 564 (7): 81-108.

Bazemore, G. 2001. Young People, Trouble, and Crime: Restorative Justice as a Normative Theory of Informal Social Control and Social Support. *Youth and Society* 33 (2): 199-226.

Bazemore, G., and M. Umbreit. 2001. *A Comparison of Four Restorative Conferencing Models*. Washington, DC: United States Department of Justice, Office of Justice Programs, Office of Juvenile Justice and Delinquency Prevention.

Bazemore, G., and L. Walgrave. 1999. Restorative Juvenile Justice: In Search of Fundamentals and an Outline for Systemic Reform. In *Restorative Juvenile Justice: Repairing the Harm of Youth Crime*, ed. G. Bazemore and L. Walgrave, pp. 45-62. Monsey, NY: Criminal Justice Press.

Blood, P., and M. Thorsborne. 2006. Overcoming Resistance to Whole-School Uptake of Restorative Practices. Paper presented at the International Institute of Restorative Practices Conference, "The Next Step: Developing Restorative Communities, Part 2." Bethlehem, PA.

Braithwaite, J. 1999. Restorative Justice: Assessing Optimistic and Pessimistic Accounts. In *Crime and Justice: A Review of Research*, ed. M. Tonry, pp. 25-30. Chicago: University of Chicago Press.

Braithwaite, J. 2002. *Restorative Justice and Responsive Regulation*. New York: Oxford University Press.

Braithwaite, J., and H. Strang. 2001. Introduction: Restorative Justice and Civil Society. In *Restorative Justice and Civil Society*, ed. H. Strang and J. Braithwaite, pp. 1-13. New York: Cambridge University Press.

Calhoun, A. 2000. Calgary Community Conferencing School Component, 1999-2000: A Year in Review. http://www.calgarycommunityconferencing.com.

Cameron, L., and M. Thorsborne. 2001. Restorative Justice and School Discipline: Mutually Exclusive? In *Restorative Justice and Civil Society*, ed. H. Strang and J. Braithwaite, pp. 180-94. New York: Cambridge University Press.

Christensen, L. 2009. Sticks, Stones, and Schoolyard Bullies: Restorative Justice, Mediation, and a New Approach to Resolution in Our Schools. *Nevada Law Journal* 9: 545-79.

Cox, E. 1995. *A Truly Civil Society*. Sydney, Australia: ABC Books.

Denver Public Schools. 2009. *School Performance Framework 2009 Stoplight Summary Score Card*. http://testing.dpsk12.org/public/spf/2009/455%20-%202009%20Stoplight%20 Scorecard.pdf.

Forgays, D., and L. DeMilio. 2005. Is Teen Court Effective for Repeat Offenders? A Test of the Restorative Approach. *International Journal of Offender Therapy and Comparative Criminology* 49: 107-18.

Hall, W. 2000. More Than Zero Tolerance: The Cost of Zero Tolerance and the Case for Restorative Justice in Schools. *University of Denver Law Review* 77: 795-812.

Hirschfeld, P. 2008. Preparing for Prison? The Criminalization of School Discipline in the USA. *Theoretical Criminology* 12: 79 – 91.

Hopkins, B. 2004. *Just Schools: A Whole School Approach to Restorative Justice*. London: Jessica Kingsley Publishers.

International Institute for Restorative Practices. 2009. *Improving School Climate: Findings from Schools Implementing Restorative Practices*. www.realjustice.org/pdf/IIRP-Improving-School-Climate.pdf.

Jennings, W., A. Gover, and D. Hitchcock. 2008. Localizing Restorative Justice: An In-Depth Look at a Denver Public School Program. *Sociology of Crime, Law, and Deviance* 11: 167-87.

Karp, D., and B. Breslin. 2001. Restorative Justice in Communities. *Youth and Society* 33: 249-72.

Lewis, R. 2009. A Multi-System Approach to Dismantling the "Cradle to Prison" Pipeline. *Houston Lawyer* 47: 28-31.

Mac Iver, M., R. Balfanz, and V. Byrnes. 2009. *Advancing the "Colorado Graduates" Agenda: Understanding the Dropout Problem and Mobilizing to Meet the Graduation Challenge*. Baltimore, MD: Center for Social Organization of Schools.

Mac Iver, M. A., and D. J. Mac Iver. 2009. *Beyond the Indicators: An Integrated School-Level Approach to Dropout Prevention*. Arlington, VA: Mid-Atlantic Equity Center, George Washington University Center for Equity and Excellence in Education.

McNeely, C., J. M. Nonnemaker, and R. W. Blum. 2002. Promoting School Connectedness: Evidence from the National Longitudinal Study of Adolescent Health. *Journal of School Health* 72 (4): 138-46.

Morrison, B. 2001. "Developing the Schools' Capacity in the Regulation of Society." In *Restorative Justice and Civil Society*, ed. H. Strang and J. Braithwaite, pp. 195-210. New York: Cambridge University Press.

Morrison, B. 2003. Regulating Safe School Communities: Being Responsive and Restorative. *Journal of Educational Administration* 41 (6): 689-704.

Morrison, B. 2007. *Restoring Safe School Communities, A Whole School Response to Bullying, Violence, and Alienation*. Sydney, Australia: Federation Press.

Morrison, B., P. Blood, and M. Thorsborne. 2005. Practicing Restorative Justice in School Communities: The Challenge of Culture Change. *Public Organization Review: A Global Journal* 5: 335-57.

Payne, A., D. Gottfredson, and G. Gottfredson. 2003. Schools as Communities: The Relationships among Communal School Organization, Student Bonding, and School Disorder. *Criminology* 41 (3): 749-77.

Riestenberg, N. 2003. *Zero and No: Some Definitions*. Roseville: Minnesota Department of Education.

Salmivalli, C. 1999. Participant Role Approach to School Bullying: Implications for Interventions. *Journal of Adolescence* 22: 453-59.

Siman, A. 2005. Challenging Zero Tolerance: Federal and State Legal Remedies for Students of Color. *Cornell Journal of Law and Public Policy* 14: 327-64.

Skiba, R., and C. Noam. 2001. *Zero Tolerance: Can Suspension and Expulsion Keep Schools Safe? New Directions for Youth Development: Theory, Practice, Research*. San Francisco: Jossey-Bass.

Skiba, R., and R. Peterson. 1999. The Dark Side of Zero Tolerance: Can Punishment Lead to Safe Schools? *Phi Delta Kappan* 80: 372-78.

Smith, C. 2009. Deconstructing the Pipeline: Evaluating School-to-Prison Pipeline Equal Protection Cases through a Structural Racism Framework. *Fordham Urban Law Journal* 36: 1009-49.

Stinchcomb, J., G. Bazemore, and N. Riestenberg. 2006. Beyond Zero Tolerance: Restoring Justice in Secondary Schools. *Youth Violence and Juvenile Justice* 4 (2): 123-47.

Suvall, C. 2009. Restorative Justice in Schools: Learning from Jena High School. *Harvard Civil Rights and Civil Liberties Law Review* 44: 547-69.

Texas Appleseed. 2010. *Texas' School-to-Prison Pipeline: The Path from Lockout to Dropout*. Austin, TX: Texas Appleseed. http://www.texasappleseed.net/index.php?option=content&task=view&id=21&Itemid=106.

Van Ness, D., and K. H. Strong. 2001. *Restoring Justice* (2nd ed.). Cincinnati, OH: Anderson.

Wachtel, T., and P. McCold. 2001. Restorative Justice in Everyday Life: Beyond Formal Ritual. In *Restorative Justice and Civil Society*, ed. H. Strang and J. Braithwaite, pp. 114-30. New York: Cambridge University Press.

Wenzel, M., T. Okimoto, N. Feather, and M. Platow. 2008. Retributive and Restorative Justice. *Law and Human Behavior* 32: 375-89.

Youth Justice Board for England and Wales. 2004. National Evaluation of the Restorative Justice in Schools Programme. http://www.youth-justice-board.gov.uk.

Zehr, H. 2002. *Little Book of Restorative Justice*. Intercourse, PA: Good Books.

12

The Line of Prevention

KHARY LAZARRE-WHITE

The Brotherhood/Sister Sol is a rites of passage–based youth development program that serves children, mostly from the neighborhood of Harlem, in New York City. We offer long-term, comprehensive, and holistic services, surrounding our members with education and developmental programming. We provide support, guidance, and love, as we teach discipline and order. Essential to our process and demonstrated successful outcomes is access to real opportunities that enable our members to develop and grow.

Much of the national dialogue on juvenile justice focuses on cases in which juveniles have committed atrocious, heinous acts of violence, acts that clearly demand that the adolescent be secured in some kind of facility. This chapter does not focus on these cases. The reality is that such incidents do not represent the majority of crimes for which young people are incarcerated in our country. Instead, all too many youth are being incarcerated for low-level criminal activity, such as nonviolent drug offenses, in which socioeconomic conditions along with poor choices have led to incarceration and for which alternatives to incarceration are possible. We have found, over fifteen years, that when we provide young people with the skills to change their conditions and help them learn critical thinking skills, the vast majority will choose a proper path. There is a fine line between a young person who commits a low-level criminal act and can be taught to correct his/her life, or even a young person who is on the verge of such acts, and a young person who crosses over that line, committing acts that lead to incarceration. This essay, and our work, focus on that line.

We have had members who have sold drugs. We have had members who have joined gangs. We have had members who have used illegal drugs. We have had members who have committed robberies. With the proper supports, with guidance, with high-level representation when they are arrested, they have all chosen alternative paths of life. No member or alumnus of the Brotherhood/Sister Sol is in prison or jail, no member is on parole, and only two, out of hundreds, are on probation.

A few years ago the president of a leading foundation attended a Brotherhood Rites of Passage workshop. A group of seven or eight alumni had returned to work with a group of nearly twenty teenaged members. This was one example, among many, of our male alumni returning to support the younger generation. They spent over two hours talking about the central issues they faced—in their communities, in their families, in their schools, and in society in general. The culmination of the workshop was that together, these young Black and Latino men, ages 15-23, created a "Survival Guide for Black and Latino Young Men in Harlem."

It is a powerful document that calls societal forces to task, speaks plainly about economic and racial injustice, takes responsibility for personal failures, acknowledges the lack of family support—and yet states, unequivocally, that while recognizing these realities, and because they know the obstacles so well, they will overcome them and be successful; there will be no excuses. It was one of many powerful sessions—the kind of unique power that comes from harnessing the passion, truth, and vision of young people, of providing space for exposure, investigation, and reflection and then directing it.

It was a hot June day, and the room where the session was held was in a school building in East Harlem. The large windows of the classroom looked out onto a busy thoroughfare and housing projects as far as the eye could see—East Harlem being the area of the United States most densely populated by public housing. Through this window one could see rolling traffic, famous graffiti walls, elevated trains, school children walking home, hard-working people laboring, and also crews of young men, some merely hanging out, some smoking weed or drinking, some possibly selling drugs, and, invariably, some gang affiliated. The visiting president of the foundation was struck by what he saw in the room that afternoon, and he asked a powerful question of one of the recent alumni. He pointed to the group of young men on the corner and said, "Why are they out there?" and then turned his finger to the young man in the room and finished, "while you are in here?" The alumnus to whom the question was directed is a son of Harlem. He is a first-generation American born to Dominican immigrant parents. He graduated from the high school where he now sat as a teacher-model. When he had graduated, he had never read a complete book as a school assignment. Never. His mother worked as a cleaning woman, sweeping the Ivy League floors of Columbia University, a few blocks away but in reality worlds away from their Harlem home. He was now a sophomore at Brown University, another Ivy League school. This alumnus responded, "They *are* in here. And we *are* out there."

BHSS works in economically distressed communities, and we engage in no sifting when choosing our membership. All who want to be a part of BHSS can be a part—our membership represents the diversity of Harlem and we work with a population that ranges between the ages of six and twenty-two, with the majority being twelve to eighteen years of age. Nearly 80 percent of our young people come from single-parent homes. Some of our youth come from stable homes where their parent or parents provide a nurturing environment and we are another hand in raising the child. Others come from families destroyed by the social ills of our times, by drugs, incarceration, homelessness, poverty, and, in some cases, poor parenting. For these children, we may be the most stable element in their life. Yet, no matter the family, all of our members face risks that can lead to them being incarcerated. They all walk the same streets that are inundated with drugs and violence, and all are confronted with the same damaging images of masculinity and femininity—with "manhood" defined primarily in terms of a capacity for violence and emotional irresponsibility and "womanhood" defined as passivity and sexual objectification. Our members attend schools that are almost all either in a state of sustained mediocrity, at best, or, at worst, serve as chaotic holding facilities. All of our youth are confronted with invasive policing and are afforded few job opportunities. Inundated by these negative forces and pressures, all are, in the phrase of James Baldwin, "expected to make peace with mediocrity."

In response, we surround our members with positive forces and opportunities. BHSS operates like a well-constructed family, with levels of responsibility and tiered achievement, with high expectations and guidance on how to reach them, with caring adults who represent different examples of success and are committed, wholeheartedly and without question, to our members' success and interests. BHSS provides single-gendered rites-of-passage programming over a period of four to six years during which our members define manhood or womanhood, leadership, and brotherhood or sisterhood, while honing a moral and ethical code by which to live.

All of our other programming is cross-gender, that is, programs serve young men and young women together, and we offer thorough five-day-a-week after-school care, school and home counseling, summer camps, job training, college preparation, employment opportunities, community organizing training, a community gardening and environmental education program, and free legal representation. In addition, BHSS continually seeks to expose our young people to new opportunities through wilderness retreats, cultural performances, college tours, and month-long intensive study programs in places such as Ghana, South Africa, Egypt, Mexico, Morocco, the Dominican Republic, Puerto Rico, and Brazil. We publish assorted curricula and collections of our members' writings and train educators throughout the nation in our approach.

We are an evidence-based program, and many of our statistical outcomes have been recognized as some of the best achieved in our field in the country, when compared to those working with a similar population. In the United States of America, 30 percent of Black men, if trends continue, will spend time in prison.[1] After fifteen years, none of our male members is incarcerated, none is on parole, and less than 1 percent are on probation. Being born to a teenaged mother greatly increases a child's chance of being incarcerated during his or her life. The teenage pregnancy rate in New York City is 9.4 percent;[2] BHSS members and alumni have a teenage pregnancy rate of less than 2 percent. Negative educational outcomes are another statistic with a direct correlation to prison contact. In New York City, where only 32 percent of Black males graduate within four years,[3] 88 percent of BHSS alumni have graduated from high school and 95 percent of BHSS alumni of this age are either working full-time or in college. For our work, and because of these outcomes, we have won awards from Oprah Winfrey, the Ford Foundation, Brown University, the New York State Department of Education, the Fund for the City of New York, Union Square Awards, and many others.

Each day Black and Latino youth navigate a multitude of negative social conditions, often with little or no positive guidance. Understanding the community context in which BHSS exists is essential to understanding what our members face and why our program works. Most of our members live in not merely underserved, but all too often completely neglected, communities where from an early age they are exposed to violence, drugs, poverty, misogyny, racism, and death. In Harlem, depending on the area of the community, between 45 percent and 56 percent of the community's children live in poverty.[4] Our neighborhood is the main distribution point in the Northeast for cocaine, supplying over 95 percent of the city.[5] Children in our program participate in a failing public education system deemed by the highest court in the state of New York as unconstitutional.[6] They witness negative images of "masculinity" and "femininity" in their communities and in the media that, unless they learn to critique them, they will surely replicate. Without having the necessary guidance and resources all young people need to shape and achieve their potential, our children are coerced into destructive lifestyles, one devastating impact often leading to the next, and resulting in a litany of distressing human statistical outcomes. We stand in the chasm.

In 2003, the Court of Appeals of the State of New York, the state's highest court, found that the education provided to New York City school children violated the state's constitutionally mandated standard of a statewide "common" level education. It found that of the 1.1 million children being educated within New York City's public school system, seven hundred thousand were at risk of failure. The court held that many of New York City's schools had half the books of their suburban counterparts, that the students attended "crumbling" schools, and that the system was underfunded by six billion dollars. In one of the most damning holdings, the court found that even those students who were graduating from the system were not being served, as the high school diploma represented only an eighth-grade level education. Those who were graduating from high school and being told they were ready to compete in college and the workforce were being sold a false bill of goods. Writing for the majority, then-Chief Justice of the New York State Court of Appeals, Judith S. Kaye, wrote, "Tens of thousands of students are placed in overcrowded classrooms, taught by unqualified teachers, and provided with inadequate facilities and equipment. The number of children in these straits is large enough to represent a systematic failure."[7] Attending failing schools and being ill prepared to compete economically is, as we know, directly connected to a greater likelihood of incarceration.

Between 1987 and 2007 the prison population of the United States tripled. The United States has the most people incarcerated in the world and the highest rate of incarceration. There are over 2.3 million people incarcerated in this country.[8] This explosion of incarceration is due to policies of getting "tough on crime" and fuels one of the largest businesses in America, the prison system. This situation is due, in part, to the Sentencing Reform Act of 1984, which created mandatory minimum sentences for drug convictions and distinguished between crack and powder cocaine. In the state of New York the situation was exacerbated by the Rockefeller Laws creating mandatory minimum sentences for nonviolent drug convictions. According to the analysis of the Advancement Project, additional policing and prosecutorial strategies responsible for this explosion included "three strikes" laws following the conviction of a third crime and the "broken windows" theory, which sought aggressive policing for previously ignored minor offenses.[9] For our population, it is this final area that has most greatly contributed to our members' interactions with police in New York City.

At BHSS we have had members arrested for being in a park, after dusk, with no identification, when they were only working out. This does not occur in Central Park, one mile away, when thousands jog in the summer heat. We have had members arrested for possession of marijuana, enough for one cigarette's worth. This does not occur half a mile from Harlem at Columbia University. We have had members told to move off street corners where three or four of them were talking, told they were "disrupting traffic," and when they did not move quickly enough, arrested for "disorderly conduct." Imagine if groups of people, standing and talking in a posh neighborhood such as Soho or in the busy Midtown area, were treated the same way. We have had members stopped and detained for moving between the trains of the subway—a ticketable offense. When they argued that thousands of people do this every day in New York City, they were arrested for disorderly conduct. We had a member stopped as he was entering the train, as an undercover officer saw a "gravity knife" attached to his belt. This is an item sold in hardware stores to open boxes. The "gravity knife" in question was given to our member due to his summer job. He was a college student in the State University of New York system, home for the summer, and working for Teach for America. Teach for America gave him the small tool to open the boxes of applications they received in the mail. Although the member explained this, he was arrested.

This kind of biased policing is rampant in Harlem and in similarly situated communities in New York City. Overwhelming numbers of anecdotes as well as comprehensive statistical studies make this reality clear. No objective review of the research could lead to another conclusion; only a subjective and predisposed analysis could lead to a finding that such policing does not occur.

According to the New York Police Department's (NYPD) annually released statistics and also according to comprehensive analysis done by the Center for Constitutional Rights, in 2009, the NYPD stopped over 575,304 New Yorkers. Of those stopped, 87 percent were Black or Latino. Of those stopped, 94 percent, or over 550,000 New Yorkers, were innocent of any criminal activity: they were completely innocent of any crime. These people had no outstanding warrants, no drugs, no weapons, and no contraband.[10] The NYPD and the political powers in New York City do not apologize for these numbers—they defend and celebrate them.

This is not a one-year phenomenon, but instead, a vetted, intentional, formal practice of the NYPD that has been documented and ongoing for more than five years, with over 90 percent of those stopped having been completely innocent of any crime.[11] Under the New York Penal Code, the police may stop and frisk a person if there is only a "reasonable suspicion of criminal action." One can only conclude that these stops were capricious and without cause if nearly 96 percent of those stopped were innocent. The stops must be unreasonable if they are inaccurately founded 96 percent of the time. If they are unreasonable and without foundation—a mere fishing expedition—then they are illegal and unconstitutional.

However, in many quarters these numbers were met with celebration due to the 6 percent of individuals who were found to have committed a crime or have an outstanding warrant. The viewpoint articulated was that guns were off the street, drugs were recovered, and therefore the stops were a success. While the arresting of criminals and removing of guns from our streets is vital to any society, we must continue to focus on the 96 percent of people, the over 550,000 law-abiding New Yorkers, citizens of the city, who were stopped capriciously and without reason. What does it say about the morality of our society when we allow this to happen to our fellow citizens?

There are virtually no male members or alumni of the Brotherhood/Sister Sol over the age of fifteen who have not had negative experiences with police officers. Within the last three years, I myself have twice been profiled: once stopped and frisked, once pulled over at gunpoint.

I recently completed work with a group of young men who started in the Brotherhood Rites of Passage Program at the age of twelve. By the age of eighteen, these fourteen young men were all on the right path. All but two are in college, including Howard University, Brandeis University, Monroe College, and assorted State University of New York and City University of New York campuses. One of the two who did not matriculate to college is now a corporal in the United States Marine Corps. None has a criminal record. None. In a conversation regarding one's rights, it was revealed that all fourteen, as well as myself and the other adult youth worker (sixteen out of sixteen Black and Latino men in the room), had been stopped and frisked by the NYPD. Every one. Our members know, as I know, that the vast majority of police are doing important and essential work each and every day. We applaud our officers for getting guns off the streets, for arresting violent criminals, and for making our city safe. We understand that their jobs are uncommonly difficult. But when the police continue to blindly defend practices such as those described above, continue to stubbornly refuse to acknowledge that there is an issue, they in fact do themselves a disservice and discredit the wide array of good and vital work they do.

We have fifteen-year-old members who are so resigned to being stopped, who have become so used to the experience, that when they are stopped and frisked while walking to our offices from school, they shrug off the experiences, stating, "It is not a problem." That it doesn't bother them, that it is par for the course of being a young Black man in New York City, that these young men have grown inured to the outrage of being stopped and frisked without cause, that they have become accustomed to having their constitutional rights violated regularly, means New York City has failed its citizens. That no member of high rank of the NYPD has declared this a problem, a serious issue in an otherwise highly professional force, but instead defends the practice visited upon their fellow citizens, is a disgrace to this city.

BHSS tries to counter such forces with a multilayered, interwoven system of services, comprehensive in nature, that provide the web of support and guidance that lead to our documented successful outcomes. We have established a set of long-range goals for our members. Through participating in one or more of our programs our members are expected to

- develop a personal self-definition that encompasses respect for themselves, their family, and the larger community;
- gain a greater understanding of and appreciation for their cultural and historical legacy as Black and Latino people;
- develop into critical thinkers who can analyze personal and societal issues and who are committed to self– and community development;
- broaden their knowledge of social issues and increase their participation in community activities;
- find their creative voice;
- develop a powerful sense of self-worth and belief in their ability to achieve;
- improve their academic performance and develop a lifelong love of learning;
- increase their involvement in the workforce, internships, and travel;
- learn the life skills essential for survival and success;
- create a personal testimony of their values, beliefs, and goals that reflects an understanding of their moral responsibility to others;
- not commit a crime, become incarcerated, become addicted to drugs, or have children before the age of twenty-one;
- graduate from high school, attend college, or gain long-term and secure employment and learn to become good parents.

Our educational philosophy, the *Framework for Analysis*, and honed curriculum are at the foundation of our success. We have worked for years to perfect the content of what we teach and the substance of our youth development model. Also at the core of our success is the greatest resource and capital of the organization—our staff. In our field, all too often, there is not enough attention given to who staffs youth development organization and how they are trained and developed. We have committed youth workers—the average tenure of our staff is seven years. This kind of consistency and commitment speaks volumes to our members. Our staff knows that this work is a calling, and our members know that we are committed to and passionate about their survival.

We have a four-tiered, intensive hiring process that allows us to sift applicants and hire the right kind of youth workers. We often have one hundred applications for a youth development position. Our first hiring tier involves vetting the resumes and conducting phone interviews to narrow the pool to about ten to fifteen candidates. Then, a second tier consisting of a 30- to 45-minute resume-based, face-to-face interview takes place to further narrow the candidates to approximately five semifinalists. The third tier of our process is called our ideological interview. By this point we have provided the applicant with our *Framework for Analysis* and the overview of our *10 Curriculum Focus Issues* (about fifteen pages) and have asked them to read these documents in advance. The candidate then meets with the executive director and one or two other program staff for a conversation lasting one and a half to two hours, during which we discuss youth development strategies and approaches to educating, guiding, and disciplining young people. During this meeting we also pose scenarios: "You receive a call at 2:00 a.m. that your member has been arrested"; "Your member tells you he thinks he has gotten his girlfriend pregnant or that she is pregnant"; "Your member, who is attending a failing school, asks why s/he should attend at all." We ask the candidate to respond. Finally, approximately three finalists have to facilitate a workshop for a population similar to the one s/he will be working with, in front of executive staff and his/her potential partners—and the youth provide responses and recommendations. Upon selection, the staff member must make a minimum three-year commitment to BHSS.

One word that is often used by our members to describe BHSS youth workers is "relentless." We are relentless in our effort to support and guide them—reaching out over and over again—always there with a trusted word of support. We are relentless in our quest to educate them in a way that speaks to them personally or to their experience and furthers their development. We are relentless in providing opportunities for them and in teaching them to develop the ability to navigate and seize hold of these opportunities. We are relentless in teaching them discipline and ways to order their lives. And, finally, we are relentless in surrounding them with love.

It is important that two distinct and different kinds of dedication are in place: long-term and wide-ranging. These two forms of dedication are essential to retention. The long-term is just that—long-term. Our young people are all too often experienced with adults who come in and out of their lives, who promise to be there for them and then disappear. BHSS youth workers cannot be this type of adult. We often go well beyond the call of duty in supporting and guiding our members. We are there when they cry and when they have wonderful moments. We are extremely careful to follow through on what we promise. If we say we will attend a game, or a graduation ceremony, or a teacher meeting, we attend. We are there. Period. They can count on us. We have assisted our members in confronting individuals who have robbed them or threatened them. We have shown up in large numbers when a gang jumping was threatened. We have made court appearances and home visits. We have attended meetings in their schools to serve as allies and advocates. We have attended games, celebrations, graduations, and funerals for their family members. We have driven them off to college for their first year and in each year following. We have shown our love and commitment in word and deed. This level of dedication is contagious and encourages reciprocation.

Of course, in this process of guiding young people, on our own journeys as staff, we make mistakes, and as adults we must continue to develop. BHSS is committed to supporting our staff in their development—to be better youth development workers, yes, but also to be better men and women. We teach that the worst thing we can call ourselves is a hypocrite. We must meet the standards of our words. We must, both chapter leaders and youth, live up to the ideals and definitions we create—Leaders, Brothers/Sisters, and Women/Men. We must wear multiple hats and play multiple roles that may be familiar to our members from various people but that they rarely see in one person: we must educate like a teacher, discipline and love like a parent, laugh with them like a friend, support them in their development about any issue like an older sibling, inspire them like a coach, and be able to bring new ideas and concepts that help them to reflect on their lives like a spiritual guide.

Too many youth workers in our community utilize an approach based only on toughness and discipline. Too many others go too far in accommodating our youth, do not maintain high standards, and do not expect discipline. We avoid these typical polarizations. We seek to be gentle, yet firm; to be supportive, yet tough; to utilize discipline and love; and to provide unconditional support and high expectations. These are the ideals we strive for. The language we use with our members also goes a long way towards maintaining their involvement in the organization. The way we talk to them is different from the way other "elders" often speak with them. We respect their opinions and talk to them as intelligent young people. We are truly interested in who they are, in what they think, and in their views on the world. Even when we are angry or disappointed with them, we speak with respect. And yet, we raise the bar—we expect that they will struggle to live more consciously and righteously, that they will not be perfect and that they will fall, but that they will get back up. And we will be there to lend a hand. One of the central lessons we have learned is that these forms of support must be holistic, comprehensive, and long-term.

BHSS intentionally connects our young people with other young people struggling to live a different way from many of their peers by building a "chapter," a collective of young people that provides a connected group. There is a sense of strength in numbers, a sense of belonging. We provide paraphernalia (BHSS-designed shirts and clothes illustrated with our logo and design and inspirational quotes) that also conveys this sense of family and unity, making our members stand out and marking them as a part of something larger. We expose them to new and exciting possibilities that are also productive and positive experiences. We do this through our international study programs to Africa and Latin America, guest speakers who display different images of Black and Latino(a) adults, professional site visit days, and attendance at plays and cultural performances. We help our members to expand their minds and follow their dreams. We teach a curriculum that is geared toward them, deals with their lived reality, and uses mediums that speak to them. We offer our members resources that allow them to know we are there for them during tough times (i.e., school or home counseling, mental health support, legal representation) and also are there during the good times. We use a weekly *Check-in* to listen to them and let them know that their lives and views are important, and this helps to counteract a sense of hopelessness. We connect the chapters to each other through outings and wilderness retreats that help them see they are a part of a large organization that will support them, love them, and protect them.

We support our members and recent alumni financially as we have learned how relatively small investments of money can make the difference between staying in college or dropping out; between obtaining a job or not; between making it or falling through the cracks. Because so many of our members come from such economically distressed backgrounds, we regularly cover such needs as clothes and food, travel support (to get to and from jobs and college), medical costs, rent, eyeglasses, and other necessities, as needed. Due to the economic crisis, many colleges and universities saw a great decline in their endowments, and in turn in the financial aid packages they were able to provide students. Their advice to students in need was to seek private loans from banks to cover the shortfall reflected in their packages. With the lack of liquidity in the markets, the standards as to who could secure loans were tightened. Our members would not qualify on their own merits and most, due to unemployment or poor credit, had no "cosigner" at home to help secure the loan. Our support has ensured that members remained in college, while also providing computers and money for books and supplies. BHSS has also provided members and alumni with legal representation regarding such issues as landlord/tenant law, criminal law, and immigration issues.

We have had members who have done everything asked of them. They have graduated from high school and gained entry to college. However, after all loans were in place and all scholarship monies were offered, they were fifteen hundred dollars short on their fees and had no family members who could provide this money. They were told they could not register for classes without this additional contribution. We have paid it. Otherwise, they would not have been in college. We have had members who have gotten wonderful job opportunities, the kind of jobs that are transformative to middle-class youth across the country—ones that develop skills, open doors, connect young people with lifelong mentors. Our members, through our connections, have had the chance to secure these jobs. However, here is where the economics of deep poverty come into play. After securing these jobs, many find they have no appropriate professional clothes, no dress pants, only one dress shirt, no dress shoes, not even a dress belt or socks. Yet, full wardrobes are often needed in order to accept the job offer. Many have no transportation money for the first two weeks of the job, until they are paid, and thus need two weeks of subway fare ($51.50 in New York City). They insist they will walk the eight miles to and from work, in the city's summer heat, in dress clothes, as they are used to trying to adjust to harsh realities. They have no money for lunch each day for two weeks, until they are paid. They say they will go without. But we at BHSS pay for these needs. Three of the members who experienced these realities were eighteen at the time, had finished their first year of college, had no money at all, and had never had a job of this type. They were from one of the most notorious housing projects in New York City, from dilapidated buildings; all had guardians and parents struggling with alcoholism; all attended a high school mired in mediocrity that ill prepared them for college. One is now studying to be an engineer; one to be a teacher; one to be a doctor.

As a nation that has become punitive toward some of our young—and it is only some of our young—due to their race and/or economic status, many fail to recognize the nuanced and subjective choice of enforcement in many of these cases. There is a judicial caste system that ensures two forms of criminal justice—one for those who possess access and agency, and one for those who do not. Those commentators who call out for stiff punishments of those who have used illegal drugs on some occasions, who state that alternatives to incarceration are too soft and that these youth need to be taught a hard lesson, would do well to remember that the present and former two presidents of the United States have admitted to the use of illegal drugs, either marijuana or cocaine.

Because we realize that it is likely that many of our members will come into contact with the police and the criminal system, we have lawyers on staff, and on our board, as well as criminal attorneys on retainer for when such situations arise. When some of our youth have been arrested, most often for a misdemeanor, or in those few instances when a felony arrest has occurred, the fact that private attorneys arrive to represent them alters the entire narrative and reality found in our courts.

On the essential issue of contact with the criminal system, we have developed an approach that allows us to prevent our members from choosing to engage in illegal activities and to develop the strength to resist negative peer pressure. In addition, the opportunities and access we offer, and the images we use to counteract those that they witness each and every day, develop the belief of our members in another way of life, instills in them the fortitude to commit to reaching high expectations. If, even with these supports, a member either commits an act that leads toward his/her arrest or is falsely arrested, then we seek to intervene aggressively on his/her behalf to ensure that such contact occurs only once and that he/she is as protected as any middle-class child would expect to be. Such members receive counseling regarding options, we meet with their families, we bring in alumni or friends of the organization to speak to them about the path they are on and how to change it, and we offer free and high-level legal representation.

It all started with the case of a boy we call Steven. In 1996, when we were first starting out, a sixteen-year-old member of the Brotherhood, Steven, was arrested. We had worked with young men on the line, young men whom we were struggling to keep on the correct path. Steven was not such a young man—he was seen as gentle by all his teachers, had never been arrested, had never had issues with behavior in school, played sports, and stayed quietly to himself. He was a new father, his girlfriend had moved in with his family, and he was a doting and gentle parent. He also had a severe learning disability that left him reading and writing on an elementary grade level. When we heard the charges we were even more stunned—felony assault of a police officer. The total charges he faced could have put him away for eleven years.

The charge was that he had thrown a large votive candle, the kind used for religious ceremonies and left on streets as memorials to those killed by violence, out of an eleventh-story housing project window, striking one police officer and the shards of the glass injuring another. The incident had made the local newspapers and the police were searching for the perpetrator. Steven claimed he was playing basketball at the time. The only evidence against him was a statement he signed. We learned later that a young man had been arrested for selling drugs; to save himself he told the police he knew who had thrown the candle that had hit the officer. He gave the name of the young man who lived below him—Steven. Steven and the young man in question had had physical fights on numerous occasions. Steven's brother and the young man's brother had fought. Steven's mother and the young man's mother had fought. Steven was arrested and interrogated for several hours and told that if he didn't sign a confession the police would have his family thrown out of public housing. After several hours Steven signed a statement filled with police language, using advanced vocabulary he did not know—a confession that ran counter to the many witnesses with whom he was playing basketball at the time of the incident.

We received a call the day after he had been arrested—Steven was in central booking, "The Tombs," and would be arraigned the next day. He would then be transferred to New York City's massive jail, Rikers Island. We arrived at his arraignment to post bail and to keep him from Rikers.

As any who have been to the supreme court of any of the counties of New York City know, you will see a parade of virtually only Black and Latino men. That day's depressing parade was no different. In most cases overwhelmed public defenders try their best to handle a massive workload that allows minimal review and preparation. At worst, disinterested attorneys push clients to settle, no matter the facts, and have a hard time remembering their client's name. I watched the attorney provide minimal representation for our member, a scared boy of sixteen.

After Steven was released on bail, the public defender began the press for Steven to take a plea. He kept aggressively pressing Steven, and when we pushed back, he snapped at us that it would be "best for Steven" to take the plea, or else he would be doing much more time. His mother and Steven sought to make the lawyer understand that Steven was innocent. He simply did not listen to them, or see Steven as more than yet another case. Anyone who has entered the court system and been poor can tell you of this invisibility. When BHSS's cofounder, Jason Warwin, argued that Steven shouldn't take a plea because he was innocent, the attorney replied, "That's a crock of shit. He's guilty." While there are many phenomenal legal aid lawyers, brave women and men fighting in the legal trenches to ensure each and every day that the constitutional right to adequate counsel is upheld, this was clearly not such a lawyer. It was time for a private attorney.

We reached out to our board of directors and asked for a reference for a defense attorney. One of our board members at the time was the late Kellis Parker, the Isidor and Seville Sulzbacher Professor of Law at Columbia Law School. He set up a meeting among myself, Steven, his mother, Jason Warwin, and the local Harlem firm of Stevens, Hinds, and White, led by the famous lawyer and Rutgers professor, Lennox Hinds. We entered the small brownstone where the walls were lined with photos of Lennox Hinds with former clients and friends: Haywood Burns, the dean of CUNY Law School at the time, Nelson Mandela, and others. As we waited, down the stairs came a white man with long gray hair who greeted us with words that bespoke his British origins. He was not what we expected from a firm in Harlem that had represented Assata Shakur and Nelson Mandela. His name was Richard Harvey, and he told us about his history and major clients over the last two years—the African National Congress and the Irish Republican Army. Jason and I looked at each other and smiled. Yes, he would do.

Richard Harvey made his first appearance in court and gave notice that he was taking over the case. The judge was clearly irritated—a new attorney taking over the case meant delays in schedule. He gave Richard half the time he had requested to review the case and lectured him on being prepared, and then said that because Steven was fifteen minutes late to court, he was doubling his bail and ordered the court officers to take him into custody. The judge clearly expected that it would take time for the family to raise the money and Steven would now in fact be going to Rikers Island. We walked across the street and took out the money from our bank and paid the bond in cash. He was released within an hour. Now the judge was steaming. Surprised, he asked Richard Harvey who was bailing Steven out, and who was paying for his services. The Brotherhood.

The case meandered though the system for over a year with assorted delays and extensions granted, disturbing Steven's schooling and his family life. After over a year the jury unanimously found him not guilty of the felony, and somehow one juror voted him not guilty on the felony assault of the officer but guilty of a misdemeanor assault. The District Attorney's Office, hungry for a conviction, then sought a retrial on the misdemeanor after the eleven-to-one vote. This second trial was a judge's trial, and it took months before it began. After the sides were argued, and closing statements made, the judge, clearly irritated, looked at the ADA and said, "Are you done?" The ADA replied, "Yes, the State rests, your honor." The judge deliberated for less than two seconds before banging his gavel—"Not guilty, this case is over, Mr. Jackson." His two-year ordeal finally completed, Steven, standing to hear the verdict, put his hands on the table in front of him and sobbed.

Fourteen years later, this father of three has worked the same job for seven years. He supervises the stock room and intake at a high-end clothing store, provides for his children, covers them with his insurance, and has never been in trouble with the law.

There are readers who will think, "What complicated and interwoven services! This surely cannot be replicated." In the state of New York, the Office of Children and Family Services spends up to $210,000 a year to incarcerate a child in one of its juvenile facilities; the City of New York also spends in excess of $200,000.[12] A longitudinal study of these children found that 89 percent of the boys and 81 percent of the girls were rearrested upon release.[13] The City of New York spends approximately $19,000 a year to educate a child.[14] BHSS spends approximately $6,000 a year to provide the services described in this chapter for each child. When discussions focus on what it takes to help precariously situated young people to overcome their reality, all too often people talk about the resources it will take to do this. They state that it costs too much to replicate high-performing schools or programs. This is a false argument and a disingenuous statement. In truth, it is simply a discussion of where society wants to invest its resources and what kind of society America wants to be. It is an objective and demonstrable fact that it costs $210,000 a year to imprison a child in the state of New York. It is an objective and demonstrable fact that with an 81-89 percent recidivism rate, this investment shows no return. And yet, there never seems to be a conversation regarding these resources—more prisons are always built, more beds always offered. No judge, upon having a juvenile offender brought before her says, "You need to be incarcerated, but there is no bed for you, so you can walk free." And yes, every day, our children need an investment of education and opportunities and are told there is no place for them. At BHSS we help our young people to analyze why society makes such a decision. We do this because we believe there is a power in this form of education, but also because we believe this knowledge will make them far less likely to make decisions that lead toward imprisonment. This is the pedagogy of BHSS.

According to the National Association of State Budgets, in 1987, the states throughout this country collectively spent $10.6 billion on corrections. Last year, the states spent more than $44 billion, a 315 percent increase. Adjusted to 2007 dollars, the increase represents an increase of 127 percent. During the same twenty-year period, adjusted spending on higher education increased by 21 percent.[15]

At BHSS we believe that it is essential to help all children, but especially some of our nation's most precariously situated young people, to understand and name the issues they face due to race and gender, due to a culture of poverty and lack of educational access, due in some cases to family structures, and due to a general dearth of opportunity for America's economic underclass. Here is the core of our work and where we part paths from so many schools and youth development organization. We teach them these realities, and when appropriate, make the necessary connections to America's history of discrimination and its intentional historic acts of subjugation. We do this openly and directly—because we believe that with this knowledge, with this understanding, our members can overcome this history and these present-day realities. It is quite difficult to overcome obstacles that are unseen or unnamed. It is much like asking a runner to navigate an obstacle course with no map in hand, or even without the knowledge that the runner is in maze.

If we are seeking to truly teach and empower young people to save their own lives, if we are seeking to help foster social change, if we are seeking to break the cycles, the dependencies, and the lack of the opportunities that have led to mass incarceration of certain sectors of our country's population, then we must hone young people's critical analysis, and delve into the systemic societal issues that are behind the symptoms. We must work to help young people understand the root of the issue and the systems in place, to become change makers who question, who follow a moral and ethical code that leads away from prison walls and toward a commitment to social change and self-development.

Their voices must enter the conversation. This is true empowerment. Young people are the most often discussed, least heard from constituency. Issues relating to young people are all over the airways—but where are they and where are their voices?

Martin Luther King Jr. was twenty-five when he led the Montgomery bus boycotts. Youth leaders all across the country were central organizers for the Student Nonviolent Coordinating Committee. Youth were central in the Soweto

Uprising and in the effort to end apartheid. These were some of the most dispossessed youth of their time and place. College students helped to bring down a United States president, Lyndon Johnson, during the Vietnam War. Eighteen – to 25-year-old women were at the vanguard of the fight for women's liberation and changed the expectations and opportunities of women forever.

At BHSS, we seek to develop these voices of changes, so that they can be heard, yes, but also because we feel this form of education has always been, and continues to be, transformative. We publish their writings, provide them the opportunity to speak at national conferences and to the media, ensure that they are placed on educational conferences, and give them opportunities to speak and perform in front of some of our society's most prominent people. We do this because we believe that the issue of education, of the access of America's underclass to have real opportunity to transform their lives, is the major civil rights issue of our time.

We are not naïve—we know that our society continues to spend more money on incarceration than on education. We are fully aware that the political discourse of the day does not focus on our fellow citizens most in need—the ones who fill failing schools, who see a pipeline to prison, who continue to feel a suffocating lack of opportunity. Yet, there is a proverb that states, "It is when the riverbed is dry that we can change the flow of the river's waters." We believe youth are educated to transform their own lives when they learn the staggering odds they face, are taught the skills to overcome these odds, and are afforded the support, guidance, access, and opportunities to overcome them. This work of educating youth to create change both within and without brings perspective—an understanding of the challenge: that the force of the river is mighty, and the effort to change its flow will be massive, but that to change its course, we must know where the river comes from, and the direction in which we wish to send it. With this knowledge comes a map to redirect their lives.

The question for us is what kind of society do we wish to be? Do we seek to be a moral and ethical society? Do we want to live in a society that recognizes that many young people will make mistakes, and may commit crimes, but that if they are not egregious we must believe in redemption through alternatives to incarceration? Or instead, do want to continue policies that are unsustainable, economically and morally? Will we recognize that we cannot incarcerate children at a cost of $210,000 in facilities that display a recidivism rate nearing 90 percent, that we cannot continue to have the largest prison population in the world, that we cannot maintain a school-to-prison pipeline, that we cannot continue to place children in environments where they have such limited access and opportunity and resources because it is immoral and inhumane? We know that with the proper support systems and education, with guidance and opportunity, those young people who stand on the precipice of engaging in illegal acts, those who are faced with a path of crime and damaging life choices, will choose another way. We know that while the necessary investments in educational and youth programs are extensive, they pale in the face of the resources presently used to incarcerate and punish these children. The choice is clear, and sharp, and profound. The continued prosecution and imprisonment of our children does not speak to their lack of morality, but to our own.

NOTES

1. Stuart Taylor Jr., "America's Prison Spree Has Brutal Impact," *National Journal Magazine*, Saturday, November 14, 2009.

2. Clare Trapasso, "Bronx Teenage Pregnancy Rate Soars," *Daily News*, March 4, 2008.

3. The Schott Foundation. 2008. *Given Half a Chance: The Schott 50-State Report on Public Education and Black Males*. http://www.blackboysreport.org/files/schott50statereport-execsummary.pdf.

4. Citizen's Committee for Children of New York, Inc. 2010. *Keeping Track of New York City's Children, Status Report 2010*.

5. Michelle McPhee, "Cocaine Crackdown Comes to Harlem," *Daily News*, July 21, 2002.

6. Campaign for Fiscal Equity v. New York. 2003. 100 N.Y. 2d 893.

7. Campaign for Fiscal Equity v. New York. 2003. 100 N.Y. 2d 893.

8. Advancement Project. 2010. *Test, Punish, and Push Out: How "Zero Tolerance" and High-Stakes Testing Funnel Youth into the School-to-Prison Pipeline*.

9. Advancement Project. 2010. *Test, Punish, and Push Out: How "Zero Tolerance" and High-Stakes Testing Funnel Youth into the School-to-Prison Pipeline*.

10. Center for Constitutional Rights, "New NYPD Data for 2009 Shows Significant Rise in Stop-and-Frisks: More Than Half Million New Yorkers Stopped Last Year," February 17, 2010. http://ccrjustice.org/newsroom/press-releases/new-nypd-data-2009-shows-significant-rise-stop-and-frisks%3A-more-half-million.

11. Center for Constitutional Rights, "New NYPD Data for 2009 Shows Significant Rise in Stop-and-Frisks: More Than Half Million New Yorkers Stopped Last Year," February 17, 2010. http://ccrjustice.org/newsroom/press-releases/new-nypd-data-2009-shows-significant-rise-stop-and-frisks%3A-more-half-million; Bob Herbert, "An Easy Call," *New York Times*, July 5, 2010. http://ccrjustice.org/newsroom/press-releases/new-nypd-data-2009-shows-significant-rise-stop-and-frisks%3A-more-half-million.

12. The New York City Association of Homeless and Street-Involved Youth Organizations. 2007. *The State of the City's Homeless Youth Report*. http://www.empirestatecoalition.org/main/pdf/State%20of%20the%20City%20Report%20FINAL%201-21-10.pdf; Task Force on Transforming Juvenile Justice. 2009. *Charting a New Course: A Blueprint for Transforming Juvenile Justice in New York State*. http://www.vera.org/paterson-task-force-juvenile-justice-report.

13. New York Juvenile Justice Coalition. 2010. "Downsize and Reinvest." Correctional Association of New York.

14. Citizen's Committee for Children of New York, Inc. 2010. *Keeping Track of New York City's Children, Status Report 2010.*

15. The PEW Center on the States. 2008. One in 100: Behind Bars in America in 2008. http://www.pewcenteronthestates.org/uploadedFiles/8015PCTS_Prison08_FINAL_2-1-1_FORWEB.pdf.

13

What It Takes to Transform a School inside a Juvenile Justice Facility

The Story of the Maya Angelou Academy

DAVID DOMENICI AND JAMES FORMAN JR.

"Do you want to apply to run the school inside Oak Hill?" The question came from Vincent Schiraldi, the new head of Washington, D.C.'s juvenile justice agency, in November 2006. He wasn't making any promises—there would be a formal Request for Proposals before any decisions were made—but he wanted to gauge our interest.

Schiraldi was not a typical juvenile justice administrator. He was a former social worker who had spent the bulk of his career as a critic of the way our nation treats incarcerated youth. Schiraldi understood education's transformative potential, and one of his first priorities was to improve the school at Oak Hill, the city's facility for juveniles who had been adjudicated delinquent.

Incarcerated teens suffer tremendous educational deficits: they disproportionately have attended failing schools, typically read and do math at the elementary school level, and often have dropped out or been kicked out of school before being arrested (Sedlak and McPherson 2010; Balfanz et al. 2003). In theory, commitment to a state facility offers them an opportunity to receive an education. In practice, however, most schools in correctional facilities are woefully inadequate (Dohrn 2002). In a typical facility, academic expectations are low, the curriculum is not rigorous, special education services are wanting, and the teaching staff is underskilled and demoralized. What Franklin Zimring said almost thirty years ago is still largely the case: "the training school neither trains much nor schools effectively" (Zimring 1982, 72).

Oak Hill was no exception. The all-male facility had long been a horror show—assaults were commonplace and drugs and weapons were easy to find. The *Washington Post* warned that it had become "little more than a warehouse that rehabilitates no one" ("DYRS" 2010). The school within Oak Hill—then called the Oak Hill Academy—was little better. Everything about the place told the young men incarcerated in Oak Hill that education was not a priority: guards sat in classrooms with walkie-talkies blaring, students came, went, or slept without interruption, and fights were routine.

Schiraldi was determined to change this. In an innovative move, he solicited proposals from successful educators to run the Oak Hill Academy, which until then had been part of the D.C. Public Schools (DCPS). Schiraldi called us because since the late 1990s we had run two charter high schools that worked with some of the city's most underserved kids. Our schools—both named after the poet Maya Angelou—are open to any who apply, but we actively recruit teens who have dropped out or been expelled, have truancy issues, or have been arrested. We also serve a higher than average number of special education students.

Despite our background, we had serious doubts about taking on the challenge of running the school at Oak Hill. After all, we had never operated a school *inside* a prison. The list of possible pitfalls was long: Would qualified teachers apply to work in a juvenile facility? How would we manage discipline? Could we create a school that felt special and welcoming, or was it naïve to think we could establish such an atmosphere within the confines of a jail? Considering how far behind the students would be academically, could we help them make significant progress when we would only work with them for about nine months?

We eventually overcame these doubts, submitted a proposal, and were chosen to run the school, which we renamed the Maya Angelou Academy. We launched our program in the original Oak Hill compound, but after two years it was relocated to the New Beginnings Youth Development Center, a brand-new facility that replaced Oak Hill. Three years after it opened, the Maya Angelou Academy is far from perfect, but outside evaluators have been impressed with the speed and extent of the turnaround. In July 2010, the monitor overseeing the court-ordered reform of Washington, D.C.'s juvenile justice agency called the school an "extraordinary educational program" (Special Arbiter's Report 2010). The educational expert the monitor hired reached a similar conclusion:

> The Maya Angelou Academy at the New Beginnings Youth Development Center is one of the best education programs in a confinement facility I have had the opportunity to observe. Scholars in the model units are receiving an excellent education. The strength of the leadership and the

staff, the people and material resources available to them, and the processes and program design all contribute to the overall effectiveness of the program. (Exhibit 6A 2010)

After decades of documenting the school's failures, the *Washington Post* finally had good news—citing the monitor's report, it noted that the school had been transformed "from one of the nation's worst programs to one of its finest" ("DYRS" 2010).

Drawing on the lessons of our collaboration with Schiraldi and D.C.'s Department of Youth Rehabilitation Services (DYRS), we have written this chapter in the hope of fostering similar transformations elsewhere. We call on juvenile justice administrators, reform activists, and policy analysts to do whatever is in their power to bring high-quality schools to youth correctional facilities. Similarly, we call on education reformers to do more to create such schools in facilities across the country. Though our focus here is on education inside juvenile facilities, we also believe there has to be a larger commitment to educating these same young people before they enter and after they are released—themes to which we will return at the end of the chapter.

At first blush, such an appeal might seem unnecessary. After all, most people know that education is critical to a young person's future, and most people assume—even if they do not know for sure—that schools in juvenile facilities are not very good. Despite this, however, we have found that the education and juvenile justice communities largely inhabit parallel universes. The two groups rarely talk to each other—when we attend a conference of educators, members of the juvenile justice community are rarely present, and educators do not typically attend juvenile justice gatherings. (At the conference that led to this book, for example, there were only a handful of educators present, and no other charter school operators.)

There are many reasons why these two groups do not collaborate, most of them understandable. Apart from a few visionary leaders like Schiraldi, juvenile justice administrators have not thought to establish educational partnerships with high-quality charter school providers (or other unconventional school operators). Juvenile justice reformers, for their part, have been largely concerned with reducing the number of young people who are incarcerated (including reducing the number tried as adults), not with developing quality schools for those who remain behind bars. More radical reformers are reluctant to invest in improving schools inside juvenile prisons because they believe that doing so reinforces a system they would like to abolish. Finally, many juvenile justice advocates are lawyers (as are we), and law schools train students to think about pretrial rights (such as right to counsel and the right against illegal searches and seizures); by contrast, few criminal procedure classes or juvenile rights classes focus on what happens *after* a young offender is convicted and sent to a facility.

It is equally understandable that education reformers have not focused on juvenile facilities. Many wonder—as we did—whether the techniques they have developed running schools in the community will work in a correctional setting. Others are just starting their schools, or expanding, and do not have the capacity to take on an additional—and somewhat different—challenge. More than a few would prefer to work with the same group of kids for multiple years, rather than the nine months to a year that juvenile offenders typically spend in a facility. And some wonder if this is the best way to spend their own limited resources. Given that there are so many law-abiding young people who need better schools, these educators opt to work with them.

We do not seek to rebut these considerations here. Indeed, we would not want to—we endorse efforts by juvenile justice reformers to reduce the number of incarcerated youth, and we are thrilled that so many education reformers are creating high-quality schools outside of juvenile facilities. We view these efforts as of a piece with our own. On the other hand, we hope that our story can motivate some juvenile justice and education reformers to work together to improve other schools for incarcerated youth. By focusing on the nitty-gritty details of running such a school, we hope to suggest concrete practices that can strengthen their efforts.

We have divided our account of the Maya Angelou Academy's development into the following sections: "People," "Culture," "Curriculum," "Instruction," and "Transition." After describing the school, we discuss our results. We conclude by examining the policy implications of our experience and asking what the education and juvenile justice communities could do differently to achieve the central aim of this book—keeping kids out of the juvenile system.

People

It is now widely believed that improving teacher quality is the single most important thing a school can do to influence academic achievement (Gordon et al. 2006; Jordan et al. 1997). As Chris Barbic, founder of the high-performing YES Prep charter school network, is fond of saying, "We bet the farm on people."

Yet teacher quality in schools in juvenile facilities is notoriously low. This does not surprise many people. We wondered ourselves whether we would be able to recruit dedicated, high-performing teachers. But we saw one ray of hope. Even though many teachers would shudder at the thought of entering a juvenile facility every day, we also suspected that there was a subset of teachers who would be drawn to our social justice mission. Those behind bars have few allies, to be sure, but there are some in our nation—including some educators—who are appalled that we have the world's largest prison system and that we lock up so many juveniles in such terrible conditions. Those were the people we needed to find.

To get them, we had to send the message that the Maya Angelou Academy was going to be a high-quality school, even though it was in a juvenile facility. So every time we opened our mouths, wrote a flyer, or sent an e-mail, our message remained the same: We were going to create the best school in the country for kids who are locked up. We were not sure this would end up being true, but we figured if we did not believe it, nobody would.

Everything about our recruitment process emphasized our mission. Our outreach materials stressed the school's uniqueness. Our job postings declared that we would "provide these students with the best education they have ever had" and that we sought only those who had "an unyielding belief that with the appropriate supports, coupled with high expectations, all students can significantly improve their academic skills."

During interviews we probed candidates about high expectations in various ways. While some of our questions were tailored specifically to our school, we modeled much of our hiring process on what we have learned from organizations like New Leaders for New Schools, and from presentations by high-performing schools at conferences sponsored by the New Schools Venture Fund. We asked candidates to provide examples of how they created a classroom culture of high expectations even in the face of obstacles. We asked how they would approach working with teenagers who could barely read, students who had been labeled as needing special education throughout their school lives, students with little understanding of what it meant to be successful in school. We also asked each teacher candidate to respond to a writing prompt and to teach a sample lesson.

Our selection process served multiple ends. Most directly, it helped us identify talent. But it also served as a recruitment tool. We were trying to signal to candidates that this would be a rigorous school, with high standards for students and teachers alike. Having a rigorous selection process was essential to that message.

The process also gave us some insight into the quality of the teaching staff at the existing school. Our contract gave us complete hiring and firing authority. Existing teachers at the Oak Hill Academy—all of whom were DCPS employees—were not guaranteed jobs at the Maya Angelou Academy. They could apply to work for us, and we promised to interview all who applied. If they chose not to apply, or if they applied but were not hired, they would be reassigned within DCPS.

About ten of the existing teachers applied for jobs, and the interviews were dispiriting. One candidate proudly stated that "crossword puzzles and word-finds keep students motivated." Another told us that because most of the students could not read, he focused his efforts on the handful that could, and let the rest sleep.

We did not hire any of these ten teachers. Looking back, we realized that—although we had not set this as a goal—we had not ended up hiring any teachers with experience in a correctional setting. In hindsight, we think this was mostly a good thing, because no one came into the job dragged down by the low expectations of most correctional schools. (In saying this, we do not mean to suggest that there are not excellent, hard-working teachers in correctional schools; we mean only that the culture of those schools makes such teachers rare.)

Make no mistake: Finding the right teachers has not been easy. But through aggressive recruiting, we have found a number of highly experienced, talented teachers who, as we thought, wanted to make a difference by working with our students.

It is worth emphasizing the "reach" of our informal recruiting network. Many of the people we hired had heard of our program through friends and colleagues, not advertisements. Our inaugural faculty included a former Teach for America (TFA) corps member who had been teaching social studies at one of D.C.'s highest-performing public charter schools. She heard about us through the Children's Defense Fund. On our current math team, we have a teacher with many years of experience at a public school in the Bronx and a special education teacher who worked in alternative settings outside of Boston. Both were attracted to our mission, and after visiting the school, they felt that we had created a place where they could be successful. And our academic dean came to us with a stellar resume—she began her teaching career as a TFA corps member, then became a TFA trainer, was a teacher at one of our schools, and spent a year coaching teachers at DCPS under Chancellor Michelle Rhee. These were the kind of people we needed if we were to build the type of school culture we wanted.

Culture

High-achieving schools are places where a culture of trust dominates. They are safe and nonviolent. Students work hard and respect the building and learning environment. Unfortunately, schools in correctional settings typically have weak, or negative, cultures. Like the old Oak Hill Academy, they are often dominated by low expectations, a culture of violence, and negative behavior by students (and too often by staff).

Fixing this was our first priority. We started with the physical environment. When we walked through the Oak Hill Academy before taking over, we were greeted by drab walls, out-of-date posters, and classrooms cluttered with unused texts and papers from students who had long ago left the school. The divider in the auditorium was nailed shut, and an inside wall was blackened and dark from a recent fire. As a result, what could have been an ideal setting for school ceremonies and performances had become a fire hazard and a place for teachers to hide. Some of the physical obstacles seemed almost gratuitous. For example, although the school was located inside a large, prisonlike facility surrounded by thirty-foot-high razor wire, the school itself was surrounded by an additional ten-foot fence, as if to say to the students, "You are not welcome here" or "This school is a prison within a prison."

Soon after we took over the school, the hallways were decorated with student art and other work, awards and plaques hung on the walls, and classrooms were tidy. The small, never-used auditorium was open, painted, and ready for our first awards ceremony. And the fence that separated the school from the rest of the grounds was bulldozed over and thrown away.

Words—especially the ones you use to refer to people—matter, too. At Maya Angelou, we call the students "scholars." This practice began during our first summer, when we partnered with the Children's Defense Fund and established a CDF Freedom School (the first ever inside a youth correctional facility). In the Freedom School model, all participants are called scholars. We adopted the term that summer and decided to stick with it. We believe that it reminds everyone—teachers, visitors, and the scholars themselves—how we view the young men in our school.

We also believe in celebrating student success. We host an awards ceremony nine times a year, at the end of each curricular unit. Teachers give awards to outstanding scholars in each class, recognizing excellence in such categories as academic performance, leadership, creativity, advocacy, and greatest improvement. Students star in these ceremonies, serving as the emcees, reading poems or essays, and performing songs or dances.

Awards ceremonies are important at all schools, but they are especially important for our scholars. Most of them have failed repeatedly in school, have been suspended multiple times, and became known to school administrators and the larger school community only when they did something wrong. For such students, being rewarded and acknowledged for working hard helps them develop a sense that school can be a place where they can shine.

Awards ceremonies have other benefits as well. At our facility, as in most youth correctional settings, students are rarely allowed to mingle together freely. Instead, they spend most of the day interacting only with other members of their residential unit. A schoolwide ceremony helps to change the culture by establishing that students can come together in one place and behave appropriately.

In addition to celebrating their success, we help our students imagine a future for themselves. Good schools serving low-income populations work relentlessly to get their students to believe that their future includes college. Such schools hang college banners in hallways and classrooms, organize college trips, and invite guest speakers to campus. Schools in correctional settings must take similar steps. Accordingly, we sponsor college trips for students who are nearing their release date. We also host college fairs in the facility and have a "How to Apply to College" bulletin board prominently displayed in the school.

Even as we look to the long term, we know that building a strong school climate also requires attending to day-to-day behavioral norms. Accordingly, we teach and reward the behaviors and attitudes we want to see in the school through a range of incentive-based programs. These programs help students develop the social/behavioral habits that are expected in school or at work.

We use a modified version of the Positive Behavioral Incentive Program (PBIS) to encourage students to demonstrate our school values: Respect, Responsibility, Integrity, Safety, Self-determination, and Empathy (R^2IS^2E).[1] School and DYRS staff give out stars to students when they exhibit one of the values; the stars are displayed on the school walls and tallied daily in our student information system. The scholars who accumulate the most stars during each curricular unit are acknowledged at our awards ceremonies, earning a Nelson Mandela leadership certificate.

In addition, all teachers provide a daily score for students based on student *participation* and *respect* in each class (PR points). Students earn weekly stipends based on their PR points, which are totaled up along with their R^2IS^2E stars in an easy-to-read report. Each Friday, scholars meet with a small team of school staff to review their progress from the past week and set goals for the upcoming week.

In all these ways, we act on our belief that a good school inside a juvenile facility shares many characteristics with good schools on the outside. But we also recognize that a school inside a facility faces some distinct issues. While we believe these are matters of tactics, rather than philosophy, they are nonetheless important. In correctional settings, for example, staff includes both school staff and "correctional" or "secure" staff. These two groups—educators and security—often clash. The tension was magnified in our case because the school staff were our employees while the secure staff worked for DYRS. When we first came to Oak Hill, the chasm between school and DYRS front-line staff was wide. Many of the DYRS staff were wary and unsupportive of us. Some believed we were naïve, others doubted our sincerity, and plenty felt we would not last long.

Today, we have largely closed the gap between the two staffs. We were able to do this because (1) we had the support of DYRS leadership, (2) we were relentless, and (3) we were optimistic. The first point is simple but overwhelmingly important. Although many front-line DYRS staff had their doubts about our new school, Schiraldi and his entire leadership team believed passionately in our educational mission. The school would not have opened or survived without them. The lesson we draw for other educators is that this work can only be done with the support of the juvenile justice agency.

Second, we were relentless. We sat down with DYRS leadership and explained what we needed front-line staff to do in order for the school to succeed. The list was basic, but in this setting, our expectations represented a major culture shift: all kids come to school, on time; students receiving medication on a regular basis take it in the morning, before coming to school, instead of disrupting class later by making trips to the nurse; walkie-talkies are turned down in the classroom; DYRS staff and students are in classrooms during school hours, not chatting in the hallways. Making the list of priorities is only the first step; school leadership must enforce the new practices. We estimate that nearly 30 percent of the principal's time during the first two years was spent walking the hallways to make sure these changes were implemented consistently.

Third, we were optimistic. We believed that if we started to turn the tide and if the school started to function like a *school*, most front-line staff would adapt to and eventually prefer the new routine. We believed that most would eventually embrace the notion that from 8:00 a.m. until 3:30 p.m. all adults in the building have one primary objective—to help our students develop the skills they need to succeed when they leave. After all, most of the DYRS staff were good people who had spent years—sometimes decades—stuck in a dysfunctional system. A few were beyond reform (we were optimists, not fools), but the majority, we believed, would like their jobs better if they could spend the day supporting students who were engaged in the learning process, rather than punishing students who were bored, irritated, and restless. Our optimism (supported by DYRS leadership's willingness to hold staff accountable for their performance in the school) has paid dividends. Although disagreements remain between the school and secure staff, the two groups now generally work closely in support of students in the school.

We recognized from the outset that if we did not get school culture right, nothing else about the school would work. A strong culture does not guarantee success (we have seen schools with strong cultures but inconsistent instructional quality, for example). But a negative school culture guarantees failure. Accordingly, each of the practices we have described—adorning hallways and classrooms with student work and inspirational messages, holding awards ceremonies, offering incentives and rewards for positive behavior, exposing students to high-quality programs and colleges before they leave—were all focused on building up a culture where learning and academic achievement can flourish.

Curriculum

In designing the curriculum at the Maya Angelou Academy, we were guided by two well-established educational principles: rigor and relevance. First, a rigorous, challenging high school curriculum is a critical determinant of postsecondary success (Adelman 2006). Second, especially for students who have struggled in school, the curriculum must be relevant to their lives (National Research Council 2003). We also knew that core classes would have to be aligned with DCPS curriculum standards if our students were to earn credits that would count when they returned to school in the community. (In many states, schools in juvenile facilities do not use a curriculum aligned to the state standards—a source of great frustration for students who leave only to find that they have not made any progress toward graduation.)

Although we were committed to these general principles, we quickly realized that our status as a school in a juvenile facility would influence curricular decisions. Because our students come and go throughout the year, a curriculum composed of semester-long units would not work. If a student arrives in

November and the next semester starts in January, it is unreasonable to tell him to study for six weeks if he knows he will not earn credit for the effort.

For this reason, we structured our curriculum as a series of eight modular units, each of which takes just over a month to complete (this schedule is supplemented by an eight-week summer program). For the past two years, the unit themes have been Relationships, Systems, Change, Choice, Power, Justice, Ethics, and Dreams. Breaking up the school year into short, manageable units serves multiple goals. Even students who have been disengaged from school can quickly delve into the curriculum. And students who are with us for only a few weeks or months can complete whole units of study—and earn transferable credits—before leaving.

Here is an example of a unit in action. In the fall of 2008, the Systems unit focused on the presidential election. In social studies, students learned about the electoral process, the history of voting rights, and governmental systems. In math, they learned data analysis by studying the Electoral College system, conducting polls inside the school, and reviewing the correlation between demographic groups and voting trends. In English, students focused on messaging, marketing, and public speaking while reading Barack Obama's memoir, *Dreams from My Father*. The unit culminated with mock presidential and local elections, while the few students who were eighteen registered and voted in the actual election.

In addition to our core curriculum, we offer a GED program for selected students. GED programs have a bad name; they are often dumping grounds for kids whose schools have given up on them. And it is easy to offer poor GED instruction—we know, because our GED program floundered during our first year. But we have since developed a rigorous, engaging program that is on an upward trajectory. We think that getting it right requires remembering two key points.

First, a school must be thoughtful about the entry requirements for its GED program. The GED program should be reserved for those students who are unlikely to graduate from high school (because of their age and accumulated credits) and who have a real chance of passing the test. The test is not easy, and students who lack the basic skills necessary for a GED prep class probably need a more intensive focus on literacy and numeracy, and should not be fooled into thinking they are ready for the GED. Accordingly, we limit enrollment in our GED program to students who are at least seventeen years old, have less than a year of high school credits, have been at New Beginnings for a minimum of four months, have developed the behavioral skills necessary to function in a class comprised of students from multiple housing units, and who—based on their performance at the academy and on standardized tests—we believe can pass the GED with three to four months of intensive work.

Second, a GED program should not be linked, as it too often is, with vocational education, or "earning a trade." There is nothing wrong (and a lot that is right) with high-quality vocational education. Indeed, we have students who have earned their GED and gone on to construction-related job-training programs. But that should not be the only way a school talks to students about a GED. We talk about a GED as a gateway to college, and each of the last two years we have sent students who passed the GED while with us directly on to college. None of these young men had seen college as a remote possibility when they first came to New Beginnings.

To understand how we approach students who arrive performing at higher academic levels, consider Jeremy,[2] a seventeen-year-old who arrived at New Beginnings in August 2009. Jeremy performed at a higher level than our average student, having scored at the eighth grade level in math and the ninth grade level in English. He entered our GED program in December 2009 and passed the test in April 2010. At this point, however, Jeremy didn't stop working to improve his academic skills (as, admittedly, some of our students do). Instead, he studied for and took the SAT. He also took a mock Philosophy 101 class that we created for a classmate and him during their last month at New Beginnings. The class structure and expectations were modeled on those of an entry-level college class, and although he did not receive any credit, Jeremy worked hard. At this writing, Jeremy leaves for college in just a few weeks, interested in pursuing a degree in architecture (which he learned about in our carpentry class).

Although Jeremy is better prepared academically and socio-emotionally than many of our students, he faces a tough road. His SAT scores are lower than those of most of his college peers, and he has major gaps in his education. Nonetheless, we believe that Jeremy deserves the chance to pursue a college degree. And through our GED program, he obtained a credential that will give him that opportunity.

Instruction

Jeremy is not our typical student, of course. The average student enters the academy just under the age of seventeen, with less than a year's worth of high school credits, and functioning at between the fifth and sixth grade levels in reading and math.[3] Just under 50 percent are identified as special education students.[4] But these averages are just that—they hide great variation among our students, including the staggering fact that nearly 20 percent of our students test at or below the third grade level in reading at entry.

A further complication is that students attend school grouped by their residential units, not by their academic proficiency. As a result, classes are mixed in terms of age, skill level, and educational history. A single class may include both nineteen-year-olds and fourteen-year-olds; students who function at the high school level and students who struggle to read; students who had been attending school regularly prior to their involvement in the juvenile justice system and students who have not been to school in years.

One of our first challenges was to build and implement consistent classroom norms and systems. We use a variety of tactics, some of them versions of the practices Doug Lemov describes in *Teach like a Champion* (Lemov 2010). All classes start the same way (students enter, get their subject binders, and turn to the warm-up section), and all classes finish with an exit ticket (usually a short question or problem that helps to wrap up the class), after which students return their binders to the shelf.

In addition, students learn that at the academy we provide immense supports but don't allow distracting behaviors or interruptions to slow us down. Each class activity is timed: a typical class begins with five minutes for the warm-up, and a clock on the SMART board pops up and starts ticking. After five minutes, the clock goes off, the warm-up ends, and the class moves to the next part of the lesson. Then the clock is reset. Fifteen minutes later, the clock chimes, and the class moves to the next activity. When we opened our first school almost fifteen years ago, this process would have been anathema to us; we would have rejected it as too rigid and controlling. But we have changed our thinking. Now we believe that paying close attention to time in this way both maximizes learning time and reinforces the sense of urgency about the educational process that we want all students to feel.

Given our population, teachers must differentiate extensively within the classroom. For example, when teachers assign a newspaper or magazine article, they will typically create multiple versions, paraphrasing complex ideas or using substitute vocabulary where necessary. This enables all students to read and discuss the same article, while ensuring that the reading level is appropriate for each student. Teachers also differentiate final assessments—each version is aligned to the core content and skills taught during the unit, but the assessments vary in their level of complexity, the degree of guidance provided, and the expectations for the writing section. In addition, some students take the assessments one on one with special education staff and may receive additional time and support.

Differentiation is closely connected to individualization. In all classes, but particularly in English and math, we have systems in place to support the development of individual students' skills within the class structure. In math, all students take a diagnostic assessment when they arrive. Using this assessment, students and teachers prioritize basic skills that students need to work on. After the class warm-up, all students refer to their Skills Log, and for ten-fifteen minutes work on math fundamentals. Once a student believes he has mastered a skill, he takes a short assessment. Students only move to the next skill if they receive a grade of 80 percent or higher. Each day, once the "skills" part of the class is over, the full class moves together to the day's objective. Using this balanced approach, students have the time and support they need to tackle long-neglected math skills, while also gaining exposure to higher-level concepts in algebra and geometry—subjects rarely offered to students in correctional settings.

As this discussion indicates, many of our classes are structured in such a way that special education is woven into the fabric of the school. We do provide pull-out classes for some students, but the vast majority of our special education instruction takes place within our standard class rotations.

Keith's story provides a good example of how we work with students who are far behind academically. Keith was placed at New Beginnings in the middle of the 2009-2010 school year. He tested at the third grade level in reading, and a little higher in math. His background included middle school years at a special education school, and a failed ninth grade year at a large public high school.

After completing his intake assessments, Keith told our director of special education that he wanted to improve his reading more than anything. He pointed to the "2.8" next to his reading fluency score and told her he was going to make that number go up, because he didn't want to read like a second grader anymore.

When asked about his struggles with reading, Keith broke down and cried, admitting that he started having problems in second grade. His teachers knew it, he said, but they didn't help him—not in elementary school, not in the special education middle school, and not at the big high school where he got into trouble. He wasn't accusatory, just sad—and, it seemed, a little embarrassed.

For the next six months, Keith worked with one of our reading coaches each day instead of going to science class, using a variety of reading improvement strategies and programs, including the Wilson Reading System. In English, he set weekly goals for learning new vocabulary words, which he would take back to his unit in the evening. During the Structured Reading

Program (SRP)—a twenty- to thirty-minute session built into our English classes, inspired by the Teachers College Reading and Writing Project—he read and responded to books he had chosen from a list of titles at his reading level. Over the next six months, he read four books in the SRP and three others in English class, often taking his books back to the unit at night. He won recognition at our awards ceremonies as a member of our "Bookworm Club"—students who complete books or improve their reading levels during a curricular unit—and became a favorite with his English teachers.

Now, just six months later, as he prepares for his release, Keith's reading fluency score is just shy of the fifth grade level. Keith will be heading to the tenth grade in the fall. Age-wise, he'll only be one year behind his peers (he is still sixteen). Academically, he is much further behind but doing his best to catch up. We are working with him to find a school where he can keep getting the intensive reading support he needs. But his family just moved to Prince George's County, Maryland, and options beyond his large, low-performing neighborhood high school are limited.

Transition

Planning for a youth's transition back to the community must begin the moment he arrives at a correctional facility. This has become something of a cliché in the world of juvenile justice. But the principle is sound and a commitment to it is essential, even if it is hard to implement consistently.

Our transition specialists have the title "advocates," and their job begins with welcoming each student into the academy and helping him to adjust. They also serve as the school's primary liaison with the DYRS staff in charge of the student's living unit. Finally, they help plan and support the student's transition to school or job training in the community. By assuming all these roles, advocates develop a strong relationship with the student—a relationship of critical importance once he leaves us and reenters a world full of challenges and temptations.

In addition to building a relationship from the start, our advocates locate accurate and up-to-date school records (including special education records where appropriate). This can be difficult and is often done poorly in juvenile facilities (Balfanz et al. 2003). But such records are tremendously helpful for developing an academic plan. In addition, the very act of working tirelessly to obtain the records signals to students that—contrary to what previous bad experiences with juvenile officials might have taught them—we care about them and want to support them.

As students move to within a few months of release, the advocates work closely with them, their parents, after-care workers, and our director of special education, as appropriate, to support their transition. Advocates help students develop a portfolio of their work, awards they have received, progress reports, and a resume. With the support of DYRS, advocates set up and accompany students on interviews with prospective schools or training programs. Advocates ensure that all students have copies of the basic documents they need for work and school (Social Security card, non-driver ID, etc.).

In addition, all students participate in mock interviews as part of their transition process. Advocates help students prepare for these interviews, and friends of the school—from business, nonprofits, and government agencies—come out to New Beginnings to conduct them. The panels score each interview by using a rubric and talk with students afterwards about their performance.

Once students leave New Beginnings, advocates provide ongoing support for ninety days (this is not enough time, but it is all that our funding currently allows). Advocates often accompany students on their first day of school, and they visit students at school or in their homes or group homes once a week. Throughout this time, advocates stay in touch with DYRS after-care workers, school officials, and family members.

We believe that our advocates succeed because of their force of will and personalities, but also because our process allows them to bond with students and provide uninterrupted care. Students at the academy rightfully see the advocate as their closest ally and a source of consistent support—from day one to release and beyond.

Advocates must listen carefully to what a student wants, but they also must be honest with the student about creating a plan that is likely to succeed. For example, sometimes a student wants to go to his neighborhood school to be with friends, even though the friends are part of his problems. Others want to go to a school where they can compete for a football scholarship to college, even though they've never played football. Others want to enroll in a job-training program with academic entry requirements they cannot meet.

Trevon's story illustrates the role that advocates play in helping our students succeed in their transition. Trevon arrived at New Beginnings in the early fall of 2009. He had just turned seventeen, and had about a year's worth of high school credits. Trevon scored at the seventh grade level in reading and the fifth grade level in math. He was quiet, unassuming, and eager to learn.

Trevon did well at the academy. He played on our flag football team, then on our basketball team (where he earned all-league honors), and passed all his classes with a B+ average. Trevon especially liked his art and English classes. His scores went up at an annualized rate of more than three grade levels in reading and 1.3 grade levels in math.

As spring approached, Trevon's advocate started talking to him about his options once he was released. He didn't want to return to his neighborhood, where he said he knew he would get into trouble; he was open to going to a small school and said he didn't mind enrolling in eleventh grade, even though he would soon turn eighteen. These were all indications that Trevon was a good candidate for one of our Maya Angelou charter schools.

In Trevon's case, his advocate created a transition plan that appealed to his interests, reduced the risk of his getting into trouble over the summer before school started, and placed him in a school where we thought he could succeed. This plan included (a) getting Trevon signed up for D.C.'s Summer Youth Employment Program (SYEP) and arranging a week-long "tryout" at a summer basketball camp, the deal being that if he did well he could work at the camp for a month and get paid through SYEP; (b) researching our databank of precollege summer programs and encouraging him to apply to a three-week program at Pace University, where he would live on campus and take an arts-focused curriculum; and (c) working with one of our charter schools to get his application in for the fall.

Trevon "passed" his tryout week and spent a month working at one of the city's top basketball camps. He completed the program at Pace (not without some struggles), and he enrolled at the Maya Angelou Public Charter School as a junior. Ensuring that each piece of this plan came to fruition exemplifies the sort of hard, detailed work our advocates undertake. In Trevon's case, the Pace experience required convincing the director of the program to admit Trevon, taking him to the train station, buying a set of summer clothes, arranging a cell phone with restricted minutes, figuring out a ride from the train station in New York City to the Pace campus (the advocate's mother, who lives in New York, was called in to pick him up at the train station and get him to Pace on his first day), calling him daily, and having lots of "I know you can do it" conversations with him. This level of support, planning, and willingness to attend to the individual needs of students in transition is what sets our advocates apart.

Results

With all of these programs and strategies in place, what has the Maya Angelou Academy achieved? Our internal data indicate success in some important areas. First, consider credit accumulation. Students in juvenile facilities are often frustrated by their inability to earn credits towards graduation while they are locked up. If the school does not use a standards-based curriculum that allows credit accumulation, many students feel that their time is being wasted—and in an important respect, they are right. At the Maya Angelou Academy, however, students accumulate credits more than three times as quickly as they did before coming to us. Our average student earns just over six high school credits for every nine months of school with us. These same students averaged just over three credits during their prior *two years* of school, or about 1.5 credits a year.

In addition to accumulating credits at a faster rate, our students are improving their reading and math skills. During the 2009-2010 school year, students on average advanced 1.4 years in reading and 1.3 years in math.[5] These numbers are especially powerful given our students' previous rate of improvement. Remember that on average our students are reading and doing math at between the fifth and sixth grade level, although most of them are old enough to be in the eleventh grade. This means that before coming to the academy, our students on average advanced half a year in reading and math for every year they were in school. At the academy, these students have advanced at nearly three times that rate in both reading and math.

Most of our students have experienced significant school failure prior to coming to New Beginnings. They typically do not like school, do not think of themselves as successful students, and do not trust teachers and other educators. We think that changing these attitudes is as important as anything else we do.

We measure students' attitudes in several areas, both at enrollment and then again when they leave. At enrollment, more than 80 percent of our students tell us they did not like school and did not think they were successful students. At departure, however, more than 75 percent of our students say they enjoyed learning and felt successful at the Maya Angelou Academy. Our students are also much more trusting of teachers when they depart. When we ask them upon arrival if they trusted the staff at their prior school to work in their best interest, more than 70 percent say they did not. But upon departure, nearly 90 percent say they trust Maya Angelou Academy staff to work in their best interest.

We also track whether students remain in school after leaving us. This is a massively important measure, although it is one that we have less control over than some others. Our results here are improving rapidly, though they are not where we would like them to be. In the first nine months we were running the school, approximately 70 students completed our program. Of those, 35 percent were still attending school or job-training programs on a regular basis ninety days after release. The retention numbers have gone up since then. Of the last 70 students who completed the program (as of April 2010), 49 percent were still attending school or job-training programs on a regular basis ninety days after release.

Implications: Reforming Education outside of Juvenile Facilities

While we are gratified when students say, "This is the best school I've ever been to," we are often saddened as well. Shouldn't our kids have had many great schools before this? And shouldn't another great school await them when they leave?

Volumes have been written about improving our education system, and we do not propose to join that debate here. Our aim is narrower—we want to talk about education policy as it relates to the kids we see at the Maya Angelou Academy, those who have been the most profoundly underserved, who are the furthest behind, and who are at the greatest risk of ending up at the margins of our society unless we (and they) make different choices.

As we noted above, nearly 20 percent of our students enter the school functioning at or below the third grade level. Even if these students improve their reading two grade levels while they are with us, they nonetheless return to the community years behind academically, functioning well below the level necessary to succeed in a traditional high school, an adult education center, or a GED program. Yet there are almost no programs in the District of Columbia designed and resourced appropriately for them. So they quit.

Why don't these students have more, and better, options? We have already identified one reason—we do not think that either the juvenile justice or education community has paid enough attention to developing meaningful educational options for this group of young people. But that's only part of the story. In effect, national and local education policies conspire *against* these students.

When people ask us about the feasibility of starting a school like the Maya Angelou Public Charter Schools—community schools serving the kids who are most in need—we are encouraging, but also honest. We remind them that under the federal No Child Left Behind law (which we believe has done some good things), schools must test their students in reading and math and that the world will judge their school according to the percentage of students who meet the state's definition of proficiency. In some states (and in Washington, D.C.), the last tests are given in tenth grade. So although people may set out to provide a second-chance school for older students, they will face tremendous pressure to avoid accepting any students in the tenth grade (after all, if they do, they will only have a few months to prepare them for the tests). Similarly, it will be in their interest to avoid accepting too many ninth graders who are far behind. In order to have greater numbers of students who are proficient, they will do well to start with a younger group. If they truly want to serve the kids who are coming out of places like the Maya Angelou Academy, we tell them, they will be forced to explain their low test scores and face criticism from people who think they are just making excuses.

But state tests and No Child Left Behind are not the only problem they will face. There is also tremendous funding pressure. Students like those we serve at the Maya Angelou Academy cost more to educate properly than students who are on grade level. They even cost more to educate than the average low-income student. They have particular needs that a good school will try to meet. But where will the money come from?

Consider Anton, a fairly typical Maya Angelou Academy student. Anton was sixteen when he arrived. He tested just below the fourth grade level in reading and just above it in math. He had not earned any high school credits, and had not attended school with any consistency since he completed the eighth grade.

He had committed a crime, but like many of our students, he had also been a victim—he had been shot the year before. His father passed away earlier this year, while Anton was at New Beginnings. Anton does not have any diagnosed learning or emotional disabilities and is not a special education student.

He is doing quite well at the academy. Anton attends classes with ten other students, and in each class there are two members of our instructional staff and two DYRS staff. He receives counseling and behavioral health support on a regular basis, has adults who ensure that he gets up and comes to school each day, and often stays after school to receive additional tutoring. He attends a school with a total of sixty students.

Anton will return to the community with better academic skills, a transition plan, more resilience, and some strategies to cope with the trauma that he has experienced. But there is a good chance that whatever school accepts Anton will lack the resources to truly help him. Anton is involved in the juvenile justice system, will be returning from nearly a year of confinement, is five to six years behind in school, and has experienced major trauma. Once released, he needs a community school that will provide what proved successful at the academy, including tutoring, small classes, intensive support with his reading and writing, and consistent mental health counseling. If Anton were a special education student, he would have a chance of finding such a school. But for non–special education students who have his needs, the options are few. Schools that provide such services are almost nonexistent, because we as a society don't provide the funding to develop and operate them.

In most states there is one more obstacle to creating high-quality schools for students like those leaving the Maya Angelou Academy. In Washington, D.C., and the vast majority of states, the only way to earn a high school diploma is to accumulate the requisite number of Carnegie units. And the only way to earn a unit is to pass a class that meets the District's seat-time requirement (literally, this means that a student must spend a specified number of hours in class—i.e., in his or her "seat").

Thus, students who come to us at age seventeen with three high school credits, work hard, and leave us at age eighteen with nine to eleven credits will nonetheless return to their communities needing two more years of high school. For students like these, whose one real success in school was at the academy and who will probably be returning to a large, underperforming public high school, this is too long, and the diploma too far away.

There is a better way. A number of states—including California, Illinois, Indiana, Maryland, New York, Oregon, and Rhode Island—offer more robust alternatives for earning a high school diploma; these include options for competency-based credit, workplace-based credit, and dual high school–community college enrollments. If our society is to provide a pathway for students such as those who leave the Maya Angelou Academy, then Washington, D.C., and other states must follow their lead.

Conclusion

This volume is dedicated to showing how we might keep our young people out of the juvenile justice system. This includes making sure that kids who enter the system do not return. In this chapter, we have argued that the juvenile justice community should do more to demand quality schools for youth in the system, and that education reformers should do more to create such schools. The story of the Maya Angelou Academy at New Beginnings is one example of how to build such a school inside a juvenile facility.

At the same time, what happens outside the walls matters just as much as what happens inside. Ensuring that young people do not return to the juvenile system will require that equally good schools are available to them when they reenter the community. This combination—of excellent education inside and outside—is what Jeremy, Keith, Trevon, Anton, and others like them need, and what we as a society have an obligation to provide.

NOTES

As used throughout this chapter, the pronoun "we" does not refer exclusively to the authors but often to the teachers and staff of the Maya Angelou Academy. Their passion and commitment are something to behold, and this chapter is dedicated to them. The authors also applaud the work of Vincent Schiraldi, Marc Schindler, David Brown, David Muhammad, and the entire DYRS team, including the front-line staff at New Beginnings Youth Center. We would like to thank Arthur Evenchik for his comments and editorial assistance, and Patrick Clark, Alana Intriere, and Michael Knobler for research assistance. Finally, we would like to thank the young men of the New Beginnings Youth Center. May you dream big, work hard, and never, ever return.

1. PBIS is a nationally recognized approach to supporting positive school culture, and it is used in many school districts. It was not specifically designed for use in juvenile facilities, although a number of such schools have adopted it.

2. We have changed all of the students' names for confidentiality purposes.

3. Here and elsewhere, our grade level equivalency estimates are based on students' scores on the Woodcock Johnson III Achievement series assessment.

4. Between September of 2009 and July of 2010 the percentage of special needs students at the academy averaged 48 percent, and varied from a high of 55 percent to a low of 39 percent.

5. Results are based on students during the 2009-2010 school year who took three sections of the Woodcock Johnson III Achievement series in both English and math at entry and prior to release. Growth rates are calculated by annualizing actual growth rates. On average, scholars were administered the test just over six months apart, and growth rates were then extrapolated to equivalent rates of growth over nine months.

REFERENCES

Adelman, C. 2006. *The Toolbox Revisited: Paths to Degree Completion from High School through College*. Washington, DC: Dept. of Education.

Balfanz, R., et al. 2003. High-Poverty Secondary Schools and the Juvenile Justice System: How Neither Helps the Other and How That Could Change. *New Directions for Youth Development* 99:71-89.

Cauvin, H. "D.C. Youth Justice Agency's School Improvements Deemed 'Remarkable,'" *Washington Post*. July 9, 2010.

Coffey, O., and M. Gemignani. 1994. *Effective Practices in Juvenile Correctional Education: A Study of the Literature and Research, 1980-1992*. Washington, DC: Office of Juvenile Justice and Delinquency Prevention, Dept. of Justice.

Davis, S. 2009. *Rights of Juveniles: The Juvenile Justice System.* Eagan, MN: West.

Dohrn, Bernardine. 2002. The School, the Child, and the Court. In *A Century of Juvenile Justice* (Margaret Rosenheim et al. eds.), 267-309. Chicago: University of Chicago Press.

"DYRS Has Made Great Strides, But More Are Needed." *Washington Post.* July 12, 2010.

Exhibit 6A to Special Arbiter's Report to the Court. 2010. Filed in Jerry M. et al. v. District of Columbia, Civil Action No. 1519-85.

Gordon, R., T. Kane, and D. Staiger. 2006. *Identifying Effective Teachers Using Performance on the Job.* Washington, DC: Brookings Institute.

Jordan, H., R. Mendro, and D. Weerasinghe. 1997. Teacher Effects on Longitudinal Student Achievement: A Report on Research in Progress. Indianapolis: CREATE Annual Meeting.

Lemov, D. 2010. *Teach like a Champion: Forty-Nine Techniques That Put Students on the Path to College.* New York: Jossey-Bass.

National Research Council. 2003. Engaging Schools: Fostering High School Students' Motivation to Learn. Washington, DC: National Academies Press.

Sedlak, A., and K. McPherson. 2010. Youths' Needs and Services: Findings from the Survey of Youth in Residential Placement. *Juvenile Justice Bulletin.* Washington, DC: Office of Juvenile Justice and Delinquency Prevention, Dept. of Justice.

The Special Arbiter's Report to the Court. 2010. Filed in Jerry M. et al. v. District of Columbia, Civil Action No. 1519-85.

Zimring, F. 1982. *The Changing Legal World of Adolescence.* New York: Free Press.

About the Contributors

BRIAN R. BARBER is a doctoral student in special education at the University of Florida. His research interests include social-emotional intervention for students with emotional and behavioral disorders.

SHAY BILCHIK is Research Professor and Director, Center for Juvenile Justice Reform, Georgetown University Public Policy Institute. He formerly served as head of the Office of Juvenile Justice and Delinquency Prevention in the Clinton administration, and as head of the Child Welfare League of America.

BENJAMIN CAIRNS, MPA, is the Restorative Justice Coordinator at North High School in Denver, Colorado.

DAVID DOMENICI is the Principal of the Maya Angelou Academy at New Beginnings and the cofounder of the Maya Angelou Schools.

NANCY E. DOWD is the David H. Levin Chair in Family Law and Director, Center on Children and Families at the University of Florida Levin College of Law.

JEFFREY FAGAN is Professor of Law and Public Health at Columbia University, and Director of the Center for Crime, Community, and Law at Columbia Law School. His research examines policing, juvenile justice, and capital punishment. He is a fellow of the American Society of Criminology.

JAMES FORMAN JR. is a Professor of Law at Georgetown University and a cofounder of the Maya Angelou Schools.

JOSEPH C. GAGNON is an Assistant Professor of Special Education at the University of Florida. His research focuses on academic and behavioral interventions for youth with high-incidence disabilities.

THERESA GLENNON is the Jack E. Feinberg Professor of Litigation at the James E. Beasley School of Law and Temple University, where her teaching and scholarship focuses on the legal rights of children and families, with particular focus on family law, education, race, and disability.

THALIA N. C. GONZÁLEZ is an Assistant Professor of Politics at Occidental College. She has authored articles on the roles of community-based lawyers and organizers in such areas as education policy reform, juvenile justice, economic development, and corporate social responsibility.

LESLIE JOAN HARRIS, the Dorothy Kliks Fones Professor at the University of Oregon School of Law, is the coauthor of textbooks about family law and children and the law. She is also the director of the Oregon Child Advocacy Project at the law school.

DAVID R. KATNER is a Professor of Clinical Law and the Felix J. Dreyfous Teaching Fellow in Juvenile Law at Tulane Law School. He has served on the boards of the National Association of Counsel for Children, the New Orleans Legal Assistance Corp., the Jefferson Parish Juvenile Services Advisory Board, and the Children's Bureau. He sits as an ad hoc judge in the Orleans Parish Juvenile Court.

KHARY LAZARRE-WHITE, JD, is the Executive Director and Cofounder of the Brotherhood/Sister Sol (BHSS), a comprehensive youth development organization founded in 1995 in Harlem.

THOMAS A. LOUGHRAN is an Assistant Professor in the Department of Criminology and Criminal Justice at the University of Maryland. His research interests include deterrence, individuals' response to sanctioning, and quantitative methods.

EDWARD P. MULVEY is a Professor of Psychiatry and Director of the Law and Psychiatry Program at Western Psychiatric Institute and Clinic at the University of Pittsburgh School of Medicine. He is currently the principal investigator for a longitudinal study, Pathways to Desistance, examining how serious adolescent offenders make the transition from adolescence to adulthood.

KENNETH B. NUNN is Professor of Law at the University of Florida Levin College of Law. He teaches criminal law and criminal procedure and writes in the areas of race, crime, and juvenile justice issues.

VANESSA PATINO is a Senior Researcher at the National Council on Crime and Delinquency Center for Girls and Young Women, where she focuses on translating research to improve the system's response to justice-involved girls.

ALEX R. PIQUERO is Professor in the School of Criminology and Criminal Justice at Florida State University; Adjunct Professor at the Key Centre for Ethics, Law, Justice, and Governance, Griffith University Australia; and Co-editor, *Journal of Quantitative Criminology*. His research interests include criminal careers, criminological theory, and quantitative research methods.

LAWANDA RAVOIRA is the Director of the National Council on Crime and Delinquency Center for Girls and Young Women and is a national expert, author, researcher, and trainer on issues specific to justice-involved girls.

STEPHEN M. REBA is an attorney at the Barton Juvenile Defender Clinic at Emory University School of Law, where he directs an Equal Justice Works project called Appeal for Youth.

SARAH VALENTINE is the Director of Student Affairs and Associate Law Library Professor at CUNY School of Law. She has written extensively on queer children and youth.

RANDEE J. WALDMAN is a Clinical Instructor and Director of the Barton Juvenile Defender Clinic at Emory University School of Law.

BARBARA BENNETT WOODHOUSE is L. Q. C. Lamar Chair of Law and Codirector of the Barton Child Law and Policy Center at Emory University School of Law.

Index

diversion programs, 165
domestic violence, 162–174. *See also* intimate-partner violence
Due process, 228, 235. *See also* Fourteenth Amendment

Early Childhood Advisory Councils (ECACs), 52
early childhood education, 4, 26, 39, 163. *See also* daycare
ecological approach/model, 6, 7, 230
Eighth Amendment, 221
Elementary and Secondary Education Act of 1965 (ESEA), 114
emotional disturbance, 10, 83–85, 97
Equal Protection Clause, 108, 120–121, 221. *See also* Fourteenth Amendment
exclusionary based policies, 246
exosystems, 6. *See also* ecological approach/ model
expectation of privacy, 223

false confession, 225, 232
Family and Schools Together (FAST) Track program, 98
foster care, 5, 10, 62–77; drift, 68; "foster-care-to-prison" pipeline, 8; Multidimensional Treatment, 30, 174; and queer youth, 185
Foster Care Non-Discrimination Act (California), 192
Fifth Amendment, 221, 225, 234
Foucault, Michael, 62–63, 71–74
Fourteenth Amendment, 108, 120–121
Fourth Amendment, 225, 234
Friere, Paulo, 141
Functional Family Therapy (FFT), 30, 174, 229–230, 234. *See also* Multisystem Theory (MST)

gangs, 254; gang-related activity, 110
Gay/Straight Alliances (GSAs), 190
Georgetown Juvenile Justice Clinic, ix
gender: contributing factors to delinquency, 161; discrimination (*see* discrimination); disparate treatment, 158, 168–174; disparities, 157; identification, 181, 191, 194; identity, 180; identity disorder, 180; non-conforming, 4, 12, 180; norms, 186; rates of incarceration, 160; roles, 186; -specific interventions, 12; -specific services, 157, 164, 169, 171–174
Gladwell, Malcolm, 135–136
Green Chimneys program, 190
Gun-Free Schools Act of 1994 (GFSA), 110

Harlem Children's Zone, ix
Harvard Child Advocacy Project, ix
heterosexism, 181, 186–187
High/Scope Perry Preschool program, 26, 45–46, 48
homelessness, 265: and queer youth, 180–185
homophobia, 181, 186–187

Improving America's Schools Act of 1994, 115
indirect control, 228
Individuals with Disabilities Education Act (IDEA), 120, 124–126
Individuals with Disabilities Education Improvement Act (IDEIA) of 2006, 84, 86, 87, 89
institutional mindfulness, 126
integrated court systems, 24, 28
interested adult, 231
internalized control, 228
interrogation, 219–235
intervention: community, 14; family, 14; individual-level, 164; positive behavioral, 15; primary, 7–8; school-based, 172; secondary, 7; selective, 10, 95; system-level, 29, 164, 169; tertiary, 7, 182
intimate partner violence (IPV), 181, 186–188, 192, 194; and queer youth, 186–188. *See also* domestic violence

Jim Crow, 1, 144, 151
Juvenile Detention Alternatives Initiative (JDAI), 29